Matthew Biggs's
COMPLETE BOOK
OF VEGETABLES

Matthew Biggs trained in horticulture at Pershore and the
Royal Botanic Gardens, Kew, where he also worked as a
guide and lecturer. From his frequent travels across the
continents, he has developed an enthusiasm for both
temperate and tropical crops and likes to experiment with
unusual varieties and try out new growing techniques. He
can be regularly seen on BBC 2's *How Does Your Garden
Grow?* and Meridian's *Grass Roots*. He also has a monthly
diary in *Garden Answers* and writes regular contributions for
Your Gardens and *Gardeners' World*.

Matthew Biggs's
COMPLETE
BOOK OF
VEGETABLES

**THE PRACTICAL SOURCEBOOK:
GROWING, HARVESTING AND
COOKING VEGETABLES**

KYLE CATHIE LIMITED

I dedicate this book to my daughter, Jessica Daisy

First published in paperback 2000
by Kyle Cathie Limited
122 Arlington Road, London NW1 7HP

Hardcover edition published 1997

2 4 6 8 10 9 7 5 3 1

ISBN 1 85626 355 X

Copyright © Matthew Biggs 1997, 2000
Photographs © Sally Maltby 1997 © Michelle Garrett 1997
For additional photographic acknowledgements see page 256

Matthew Biggs is hereby identified as the author of this
work in accordance with Section 77 of the Copyright, Designs
and Patents Act, 1988

Design by Geoff Hayes
Printed and bound in Singapore by
Sino Publishing House Ltd

A Cataloguing in Publication record for this title is available
from the British Library

Acknowledgements
With many thanks to Kyle Cathie for taking a chance, and to Candida Hall
and Penny David for their expertise, patience and encouragement.
Also to Marilyn Ward and Jill Cowley at the Royal Botanic Gardens, Kew;
Charles Grace of Pukawa Plants for information on tamarillo; Karen Box
and Peter Lipsham in New Zealand; Mike Darcy and Robert Fleming in
the USA; Simon Hickmott at the Henry Doubleday Research Association,
UK; Anita Bean, Consultant Nutritionist to the Fresh Fruit and Vegetable
Information Bureau and John Tunstall, an enthusiastic grower of unusual
vegetables, for his advice. Finally, thanks to Steve Bradley, Ray Desmond
and my wife Gill for her support and administrative skills.

Publisher's Note
An asterisk (*) beside a variety name indicates a vegetable which has
received an award from the Royal Horticultural Society (see page 248)

AUTHOR'S NOTE
Organic vs. Chemical
While I strongly urge you to practise organic cultivation, it must
also be accepted that every gardener has the right to decide
whether to use chemicals or not. Whatever your persuasion, both
organic and chemical controls are suggested in this book; the
ultimate decision is your own.

CONTENTS

INTRODUCTION

We all have to eat to survive, and there is nothing like home-grown vegetables to increase that pleasure. To some people eating was, and still is, a rather functional process, while the more privileged have developed it into a cultural experience and a pastime to be enjoyed. Plants are the basis of the food chain – even for meat-eaters – and vegetables make a meal more palatable. They are visually attractive, nutritious and essential for a balanced diet, adding a range of flavours and interest to a meal. The greater choice of vegetables we have, the more exciting our culinary experience will be.

For centuries, vegetable gardens throughout the world have been the focal point of family and community survival. From the Middle Ages onwards in rural Europe, vegetables were grown of necessity and villagers cultivated turnips, leeks, kales and cabbages as part of their simple diet. Later, cottage gardens contained a mixture of vegetables, herbs and flowers, providing food, medicine, flavouring, ornament and a nectar supply for bees. Where every plant had a part to play, flowers grown only for their ornamental value were considered a luxury.

This philosophy still prevails in France, where vegetable gardening has been refined to create the 'potager' or ornamental vegetable garden, satisfying an artistic and practical need. The finest example exists at the château garden at Villandry in the Loire Valley, where formal borders are embellished with a magnificent array of vegetables. Why not try this on a smaller scale at home? There is a wholesome beauty in a display of vegetables – a row of vibrantly coloured ruby chard, 'January King' cabbages dusted with snow, the aristocratic foliage of globe artichokes – all have a unique yet distinctive charm. I hope that this book encourages you to experiment further.

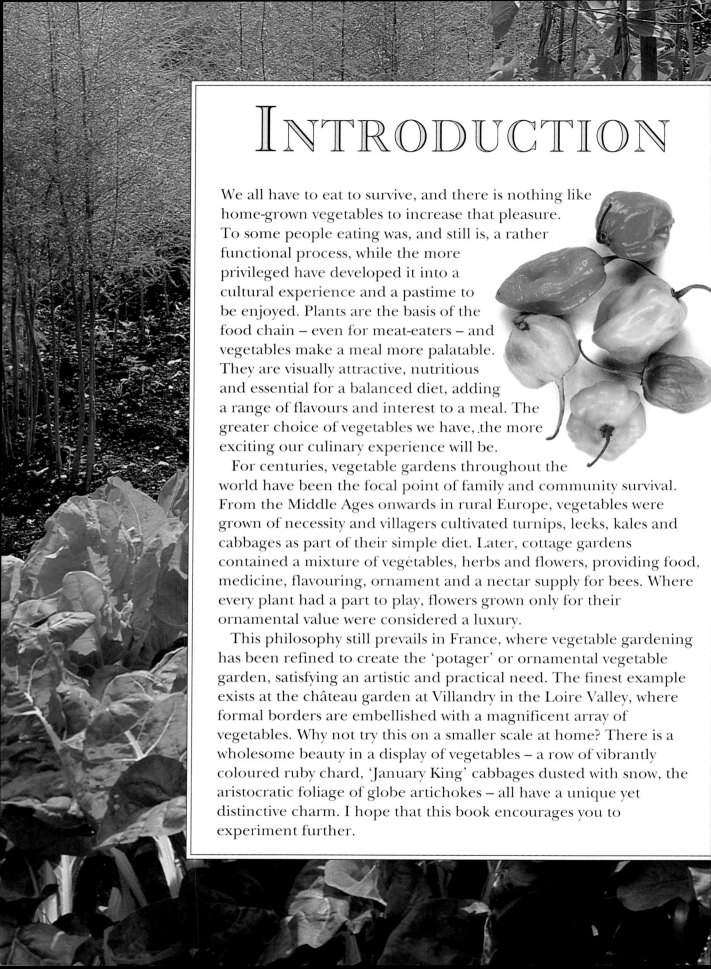

The French also revolutionized eating, changing it into an artistic experience in which every meal was considered an important occasion. After the French Revolution and the fall of the aristocracy, many chefs – finding themselves unemployed – opened restaurants and, in time, social eating became widespread. For the wealthy, fine food had always provided an opportunity to indulge in pleasures both sensual and cultural; a meal was the ideal occasion to savour the exquisite flavour of fresh vegetables, meat, fish, good wine and fruit as well as a time for conviviality and friendship. The social aspect of eating is still an essential part of the pleasure, and a satisfying meal in good company should last for many hours. It is, of course, also an opportunity for the chef to show his/her skill in the preparation and presentation of food.

But what would a meal be without vegetables? They add finesse to a dish that meat alone cannot provide. And where would a cook be without recipes? Where the gardener's skill finishes, culinary creativity takes over. While researching this book I became aware of exciting developments in cooking with vegetables, stimulated by the

The Frugal Meal **by Jozef Israels, 1824–1911**

increasing popularity of vegetarianism. Such new ideas elevate even the most basic crops to tantalizing heights: I hope you will find the recipes given here tempting.

Too many people treat the ubiquitous vegetable with indifference rather than appreciation. Yet these loyal servants not only provide our daily food, but also help maintain health and cure ills. It is believed that Henry VIII of England (1491–1547) died from malnutrition due to a predominantly carnivorous diet! Some vegetables have an ancient and fascinating past, having been developed over many centuries, while others have even influenced social and political history – most notably our good friend, the common potato.

During the Industrial Revolution many people were uprooted from their rural heritage as they turned to the cities. Now many of those working in towns and cities are seeking their rural past, returning to allotments and plots. There is certainly a resurgence of interest in vegetable growing. What's more, an increasing number of people are determined to grow vegetables organically, free from health-damaging chemicals, taking the opportunity to be 'in touch with the soil' while enjoying fresh air and exercise. Vegetable growing is more uplifting and undoubtedly more productive than a visit to the gym – what can be a better reward for your efforts than a tasty meal with fine home-grown vegetables?

I heartily recommend that everyone tries their hand at growing vegetables. You only have a balcony? Use buckets, boxes, windowboxes, tea chests or pots – almost any available container will do. Grow 'mini' vegetables or dot them among your flowers. Are you uninspired by the 'same old veg'? Experiment with lesser

A well-kept vegetable garden can be a source of pride

The Vegetable Garden, Coombe by **Paul Riley, 1988**

known varieties, oriental vegetables or exotics such as okra; enliven your salads with white cucumbers, bi-coloured beetroot, red spring onions and red-fleshed radishes. With careful planning, your vegetable garden should be productive all year round, providing an endless supply of fresh vegetables and filling your freezer. And who can argue that a commercially produced vegetable, jaded after its journey from field to supermarket, is comparable with those eaten straight from the garden, bursting with vitality and packed with goodness and flavour?

Vegetable growing is tremendously fulfilling and should not be seen as the exclusive domain of gruff old men in baggy corduroys and flat caps, pottering round allotments. Neither are vegetables inferior to flowers, as so many erroneously seem to think. To neglect them would be a great loss. Not only are they part of our history, but they greatly enrich the present and are vital to sustain our future. Don't just take my word for it. This book is intended to help, inspire and encourage you to get out into the garden. Go on, try it – and enjoy yourself!

HISTORY OF VEGETABLES

The selection of food crops is believed to have been a process of 'trial and error'. Plants were sampled and remembered for being either pleasant to the taste, or unpleasant and to be avoided. This same process must have also led to the selection of medicinal plants. There would have been times of considerable hardship, and even fatalities, as people gradually found out what could be eaten and how it should be prepared – as with the discovery that manioc was edible only after washing several times to remove the injurious calcium oxalate crystals.

Early humans collected food from the surrounding countryside and followed migrating animals. The first settlements were established in areas where food was plentiful all year round; one of the earliest, found in Tehuacan in southern central Mexico, dates from 5000BC. Later came the discovery that seeds could be planted and nurtured to ensure an easily accessible supply of food.

Cereals and peas were the first crops to be domesticated. Cultivated wheat and barley have been found dating from 8000 to 7000BC and peas from 6500BC, while rice was recorded as a staple in China by 2800BC. Later crops like oats, which have been in cultivation only since 2000BC, may well have originated as weeds among cultivated crops.

The most productive areas were along great rivers, where the vast flood plains were ideal for constructing dwellings and growing crops. Here civilizations developed like those in the 'Fertile Crescent' of Mesopotamia, in

Winter vegetables

the flood plains of the Euphrates and Tigris, and in Egypt, along the Nile and its delta. Annual flooding brought deposits of rich, fertile alluvial soil and the rivers together with their gods were respected and revered for their bounty. Agriculture became highly developed and complex irrigation systems were established. The sophistication of these societies seems to indicate that once a regular, plentiful food supply was guaranteed, other parts of their culture were developed – in Egypt many cultivated vegetables were an integral part of the system of medicine.

With domestication came early selection of plants for beneficial characteristics such as yield, disease resistance and ease of germination. These were the first cultivated varieties, or 'cultivars'. This has continued extensively and by the eighteenth century in

Europe, seed selection became a fine art in the hands of skilled gardeners. Gregor Mendel's work with peas in 1855–64 in his monastery garden at Brno in Moravia was one of the most significant discoveries, leading to the development of hybrids and scientific selection. This has evolved to the extent that plant breeders are now able to change the genetic make-up of plants using X–rays and colchicine, a chemical extracted from the autumn crocus or Colchicum. Most development has centred on the major food crops. Minor crops like seakale have changed very little, apart from the selection of a few cultivars. Others, like most carrots, are similar to their wild relatives, but the roots are larger and more tender.

A Russian botanist, Nikolai Vavilov, concluded there were up to twelve main centres of origin including North Africa, the Mediterranean and Asia. Food crops travelled from one central point with expanding populations and invading armies. Migrating peoples took maize from the Andes to Central and later North America, while the Romans (who were certainly cultivating beetroot, cabbage, kale and asparagus) took vegetables, including peas, to distant parts of their empire. In later years settlers took their crops to new lands. Polynesians took the sweet potato to New Zealand, where it became a staple, and Europeans took their crops to Australia, where prior to their arrival in 1788, the Aborigines were 'hunter-gatherers' and had no domesticated crops.

The greatest exchange of foods began in 1492 with the discovery of the 'New World'.

Large kitchen gardens were formerly attached to great houses: *Vegetable Garden at Charlton Park* by Thomas Robins, 1716–70

Columbus returned with maize and took European crops to the new lands. Less than one hundred years later potatoes were being sold in Spain; by the end of the seventeenth century, maize was a staple crop in the Iberian peninsula and chillies were being added to the curries in India.

There are estimated to be between 250 and 350 plant families, yet our main food crops are derived from just ten. From one single species, Brassica oleracea, comes a diverse variety of vegetables: kale and cabbage are grown for the leaves; cauliflower, broccoli and calabrese for the immature flower heads, and kohlrabi for the swollen stem bases. Leguminosae provide us with peas and many kinds of beans, Gramineae with cereals like wheat and barley, plus maize and rice, and Solanaceae contribute potatoes, tomatoes, sweet peppers and chillies.

In the past, varieties were maintained by saving seed after harvest for sowing the following year. Many were local or regional cultivars which had been bred or selected specifically to flourish in the soil, climate and other growing conditions of the area. Staple crops like the potato were widely developed and there are many regional varieties, like 'Edzell Blue' from Edzell near Forfar in Scotland. Others were developed by enthusiasts like Donald Mackelvie on the Isle of Arran in Scotland, who sold his general store and became a full-time potato breeder. He introduced about twenty different varieties, the most famous of these being 'Arran Pilot'.

Yet the existence of such diversity and genetic richness is under threat. If varieties are lost, material for breeding new cultivars will disappear. Many old types have fallen from favour, displaced by modern, standardized cultivars in bright, glossy packets. Others fail to reach standards set by European legislation and cannot be

St. Paul de Vence by **Margaret Loxton**

marketed. This valuable resource is protected by enthusiasts and societies like the Henry Doubleday Research Association in the UK, Seed Savers in the USA and Seed Savers International. The future of crop breeding is in their hands and they deserve our support.

Recently, another exchange of vegetables has taken place. Since the Berlin Wall fell, another 'new world' has been discovered as new varieties, like cold-resistant tomatoes, have emerged from the Eastern bloc. This and the advent of refrigeration and air transport, allowing even the most perishable of vegetables to travel, has introduced new cultivars and 'exotic' vegetables to the West. Chinese, West Indian and Asian settlers in Europe enjoy their culinary heritage, enriching the diet of those around them. Many grow their own crops which, I am certain, will gradually become more widely accepted – the potato and tomato were once 'exotics'. For vegetable growers and lovers of good food, the future looks tasty indeed!

FADS AND FASHIONS

While some vegetables have remained universally popular, others have waxed and waned, remained peripheral or become regional specialities. Consistently high yields over a long harvesting season – particularly when few other vegetables are available – coupled with versatility, have guaranteed the establishment of many vegetables. Winter brassicas are a good example of this.

Regional popularity can be attributed to several factors, one of which is climatic suitability. Hamburg parsley, for instance, has been widely grown in central Europe (notably, Germany) for centuries because of its robust nature and ability to crop successfully in such a climate.

Yet it never achieved the same status in other countries, even if the conditions were equally favourable. Why not?

It could be argued that a taste for it was never 'acquired'. When it was introduced to Britain, similar, better-quality vegetables such as parsnip with its larger roots and the more refined curled parsley were already well established. The level of popularity enjoyed by Hamburg parsley was never enough to persuade those who cultivated it to save and distribute widely. And so it simply remained a 'trendy' vegetable which never gained a footing in Britain.

Trends are set by commercial producers seeking marketing opportunities or by innovative, wealthy or famous people whose opinions are valued and actions mimicked because they are considered to be 'arbiters of taste'. This applies to trends in clothes, fine wines and many forms of entertainment, and extends to the adoption of another

Leeks, carrots and cabbage have long since ceased to be 'trendy'

country's cuisine. The cuisine of France and Italy, for instance, is regarded as the height of good taste and so many seek to imitate it. Endive, rocket (or roquette!) and chicory are perfect illustrations of current 'trendy' salad crops – though rocket should beware! Still extensively grown around the Mediterranean, it was once fashionable in Britain but quickly lost its appeal. It remains to be seen if, finally, it is established after its recent resurgence, or if it is destined to decline into obscurity and become, once again, a peripheral vegetable.

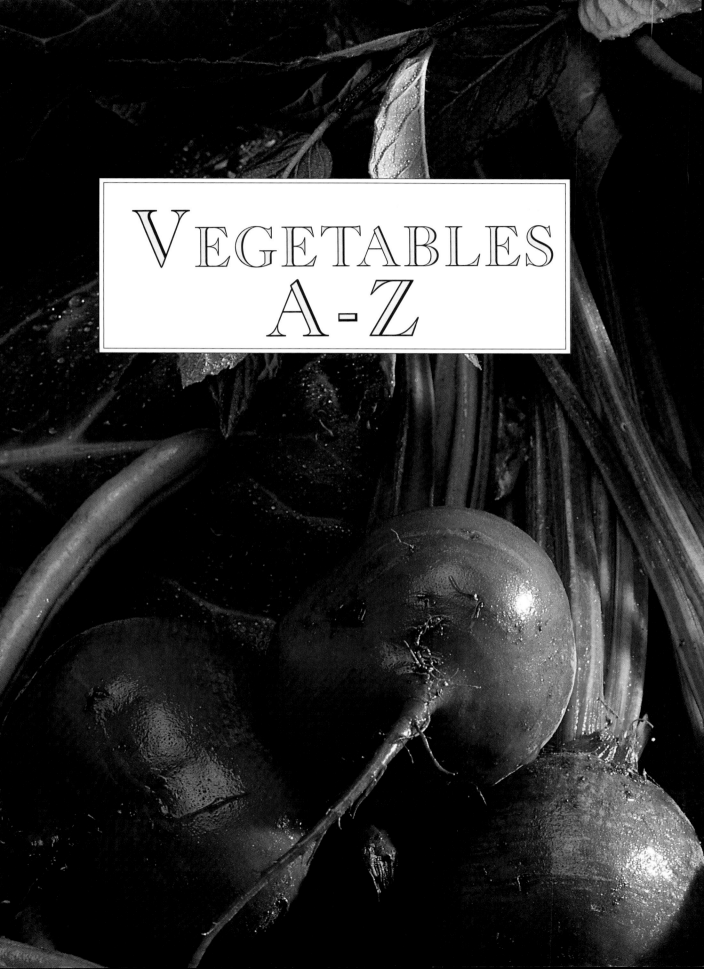

VEGETABLES
A-Z

Allium cepa. Liliaceae

ONION

Biennial grown as annual for swollen bulbs. Half hardy. Value: small amounts of most vitamins and minerals.

A vegetable of antiquity, onions were cultivated by the Egyptians not only as food, but also to place in the thorax, pelvis or near the eyes during mummification. Pliny recorded six varieties in ancient Rome. The onion was highly regarded for its antiseptic properties, but many other legends became attached to it. In parts of Ireland it was said to cure baldness: 'Rub the sap mixed with honey into a bald patch, keep on rubbing until the spot gets red. This concoction if properly applied would grow hair on a duck's egg.' Many varieties have been bred over the centuries; some, like 'The Kelsae', are famous for their size, while newer varieties have incorporated hardiness, disease resistance and colour.

'First Early'

VARIETIES

Varieties of *Allium cepa* fall into several different groups according to their colour, shape and use. The bulb or common onion has brown, yellow or red skin and is round, elongated or spindle-shaped, or flattened. (Grouped with these are Japanese onions, a type of the perennial *Allium fistulosum*, which are grown as an annual for overwintering.) Spring or bunching onions are harvested small for salads, and pickling varieties (also known as 'silverskin', 'mini' or 'button' onions) are allowed to grow larger before harvesting.

Bulb or Common Onions
'Ailsa Craig', an old favourite, is a large variety, round and straw-coloured with a mild flavour. **'Albion'** is a round onion with a white bulb of medium size. **'Buffalo'*** is high-yielding, for sowing in summer and harvesting the following year. The round, firm bulbs are well flavoured. **'Express Yellow O-X'** is a Japanese onion for sowing in summer and harvesting the following year. **'Marshalls Giant Fen Globe'*** is an old, heavy-cropping variety with a mild flavour. **'Red Baron'**

is a gorgeous dark red-skinned onion with a strong flavour and red outer flesh to each ring. Good for storing. **'Rijnsberger'** is large, pale yellow and round; this is an excellent keeper. **'Senshyu Semi-Globe Yellow'** is a Japanese onion with a deep yellow skin. **'Sturon'**, an old, high-yielding variety, has straw-coloured skin and an excellent resistance to running to seed. **'Stuttgarter Giant'** is a reliable variety with flattened bulbs and a mild flavour. A good keeper and slow to bolt. **'The Kelsae'**, a large, round onion with mild flesh, does not store well. **'Torpedo'** is a spindle-shaped onion that is mild-flavoured, but does not store well.

'Torpedo', or 'Red Italian'

Bunching, Spring or Salad Onions
'Beltsville Bunching' is a vigorous, mild-tasting variety, tolerant of both winter cold and hot, dry weather. **'Ishikura'**, a cross between a leek and coarse chives, is prolific, tender and a rapid grower with upright, white stems and dark green leaves. It can be left in the ground to thicken and still retains its taste. **'Kyoto Market'** is mild, easy to germinate and excellent for early sowings. **'Redmate'** is a colourful variety which is red towards the base, and is ideal for livening up salads. This can be thinned to 7.5cm (3in) apart for mild bulb onions. **'Santa Claus'**, another red variety, is ready from about 6 weeks, keeps its taste well and can be

Spring onions add bite to salads

harvested until the size of a leek. The colour is stronger during cold weather, and when they are earthed up. **'White Lisbon'*** is a tasty, popular and reliable variety. It is fast-growing and very hardy. **'Winter-Over'*** is a well-flavoured, extremely hardy variety for sowing in autumn. **'Winter White Bunching'*** has slim stalks, stiff leaves and a mild flavour. It is hardy and overwinters well.

Pickling Onions
'Brown Pickling SY300' is a pale brown-skinned early variety. It stores well and remains firm when pickled. **'Paris Silverskin'** is a popular, excellent 'cocktail' onion, which grows rapidly and thrives in poor soil. Sow from mid-spring and lift when about the size of your thumbnail. **'Shakespear'** is a tasty, small brown onion which is perfect for pickling.

Onions for pickling should be peeled thoroughly before storing

CULTIVATION

Onions require an open, sunny site, fertile soil and free drainage. 'Sets' (immature bulbs which have been specifically grown for planting) are more tolerant than seedlings and do not need a fine soil or such high levels of fertility. Pickling onions tolerate poorer soil than other types. Rotate crops annually.

Propagation
For a constant supply, two plantings or sowings are needed, one in spring and another in autumn, when old varieties or newer hardy Japanese varieties are used.

Onion sets have several advantages over seed. They are quick to mature, are better in cooler areas with shorter growing seasons, they grow well in poorer soils and are not attacked by onion fly or mildew. They are easy to grow and mature earlier, but are more expensive and prone to run to seed. (Buying modern varieties and heat-treated sets about 2cm (¾in) in diameter reduces that risk.) There is a greater choice of varieties when growing from seed. If planting is delayed, spread out sets in a cool, well-lit place to prevent

'Sturon' drying. Check stored onions regularly, removing any that are diseased or damaged

premature sprouting. It is possible to save your own sets from bulbs grown the previous year. Plant onion sets when the soil warms from late winter to mid-spring. Sets which have been heat-treated should not be planted until late spring. Plant in shallow drills or push them gently into the soil until only the tips are above the surface. For medium-sized onions, plant 5cm (2in) apart in rows 25cm (10in) apart; for larger onions space sets 10cm (4in) apart in the rows.

Sow seed indoors in late winter at 10–16°C (50–60°F) in seed trays, pots or modules (about 6 seeds in each module). Harden off the seedlings carefully by gradually increasing ventilation, then plant out in early spring when the seedlings have 2 true leaves. When transplanting those raised in modules and pots, ensure that the roots fall down into the planting hole and that the base of the bulb is about 1cm (½in) below the surface.

Onions can also be sown outdoors in a seedbed in early to mid-spring in cool temperate zones. Use cloches or polythene to ensure the soil is warm, as cold, wet soil leads to poor germination and disease. Use treated seed to protect against fungal disease.

When the soil is moist and crumbly, rake in a general

fertilizer about 2 weeks before sowing and walk over the plot to create a firm seedbed, then sow onions 12–20mm (½–¾in) deep in rows 30cm (12in) apart. Once they germinate, thin to 4cm (1–1½in) apart for medium-sized onions and 7.5–10cm (3–4in) for large onions. Thin when the soil is moist to deter onion fly. Plant multi-sown blocks 25–30cm (10–12in) apart. Plant firmly.

Sowing times for Japanese onions are critical; sown too early, they run to seed; sown too late, they are too weak to survive the winter. To cover for losses over winter, sow seeds about 2.5cm (1in) apart in rows 30cm (12in) apart. Top-dress with nitrogen in mid-winter.

Sow pickling onions in spring, either broadcast or in drills the width of a hoe and about 10cm (4in) apart. Thin according to the size of onions required and harvest them when the leaves have died back.

Sow salad or bunching onions thinly, watering the drills before sowing in dry weather. Rows should be 10cm (4in) apart; thin to a final spacing of 1–2.5cm (½–1in) when the seedlings are large enough to handle for good-sized onions. For a regular supply sow at 2 to 3 week intervals through late spring and early summer, watering thoroughly during dry weather.

'Senshyu', a very attractive and reliable variety

Growing
Dig thoroughly during early winter, incorporating liberal quantities of well-rotted manure or compost if needed. Do not grow on freshly manured ground. Lime acid soils. Before planting, rake the surface level, removing any debris and adding a general granular fertilizer to it at 60g/sq m (2oz/sq yd). In summer pull back the earth or mulch from around the bulb to expose it to the sun.

Maintenance
Spring Plant sets or seeds. Keep weed-free, particularly in the early stages of growth.
Summer Mulch to reduce water loss and weeds. Watering is only vital during drought.
Autumn Lift early autumn.
Winter Push back any sets which have been lifted by frost or birds.

Protected Cropping
Onions do not need protection, although early sowings in cold weather and overwintering onions benefit from cloching or from horticultural fleece in exceptionally cold or wet weather.

Early sowings of salad or bunching onions can be made in late summer or early autumn and protected with cloches during severe weather for harvesting the following spring.

Container Growing
Bulb onions can be grown in containers, but yields will be small and not really worth the trouble.

Harvesting & Storing
Harvesting commences when the tops bend over naturally and the leaves begin to dry out. Do not bend the leaves over. Allow the bulbs and leaves to dry out while still in the ground during fine weather; wait until the dried foliage rustles before lifting. In adverse weather, spread out the bulbs on sacking or in trays in cold frames, cloches or a shed, turning them regularly. Handle bulbs carefully to avoid damage and disease. Before storing, be sure to remove any damaged, soft, spotted or thick-necked onions and use them immediately. Onions can be stored in trays, net bags or tights, or tied to a length of cord as onion ropes in a cool place.

Harvest salad or bunching onions before the bases swell. During dry weather, water before harvesting to make pulling easier.

Making an onion rope
Storing onions on a rope enables the air to circulate, reducing the possibility of diseases. It is attractive and a convenient method of storage. You can plait the stems to form a rope as with garlic, but they are usually too short and are better tied to raffia or strong string.

Firmly tie in 2 onions at the base, then wind the leaves of each onion firmly round the string, with each bulb just resting on the onions below. When you reach the top of the string, tie a firm knot around the bulbs at the top, then hang them up to dry. Cut onions from the rope as they are needed.

Pests & Diseases
If **birds** are a nuisance, protect plants with black thread or netting.

The larvae of **onion fly** tunnel into bulbs, causing the stems to wilt and become yellow. Seedlings and small plants may die. Cultivate the ground thoroughly over winter; apply a soil insecticide before sowing. Remove and destroy affected plants and rotate crops.

White rot can be a problem, particularly on salad onions. White mould like cotton-wool, dotted with tiny, black spots, appears round the base. Leaves turn yellow and die. It is almost impossible to eradicate. Remove affected onions with as much of the soil round them as possible, dispose of plants and any debris – do not put them on the compost heap. As a preventive measure, dust the drills with an appropriate fungicide. Grow on a new site and from seed.

When attacked by **stem eelworm**, bulbs become distorted, crack, soften, then die. Grow plants from seed; rotate crops; in severe cases do not grow in the same place again. Dispose of plant debris thoroughly and remove any affected plants.

COMPANION PLANTING

Parsley sown with onions is said to keep onion fly away.

MEDICINAL

Used as an antiseptic and diuretic, the juice is good for coughs and colds. The bulbs and stems were applied as poultices to carbuncles.

The traditional way of storing onions is also highly decorative

CULINARY

So indispensable are onions for flavouring sauces, stocks, stews and casseroles that there is hardly a recipe that does not start with some variant of 'fry [or sauté or sweat] the onion in the oil or fat until soft...' They also make a delicious vegetable or garnish in their own right: roasted or boiled whole, cut into rings, battered and deep-fried, or sliced and slowly softened into a meltingly sweet 'marmalade'. Finely chopped raw onion adds zing to dishes like rice salad; you can also use the thinnings to flavour salads.

'Bunching' onions are perfect for salads, pastas, soups and flans. In France they are chopped, sautéed in butter and added to chicken consommé with vermicelli.

Pickled onions are an excellent accompaniment to bread, strong cheese and pickled beetroot – the traditional 'Ploughman's Lunch'. Besides being pickled, pickling varieties can be used fresh in salads and stir-fries, added to stews or else threaded on to kebab skewers for barbecuing.

Onion & Walnut Muffins
Makes 20

This wonderful recipe comes from chef Wally Malouf's *Hudson Valley Cookbook*.

1 large onion
250g (8oz) unsalted butter, melted
2 large eggs
6 tablespoons sugar
1 teaspoon sea salt
1 teaspoon baking powder
300g (10oz) shelled walnuts, coarsely crushed
350g (12oz) plain flour

Preheat the oven to 220°C, 425°F, gas 7. Peel the onion, cut it into quarters and purée it finely in a food processor. Measure the purée to achieve 250g (8oz). Beat together the butter, eggs and sugar and add the onion purée. Stir in the remaining ingredients one by one and mix thoroughly. Fill the muffin tins almost full. Bake them for 20 minutes, or until they are puffed and well browned. Serve warm.

Onion & Walnut Muffins

Onion Tart
Serves 4

This Alsatian dish is full of flavour and very filling. Enjoy it with a simple fresh green salad.

90g (3oz) lard or olive oil
1kg (2lb) onions, sliced into rings
90g (3 oz) smoked bacon, diced
240ml (8fl oz) double cream
3 eggs, lightly beaten
Salt & freshly ground black pepper
Shortcrust pastry to line a 20–23cm (8–9in) tart tin

In a heavy pan, heat the lard or oil and sauté the onions until soft but not browned. Drain well on kitchen paper. Add the bacon to the pan and cook briskly for a couple of minutes, then drain off the fat. Next, mix the cream and the eggs and season well. Then stir in the onions and the bacon and fill the pastry case.

Onion Tart

Bake in a preheated oven at 220°C, 425°F, gas 7 for 10–15 minutes, turning the heat down to 190°C, 375°F, gas 5 for a further 15 minutes, or until the filling is set. Serve warm.

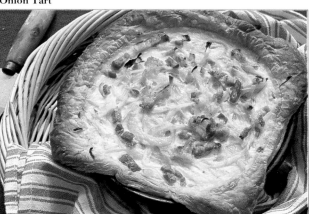

Allium cepa Aggregatum Group. *Liliaceae*

SHALLOT

Small onion, grown as an annual, forming several new bulbs. Hardy.
Value: small amounts of most vitamins and minerals.

Shallots are hardy, mature rapidly, are good for colder climates, tolerate heat and will grow on poorer soils than common onions. Sets are more expensive than seed and are inclined to bolt unless they are heat-treated; buy virus-free stock which is higher-yielding and vigorous, or save healthy bulbs of your own for the following year.

VARIETIES

'Atlantic'* can be sown early and produces heavy yields of moderate to large bulbs which are crisp, tasty and store well. 'Creation' F1, a seed-grown variety, is delicious, highly resistant to bolting and stores well. 'Drittler White Nest', an old variety, produces tasty bulbs of variable size. 'Giant Yellow Improved'* is well worth considering. The bulbs have yellow-brown skins, are consistently large and high-yielding. 'Golden Gourmet' is a mild-tasting shallot for casseroles and salads. It is reliable and high-yielding, stores well and produces good edible shoots. 'Hative de Niort' is an extremely attractive variety with elongated, pear-shaped bulbs, dark brown skins and white flesh. 'Pikant'* is prolific and resistant to bolting. Its skin is dark reddish-brown, the flesh strongly flavoured and firm. 'Red Potato Onion' is extremely hardy, with bronze-red skin and pink flesh which keeps well. 'Sante'* is large and round with brown skin and pinkish-white flesh which is packed with flavour. Yields are high and it stores well. However, it is inclined to bolt and should only be planted from mid- to late spring when conditions improve. 'Topper' is a mild-tasting, vigorous, golden-yellow variety for planting from late winter. It stores well.

CULTIVATION

Propagation
The ideal size for sets is about 2cm (¾in) diameter, which will result in a high yield of good-sized shallots; larger sets will produce a greater number of smaller shallots.

Plant from late winter or early spring, as soon as soil conditions are suitable. Shallots can also be planted from late autumn to mid-winter for early crops. Cover the soil with cloches, fleece or polythene about 2 weeks before planting to warm the soil. If the weather is unfavourable, bulbs can be planted in 10cm (4in) pots of compost and transplanted when conditions improve.

Space sets 23cm (9in) apart with 30–38cm (12–15in) between the rows. Make small holes with a trowel rather than pushing bulbs into the ground (the compaction this causes, particularly in heavier soils, can act as a barrier to young roots). Leave the tips of the bulbs just above the soil. Alternatively, plant in drills, 1cm (½in) deep, 18cm (7in) apart, then cover with soil.

F1 hybrids which are grown from seed produce one bulb, rather than several. From early to mid-spring, as soon as soil conditions allow, sow seed thinly 1cm (½in) deep in broad drills, the width of a hoe, thinning until there is 2.5–5cm (1–2in) around each plant. If spaced farther apart, clusters of bulbs are more likely to form.

Undersized shallots can be grown for their leaves, or you can pick a few leaves from those being grown for bulbs. Plant from autumn to spring under cloches for earlier crops, in seed trays or pots of compost under cover and outdoors when the soil becomes workable. Each bulb should be about 2.5cm (1in) apart.

Growing
Shallots flourish in a sheltered, sunny position on moist, free-draining soil, preferably one which has been manured for the previous crop.

Alternatively, double dig the area in early autumn, incorporating plenty of

Shallots are small and mild enough to be added whole to casseroles

Unlike onions, shallots develop in small clusters

well-rotted organic matter into the lower spit.

Before planting, level the soil and rake in a general fertilizer at 110g/sq m (4oz/sq yd). If you are sowing sets, a rough tilth will suffice, but seeds need a seedbed of a finer texture.

Water during dry periods and keep crops weed-free, particularly while becoming established. Use an onion hoe with care, as damaged bulbs cannot be stored.

Maintenance
Spring Plant sets when soil conditions allow. Sow seed when the soil warms up.
Summer Keep crops weed-free. Water during dry periods.
Autumn Dig in well-rotted organic matter if needed. Plant sets for early crops.
Winter Plant sets from late winter onwards.

Protected Cropping
Shallots are extremely hardy, but early plantings benefit from temporary protection during periods of severe winter weather, particularly if the soil is poorly drained.

Container Growing
Shallots will grow in large pots or containers of soil-based compost. Add slow-release fertilizer to the mix and put a good layer of broken crocks or polystyrene in the bottom of the pot, for drainage. Keep plants well watered in dry periods.

Harvesting & Storing
From mid-summer onwards, as the leaves die back, carefully lift the bulbs and in dry weather leave them on the surface for about a week to dry out; otherwise dry them as onions. Do not cut off the green foliage as this may cause fungal infection, spoiling the bulbs for storage. Break up the bulbs in each clump, remove any soil and loose leaves, then store them in a dry, cool, well-ventilated place. Store on slatted trays, in net bags or in a pair of old tights. Shallots grown for their foliage should be harvested when the leaves are about 10cm (4in) high.

Pests & Diseases
Shallots are usually free of pests and diseases. **Bolting** may be a problem in early plantings or if temperatures fluctuate. Use resistant varieties for early plantings.

Bulbs infected with **virus** are stunted and yields are poor. Use disease-free stock. If **mildew** is a problem, treat as for onions.

Birds can be a nuisance, pulling sets from the ground. Sprinkling a layer of fine soil over the tips can help; otherwise protect the crop with humming wire or similar bird scarers.

Bulbs lifted by **frost** should be carefully replanted immediately.

Eelworms and **onion fly** should be treated in the same way as for onions.

COMPANION PLANTING

Shallots make good companions for apples and strawberry plants; storing sulphur, they are believed to have a fungicidal effect.

CULINARY

Shallots have a milder taste than onions; generally, the yellow-skinned varieties are larger and keep better, while red types are smaller and have the best flavour. The bulbs can be eaten raw or pickled and the leaves used like spring onions.

Shallots can be finely chopped and added to fried steak just before serving. Do not brown them, as it makes them bitter. Béarnaise sauce is made by reducing shallots and herbs in wine vinegar before thickening with egg and butter.

Shallots keep better than ordinary onions

Allium ampeloprasum. Liliaceae

LEEK

Biennial grown as annual for blanched leaf bases. Hardy. Value: good source of potassium and iron, smaller amounts of beta carotene and vitamin C, particularly in green leaves.

The Bible mentions 'the cucumbers, and the melons, and the leeks, and the onions and the garlic' which grew in Egypt, where the leek was held as a sacred plant and to swear by the leek was the equivalent to swearing by one of the gods. This ancient crop still stirs passions. Giant leek contests have been held in pubs and clubs throughout the north-east of England since the mid-1880s. At one show in 1895, W. Robson was awarded a second prize of £1 and a sheep's heart; now the world championships have a first prize of over £1,300. Alongside the daffodil, the leek is one of the national symbols of Wales. Currently the European Community produces over 7 million tonnes per year and France is the chief grower.

VARIETIES

Older varieties are divided into two main groups, long thin and short stout types. In many modern cultivars, such differences are less obvious. There are also early, mid-season and late varieties.

'**King Richard**' is a high-yielding, mild-tasting, early variety with a long shank. Good for growing at close spacing for 'mini leeks'.

'**Prelina**' is harvested in early autumn and has a moderate-length shank. '**Autumn Giant – Cobra**'* is a mid- to late-harvest, medium-length variety with good bolting resistance. '**Autumn Mammoth 2 – Argenta**' and the similar '**Goliath**' mature in late autumn and can be harvested until mid-spring. A high-yielding leek with a medium shank length and thick stems. '**Cortina**' can be harvested through the winter and yields moderate crops. '**Bleu de Solaise**', a French winter variety, can be harvested until spring.

CULTIVATION

Leeks flourish in a sunny, sheltered site on well-drained, neutral to slightly acid soil.

Propagation
Leeks need a minimum soil or compost temperature of at least 7°C (45°F) to germinate, so you will achieve more consistent results, particularly with early crops, when they are sown under cover. For rapid germination, sow early varieties indoors during late winter at 13–16°C (55–60°F) in trays, pots or modules of seed compost. Pot on those grown in trays or pots, spacing them about 5cm (2in) apart, when two true leaves are produced or when they begin to bend over. Harden off gradually before planting out in late spring.

Leeks can also be sown in unheated glasshouses, in cold frames or under cloches. Sow seeds from late winter to early spring, pot on, harden off and transplant in late spring.

Although all varieties are suitable, later sowings of mid-season and later types are particularly successful in seedbeds. Warm the soil using cloches, black polythene or horticultural fleece and rake the seedbed to a fine tilth. Sow thinly in rows 15cm (6in) apart and 2.5cm (1in) deep, providing protection during cold spells. They can also be sown directly in the vegetable plot, 2.5cm (1in) deep in rows 30cm (12in) apart, thinning when seedlings have two or three leaves.

Sowing seeds in modules – either in pairs or singly – keeping the most vigorous of the two, and multi-sowing three to five per cell, avoids the necessity of 'pricking out' or thinning.

Growing
Fertile, moisture-retentive soil is essential, so dig in plenty of organic matter the winter before planting, particularly on light soils. On heavy soils, add organic matter and horticultural sand to improve drainage as crops are poor on heavy or waterlogged soil. Rake, level and firm the soil before planting in spring. As they are a long-term, high-nitrogen crop, apply a general fertilizer, fish, blood and bone or ammonium sulphate at 60–90g/sq m

A fine display of leeks grown in a deep raised bed for showing

Leek flowers are invaluable for attracting beneficial insects

(2–3oz/sq yd) 1 or 2 weeks before planting.

Transplant leeks when they are 15–20cm (6–8in) tall. Trim the leaf tips back if they drag on the ground, but not the roots, as is often recommended. If the soil is dry, water the area thoroughly before planting. Planting 15cm (6in) apart in rows 30cm (12in) apart provides a high yield of moderately-sized leeks. Planting them 7.5–10cm (3–4in) apart in rows gives a high yield of slim leeks. A spacing of 15–17.5cm (6–7in) each way provides a reasonable crop of medium-sized leeks. Leeks grown in modules should be planted 23cm (9in) apart each way.

There are two methods of planting to ensure well-blanched stems. I find the first method better, as deeply-planted leeks are more drought-resistant and soil is less likely to fall down between the leaves. Make a hole 15–20cm (6–8in) deep with a dibber, drop the plant into it and fill the hole with water (this washes some soil into the bottom of the hole), but do not fill any further.

Alternatively, plant leeks 7.5cm (3in) deep and several times through the season pull the earth up around the stems, 5–7.5cm (2–3in) at a time, with a draw hoe. Stop earthing up when the plants reach maturity and make sure that the soil does not fall down between the leaves. Earthing up is easier on light soil.

Whichever method you use, after planting, water gently with a seaweed-based fertilizer. If there is a dry period after planting, water leeks daily until the plants are well established and thereafter only during drought conditions. Hand weed or hoe carefully to keep down weeds, using an onion hoe around younger plants to avoid any damage. In poorer soils, feed weekly in summer with a liquid seaweed or comfrey fertilizer.

Maintenance
Spring Pot on leeks grown under glass; sow seed outdoors.
Summer Transplant seedlings, water and feed. Keep crops weed-free by hoeing or mulching.
Autumn Harvest crops as required.
Winter Harvest mid- and late-season crops. Sow seed under glass in late winter.

Protected Cropping
Apart from early sowings in the greenhouse or cold frame or under cloches and horticultural fleece, leeks are an extremely hardy outdoor crop.

Harvesting & Storing
Early varieties are ready for lifting from early to mid-autumn, mid-season types from early to mid-winter and lates from early to mid-spring. Lift leeks carefully with a garden fork and ensure that you dispose of any leaf debris to reduce the risk of disease in the future. Late varieties taking up space in the vegetable garden which is needed for spring planting, can be stored for several weeks in a shallow, angled trench 15–20cm (6–8in) deep; cover them lightly with soil and leave the tops exposed. If inclement weather is likely to hinder harvest, they can be lifted and packed closely together in a cold frame. The top should be raised to provide ventilation on warmer days.

PESTS & DISEASES

Leeks share many diseases with their close relatives, onions. **Leek rust** appears as orange pustules on the leaves during summer and is worse in wet seasons. Foliage developing later in the season is healthy. Feed with high-potash fertilizer, remove infected plants and debris. Improve drainage; do not plant leeks on the site for 4 to 5 years; grow

Leeks grown in tile drains for early lifting

partially resistant varieties like 'Autumn Mammoth', 'Titan' or 'Gennevilliers-Splendid'. **Slugs** can be damaging. Collect them at night, use biological control, set traps or use aluminium sulphate pellets. Mature leeks usually survive slug damage. **Stem eelworm** causes swelling at the base and distorted leaves. Destroy affected plants immediately and rotate crops. **Leaf rot** is common during periods of high humidity, particularly on high-nitrogen soils. White spots appear on the leaf tips, followed by shrivelling leaf tips. Spray with fungicide, increase the spacing between plants to improve air circulation and apply high-potash fertilizer.

COMPANION PLANTING

Leeks grow well with celery. When planted with onions and carrots they discourage onion and carrot fly. Grow leeks in your rotation programme alongside garlic, onions and shallots. Leeks are a useful crop after early potatoes and if they are grown at a 30cm (12in) spacing, their upright growth makes them ideal for intercropping with lettuces like 'Tom Thumb', land cress or winter purslane.

The blue-tinged 'Bleu de Solaise' is ideal for the ornamental border

CULINARY

Leeks can be boiled or steamed, made into terrines, cooked in casseroles, added to pasta dishes, wrapped in suet pastry and baked. They are a useful addition to soups and an important ingredient in 'Cock-a-leekie' soup and in French Vichyssoise. Braise in stock with a little wine added and bake in a moderate oven. Partially cook trimmed leeks in boiling water, drain well and roll in slices of good country ham and lay them in a dish; cover with a well-flavoured cheese sauce and bake in a hot oven until well browned. Slice or chop young leeks and use raw as a spring onion substitute in salads.

Leek & Ricotta Pie
Serves 4

4 largish leeks, trimmed
2 tablespoons olive oil
2 cloves garlic, finely chopped
225g (8oz) ricotta
2 tablespoons pine nuts
3 tablespoons raisins, softened
  in warm water
1 egg
Salt & freshly ground black
  pepper

For the pastry:
90g (3oz) butter
175g (6oz) plain flour
3 tablespoons water
Pinch salt

Make the pastry by crumbling the butter into the flour and then adding water to make a dough. Add the salt and sprinkle with flour. Wrap in cling film and chill in the fridge for 30 minutes.

Roughly chop the leeks. Steam gently for about 10 minutes and drain well.

Preheat the oven to 190°C, 375°F, gas mark 5. In a heavy frying pan heat the oil and gently fry the garlic. Then add the leeks and stir to coat well with oil; allow them to cook for about 5 minutes, stirring occasionally.

Remove from the heat. In a bowl mix the ricotta with the pine nuts and raisins, and bind with an egg. Add the leeks, mix well and season.

Gently roll out the pastry to fit a 20cm (8in) tart tin. Prick the base and bake blind for 10–15 minutes. Fill the tart with the leek and ricotta mixture and continue cooking for 30 minutes.

Serve the pie with a green salad.

Leeks wrapped in country ham and baked with a covering of cheese sauce

Barbarea verna (B. praecox). Cruciferae

LAND CRESS

***(American cress) Biennial or short-lived perennial grown as annual for young leaves. Hardy.
Value: low in calories, good source of iron, calcium, beta carotene and vitamin C.***

The genus *Barbarea* was known as *herba Sanctae Barbarae*, the 'herb of St Barbara', patron saint of miners and artillerymen and protectress from thunderstorms! Land cress is a fast-growing, hardy biennial with a rosette of deeply lobed, shiny leaves and yellow flowers. Native to south-western Europe, it has been grown as a salad crop since the seventeenth century; by the eighteenth century, extensive cultivation had died out in England, though plants became naturalized and are still common in the wild. In America it is still a popular annual crop. The peppery-tasting leaves make a fine substitute for watercress – and are a good deal more practical for most gardeners to grow.

CULTIVATION

Land cress grows in wet shady conditions, but is best in moist fertile soil; in summer plant in light shade, under deciduous trees.

Propagation
Sow immediately the soil becomes workable, in early spring to early summer for a summer crop and in mid- to late summer for autumn to

Plants flower in early spring

spring crops. Sow in seed trays or modules for transplanting when large enough to handle, or in drills 1cm (½in) deep, thinning the seedlings to 15–20cm (6–8in). Germination takes about 3 weeks in spring but in mid-summer half that time. If a few plants are left to run to seed in late spring to early summer the following year, they will seed freely; transplant seedlings into rows and water well.

Growing
Before sowing, dig in well-rotted manure or compost. Transplant seedlings sown in late summer under glass. In heat and drought they run to seed, so water often. Pick flower stalks as they appear.

Maintenance
Spring Sow seed, water well.
Summer Water as necessary so plants do not run to seed.
Autumn Sow winter crops and transplant plantlets under glass.
Winter Prepare beds for spring sowing; harvest protected crops.

Protected Cropping
Improve the quality of autumn and winter crops by growing in an unheated greenhouse or cold frame, or under cloches.

Container Growing
Grow in moisture-retentive, peat-substitute compost, water well and feed with a dilute general liquid fertilizer every 3 weeks.

Harvesting
Harvest after 7 weeks when plants are 7–10cm (3–4in) long. Pick or cut the tender young leaves about 2.5cm (1in) above ground. Do not harvest heavily until the plant is established. Soak in water to loosen dirt, then wash it off.

Pests & Diseases
Flea beetle may affect young plants; dust seedlings with derris.

COMPANION PLANTING

Makes a good edging plant for borders. Can be grown between taller crops, e.g. sweet corn and brassicas.

CULINARY

Use its peppery-tasting leaves as a watercress substitute – as a garnish, in salads and sandwiches. Or cook them like spinach and make into soup. Good in rice, pasta salads and stir-fries.

Cress, Anchovy & Barley Salad
Serves 4

300g (10oz) pearl barley
4 tablespoons virgin olive oil
2 tablespoons white wine vinegar
2 tablespoons finely chopped dill
4 anchovy fillets, roughly chopped
350g (12oz) cress, washed & dried
1 cucumber, diced
Salt & freshly ground pepper

Cook the barley in boiling water until tender and drain. Set aside. Make the dressing: mix the oil and vinegar with the dill and seasoning. In a separate bowl, mix the barley with the anchovy, add the cress and cucumber, and pour over the dressing. Toss well.

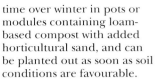

Allium sativum. Alliaceae

GARLIC

Perennial grown as annual for strongly aromatic bulbs. Half hardy. Value: contains small quantities of vitamins and minerals.

Prized throughout the world for its culinary and medicinal properties, garlic, now known only as a cultivated plant, is thought to have originated in western Asia. It has been grown since Egyptian times and for centuries in China and India. Its reputation as a 'cure all' has been endorsed by modern science. The Egyptians placed it in their tombs and gave it to the slaves who built the pyramids to ward off infection, while Hippocrates prescribed it for uterine tumours. In medieval Europe it was hung outside doors to deter witches. Today almost 3 million tonnes per annum are produced globally.

VARIETIES

Many garlic clones exist which are adapted to regional variations in climate and day length. Buy cloves which are compatible with your area. 'California Late' is very reliable in Mediterranean conditions. It keeps well. 'Cristo' is an excellent, large, long-dormancy variety producing up to 15 cloves per bulb. 'Germidor' crops early, producing large cloves and purple bulbs. It must be planted before the end of the year.

   Allium sativum var. *ophioscordon* is sold as 'Rocambole' and is also called 'Serpent Garlic' on account of its coiled, bulbil-producing stem. The bulbs are red in colour. 'Long Keeper' is well adapted to a cool temperate climate. The bulbs are white-skinned and firm. 'Solent Wight', a new variety producing large cloves with a mild flavour, is heavy-cropping.

CULTIVATION

Propagation
Garlic is usually grown from healthy, plump bulb segments ('cloves') saved from a previous crop. Where possible, buy nematode and virus-resistant stock.

   Plant cloves, a minimum of 13mm (½in) diameter, in late autumn or early spring, at a depth of 2.5cm (1in) and 10cm (4in) apart, with the rows 15–20cm (6–8in) apart.

   Garlic is surprisingly hardy and needs a cold, dormant period of 1 or 2 months when temperatures are 0–10°C (32–50°F) to yield decent sized bulbs; for this reason it is generally better planted in late autumn. A long growing period is also beneficial for the ripening process.

   In areas with heavy soil, cloves can be planted any

Garlic 'Solent Wight'

time over winter in pots or modules containing loam-based compost with added horticultural sand, and can be planted out as soon as soil conditions are favourable.

   Plant cloves vertically with the flattened base plate at the bottom, twice the depth of the clove with at least 2.5cm (1in) of soil above the tip. On good soils, planting up to 10cm (4in) deep increases the yield. When planting, you should handle the cloves lightly: do not press them into the soil as this reduces root development.

   The amount of leaf growth dictates the size of the mature bulb which develops during long summer days.

Growing
Garlic favours an open, sunny position on light, well-drained soil. On heavier soil, grow in ridges or improve the drainage by working horticultural sand or grit in to the topsoil.

   Garlic is less successful in areas of heavy rainfall. On poor soils, it is beneficial to rake in a general fertilizer about 10 days before planting. Garlic can be grown on soil manured for the previous crop as well as lime acid soils.

   Rotate the crop and do not grow in sites where onions have been planted the previous year. Keep the bulbs weed-free throughout the growing season.

Maintenance
Spring Mulch to suppress weeds. Water if necessary.
Summer Keep weed-free.
Autumn Plant cloves.
Winter Plant cloves in containers for planting out in spring.

Protected Cropping
Garlic can be grown in an unheated greenhouse for an early crop.

Container Growing
Garlic can be grown in pots, windowboxes or containers, in a moisture-retentive, free-draining compost. Water

regularly to produce decent-sized bulbs and place the container in a sunny position to allow the bulbs to develop.

Harvesting & Storing

From mid to late summer, as soon as the leaves and stems begin to yellow, lift the bulbs carefully with a fork and leave them to dry off in the sun. Delaying harvest causes the bulbs to shrivel and increases the possibility of disease during storage. Handle them delicately as they are easily bruised.

In inclement weather, dry them under cover on trays. Store them in cool, dry conditions indoors or in a shed or garage. Hang them in bunches tied by the leaves, in string bags or plait the stems together. Plants which have gone to seed can still produce usable bulbs for the kitchen.

PESTS & DISEASES

Onion fly lay their eggs around the base of garlic, the larvae tunnel into the bulb and the plant turns yellow and dies. Rotate crops, dig the plot over winter, grow under horticultural fleece and apply chemicals to the soil before sowing.

Downy mildew is a common problem in wet seasons. Grey patches appear on the leaves.

White rot, a grey fungus on the roots, turns the leaves yellow. Lift and destroy infected plants, and do not grow garlic or onions on the site for 8 years.

Stem and bulb eelworm seedlings become blunted, bloated and distorted, and stems rot. Lift and destroy affected plants. Rotate crops.

Planting garlic in Thailand

COMPANION PLANTING

Planted beside rose bushes, garlic controls greenfly. Good companions are lettuce, beetroot, summer savory, Swiss chard and strawberries. It should not be planted with peas and beans.

MEDICINAL

Garlic has powerful anti-viral, anti-bacterial and anti-fungal properties, and is effective for digestive complaints, bowel disorders and insect stings. It contains 2 chemicals which combine to form the bactericide allicin, which gives it the characteristic odour. Modern herbalists believe a cold will be cured by rubbing garlic on the soles of feet. What a combination of odours! Current research indicates its ability to reduce blood cholesterol levels and the chance of heart attack. There is also a lower incidence of colonic and other types of cancer where it is part of the daily diet.

CULINARY

Garlic is used almost exclusively as a seasoning in a range of dishes from curries and stews to pasta. For the daring, the whole immature plants can be added to salads.

La Gasconnade
Serves 6–8

Jeanne Strang gives this recipe from Gascony in *Goose Fat and Garlic*:

1 leg lamb
12 anchovy fillets
500g (1lb) garlic
175ml (6fl oz) bouillon

The *gigot* (lamb) is spiked not only with the usual few cloves of garlic but with anchovy fillets as well. You will need to cut them into small pieces in order to slide them into the slits in the meat.

Lay the fillets across the top of the roast. During the cooking they will melt over the meat and give it the same effect as if it were roasted revolving on a spit.

Cook the joint in a pre-heated oven, 230°C, 450°F, gas 8 for 20 minutes, then reduce the heat to 180°C, 350°F, gas 4. Allow to cook for 15 minutes to 500g (1lb) from start to finish.

While the joint is cooking, peel the rest of the garlic and blanch in boiling water until the cloves are almost cooked, then throw them into cold water for 20 seconds and drain. Heat the *bouillon* in a saucepan, add any pan juices and the garlic and reduce the sauce until it is nearly a purée. Serve as a garnish to the *gigot*.

Pestou

This is a version of the classic garlic and basil butter which is extremely good over pasta and which the Italians eat with fish. For 50g (2oz) butter, have 2 plump cloves garlic, 5–6 sprigs of fresh basil, 2 tablespoons Parmesan and a pinch of salt. Pound the garlic in a mortar, tear the basil leaves roughly, then add to the garlic with the butter and cheese. Pound to mix.

Aioli

Mayonnaise flavoured with garlic enriches many delicious soups and stews such as *Bouillabaisse*. Pound 2 cloves of garlic in a mortar, stir in the yolks of 2 eggs, pour into a blender and add 300ml (½pt) oil drop by drop at first, faster as the mixture begins to thicken. This will make just over 400ml (⅔pt).

La Gasconnade

Apium graveolens var. *dulce. Umbelliferae*

CELERY

Biennial grown as annual for fleshy leaf stems and leaves. Hardy. Value: low in carbohydrate and calories, high in potassium.

The species is a biennial plant, native to Europe and Asia. It is usually found on marshy ground by rivers, particularly where the water is slightly saline. Its Latin generic name *Apium* is derived from the Celtic *apon*, water, referring to its favoured habitat, while *graveolens* means heavily scented, alluding to its aroma. The stems of the wild plant are very bitter, distinguishing it from *var. dulce* – meaning sweet or pleasant – from which the culinary varieties have been bred. Celery became popular in Italy in the seventeenth century and during the following two hundred years spread throughout Europe to North America. 'Trench celery' (so called from the method used for blanching the stems) is very hardy and is harvested from late autumn to early spring, while the more recently developed self-blanching and American green types have a shorter growing season and are less hardy, cropping from mid-summer until mid-autumn. Less succulent, but full of flavour, is the smaller-stemmed 'cutting celery'.

VARIETIES

Trench celery
This is grouped into white, pink and the hardier red varieties:
'Giant Pink' is a hardy variety harvested from mid- to late winter. The crisp, pale pink stalks blanch easily. **'Giant Red'** is hardy and vigorous; the outer stalks turn shell-pink when blanched. **'Giant White'** is an old, tall, white celery variety with crisp stems and a solid, well-flavoured heart. It needs good growing conditions to flourish. **'Hopkins Fenlander'** is a late-maturing green celery with sticks of medium length and free from string. It has a good flavour. **'Standard Bearer'** red celery has the reputation of being the latest of all to reach maturity.

Self-blanching and American green celery varieties
These include: **'Celebrity'***, an early-maturing variety, has crisp, long stems and a nutty-flavoured heart. It has good bolting resistance and is one of the least stringy self-blanching varieties. **'Golden Self Blanching'** is compact

American green varieties do not need blanching

with firm golden-yellow hearts which are crisp and tasty. Does not become stringy. **'Greensleeves'**, a green variety, produces tasty green sticks. **'Ivory Tower'*** has long white 'stringless' crisp stems. **'Lathom Self Blanching'*** is a vigorous, well flavoured early variety with crisp stems. **'Tall Utah Triumph'** has long, succulent, tender green stems. It crops from late summer to early autumn but the season can be extended by growing under cloches.

Leaf, cutting or soup celery
This produces leaves and stems over a long period and is very hardy. It is usually sold as seed mixes, but cultivars are available: **'French Dinant'** is excellent for drying and full of flavour. **'Soup Celery**

Celery maturing under glass

A healthy, well-grown row of celery is a tempting proposition

d'Amsterdam' is aromatic and prolific, producing thin stems and lots of leaves. *Apium graveolens*, known as smallage or wild celery, is similar in appearance to cutting celery. It tastes bitter and has medicinal rather than culinary uses.

CULTIVATION

Celery is a crop for cool temperate conditions, flourishing at 15–21°C (59–70°F) on an open site. It requires rich, fertile soil which is constantly moist yet well drained and a pH of 6.5–7.5. Lime acid soils before planting.

Propagation
Sow celery from mid- to late spring, in trays of moist seed compost, scattering the seed thinly over the surface; do not cover it with compost, as light is needed for germination. Keep the tray in a propagator or in a greenhouse at 13–16°C (55–60°F); germination can take several weeks, so be as patient as possible.

When two true leaves appear, transplant the seedlings into trays of moist seed compost about 6cm (2½in) apart or individually into 7.5cm (3in) pots and allow them to establish. Harden off before planting outdoors from late spring to early summer when they have 5 to 7 true leaves.

Low temperatures after germination sometimes cause bolting later in life; temperatures should not fall below 10°C (50°F) for longer than 12 hours until the seedlings have become established. They are particularly sensitive at trans-planting size, so cover them with cloches and do not try to slow down the growth of advanced seedlings by putting them outdoors. It is much better to trim plants back to about 7.5cm (3in) with sharp scissors and keep them in the warm until outdoor temperatures are satisfactory. Cutting back also seems to lead to more successful transplanting. Planting in modules of seed compost lessens trans-planting shock, which can also result in bolting. If you are unable to provide the necessary conditions, plantlets can always be bought.

Celery can also be sown *in situ* but germination is usually erratic and it is not worth the trouble. Celery's low germination rate can be improved by 'fluid sowing'. If possible, use treated seed to control celery leaf spot. Several sowings at 3-week intervals lengthens the harvesting season.

Sow cutting celery in trays of seed compost from late spring to late summer before hardening off and planting out 15cm (6in) apart each way. Alternatively, multi-sow in modules, about 6–8 seeds in each, and plant each module group 20cm (8in) apart. Leave a few plants to run to seed the following year, then trans-plant self-sown seedlings at the recommended spacing.

Growing
The planting method is different for 'trench celery' and self-blanching types. For the first, dig a trench 38–50cm (15–20in) wide and 30cm (12in) deep in late autumn or early spring and incorporate as much well-rotted manure or compost as you can find. If more than one trench is needed, their centres should be 120cm (4ft) apart. Trench celery can also be grown by filling in the trench to a depth of about 7.5–10cm (3–4in) and leaving the remaining soil alongside for earthing up. A week or 10 days before planting, rake in a balanced general fertilizer at rate of 60–90g/sq m (2–3oz/sq yd) into the bottom of the trench. Celery is easier to manage when planted in single rows with plants 30–45cm (12–18in) apart. If you plant in double rows, set the plants 23cm (9in) apart in pairs, rather than staggered. This makes blanching easier. Water thoroughly after planting.

Blanch by earthing up plants when they are about 30cm (12in) high. Before you start, tie the stems loosely, just below the leaves,

Where space is limited, celery can be grown in deep containers

using raffia or soft string and make sure the soil is moist, watering if necessary (or earth up after rain). Draw soil up the stems about 7.5cm (3in) at a time, repeating this two or three times at 3-week intervals until only the tops of plants are exposed. Do not earth up higher than the leaves, neither should you let soil fall into the heart of the plant. If heavy frosts are forecast in winter, place bracken, straw or other protective material over plants to keep in good condition for as long as possible.

Plants can also be blanched with 'collars'. Use 23–25cm (9–10in) strips of thick paper like newspaper, corrugated cardboard, brown wrapping paper or thick black polythene. (Ideally this should be lined with paper to prevent sweating.) I have also seen tile drainpipes and plastic guttering being used to good effect.

Begin blanching when plants are about 30cm (12in) high, tying the collar quite loosely around the plant to give it room to expand and leaving about one-third of the plant exposed. Further collars can be added every 2 to 3 weeks as the plants grow.

Remember to unwrap them periodically to remove any slugs hiding beneath. If collars are used in exposed sites, support them by staking with a cane. Cover the top of the cane with a flower pot, film case or ping-pong ball to avoid inflicting any damage to your eyes.

Labour-saving self-blanching types do not need earthing up. They also tolerate a wider range of soils, and are particularly good where the ground is heavy and trenching or waterlogging would be a problem. They are, however, shallow-rooted and should be fed and watered regularly throughout the growing season. Self-blanching celery is planted at ground level. Dig in generous amounts of well-rotted organic matter in spring before planting. The spacing varies according to your requirements and plants should be arranged in a square pattern, not staggered rows. Spacing about 15cm (6in) apart gives a high yield of very tender, small-stemmed sticks; 27cm (11in) apart each way, the optimum spacing, gives high yields of longer, well-blanched sticks and 23cm (9in) apart each way gives moderate stem growth. Plant with the crown at soil level and put straw around the outer plants when they mature to help blanching.

For good-quality crops celery must be watered copiously throughout the growing season and the soil should not be allowed to dry out. Apply up to 22 litres/sq m (5 gal/sq yd) per week during dry periods. Mulching with straw or compost once plants have established conserves moisture and suppresses weeds. Feed with a granular or liquid general fertilizer about 4 to 6 weeks after transplanting. Rotate crops, but do not plant next to parsnip, as both are attacked by celery fly. Avoid anything which checks plant growth throughout the season as this can cause bolting, so transplant the seedlings when the soil is warm, water and feed them regularly, and always mulch or hoe round the plants very carefully.

Maintenance

Spring Prepare the ground for planting. Sow seed and plant earlier crops out under cloches.
Summer Plant out in early summer, keep soil moist and weed regularly. Check for pests and diseases.
Autumn Harvest with care using a garden fork.
Winter Cover with straw, bracken or similar materials to allow harvest to continue during heavy frosts.

The dense foliage of maturing celery suppresses weed growth

Protected Cropping

Protect newly transplanted plantlets with cloches or horticultural fleece for several weeks after planting, until they become established. This is particularly necessary in cooler conditions.

Harvesting & Storing

Lift celery carefully with a garden fork, easing the roots from the ground. Bracken, straw or other protective material placed over trenches assists lifting in frosty weather.

Self-blanching celery can be harvested from mid-summer to early autumn. Before the first frosts, lift and store any remaining plants and put them in a cool, frost-free shed. They will keep for several weeks.

Harvest cutting celery regularly from about 5 weeks after planting.

Lush leaves top celery stems

MEDICINAL

Cultivated varieties are said to be beneficial in the treatment of rheumatism and as a diuretic.

PESTS & DISEASES

Celery leaf miner or **celery fly larvae** tunnel through the leaves leaving brown blisters. Severe attacks check growth. Grow under horticultural fleece, pinch out affected leaves, do not plant seedlings which have affected leaves, or spray with systemic insecticide at the first signs of attack. Do not plant near to parsnips as they can be affected.

Slugs are a major problem, particularly on heavy soil. Use biological control, traps, hand pick or use aluminium-sulphate based slug pellets.

Carrot fly attack the roots and stem bases, stunting growth. Rake insecticide into the soil before planting, grow under fleece or put fine mesh netting barriers 45–75cm (18–30in) high around the crop before or straight after transplanting.

Celery leaf spot shows as brown spots on older leaves, spreading to younger ones. Severe attacks can stunt growth; use treated seed or spray with fungicide.

Celery pale leaf spot (early blight) appears as tiny yellow spots on the leaf surfaces with accompanying grey mould in damp conditions. This disease spreads rapidly. Spray with Bordeaux mixture or similar fungicide. Destroy any plant debris at the end of the season.

COMPANION PLANTING

Celery helps brassicas by deterring damaging butterflies. It grows well with beans, tomatoes and particularly leeks. If left to flower, celery attracts beneficial insects.

CULINARY

Usually eaten raw rather than cooked, celery adds welcome crunchiness to salads, particularly in winter months. It is a key ingredient of Waldorf Salad, made with equal quantities of chopped red-skinned apples and celery, combined with walnuts and bound with mayonnaise.

Celery goes well with cheese – sticks filled with cream cheese or pâté are an appetizing 'nibble'. The 'heart' is particularly tasty. Cook celery in soups and stews, or stir-fry. Braise hearts by simmering in boiling water for 10 minutes, then cook in a covered dish for 45 minutes in a low oven to accompany roasts.

Add leaves to meat dishes, like parsley. Fresh or dried leaves flavour soups and stuffings. Cutting celery is a flavouring for salads, soups and stews; the seeds can also be used.

Celery will stay fresh in a polythene bag in the refrigerator for up to 3 days. Do not stand in water for long periods, or the freshness is lost.

Freeze celery by washing and cutting the sticks into 2.5cm (1in) lengths, blanch for 3 minutes, cool, drain and pack into polythene bags. Use frozen celery only in cooked dishes.

Celery & Courgette with Blue Cheese Dip
Serves 4

2 tablespoons olive oil
1 teaspoon chilli powder
½ teaspoon paprika
1 clove garlic, crushed
4 basil leaves, roughly chopped
4 courgettes, sliced lengthwise into quarters
4 stalks celery, cut into 7.5cm (3in) lengths
Chives, to garnish

For the dip:
4 tablespoons cottage cheese
2 tablespoons crumbled Roquefort cheese
50g (2oz) yoghurt
Salt & freshly ground pepper

In a heavy frying pan over a gentle heat, mix the oil with the chilli powder, paprika, garlic and basil. Turn up the heat and fry the courgette slices, cut side down, until browned and turn them to brown the second side.

In a small bowl mix together all the dip ingredients. On 4 small plates, arrange a fan of alternating courgette and celery sticks and fill the centre with the dip. Garnish with finely snipped chives and serve.

Apium graveolens var. *rapaceum. Umbelliferae*

CELERIAC

**(Celery Root) Biennial usually grown as annual for edible root.
Hardy. Value: rich in potassium; moderate amounts of vitamin C.**

If you have never grown this vegetable, do so immediately; it is absolutely delicious. This swollen-stemmed relative of celery has long been popular in Europe. It was introduced to Britain in the early eighteenth century by the writer and seedsman Stephen Switzer, who brought seed from Alexandria and wrote about the vegetable in his book, *Growing Foreign Kitchen Vegetables*. It is an excellent, versatile winter vegetable, hardier and more disease-resistant than celery, but with similar flavour and aroma.

VARIETIES

The lowest part of the stem, known as the 'bulb' is eaten; the roots which grow below are removed.
   'Iram' is a medium sized 'bulb', with few side shoots. It stores well and the flesh remains white when cooked. **'Marble Ball'** This well known variety is medium sized, globular and strongly flavoured. It stores well. **'Alabaster'** is a high-yielding variety with upright foliage, round bulbs and good resistance to running to seed. **'Tellus'** is a quick-growing variety which remains white after boiling. It has firm flesh and a smoother skin than many varieties. **'Balder'** has a good flavour with round medium sized roots, which are excellent when cooked or raw. The 'bulb' of **'Brilliant'*** is smooth with white flesh and does not discolour. **'Monarch'*** is a popular variety with smooth skin and succulent flesh. **'Regent'** produces large, firm roots with white flesh. It does not discolour when cooked.

CULTIVATION

Propagation
Celeriac needs a long growing season. Sow in late winter to early spring in a propagator at 18°C (65°F) or in mid to late spring in a cold greenhouse, under cloches or in a cold frame. Plant seeds in peat substitute based compost either several to a pot or in seed boxes or modules. Germination is notoriously erratic. Pot on strong seedlings when they are about 1cm (½in) tall and large enough to handle. Plant them into single 7.5cm (3in) pots, modules or in seedtrays at 6cm (2Hin) intervals, keeping the temperature at 13–16°C (55–60°F). Harden off when the weather becomes warm in late spring and plant outdoors once there is no danger of frost.
   Celeriac is sensitive to cold at the transplanting stage; do not try to slow the growth of fast-growing seedlings by lowering the temperature, as this will encourage them to run to seed later in the season. Maintain the temperature and cut off the tops of the plants with sharp scissors to 8cm (3in) – the ideal size for transplanting.

Growing
Celeriac needs rich, fertile, moisture-retentive soil and is ideal for damper parts of the garden. In autumn, incorporate as much well-rotted manure or compost as possible. Space plants 30–38cm (12–15in) apart each way. Do not bury the crowns; they should be planted at ground level. Plant firmly and water thoroughly and continually. In mid-summer remove the outer leaves to expose the crown and encourage the bulb to develop, and remove side shoots if they appear.

Maintenance
Spring Plant out seedlings – harden off. Keep weed free.
Summer Water in dry weather. Mulch to conserve moisture; feed weekly with a liquid manure, particularly in poorer soils.
Autumn Begin harvesting. Cover with straw for ease of lifting.
Winter Prepare ground. Sow seeds under glass.

Protected Cropping
Celeriac only benefits from protection when it is at the seedling stage.

Celeriac 'Iram'

Harvesting & Storing

Celeriac can be harvested through the winter. Harvest when the plants are 7–13cm (3–5in) diameter, though they can be lifted when larger with no loss of flavour. Ideally they should remain in the ground until required. Before the onset of severe winter weather, protect plants with a layer of straw, bracken or with horticultural fleece to prevent the ground from freezing. If the soil is heavy, the site exposed or needed for another crop, lift and remove the outer leaves keeping the central tuft attached; cut off the roots and store in a cool shed in boxes of damp peat substitute or sand.

Alternatively, lift and 'heel in' or transplant the crop in another part of the garden, laying them close together in a trench and covering the bulbs with soil. They last for several weeks when stored in this manner.

Bulbs can be frozen; cut into cubes, blanch for 3 minutes, dry, store in polythene bags and put in the freezer. They will keep for a week in the salad drawer of a refrigerator.

PESTS & DISEASES

Celeriac has the same problems as celery. **Protect against slugs**; use aluminium sulphate-based slug pellets, pick off slugs at night and encourage natural predators. Slugs congregate under lettuce leaves or wet paper; pick off and destroy.

Carrot fly is often a pest when established on carrots. Rake bromophos into the soil before planting. Grow under fleece or place a barrier 75cm (2½ft) high made of fine netting or polythene, erected before or just after sowing.

Celery fly is less of a problem than on celery. Pick off any brown, blistered leaflets or grow under horticultural fleece.

COMPANION PLANTING

Celeriac grows well where legumes have been planted the previous year and benefits from being placed alongside beans, brassicas, leeks, tomatoes and onions.

MEDICINAL

Celeriac oil has a calming effect and is a traditional remedy for skin complaints and rheumatism. It is also said to restore sexual potency after illness! Celeriac is rich in calcium, phosphorus and vitamin C.

WARNING

Celeriac is a diuretic. Pregnant women and those with a kidney disorder should avoid eating it in large quantities.

CULINARY

Containing only 14 cal per 100g, celeriac is excellent for anyone on a diet.

Scrub the 'bulb' thoroughly to remove dirt before peeling. It discolours rapidly when cut; put immediately into acidulated water. Grated celeriac can be added raw to winter salads. Alternatively, blanch the slices or cubes in boiling water for a few seconds beforehand. In France it is cut into cubes and mixed with mayonnaise and Dijon mustard to make *Céleri-rave rémoulade*.

The 'bulb' adds flavour to soups or stews and is good with lamb or beef; puréed or seasoned with pepper, salt and butter, it is an ideal accompaniment for stronger flavoured game.

The leaves are strongly flavoured and can be used sparingly to garnish salads or dried for use in cooking.

The stems can be cooked and eaten like seakale.

Celeriac can be made into delicious chips: boil a whole, peeled root in salted water until just tender and then cut into chips and fry in a mixture of butter and oil until lightly browned. These chips make an excellent accompaniment to game or plain grilled steaks.

Boiled and sliced, celeriac can be covered with a cheese sauce well flavoured with French mustard. It also makes an excellent soup.

Monkfish with Celeriac
Serves 4

750g (1½lb) monkfish, cut into chunks
1 large onion, finely sliced
1 carrot, peeled and cut into julienne strips
50g (2oz) celeriac, cut into julienne strips
75g (3oz) butter
1 tablespoon flour
2 teaspoons French mustard
2 tablespoons Greek yoghurt
1 tablespoon double cream
Salt & freshly ground black pepper

Season the monkfish and prepare the vegetables. Heat half the butter in a heavy frying pan and cook the monkfish gently for about 7–8 minutes, turning it until just tender. Remove from the pan and keep warm. Using the rest of the butter, add the vegetables to the pan and sauté until soft. Stir in the flour and cook for a couple of minutes; then add the mustard, yoghurt and cream. Stir well and heat through gently. Put the fish pieces in, stir to coat well and serve piping hot.

Armoracia rusticana. Cruciferae

HORSERADISH

Perennial herb sometimes grown as annual for strong-flavoured fleshy roots. Hardy. Value: rich in vitamin C and calcium, moderate in carbohydrates.

Thought to be native of southern Russia and the eastern Ukraine, horseradish is now found throughout the temperate zones of the world. Cultivated since classical times, horseradish was probably carried round Europe by the Romans, who used it as a medicine and flavouring. Parkinson noted in 1640, 'it is too strong for tender and gentle stomachs', yet it was extensively eaten by country folk in Germany; it is known in France as *moutarde des Allemands*. Its hardiness and ability to regenerate from the smallest particle of root has ensured its success – and sometimes makes it a pernicious weed both in and outside the garden. The common name 'horseradish' distinguishes it from the salad radish, 'horse' signifying coarse.

Horseradish is easily identified by its paddle-shaped leaves

VARIETIES

The species **Armoracia rusticana** grows up to 90cm (36in) tall; the broad, oblong, dark green leaves have serrated margins. The thick tapering roots penetrate 60cm or more (24in) into the soil. **A.r. 'Variegata'** has leaves splashed with cream and is of ornamental merit, though its flavour is not as good as the species.

CULTIVATION

As horseradish is difficult to eradicate once established, lift all plants from late autumn to early winter, keeping some side roots for propagation the following spring. Alternatively, let it grow as a perennial for some years and divide in spring.

Propagation

Grow from root cuttings or young plants. In late autumn or winter lift crowns, remove side shoots of pencil thickness about 15–20cm (6–8in) long and store them in damp sand in a cool, frost-free shed. In mid-spring, make holes with a dibber 60cm (24in) apart, deep enough for the top of the root cutting to be covered with soil to a depth of 5–7cm (2–2½in); insert a piece of root into each hole with the thickest end uppermost and fill with soil.

Growing

Horseradish dislikes heavy shade but grows on any soil with reasonable drainage; roots flourish in deep, rich, well-drained soils. Dig in well-rotted organic matter the winter before planting; where crops are rotated, horseradish should follow a heavily manured crop like beans. After planting, apply a general fertilizer, water as needed, particularly during drought. Keep weed-free.

Maintenance

Spring Plant root cuttings.
Summer Feed, water and keep the crop weed-free.
Autumn Lift whole crowns, keep large roots for use in the kitchen, use others for propagation.
Winter Prepare the ground for replanting.

Container Growing

Restrict the growth of horseradish as a perennial by planting in a bucket or dustbin (with drainage holes in the base) sunk into the ground. Use soil with plenty of rotted organic matter or a loam-based compost with a moderate fertilizer content. Water well. Divide in autumn and winter as necessary.

Harvesting & Storing
Lift and harvest the crowns in autumn when the flavour is strongest and use stored roots over winter and spring. As exposure to light causes greening, store roots in the cool and dark. In summer, lift roots as required.

Pests & Diseases
Do not plant in soil affected by clubroot.

Horseradish pale leaf spot – near-white spots with dark margins on the leaves – does not affect the roots and no treatment is needed.

COMPANION PLANTING

It improves the disease resistance of potatoes.

Variegated horseradish makes an unusual ornamental

MEDICINAL

Horseradish is a diaphoretic, digestive, diuretic and stimulant. Modern research has indicated anti-microbial activity against some micro-organisms. It is also said to staunch bleeding, prevent scarring and cure stomach cramp. In folk medicine the vapour from grated roots was inhaled to treat colds. It contains high levels of sulphur and potassium.

WARNING

Grate horseradish using the shredder attachment of a food processor to prevent your eyes watering.

Apricot & Horseradish Sauce

CULINARY

The root stays fresh for about 2 weeks in the salad drawer of a refrigerator, but it is better to freeze grated root in polythene bags and use as required. Trim off the rootlets, scrub or scrape under the cold tap to remove soil. Finely grate or use a food processor, discarding the central core. Or store by grating into white vinegar (red wine or cider vinegar discolours the root).

Horseradish sauce, made with milk or oil and vinegar, is the traditional accompaniment for roast beef, asparagus and smoked fish like mackerel. Fold into whipping cream, yoghurt or sour cream and season with salt, sugar and a little vinegar to make horseradish cream. Don't grate until just before serving or it will lose its flavour. My father made his horseradish sauce just before the roast beef was carved: a teaspoonful was absolutely lethal and sent us running for a glass of cold water! Serve with ham, on baked potatoes or cold meats. Grated horseradish can be used in steak tartare, or added to coleslaw, dips and sauces.

Blended with butter and chilled it is an alternative to garlic butter to accompany grilled steak.

Apricot & Horseradish Sauce

Serve this more delicate sauce to accompany roast chicken. With fish, use fennel rather than tarragon.

500g (1lb) apricots, stoned
Juice of half a lemon
Caster sugar
1–2 tablespoons freshly grated horseradish
1 tablespoon freshly chopped tarragon
Salt & freshly ground white pepper

Soften the apricots in a little water and purée. To the purée, add the lemon juice, sugar to taste, horseradish and tarragon. Season to taste.

Asparagus officinalis. Liliaceae

ASPARAGUS

Long-lived perennial grown for slender young shoots and ornamental foliage. Half hardy. Value: high in potassium and folic acid, moderate source of beta carotene and vitamin E.

The genus *Asparagus* provides us with a range of robust foliage houseplants and one of the world's most desirable vegetables. The delicious taste, succulent texture and suggestive shape of the emergent shoots combine to create an eating experience verging on the decadent which has been celebrated for over 2,000 years. Pliny the Elder describes cultivation methods used by the Romans for producing plants with blanched stems, and mentions a cultivar of which three 'spears' weighed a pound. These spears were once believed to arise from rams' horns buried in the soil. Wild asparagus grows in Europe, Asia and north-west Africa, in habitats including dry meadows, sand dunes, limestone cliffs and volcanic hillsides.

VARIETIES

'Connover's Colossal'*, an early, heavy-cropping old variety producing large tasty spears, is suitable for light soils and freezes well. 'Franklim' is heavy-cropping with thick spears. A few can be harvested from 2-year-old crowns. 'Giant Mammoth', with similar characteristics to 'Connover's Colossal', is more suitable for heavy soils. 'Lucullus'* crops heavily, and has long, slim, straight spears. 'Martha Washington', an established favourite in USA, crops heavily, has long spears and is rust-resistant.

The autumn fruits of 'Connover's Colossal'. Although the ripe fruits of female varieties are attractive, they tend to germinate more freely

CULTIVATION

Asparagus thrives in an open, sheltered position on well-drained soil. As a bed can be productive for up to 20 years, thorough preparation is essential.

Propagation

Asparagus can be grown from seed, though it is easier and less time-consuming to plant crowns. Soak seed for 2 days before sowing in mid-spring, 2.5cm (1in) deep in drills 45cm (18in) apart. Thin seedlings when they are 7.5cm (3in) tall until they are 15cm (6in) apart. Alternatively, sow indoors in late winter at 13–16°C

(55–60°F) directly into modules, pots or trays. Pot on, harden off and plant outdoors in early summer. Male plants are the more productive, so the following year, remove any females (identifiable by their fruits) before they shed their fruits. Transplant the remaining male crowns into their permanent position in mid-spring the following year.

Growing

The autumn or winter before planting, dig in plenty of well-rotted organic matter; lime acid soil to create a pH of 6.5–7.5. It is vital to remove perennial weeds. Fork over the soil 1 or 2 weeks before planting and rake in a general fertilizer at approximately 90g/sq m (3oz/sq yd).

One-year-old crowns establish quickly; 2- and 3-year-old crowns tend to suffer from a growth check after transplanting. Plant in mid-spring, once the soil is warm. The roots desiccate quickly and are easily damaged, so cover with sacking until ready to plant, then handle with care.

Either plant in single rows with the crowns 30–45cm (12–18in) apart or in beds with 2 or 3 rows 30cm (12in) apart. For several beds, set them 90cm (3ft) apart. Before planting dig a trench 30cm (12in) by 20cm (8in) and make a 4in (10cm) mound of soil in the base; plant crowns along the top, spreading out the roots, and cover them with 5cm (2in) of sifted soil. As the stems grow, gradually cover with soil; by autumn, the trench should be filled with soil. Keep beds weed-free by hand weeding or hoeing carefully to avoid damaging the shallow roots. On more exposed sites, support the 'ferns' when windy to avoid damage to the crown and water during dry weather.

After harvesting, apply a general fertilizer to nurture stem growth and build up the plants for the following

Cutting off asparagus roots

year. In autumn, when stems have turned yellow, cut back to within 2.5–5cm (1–2in) of the surface and tidy up the bed. Ferns can be shredded and composted. Each spring apply a general fertilizer as growth begins. Mulching with manure has little value beyond suppressing weeds and conserving moisture.

Maintenance
Spring Sow seed and plant crowns. Harvest late spring.
Summer Keep weed-free and water as necessary. Stop harvesting by mid-summer.
Autumn Cut back yellowing ferns and tidy beds.
Winter Prepare new beds: mix in organic matter and remove perennial weeds.

Protected Cropping
Protect the crowns from late frosts with horticultural fleece or cloches.

Harvesting & Storing
However tempting, do not cut spears until the third year after planting (except possibly with 'Franklim'). Harvesting lasts for 6 weeks in the first year and 8 weeks in subsequent years. Do not harvest after mid-summer: it can result in thin spears the

following year. When spears are 10–17.5cm (4–7in) long, cut them obliquely about 2.5–5cm (1–2in) below the surface with a sharp knife or a serrated asparagus knife.

Pests & Diseases
The black and yellow adults and small greyish larvae of **asparagus beetles** appear from late summer, stripping stems and foliage.

COMPANION PLANTING

Where growing conditions allow, asparagus is compatible with tomatoes, parsley and basil.

MEDICINAL

Asparagus is used to treat rheumatism, gout and cystitis. Anyone who lacks the gene to break down asparagin produces urine with a strong odour – a disconcerting but harmless phenomenon.

WARNING

The berries are poisonous.

CULINARY

Asparagus spears should be used as fresh as possible, preferably within an hour of harvesting. They can be refrigerated in a polythene bag for up to 3 days. To freeze, tie into bundles and blanch thick spears for 4 minutes, thin for 2. Freeze in a plastic container.

Asparagus is best eaten steamed or boiled and served hot with butter. Also good cold with vinaigrette, Parmesan or mayonnaise. Asparagus tips can be added to salads and pizza toppings.

To boil, wash spears, peel away the skin below the tips, and soak in cold water until all have been prepared. Sort into stalks of even length (perhaps 20 stalks if thin varieties and 6–8 if thicker-stemmed), and tie with soft string or raffia, one close to the base and another just below the

tip. Stand bundles upright in boiling salted water, with the tips above water level. Cover and boil gently for 10–15 minutes until *al dente*, then drain and serve. Don't overcook: the tips should be firm, and the spears should not bend when held at the base. The water can be used in soup.

Asparagus Risotto
Serves 4

6 morels, fresh or dried
1 big bunch thin asparagus, cut into 2.5cm (1in) pieces
25g (1oz) unsalted butter
1½ tablespoons olive oil
2 red onions, finely chopped
300g (10oz) arborio rice
600ml (1pt) chicken stock, boiling
1 tablespoon fresh marjoram (or 1 teaspoon dried)
2 tablespoons mascarpone
Salt & freshly ground black pepper
Freshly grated Parmesan (optional)

Soak fresh morels in salted water for 10 minutes and wash thoroughly. Pat dry and cut each into several

pieces. If using dried morels, soak in warm water for 30 minutes before cutting up.

Blanch the asparagus in boiling water for 1 minute, drain and set aside.

Heat the butter and oil in a heavy-bottomed pan and sauté the onion and morels until soft. Stir in the rice and coat it well with the oil and butter. Pour in a cup of the

stock and the marjoram and cook over a low heat, stirring frequently, until the liquid is absorbed. Add more cupfuls of stock one at a time and continue cooking until the rice is just tender and the consistency is creamy. Stir in the asparagus and the mascarpone and season well. Serve with Parmesan.

Asparagus Risotto

Beta vulgaris subsp. *cicula. Chenopodiaceae*

SWISS CHARD

(Silver Chard, Silver Beet, Seakale Beet) Biennial grown as annual for leaves and midribs. Hardy. Value: high in sodium, potassium, iron, and an exceptional source of Beta carotene, the precursor of vitamin A.

Perpetual spinach is highly resistant to bolting

The umbrella name 'leaf beet' includes Swiss chard and also encompasses perpetual spinach or spinach beet. (The 'true' spinach and New Zealand spinach both belong to other genera.) A close relative of the beetroot, leaf beet is an ancient vegetable cultivated for its attractive, tasty leaves. Native to the Mediterranean, it was well known to the Greeks, who also ate its roots with mustard, lentils and beans. Aristotle wrote of red chard in the fourth century BC, and Theophrastus recorded both light and dark green varieties. The Romans introduced it to central and northern Europe and from there it slowly spread, reaching the Far East in the Middle Ages and China in the seventeenth century. The name 'chard' comes from the French *carde* and derives from the resemblance of the leafstalks to those of globe artichokes and cardoons. In 1596 John Gerard wrote in his *Herball,* '... it grew with me to the height of eight cubits and did bring forth his rough seeds very plentifully.' If the measurement is correct, his Swiss Chard would be approximately 3m (9ft) tall. I wonder where that variety is today – or was his yardstick wrongly calibrated?

CULTIVATION

Though they tolerate a wide range of soils, the best growing conditions are sunny or lightly shaded positions in rich, moisture-retentive, free-draining soil. On impoverished soils, bolting can be a problem, so dig in plenty of well-rotted organic matter the winter before planting. The ideal pH is 6.5–7.5 and acid soils should be limed.

The ideal growing temperature is 16–18°C (60–65°F), though the range of tolerance is remarkably broad. They survive in winter temperatures down to about −14°C (7°F) and are more tolerant of higher summer temperatures than true spinach, which is inclined to bolt.

Propagation
For a constant supply throughout the year, make two sowings, one in mid-spring for a summer harvest and another in mid- to late summer. The later crop is usually lower-yielding.

Sow 3–4 seeds in 'stations' 23cm (9in) apart, in drills 1–2cm (½–¾in) deep. Swiss chard needs 45cm (18in) between the rows, and perpetual spinach 38cm (15in). Thin seedlings when large enough to handle to

VARIETIES

Swiss chard has broad red or white leaf stems and midribs. **'Fordhook Giant'** has huge, glossy green leaves with white veins and stems. It is tasty and high-yielding, producing bumper crops even at high temperatures. **'Lucullus'** is vigorous and crops heavily, producing pale yellow-green leaves with fleshy midribs. Tolerant of high temperatures, it does not bolt. **'Rhubarb Chard'** (**'Ruby Chard'**) is noted for its magnificent bright crimson

The bright stems of 'Ruby Chard' are spectacular

leaf stalks and dark green puckered leaves. Ideal for the ornamental border or 'potager', it needs growing with care, as it is prone to bolting. **'Vulcan'** is another cultivar with beautiful red stems and dark green, sweet tasting leaves.

'Perpetual Spinach', or spinach beet, is similar but smaller, with narrower stems, dark, fleshy leaves and is very resistant to bolting. **'Erbette'**, an Italian variety, is well flavoured and has an excellent texture. It is good as a 'cut and come again' crop.

leave the strongest seedling. Alternatively, sow in modules or trays and transplant to their final spacing when they are large enough to handle. Swiss chard is particularly successful as a 'cut and come again' crop. Prepare the seedbed thoroughly and broadcast or sow seed in drills the width of a hoe.

Growing
Keep crops weed-free by hoeing or, preferably, mulching with well-rotted organic matter and keep the soil continually moist. In dry conditions, plants will need 9–13.5 litres (2–3 gal) per week, but are surprisingly drought-tolerant. A dressing of general granular or liquid fertilizer can be given to plants needing a boost.

Maintenance
Spring Sow the first crop in mid-spring in 'stations'; thin to leave strongest seedling. *Summer* Weed, water and feed as necessary. Sow a second crop in mid- to late summer. Harvest as needed. *Autumn* Protect with cloches or fleece in late autumn for good-quality growth. *Winter* Dig over the area where the following year's crop is to be planted. Harvest overwintering crops.

Protected Cropping
Though they are hardy enough to withstand winters outdoors, plants protected in cloches, cold frames, polythene tunnels or fleece produce better crops of higher-quality leaves.

Container Growing
Swiss chard can be grown in containers and makes a fine ornamental feature. Either transplant seedlings or sow directly into loam-based compost or garden soil, with added organic matter.

Harvesting & Storing
Seeds sown in mid-spring are ready to harvest from early to mid-summer. Harvest the outer leaves first,

working towards the centre of the plant and cutting at the base of each stem: snapping them off is likely to disturb the roots. Choose firm leaves and discard any which are damaged or wilted. Pick regularly to ensure a constant supply of tender regrowth, so harvest even if you are unable to use them – they are certain to be welcomed by friends.

They can also be grown as 'cut and come again' crops from seedling stage through to maturity. Cut seedlings when about 5cm (2in) tall. After 2–3 crops have been harvested, allow them to regrow to about 7.5cm (5in). Semi–mature plants are harvested leaf by leaf and mature plants can be cut about 2.5cm (1in) above the ground; from this, new growth appears.

Swiss chard and perpetual spinach are best eaten straight from the plant. Leaves (minus the stalks) keep in a refrigerator in the salad compartment or in polythene bags for 2–3 days.

Swiss chard is highly productive

PESTS & DISEASES

They are relatively trouble-free, though beware of **downy mildew** when dense patches of seedlings are sown for 'cut and come again' crops. It appears as brown patches on leaves.

Birds sometimes attack seedlings, so protect crops; growing plants under brassicas or beans also gives them some protection.

COMPANION PLANTING

They grow well with all beans except runners, and flourish alongside brassicas, onions and lettuce. Herbs like sage, thyme, mint, dill, hyssop, rosemary and garlic are also compatible.

MEDICINAL

Leaves are vitamin- and mineral-rich with high levels of iron and magnesium. In folk medicine the juice is used as a decongestant; the leaves are said to neutralize acid and have a purgative effect. Beware of eating it in large quantities!

CULINARY

Perpetual spinach can be lightly boiled, steamed or eaten raw. Swiss chard takes longer to cook: try it steamed, served with butter or sorrel. Soup can be made from the leaves and its midribs cooked and served like asparagus, or added to pork pies. 'Rhubarb Chard' tastes milder than white-stemmed varieties.

Spinach Beet Fritters
Serves 4
These robust fritters go well with salmon or cod.

750g (1½lb) spinach beet, well washed
Knob of butter
2 large eggs, separated
1 tablespoon grated Parmesan
1 teaspoon grated lemon peel
Olive oil for frying
Salt & freshly ground black pepper
Pinch of nutmeg

Prepare the leaves, removing the midribs, and chop roughly. Cook in the water that clings to the leaves until wilted – 2–3 minutes – and drain well. Chop finely and return to the pan with the

butter, cooking until all the liquid evaporates. Leave to cool for 5 minutes and stir in the egg yolks, Parmesan and lemon peel. When almost cold, fold in the stiffly beaten egg whites and season with salt, pepper and nutmeg to taste.

Drop spoonfuls into hot fat, heated in a heavy frying pan, and cook for a minute or two, turning halfway. Drain well and serve hot.

Beta vulgaris subsp. *vulgaris. Chenopodiaceae*

BEETROOT

(Beet) Biennial grown as annual for swollen root and young leaves. Hardy.
Value: slightly higher in carbohydrates than most vegetables,
good source of folic acid and potassium.

Beetroot is a form of the maritime sea beet which has been selected over many centuries for its edible roots. From the same origin come mangold (a cattle fodder), the beet used for commercial sugar production and Swiss chard. Grown since Assyrian times, the vegetable was highly esteemed by the ancient Greeks and was used in offerings to Apollo. There were many Roman recipes for beetroot, which they regarded more highly than the greatly revered cabbage. It appeared in fourteenth-century English recipes and was first described as the beetroot we know today in Germany in 1558, though it was a rarity at that time in northern Europe. The typical red coloration comes from its cell sap, but there are also varieties in other colours.

VARIETIES

Beetroots are grouped according to shape – round or globe-shaped, tapered or long, and flat or oval. To reduce the amount of thinning needed, breeders have introduced 'monogerm' varieties.

Globe
'Boltardy'* is a delicious, well-textured, smooth-skinned variety, an excellent early cropper as it is very resistant to bolting, and good in containers. **'Bonel'** has deep red, succulent, tasty roots and is high-yielding. It crops over a long period and is resistant to bolting. **'Detroit 2 Little Ball'** produces deep red, smooth-

'Burpees Golden' is an especially tasty variety

skinned 'baby beet' which are ideal for pickling, bottling or freezing. A good crop for late sowing and for storing. **'Detroit 2 Dark Red'** has dark red flesh, a good flavour and stores well. **'Monogram'** is dark red, well-flavoured and vigorous, with smooth skin and rich red flesh. It is a 'monogerm' variety. **'Monopoly'*** is also a

'monogerm' and is resistant to bolting, with a good colour and rough skin. **'Regala'*** has very dark roots and is quite small, even at maturity. An excellent variety for containers, and resistant to bolting.

Tapered
'Cheltenham Green Top'* is a tasty, old variety with rough skin and long roots. It stores well. **'Cheltenham Mono'** is a tasty, medium-sized 'monogerm' which is resistant to bolting, good for slicing and stores well.

Others
'Albina Vereduna' (**'Snowhite'**) is a wonderful globe-shaped white variety, with smooth skin and sweet flesh; it has the advantage that it does not stain. The curly leaves can be used as 'greens' and are full of vitamins. It does not store

well and is prone to bolting. **'Barbabietola di Chioggia'** is a mild, traditional Italian variety. Sliced, it reveals unusual white internal 'rings'. It gives an exotic look to salads, certain to provoke comment. When cooked, it becomes pale pink. Sow from mid-spring. **'Burpees Golden'*** has beautiful orange skin and tasty yellow flesh; it is better harvested when small. It looks great in salads, keeps its colour when cooked, does not bleed when cut and the leaves can be used as 'greens'. It stores well and has good bolting resistance. **'Egyptian Turnip Rooted'** (**'D'Egypte'**, **'Egyptian Flat'**) has smooth roots with deep red, delicious flesh. An American introduction, it was first grown around Boston about 1869. **'Forono'*** is very tasty, with large, cylindrical roots, smooth skin and good colour. Slow to go woody, it is ideal for slicing, for summer salads, and stores well. Susceptible to bolting, it should be sown from mid-spring. **'Cylindra'** has sweet-tasting, dark, oval roots with excellent keeping qualities and good flavour. Because of its shape, it is perfect for slicing and cooks well. Harvest when young.

Varieties of 'mini vegetables' include **'Pronto'**, **'Action'** and **'Monaco'**.

'Cylindrica' is ideal for slicing

'Boltardy' is a reliable variety

CULTIVATION

Propagation

In most varieties each 'seed' is a corky fruit containing 2 or 3 seeds, so a considerable amount of thinning is required. 'Monogerm' varieties, each containing a single seed, reduce such a work load. They also contain a natural inhibitor which slows or even prevents germination. Remove this by soaking seeds or washing them in running water for ½ to 1 hour before sowing.

At soil temperatures below 7°C (45°F) germination is slow and erratic. To overcome this, sow early crops in modules, 'fluid sow' or sow in drills or stations after warming the soil with cloches. These can be left in place after sowing until the weather warms up. Use bolting-resistant varieties until mid-spring; after that, any variety can be used.

Sow the first crops under cloches from late winter to early spring 12mm–2cm (½–¾in) deep and 2.5cm (1in) apart with 23cm (9in) between rows. Thin to a final spacing of 10cm (4in) between plants. Alternatively sow 2–3 seeds at 'stations' 10cm (4in) apart, thinning to leave the strongest seedling when the first true leaf appears. 'Round' varieties can be 'multi-sown' in a cool greenhouse planting 3 seeds per module, thinning to 4–5 seedlings, then planting the modules 10cm (4in) apart when about 5cm (2in) high. Early crops can also be sown thinly in broad flat drills 12mm–2cm (½–¾in) deep, in a similar way to peas. Thin as soon as seedlings are touching and keep thinning as plants grow: those large enough can be used whole. If you grow beetroot under horticultural fleece or a similar cover (put in place once the seedlings have established), yields can be increased by up to 50%. Remove protection 4–6 weeks after sowing. From mid-spring, if the weather is warm seeds can be sown without the protection of cloches, thinning to 7.5–10cm (3–4in) apart.

Beetroot grown for pickling need to be about 5cm (2in) in diameter. Sowing in rows 7.5cm (3in) apart, thinning plants to 6.5cm (2½in) apart will give you the correct size.

From late spring to early summer sow the main crop, using any round or long variety. Harvest throughout the summer and for winter storing. Sow in drills or at 'stations', thinning to leave a final spacing of 7.5cm (3in) apart in rows 20cm (8in) apart or 12.5–15cm (5–6in) in and between the rows.

For a constant supply of beetroot, sow round cultivars under glass from late winter at 4-week intervals for mid-spring crops; and for a late autumn crop sow from early to mid-summer in mild areas (for lifting during winter thin to 10cm/4in).

For winter storage sow in late May, early June.

Growing

Beetroot needs an open site with fertile, well-drained light soil which has been manured for the previous crop. The pH should be 6.5–7.5, so acid soils will need liming. Autumn-maturing varieties tolerate heavier conditions and long-rooted varieties require a deeper soil. The best-quality grow in moderate temperatures around 16°C (61°F).

Scatter a slow-release general fertilizer at 30–60g/sq m (2–3oz/sq yd) 2–3 weeks before sowing, raking the seedbed to a fine tilth.

For good-quality beetroot, it is important to avoid any check in growth; at the onset of drought, water at a rate of 11 litres/sq m (2½ gal/sq yd) every 2 weeks. Do not over-water as this results in excessive leaf growth and small roots. If watering is neglected, yields are low, roots become woody and when it rains or you water

'Red Ace' is a vigorous grower

suddenly, the roots will split. Keep weed-free and hoe with care as damage causes the roots to bleed: use an onion hoe or mulch round the plants. Mulching with a 5cm (2in) layer of well-rotted compost or spent mushroom compost will conserve moisture.

Maintenance

Spring Sow early crops under glass or cloches. Mid-spring crops can be sown without protection.
Summer Sow successively every month, harvest earlier crops, keep the plot weed-free and water as required. Sow main crops.
Autumn Lift later crops and those for storage.
Winter In mild areas leave overwintering crops outdoors and protect with bracken, straw or similar materials. Alternatively, lift and store indoors.

Protected Cropping

Grow early crops under glass in modules and transplant under cloches. Alternatively, grow under cloches or crop covers and remove these about 6 weeks after sowing.

Container Growing

Unless growing for exhibition, grow only globe varieties in containers – about 20cm (8in) deep – or troughs or growbags. Sow seed thinly 1.2–2cm (½–¾in) deep from mid-spring to mid-summer, thinning to 10–12.5cm (4–5in) apart. Water regularly, harvest when the size of a tennis ball and keep weed-free.

Harvesting & Storing

Beetroot takes 60–90 days to mature. It must always be harvested before it becomes woody and inedible. Harvest salad beetroot from late spring to mid-autumn and maincrop varieties from mid-summer onwards. Early varieties are best harvested when the size of a golf ball; when later crops reach that size, lift every other plant and use for cooking, leaving the rest for lifting when they reach cricket ball-size.

Lift roots carefully with a fork, shake off soil and twist off the leaves. Do not cut off the leaves: it causes bleeding and makes a terrible mess! Use any damaged roots immediately. Lift beet for storage by mid-autumn and put in stout boxes of moist peat substitute, sand or sawdust, leaving a gap between each root. Store in a cool, frost-free shed or garage. Roots should keep until mid-spring the following year but check regularly and remove any which deteriorate. The long-rooted types are traditionally grown for storage, but most varieties store successfully.

In mild areas and on well drained soil they can be left over winter, but need a dense protective covering of straw or similar material before the frosts. This also makes lifting easier.

PESTS & DISEASES

Beetroot are generally trouble-free but may suffer from the following problems:

Black bean aphid forms dense colonies on the leaves. Yellow blotches between the veins, the symptom of **manganese deficiency**, appear on older leaves first and can be a problem on extremely alkaline soil.

Rough patches on the surface of the root and water-logged brown patches and rings at its centre are a sign of **boron deficiency**. There may also be corky 'growths' on the shoots and leaf stalks.

Make sure that beetroot seedlings are protected against **birds**.

Slugs make holes in leaves. The problem is worse in damp conditions.

COMPANION PLANTING

Beetroot flourish in the company of kohlrabi, carrots, cucumber, lettuce, onions, brassicas and most beans (not runners). Dill or Florence fennel planted nearby attracts predators. Because they combine well with so many other crops and small roots mature within 9–13 weeks, beetroots are good for intercropping and useful catch-crops.

OTHER USES

The foliage is attractive and ideal for inclusion in an ornamental border or 'potager', particularly varieties like 'Bull's Blood'. The leaf mineral content is 25% magnesium, making it useful on the compost heap.

MEDICINAL

Used in folk medicine as a blood tonic for gastritis, piles and constipation; mildly cardio-tonic. Recent research has shown that taking at least one glass of raw beetroot juice a day helps control cancer.

WARNING

The sap stains very badly and is difficult to remove from clothing and skin.

CULINARY

The roots are eaten raw – try them grated as a *crudité* – or cooked and served fresh or pickled. Young 'tops' can be cooked like spinach and used as 'greens'.

They add colour and flavour to salads, particularly the red, yellow, white and bicoloured varieties. Bean and beetroot salad is particularly tasty. Wash in cold water, keeping root and stems intact: do not 'top and tail' or damage the skin, as bleeding causes loss of flavour and colour. Boil for up to 2 hours in salt water, depending on the size, then carefully rub off the skin. It is delicious served hot as a vegetable, otherwise cool for pickling or for a fresh salad.

Beetroot can also be baked, and is the basis for bortsch soup when cooked with white stock. It also makes excellent chutney and wine.

Freeze small beets which are no more than 5cm (2in) across. Wash and boil, skin and cool, then cut roots into slices or cubes and freeze in a rigid container. You should use within 6 months.

In a polythene bag or salad compartment of the fridge, they stay fresh for up to 2 weeks.

Spicy Beetroot Salad
Serves 4

750g (1½lb) beetroots, washed & trimmed
Juice of half a lemon
½ teaspoon cumin
½ teaspoon cinnamon
½ teaspoon paprika pepper
1 tablespoon orange-flower water
2 tablespoons olive oil
Salt & freshly ground black pepper
2 tablespoons chopped parsley
Lettuce (coloured varieties mixed with green leaves such as lamb's lettuce)

Cook the beetroots in a steamer for 20 or 30 minutes until tender. Peel and slice them when cool, reserving the liquid that accumulates on the plate.

Toss them in lemon juice and coat with the spices, orange-flower water and olive oil, together with the liquid. Season, cover and chill. To serve, toss with the parsley and arrange on individual plates on a bed of lettuce leaves.

Spicy Beetroot Salad

Brassica oleracea Gemmifera Group. *Cruciferae*

BRUSSELS SPROUT

Biennial grown as annual for leafy buds and 'tops'. Hardy. Value: excellent source of vitamin C, rich in beta carotene, folic acid, vitamin E and potassium.

First recorded as a spontaneous sport from a cabbage plant found in the Brussels region of Belgium around 1750, this vegetable had reached England and France by 1800. The Brussels version may not have been the first occurrence: a plant described as '*Brassica capitata polycephalos*' (a many-headed brassica with knob-like heads) was illustrated in D'Alechaps's *Historia Generalis Plantarum* in 1587. A stalwart among winter vegetables in cool temperate climates, sprouts are extremely hardy and crop heavily, but are rather fiddly to prepare. As with all vegetables, homegrown ones taste far better than those bought from a shop. If you have never eaten sprouts harvested fresh from the garden, try them: they are absolutely delicious.

Harvest the buttons while firm

VARIETIES

Sprouts are divided into early, mid-season and late varieties, harvested from early to mid-autumn, mid-autumn to mid-winter and mid-winter to early spring respectively. 'Earlies' are shorter and faster-growing than the hardier 'lates', which are taller with higher yields. To extend the season, grow one variety from each group if you have space; alternatively, grow mid-season and late types for mid-winter to early spring crops, when other vegetables are scarce.

Although older open-pollinated varieties are very tasty, it is generally accepted that the modern, compact F_1 hybrids are a better buy. They produce a heavy crop of uniform 'buttons' all the way up the stem, which remain in good condition for a long period without 'blowing'; plants are also less likely to fall over.

'**Citadel**' (mid-season) produces moderately-sized dark green sprouts which freeze well. '**Falstaff**' is a vigorous, high-yielding red cultivar with tasty 'buttons'. The red coloration disappears when boiled, so steaming is a better method of cooking. '**Oliver**'* (very early) is a high-yielding variety producing large tasty sprouts. Good resistance to powdery mildew. '**Peer Gynt**'* (early to mid-season) produces medium-sized sprouts. Lower 'buttons' have a tendency not to open if mature sprouts are left on the plant. Harvest regularly. '**Rampart**'* (late) has good-tasting sprouts that last for a long time before 'blowing' but tend to become bitter late in the season. Good resistance to powdery mildew and some resistance to ringspot. '**Rubine**', a red form, is worth a place in an ornamental border and produces small crops of tasty sprouts. '**Widgeon**'* (mid-season) is a good-flavoured variety producing moderately-sized sprouts.

'Rubine', a magnificent red variety, is an excellent ornamental plant

'Oliver' in full crop

CULTIVATION

Sprouts need a sheltered, sunny spot; wind rock can be a problem in exposed sites. Soil should be moisture-retentive yet free-draining, with a pH of 6.5.

Propagation

Sow early varieties from late winter to early spring, mid-season varieties from mid- to late spring and late varieties from mid-spring. Sow seeds thinly, 2cm (¾in) deep in a half tray of moist seed or multi-purpose compost and put them in an unheated greenhouse, cold frame or sheltered spot outdoors to germinate. Transplant seedlings when they are large enough to handle into a larger seed tray, in potting or multi-purpose compost, about 4–5cm (1½–2in) apart.

Sowing in modules reduces root disturbance when transplanting. Put 2 seeds in each module and retain the strongest after germination. Sow early varieties from late winter in a propagator at 10–13°C (50–55°F) and transplant them into their permanent position after hardening off. Some taller varieties are prone to falling over when grown in modules, but when planted deeply, a long tap root develops.

The previous two methods are preferable to sowing in a seedbed, which takes up space that could be used for other crops, and leaves seedlings vulnerable to pests and diseases; I do not recommend it. If necessary, warm the soil with cloches or black polythene. Protect earlier sowings from cold weather; later sowings can be made without shelter. Water before sowing if the soil is dry. Level, firm and rake the seedbed to a fine tilth before sowing seed thinly, 2cm (¾in) deep in rows 20cm (8in) apart, thinning seedlings to 7.5–10cm (3–4in) apart when they are large enough to handle. Transplant into their final position when they are about 10–15cm (4–6in) tall.

Gradually harden off those grown under cover before planting them in their final positions.

Growing

Dig in plenty of well-rotted manure or compost several months before planting, particularly on light, poor or heavy soils. The ground should not be freshly manured, as excessive nitrogen causes sprouts to 'blow'.

Plant earlier, smaller varieties about 60cm (2ft) apart each way, those of moderate size 75cm (2½ft) apart and taller varieties 90cm (3ft) apart. Wider spacing encourages larger sprouts, improves air circulation and reduces fungal problems, while closer spacing means smaller, compact 'buttons' which will mature at the same time.

Plant with the lowest leaves just above the soil surface. Tug a leaf – if the whole plant moves it has not been planted firmly enough. On light soils, make a drill 7.5–10cm (3–4in) deep, plant sprouts in the bottom and refill it with soil. The extra support makes the plants more stable. Water immediately after transplanting for 3–4 weeks until plants have become established and, if available, mulch with straw to a depth of 5–7.5cm (2–3in).

Keep the beds weed-free. Watering is not normally needed once plants are established except during drought, when each plant can be given up to 142ml (¼pt) per day to maintain the constant growth necessary for good cropping. Remove any diseased or yellowing leaves as they appear. Earthing up round the stem base to a depth of 7.5–12.5cm (3–5in) provides extra support against winter winds, although tall varieties will usually need staking. In exposed gardens, even dwarf varieties need staking.

'Stopping' by removing the growing point is only beneficial for autumn-maturing F₁ cultivars being grown for freezing. Plants can be stopped when lowest

Brussels sprouts at RHS Wisley, in the snow, proving their hardiness

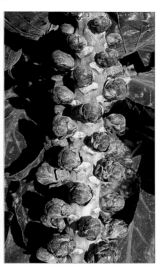

'Falstaff' – what would Shakespeare have thought?

sprouts reach 1cm (½in) diameter, to encourage even development of sprouts on the stem. When left unstopped, sprouts can be picked over a longer period.

Grow sprouts on a 3- or 4-year rotation, preferably following peas and beans (where they benefit from the nitrogen left in the soil). In late summer, feeding with a liquid high-potash fertilizer gives plants a useful boost. Plant small lettuces like 'Little Gem' between sprouts for summer and autumn cropping, and winter purslane or land cress for early winter crops.

Lift plants immediately after harvesting, put leaves on the compost heap and shred the stems.

Maintenance
Spring Sow outdoors in seedbeds, thin and keep weed-free.
Summer Transplant outdoors and water during drought.
Autumn Harvest early varieties; stake tall varieties if needed.
Winter Sow early varieties indoors. Harvest later crops.

Protected Cropping
Earlier sowings made outdoors in a seedbed should be protected with cloches or fleece. Continued protection with horticultural fleece provides a physical barrier against pests such as cabbage root fly, flea beetle, aphids and birds.

Harvesting & Storing
Pick sprouts when those at the base are walnut-sized and tightly closed. Snap them off with a sharp downward tug or cut with a knife, removing 'blown' sprouts and any yellow, diseased leaves. When harvest is over, the tops can be cooked as cabbage. During severe winter weather, lift a few plants to hang in a shed where they can be easily harvested. They will last for several weeks.

PESTS & DISEASES

Sprouts are very robust yet subject to the usual brassica problems.

Downy mildew shows as yellow patches on the leaves, with patches of fluffy mould on the underside in humid conditions. Remove all affected leaves or spray with fungicide. If downy mildew appears on seedlings, improve ventilation and increase spacing.

Powdery mildew is a white powdery deposit over shoots, stems and leaves. In severe cases, plants become yellow and die. It is more of a problem when plants are dry at the roots. Water and mulch, remove diseased leaves and spray with fungicide.

Clubroot, affecting members of the family Cruciferae, is a disease to be avoided at all costs. Roots swell and distort, young plants wilt on hot days but recover overnight, growth is stunted and crops ruined. It is more of a problem on poorly drained, acid soils. Spores remain in the soil for up to 20 years. Never buy brassicas from unknown sources: grow them yourself. Potting plants on into 10–15cm (4–6in) pots allows the roots to become established before they are planted out, which lessens the effects of clubroot. Improve drainage; lime acid soils to create a neutral pH. Earthing up often encourages new roots to form and reduces the effects. Remove all diseased plants, with the whole root system if possible, and destroy them.

Ringspot is worse in cool wet seasons and on well-manured land. It is most evident on older leaves as round brown spots with dark centres. Remove and burn any affected plants and rotate crops.

CULINARY

Steam or boil sprouts briskly for the minimum time required to cook through – they should not turn mushy. Small sprouts can be shredded in salads – 'Rubine' and 'Falstaff' are particularly attractive.

They can be stored for up to 3 days in a polythene bag in the refrigerator. Freeze sprouts only if they are small. Blanch for 3 minutes, cool and drain before drying and packing them into polythene bags.

Stir-fried Sprouts
Serves 4
This can look quite spectacular made with a red variety such as 'Falstaff' or 'Rubine'.

2 tablespoons vegetable oil
2 tablespoons soya sauce
500g (1lb) Brussels sprouts, prepared & finely sliced
2 tablespoons hazelnuts, roughly ground
Salt & freshly ground black pepper

Heat the oil in a wok, stir in the soy sauce and, over a high heat, cook the sprouts for 2–3 minutes. Sprinkle over the hazelnuts. Season and serve.

Stir-fried Sprouts

COMPANION PLANTING

When planted among maturing onions, sprouts benefit from their root residues and the firm soil.

Brassica napus Rapifera Group. *Cruciferae*

TURNIP

Biennial grown as an annual for globular/swollen root and young leaves. Hardy. Value: low in calories and carbohydrate; small amounts of vitamins and minerals.

This ancient root crop was known to Theophrastus in 400BC and many early varieties were given Greek place names. Pliny listed 12 distinct types under *rapa* and *napus* – which became *naep* in Anglo-Saxon, and together with the word 'turn' (meaning 'made round'), gave us the common name. Introduced to Canada in 1541, the turnip was brought to Virginia by the colonists in 1609 and was rapidly adopted by the native Americans. In Britain they have found a role in folklore. In Northern Ireland, turnips were made into lamps for Hallowe'en (31 October), and in the Shetland Islands of Scotland slices were shaped into letters and put into a tub of water for young revellers to retrieve with their mouths; they usually tried to pick the initial of someone they loved.

VARIETIES

Turnips are simple to grow and tasty. The leaves (turnip tops) are also delicious.

Earlies
'Purple Top Milan'* produces flattish roots with purple markings and white flesh. Tender when young, early maturing and good for overwintering, it has an excellent flavour. **'Purple Top White Globe'** (**'Veitch's Red Globe'**) is an attractive old cultivar with round or slightly flattened roots. It is reddish-purple above ground and white below. **'Snowball'** is a delicately flavoured, fast-maturing

white variety with cut leaves. **'Tokyo Cross'*** is an excellent F1 hybrid that produces small tasty white globes and matures rapidly, in about 35–40 days. A 'mini vegetable' which is also tasty when larger, it is suitable as a late summer to early autumn crop.

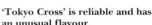
'Tokyo Cross' is reliable and has an unusual flavour

Maincrops
'Golden Ball' (**'Golden Perfection'** or **'Orange Jelly'**) is a small, round yellow variety which should be grown quickly to keep the flesh succulent. Tasty, hardy and excellent for storing. **'Manchester Market'*** has round roots, green skin, white flesh and stores well. **'Green Globe'** is white-fleshed with round roots; excellent for turnip tops.

'Purple Top Milan'

CULTIVATION

Turnips flourish at about 20°C (68°F) and prefer a sheltered, open site in light, fertile, well-drained but moisture-retentive soil. Summer sowings can be made in moderate shade provided they receive sufficient moisture. Turnips prefer a pH of 5.5–7.0; very acid soil will need liming.

Propagation
Sow early turnips in mid-spring, as soon as the ground is workable, or in late winter or early spring under cloches or fleece.

Prepare the seedbed carefully and sow early turnips thinly in drills about 2–2.5cm (¾–1in) deep, in rows 23cm (9in) apart. Then thin to a final spacing of 10–12.5cm (4–5in). They can also be grown in a grid pattern: mark 12.5cm (5in) squares in the ground with a cane and sow 3 seeds where the 'stations' cross, thinning after germination to leave the strongest seedling.

Sow maincrop varieties from mid- to late summer in drills 2cm (¾in) deep and 30cm (12in) apart, thinning to 15–23cm (6–9in) apart. It is important to thin seedlings when no more than 2.5cm (¾in) high, when the first true leaves appear, to ensure the roots develop properly. Firm the soil after thinning; do not thin turnips grown for tops.

When growing for their tops, prepare the seedbed and broadcast seed over a small area or sow thinly in rows 4–6in (10–15cm) apart as soon as soil conditions allow. Sow early cultivars in spring for summer cropping and hardy varieties in late summer or early autumn. Small seedlings of 'main-crops' overwinter and grow rapidly in spring, making them a useful early crop,

'Snowball', a popular variety

particularly when covered with cloches or fleece. To ensure a prolonged harvest, make successional sowings of 'earlies' from early spring until early summer.

Growing
If the ground has not been manured for the previous crop, double dig in autumn, working plenty of well-rotted organic matter into the soil and allowing it to weather over winter. About a week to 10 days before sowing, remove any weeds or debris and rake general fertilizer into the soil at 60g/sq m (2oz/sq yd). In common with other brassicas, turnips grow poorly on loose soil, so rake the soil to a fine tilth and firm it with the head of a rake or by carefully treading. If the soil is dry, water thoroughly before sowing and stand on a planting board to avoid compacting the soil. Mark each row with canes or twigs, and label and date the crop.

Keep crops weed-free by hand weeding or careful hoeing. Turnips must have a constant supply of water throughout the growing season, otherwise they tend to run to seed or produce small woody roots, while sudden watering or rain after a period of drought causes them to split. They will need up to 9 litres/sq m (2 gal/sq yd) per week during dry periods. This improves the size and quality of the crop, but usually reduces the flavour.

Turnips should be rotated with other brassicas.

Maintenance
Spring Prepare seedbed, sow early varieties under cloches. *Summer* Sow earlies every 2–3 weeks for successional cropping. Keep crops weed-free and water as necessary. From mid- to late summer, sow maincrop varieties. *Autumn* Sow 'earlies' under cloches mid- to late autumn. Thin maincrop varieties. *Winter* Harvest and store maincrop turnips.

Protected Cropping
Cover ground with cloches, fleece or black polythene for 2–3 weeks in late winter to early spring to warm the ground before sowing early crops. In late summer protect sowings of early cultivars. Maincrop turnips grown for their tops can be grown under cloches after sowing in autumn and picked during winter.

Container Growing
Fast-maturing early varieties grow well in large containers of well-drained, soil-based compost with added organic matter. Water crops well.

Harvesting & Storing
Harvest early varieties when young and tender. Gather those to be eaten raw when they are the size of a golf ball; any time up to tennis ball-size if they are to be cooked. Hand pull them in the same way as radishes.

Maincrop turnips which are lifted in mid-autumn for winter use are much larger, hardier and slower to mature. To keep the flavour, harvest at maturity as they soon become woody and unpalatable. Turnips can be left in the soil and lifted as required using a garden fork. Keep them in a cool place and use within a few days. In cold wet climates, roots are better lifted to prevent deterioration. Twist off the leaves, remove any soil, put the roots between layers of dry peat substitute, sawdust or sand in a box, then store in a cool shed.

Turnips grown for their tops can be harvested when about 10–15cm (4–6in) high, cutting about 2.5cm (1in) above ground level. Keep soil moist and they will resprout several times before finally running to seed.

Pests & Diseases
Flea beetle, 3mm (⅛in) long and black with yellow stripes, nibble holes in leaves of seedlings, checking growth. Large infestations of **mealy aphid** may kill young plants or cause black 'sooty mould' on leaves. **Cabbage root fly** larvae feed on roots; transplanted brassicas are particularly vulnerable. **Powdery mildew**, a white deposit over shoots, stems and leaves, causes stunted growth. In severe cases leaves yellow and die.

COMPANION PLANTING

Growing with peas and hairy tares deters aphids. Turnips are useful for intercropping between taller crops and for catch-cropping.

MEDICINAL

The liquor from turnips sprinkled with demerara sugar was used in folk medicine to cure colds.

Glazed Turnips

CULINARY

Eat early turnips raw in salads or boiled, tossed in butter and chopped parsley.

Peel maincrop turnips before cooking. They are good mashed, roasted and in casseroles and soups.

Glazed Turnips
Use small young turnips. Scrub them and cut into 1cm (½in) dice (or use whole). Drop into boiling water for 3 minutes. Drain. Melt a little butter and olive oil in a frying pan, add the turnips, sprinkled with a little sugar, and fry over a high heat, stirring constantly, until browned and caramelized. This is particularly delicious with the 'Snowball' variety.

Turnip Tops
Wash well, removing stringy stalks. Chop roughly into manageable pieces. Steam over boiling water until just tender. Serve warm, tossed in olive oil and lemon juice vinaigrette, sprinkled with a finely chopped garlic clove. Or cook like spinach: put the washed leaves in a pan, add salt, pepper and a small knob of butter and steam for 10 minutes in only the water remaining on the leaves. Drain thoroughly and serve immediately.

Brassica napus Napobrassica Group. *Cruciferae*

SWEDE

(Rutabaga, Swedish turnip) Biennial grown as annual for globular/swollen root and young leaves. Hardy.
Value: small amounts of niacin (vitamin B) and vitamin C, low in calories and carbohydrates.

Swede is one of the hardiest of all root crops and is the perfect winter vegetable for cool temperate climates. An abbreviation of 'Swedish turnip', its name indicates its origins. Eaten in France and southern Europe in the sixteenth century, it came to Britain from Holland in 1755 and rapidly became popular as the 'turnip-rooted cabbage'. Along with the turnip, it was first used as winter fodder for sheep and cattle, improving milk production during a traditionally lean period. During times of famine, swedes were eaten by country folk and still have the reputation among many as 'peasant food'.

To despise them is your loss; they are robust, undemanding and one of the easiest vegetables to grow. New varieties are disease-resistant, tasty and a wonderful accompaniment to sprouts as a winter vegetable – particularly when mashed with butter, cream and spices.

VARIETIES

'Acme' has round roots with pale purple skin. Its tops are prone to powdery mildew. 'Angela' produces purple roots and is resistant to powdery mildew. 'Best of All' is a yellow-fleshed, purple-topped, globe-shaped cultivar with excellent texture and mild flavour. Very hardy. 'Lizzy' is a round variety with purple tops and yellow flesh, a soft texture and sweet, nutty flavour. Resistant to bolting and cracking. 'Marian' is purple with yellow flesh, very tasty and quick-growing. It produces large roots and has good resistance to clubroot and powdery mildew.

CULTIVATION

Propagation
Swedes need a long growing season and should be sown from early spring in cooler climates to early summer where temperatures are warmer and germination and growth are rapid. Sow in drills 2cm (¾in) deep and 40–45cm (16–18in) apart, thinning seedlings to 23–30cm (9–12in). Thin when there are no more than 2.5cm (1in) high, when the first true leaves appear, to ensure that the roots develop properly. Firm the soil after thinning.

Growing
Swedes prefer a sheltered and open site in fertile, well-drained but moisture-retentive soil. Good drainage is essential. Summer sowings can be made in moderate shade, provided they receive sufficient moisture. Swedes prefer a pH of 5.5–7.0, so very acid soil will need liming. If the ground has not been manured for the previous crop, double dig in autumn, incorporate plenty of well-rotted organic matter and allow the soil to 'weather' over winter. About a week prior to sowing, remove any weeds or debris and rake general fertilizer into the soil at 60g/sq m (2oz/sq yd). In common with other brassicas, swedes grow poorly on loose soil, so rake the soil to a fine tilth and firm it with the head of a rake or by carefully treading. If the soil is dry, water thoroughly before sowing and stand on a planting board to avoid compacting the soil. Mark

Correct spacing between plants is vital for vigorous growth

each row with canes or twigs, and label and date the crop.

Keep crops weed-free by hand weeding and careful hoeing. Swedes need a constant supply of water throughout the growing season, otherwise they tend to run to seed or produce small, woody roots. Sudden watering or rain after a period of drought causes the roots to split, so they will need up to 10 litres/sq m (2 gal/sq yd) per week in dry periods. This improves the size and quality but usually reduces the flavour.

Rotate swedes with other brassicas.

Swede tops can be blanched for eating raw as a winter salad vegetable. Lift a few roots in early to mid-winter, cut back the leaves and plant the roots under the greenhouse staging, or stand them upright in boxes or wooden trays filled with peat substitute, humus-rich garden soil or with a thick layer of straw. Cover with upturned boxes or black polythene to exclude the light and put them in a cellar, garage or shed. After 3–4 weeks shoots will appear and can be cut when they are 10–12.5cm (4–5in) long.

Maintenance
Spring Warm soil under cloches for early sowings.
Summer Water crops and keep weed-free.
Autumn Harvest early varieties.
Winter Lift and store crops before severe weather starts.

Protected Cropping
Cover ground with cloches, fleece or black polythene for 2–3 weeks in late winter to early spring to warm the ground before sowing early crops. Seedlings should be protected until they are well-established.

Harvesting & Storing
Harvest begins any time from early to mid-autumn. Swedes are extremely hardy and can be left in the ground until needed,

though it is advisable not to leave them for too long or they will become woody. Lift when they are about the size of a grapefruit. They can be stored in boxes in a garage or cool shed. Twist off the leaves and place roots between layers of peat substitute, sawdust or sand in a stout box.

Smaller swedes are more tasty and succulent, so begin lifting as soon as the roots are large enough to use, before they reach their maximum size.

Pests & Diseases
Swedes are affected by the same problems as turnips.

Powdery mildew is common. It appears as a white powdery deposit over shoots, stems and leaves, causing stunted growth. In severe cases leaves become yellow and die. It is more of a problem when plants are dry at the roots and if it is cold at night and warm and dry in the day.

Swedes are susceptible to **club root** – a disease to be avoided at all costs. Roots swell and distort, young plants wilt on hot days but recover overnight, growth is stunted and crops ruined. It is more of a problem on poorly drained, acid soils. Spores remain in the soil for up to 20 years.

Flea beetles are 3mm (⅛in) long and black with yellow stripes. They nibble leaves of seedlings, checking growth.

'Acme', showing its subtle colour and extensive tap roots

COMPANION PLANTING

Swedes grow well with peas.

MEDICINAL

Swedes have been used in folk medicine for the treatment of coughs, kidney stones and whooping cough, though their efficacy has not been recorded.

CULINARY

Swedes can be sliced or cubed and roasted like parsnips, or added to casseroles and stews.

Otherwise, they are delicious mashed with potatoes and served with meat or fish.

To boil, peel off the outer 'skin', cut into slices or cubes and boil for 30 minutes. Drain thoroughly before serving.

Neeps, Tatties and Haggis

Neeps
Serves 4

This is the traditional accompaniment for haggis and tatties (mashed potatoes), washed down with plenty of whisky, on Burns Night in Scotland.

750g (1½lb) swedes
Salt & black pepper
Pinch nutmeg
Butter or olive oil

Clean the swedes, cut them up and boil in enough water to prevent them from burning until tender. Process in a blender or put through a sieve, discarding the juices. Season, and reheat with either butter or olive oil.

Brassica oleracea Acephela Group. *Cruciferae*

KALE

(Borecole, Collards, Colewort, Sprouts)
*Biennial grown as annual for young leaves and shoots.
Hardy. Value: good source of calcium, iron,
beta carotene, vitamins E and C.*

Kales are exceptionally robust, making an ideal winter crop. In addition, they are untroubled by common brassica problems. A type of primitive cabbage, kales are among the earliest cultivated brassicas (the Romans grew several types), with many similarities to the wild *Brassica oleracea* on the western coasts of Europe. The Celtic 'kale' derives from 'coles' or 'caulis' used by the Greeks and Romans to describe brassicas; the German *Kohl* has the same origin. First recorded in North America by 1669, kales are thought to have been introduced much earlier.

VARIETIES

Varieties are classified into groups, including the true kale, Siberian kale and 'Collards'. These are popular in the southern states of America and other warm climates.

Kales vary in height from dwarf types, about 30–40cm (12–16in) high, to tall varieties growing to 90cm (3ft) and spreading to 60cm (24in). The novelty **'Jersey Kale'** ('Walking Stick Cabbage') is grown for its straight stems to 2.25m (7ft), which can be dried and made into walking sticks.

'Siberian kale', 'Rape Kale' or 'Curled Kitchen Kale' (Brassica napus Pabularia Group)
This is a relative of the Swede or rutabaga, grown for the leaves, not the roots. This is variable in form and colour, with broader leaves than kale, which are sometimes curled or frilled. This must be sown *in situ*, not transplanted, cropping when true kales have finished. **'Hungry Gap'** is a late variety, cropping mid- to late spring. **'Laciniato'**, an Italian variety, has deeply cut flat leaves. **'Ragged Jack'** has pink-tinged leaves and midribs. **'Red Russian'** has green/red frilly leaves; excellent flavour. **'True Siberian'** is fast-growing, with blue/green frilly leaves. Can harvest continually throughout winter.

Kale (Scotch Kale, Curly-leaved Kale or Borecole)
True kale usually has dark green or glaucous leaves with heavily frilled margins. **'Darkibor'** is exceptionally hardy with dark green curled leaves. **'Dwarf Blue Curled Scotch'** ('Dwarf Blue Curled Vates') is low-growing, with glaucous leaves, extremely hardy and slow to bolt. **'Dwarf Green Curled'** is compact, hardy and easy to grow; ideal for the small garden or windswept sites. **'Fribor'*** is hardy, to about 45cm (18in), maturing from late autumn to late winter. **'Pentland Brig'**, a cross between curly and plain-leaved kale, is grown for the young leaves, side shoots and immature flower heads (which are cooked like broccoli). An excellent vegetable. **'Showbor'** is a 'mini vegetable'. **'Spurt'** produces tender, deep green, curly

'Ragged Jack' is appropriately named, its leaves an interesting contrast to curly-leaved kale

leaves. Ready to harvest 6–8 weeks after sowing, it crops for a long period. Grow as a 'cut and come again' crop. **'Tall Green Curled'** ('Tall Scotch Curled') is excellent for freezing, and shows good resistance to clubroot and cabbage root fly. **'Thousand Head'** is a plain-leaved, tall, old variety and exceptionally hardy. For harvesting through winter and spring.

Collards (or Greens)
These have smooth, thinner leaves than true kale, taste milder and are more heat-tolerant. **'Champion'** has dark green, cabbage-like leaves and is hardy, with good resistance to bolting. **'Georgia'** has glaucous, white-veined leaves; it tolerates poor soil and extreme heat. **'Hicrop Hybrid'** is mild, sweet and slow to bolt.

CULTIVATION

Propagation
Sow in early spring in trays of moist seed compost or modules, or outdoors in seedbeds in milder areas, for summer crops. Sow from late spring for autumn and winter crops. Alternatively, sow thinly in drills 1cm (½in) deep *in situ*, gradually thinning to final spacing, or sow 3 seeds in 'stations' at

The stout stem of curly-leaved kale, topped by its leaves, makes it look like a miniature tree

the final spacing, thinning to leave the strongest seedling. When 10–15cm (4–6in) high, water the rows the day before, then transplant in the early evening, keeping the lowest leaves just above the soil surface. Water well with liquid seaweed after planting and until they become established. The final spacing for dwarf varieties should be 45cm (18in) apart, with taller types 60–75cm (24–30in) apart.

Collards are sown in late spring in areas with cool summers and in late summer in hotter climates.

Sow Siberian kale thinly in early summer, *in situ*, in drills 45cm (18in) apart, thinning when large enough to handle to a final spacing of 45cm (18in) apart.

Growing

Kales are very hardy: some survive temperatures down to −15°C (5°F); others tolerate high summer temperatures. They grow in poorer soils than most brassicas, but flourish in a sunny position on well-drained soil with moderate nitrogen levels. Excessive nitrogen encourages soft growth, making plants prone to damage. Lime acid soils.

Prepare the seedbed when the soil is moist. Lightly fork the surface, remove any weeds, then firm (but do not compact) the soil.

Overwintering crops need top-dressing with high-nitrogen liquid or granular fertilizer at 60g/sq m (2oz/sq yd) in spring to encourage side shoots.

Keep crops weed-free, water thoroughly before the onset of dry weather, mulch with a 5cm (2in) layer of organic matter and in autumn, firm or earth up round the base of taller plants to prevent wind rock. On more exposed sites, they may need staking.

Kales are good where peas, early potatoes or very early crops have been grown. Rotate with brassicas.

'Tall Green Curled'

Maintenance

Spring Sow early crops under cover; in mid-spring sow in trays or modules, or outdoors in a seedbed.
Summer Transplant seedlings, feed and water well during dry spells. Keep weed-free. Harvest regularly.
Autumn Firm round plant bases; stake if necessary.
Winter Harvest regularly.

Protected Cropping

Make early sowings as a 'cut and come again' crop in the greenhouse border or in mild areas outdoors under cloches, from mid- to late winter. Sow in drills the width of a hoe, broadcast thinly, or sow sparingly in drills, thinning to 7.5cm (3in) apart.

Sow kale under cover in mid- to late winter for transplanting from mid-spring onwards when soil conditions are suitable.

Harvesting & Storing

Harvest by removing young leaves with a knife when they are 10–12.5cm (4–5in) long. Cut from several plants for an adequate picking.

Harvest regularly for constant young growth and a long cropping season; older shoots become bitter and tough. Harvest early sowings of 'cut and come again' crop when about 5–7.5cm (2–3in) high, or thin to 10cm (4in) and harvest when 12.5–15cm (5–6in) high.

Pests & Diseases

Kale is resistant to cabbage root fly and clubroot, and is usually ignored by pigeons.

Take necessary precautions against **whitefly**, **cabbage caterpillar** and **flea beetle**. Caterpillars eat irregular holes in the leaves: check regularly for eggs, squashing them. Beware of infestations of **cabbage aphids**, which check growth and may kill young plants.

CULINARY

Young leaves of later varieties taste better after being frosted.

Wash well and boil in 2.5cm (1in) of water for 8 minutes at most. Serve with butter or white sauce – an excellent accompaniment for poached eggs, fried fish, bacon and other fatty meats. Kale is also good with plain fish dishes such as salmon or cod. In parts of North America kale is served with hog jowls, and the juice is eaten with hot corn bread.

Kale can also be used in salads, soups and stews; it can be creamed, or braised with onions, parsley, spices and bacon or ham.

Before freezing, blanch young shoots for 1 minute, then cool, drain and chop. Kale stays fresh for about 3 days in the fridge or in a polythene bag.

Stir-fried Kale
Serves 4

750g (1½lb) young kale
3 tablespoons peanut or olive oil
Salt & freshly ground black pepper
Juice of half a lemon

Thoroughly wash and dry the kale in a salad spinner. Chop it roughly. Pour the oil in a wok or heavy frying pan over a high heat and, when the oil is steaming, toss in the kale and cook for 3 minutes, stirring constantly. Season and add the lemon juice, adding shavings of lemon peel for decoration if you wish. Serve piping hot with stews or roasted meats.

Stir-fried Kale

COMPANION PLANTING

Kale can be planted with corn and peas.

Brassica oleracea Botrytis Group. *Cruciferae*

CAULIFLOWER

Annual or perennial grown for immature flowerheads. Hardy or half hardy.
Value: good source of vitamin C; traces of most other vitamins.

Cauliflowers are believed to have originated in Cyprus and the oldest record dates from the sixth century BC. One thousand years later they were still widely grown there, being known in England as 'Cyprus coleworts'. A Jewish-Italian traveller wrote from Cyprus in 1593 that cabbages and cauliflowers were to be found growing in profusion, and, 'For a quattrino one can get more almost than one can carry.' Gerard in his *Herball* of 1597 calls them 'Cole flowery'. Moorish scholars in twelfth-century Spain described three varieties as introductions from Syria, where it had been grown for over a thousand years and was much developed by the Arabs. Even in 1699, John Evelyn suggested that the best seed came from Aleppo (now Halab, in northern Syria). Cultivation methods improved after 1700, and by the end of the eighteenth century the cauliflower was highly regarded throughout Europe. Dr Johnson is said to have remarked, 'Of all the flowers in the garden, I like the cauliflower.' But Mark Twain wrote disdainfully, 'Cauliflower is nothing but cabbage with a college education.' This, of course, is a matter of opinion.

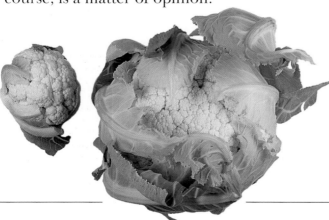

'Dok Elgon', a robust variety for autumn harvest

VARIETIES

There are four main groups for spring, summer, autumn and winter, but many overlap the seasons.

'All the Year Round' is sown in late autumn or spring for spring or summer harvest. Produces good-quality white heads. Excellent for successional sowing. 'Alverda'* has yellow-green heads. Sow late spring to mid-summer for autumn cropping. 'Autumn Giant 3' has beautiful white, firm heads. Excellent for late autumn and winter cropping. 'Castlegrant'* produces deep curds which are well protected from frost. 'Dok Elgon'* is a reliable variety for early and late autumn cropping with firm snow-white heads. 'Early Snowball' is dwarf and compact, growing well in mild climates. Heads do not discolour in bad weather.

'Limelight'* is an attractive soft green cauliflower for autumn harvest. 'Minaret'* has small, tasty, lime-green florets. Crops in late autumn. 'Orange Bouquet' is pale gold and keeps its colour. 'Purple Cape' is a hardy overwintering purple type cropping from late winter to mid-spring. Good raw or cooked; the head turns green when cooked. 'Snowball Self Blanching' is high-yielding, and the leaves naturally blanch the curds. 'Snowcap' is a very late variety, for harvest in mid- to late winter. 'Veitch's Autumn Giant' is a huge plant with large leaves and massive heads to 30cm (12in) in diameter. Very tasty; stores well. 'Walcheren Winter 3 – Armando April' is an overwintering variety. Hardy, frost-resistant and tasty. 'Walcheren Winter 4 – Markanta' is one of the hardiest of all overwintering varieties, with pure white heads. 'White Rock'* produces plenty of leaves to protect the curd. It is a very versatile variety.

CULTIVATION

Propagation
Start off crops as described in 'protected cropping' unless stated. Plants are ready for transplanting when they have 5–6 leaves; water before moving and retain as much soil as possible around the roots.

Sow successively to ensure regular cropping all year round.

Sow early summer crops in mid-autumn and leave them to overwinter under cover. Harden off in late winter, transplant from mid-spring as soon as the soil is workable and warm. Space plants 50cm (20in) apart with 60cm (24in) between the rows or with 50cm (20in) between the rows and plants. Protect with crop covers until established.

Sow summer cauliflowers in early spring under cover or in a seedbed outdoors if the soil is warm and workable, for transplanting in mid-spring and harvesting from mid-summer to autumn. Spacing as above.

Sow early autumn cauliflowers in mid-spring for transplanting in early summer and harvesting for late summer to early autumn. Space 52cm (21in) apart in and between rows, or 50cm (20in) between plants and 60cm (24in) between rows.

Sow autumn cauliflowers in late spring for transplanting in mid-summer and harvesting from mid- to late autumn. Space plants 60cm (24in) apart in and between rows.

If you have available space, sow overwintering cauliflowers, but remember that they can be in the ground for almost a year. Sow in seedbeds outdoors and transplant in mid-summer. Winter cauliflowers for harvesting from mid-winter to early spring should be 65cm (26in) apart each way; those for cutting from mid-spring to early summer should be spaced 60cm (24in) apart in and between the rows. Most varieties need frost protection to avoid damage to the heads.

Commercially grown cauliflowers harvested from Britain's Fenlands

Growing
Cauliflowers need a sheltered sunny site on deep, moisture-retentive, free-draining soil with pH of 6.5–7.5. Dig in plenty of well-rotted organic matter in autumn before planting and lime acid soils where necessary. Avoid planting overwintering types in frost pockets. Rake over the area before planting: the ground should be firm, but not compacted.

Keep plants well watered from germination to harvest, as checks in growth spoil the quality of the heads. They need at least 22 litres/sq m (4 gal/sq yd) every 2 weeks.

Cauliflowers also need moderate nitrogen levels, though excessive amounts encourage soft leafy growth. Overwintering cauliflowers require low nitrogen levels, or they will be too soft to survive colder weather.

Keep crops weed-free with regular hoeing or mulching.

Bend a few leaves over the heads of summer varieties to protect them from sunshine; do the same with winter crops to protect plants from frost and snow. Leaves can be easily tied in place with garden twine.

If the weather is hot and dry, mist plants every now and then to maintain humidity and cool temperatures. Unwrap heads occasionally to check for hiding pests. After cutting the head, feed with a general liquid fertilizer or scatter a granular general fertilizer at 15g/sq m (½oz/sq yd) to encourage the sideshoots to grow.

Rotate crops.

The dark florets of 'Purple Cape' do not affect the taste

A mass of leaves hug the developing curds

Ventilate on warm days, then harden off and transplant as required.

Harvesting & Storing
Harvest cauliflowers successively while they are small, rather than waiting until they all mature. If the heads become brown or if florets start to separate, it is too late: they should be cut. Harvest in the morning, except in frosty conditions when you should wait until midday.

Cauliflowers can be stored for up to 3 weeks by lifting whole plants, shaking the soil off the roots and hanging upside down in a cool shed; mist the heads occasionally to maintain freshness.

Freeze tight heads only. To prepare, divide into sprigs, blanch for 3 minutes in water with a squeeze of lemon juice. Cool, drain, pack carefully and freeze in polythene bags.

Cauliflowers will store, wrapped, in the salad drawer of a refrigerator for up to one week.

PESTS & DISEASES

Beware of **clubroot**, **cabbage root fly**, **caterpillars** and **birds**.

COMPANION PLANTING

Plant with rosemary, thyme, sage, onions, garlic, beet and chards.

MEDICINAL

This is another vegetable reputedly good for reducing the risk of cancer, especially of the colon and stomach.

Maintenance
Spring Sow early crops under glass and outdoors in seedbeds. Keep well watered and weed-free. Transplant.
Summer Sow indoors or outdoors in seedbeds. Transplant, harvest.
Autumn Sow overwintering crops. Harvest.
Winter Prepare ground for the following year. Harvest.

Protected Cropping
Sow under a cold frame or under cloches and thin after germination to about 5cm (2in), or sow 2–3 seeds in 'stations' at the required spacing and thin to leave the strongest seedling. Grow on in the seedbed or transplant into small pots or modules. Alternatively, sow directly in small pots or modules and germinate in a propagator or an unheated greenhouse according to the time of year. Pot on when they are large enough to handle.

'All Year Round', a popular commercial variety

CULINARY

Separate into florets, boil or steam and serve with cheese or white sauce and grated nutmeg or flaked almonds. Alternatively, dip in batter, fry and eat as fritters.

Sprigs can be served raw with mayonnaise and other dips, or added to soups, soufflés and pickles.

Cauliflower with Chillies & Black Mustard Seeds
Serves 4

In Indian cuisine, cauliflower can be cooked into curries but it is more often served dry, as in this recipe from southern India, given to me by the chef at Madras' Chola Hotel. For this dish, buy the washed or white dahl.

5 tablespoons vegetable oil
½ teaspoon asafetida
1 teaspoon whole black mustard seeds
1 teaspoon urad dhal
2 dried hot red chillies, left whole
6 fresh hot green chillies, left whole
750g (1½lb) cauliflower, broken into bite-size florets
Salt
2 tablespoons fresh coconut, grated

Either use a *karhari* or a heavy frying pan. Heat the oil over high heat and add the asafetida, then the mustard seeds. When the seeds pop, add the dhal; this will turn red, at which point add the chillies and cook until the red ones start to darken. Then stir in the cauliflower and cook for a minute or so. Add a tablespoon of water, season with salt and keep stirring, adding more water as necessary; you will probably need to cook for 4–5 minutes, using 4–5 tablespoons water. At this point, turn the heat right down and cook, covered, for a further 5 minutes, until all the liquid has evaporated. Take care not to let the cauliflower burn.

Stir in the coconut and serve, discarding the chillies unless you like really hot food. You have been warned!

Cauliflower with Chillies & Black Mustard Seeds

Cauliflower Soufflé
Serves 4

500g (1lb) cauliflower florets
1 tablespoon butter
1 tablespoon plain flour
150ml (¼ pt) milk
3 large eggs, separated
4 tablespoons grated cheddar
Pinch of nutmeg
Salt & freshly ground pepper

Steam or boil the cauliflower in salted water until just tender. Drain and dice finely. Keep warm. In a heavy saucepan, make a roux from the butter and flour and cook for 1 minute. Stir in the milk and bring to the boil, stirring constantly, to thicken the sauce. Then remove from the heat and stir in the egg yolks. Beat well and add the cheddar and cauliflower, seasoning well. Whisk the egg whites until stiff, then, using a metal spoon, fold into the cauliflower mixture.

Pour into a buttered soufflé dish and cook on the middle shelf of a preheated oven, 190°C, 375°F, gas 5, until the top is gloriously browned.

This should take about 30–35 minutes. Serve the soufflé immediately.

Brassica oleracea Capitata Group. *Cruciferae.*

CABBAGE

Biennial grown as annual for leaves and hearts. Half hardy/hardy. Value: rich in beta carotene and vitamin C – especially green varieties and outer leaves; outer leaves contain vitamin E.

The overwintering cabbage 'January King' will survive even the harshest winters

The Latin *Brassica* comes from *bresic*, the Celtic word for cabbage, a plant cultivated for centuries in the eastern Mediterranean and Asia Minor. The Romans believed that cabbages rose from Jupiter's sweat as he laboured to explain two contradicting oracles – esteeming wild and cultivated cabbages as a cure-all as well as recommending them to prevent unseemly drunkenness.

Many varieties have been developed over the centuries. Heat-tolerant types were bred in southern Europe, while many hard-headed varieties were introduced by the Celts and Scandinavians. White cabbages appeared after AD814 and German literature records the cultivation of red cabbages in 1150; in the sixteenth century Estienne and Liébault believed these were made by watering cabbages with red wine or by growing them in hot places. By the thirteenth century 'headed cabbage' was well known, and three kinds of 'Savoy' were mentioned in a German herbal of 1543.

VARIETIES

Cabbages are usually grouped according to the season when they are harvested. They range from fairly loose-leaved heads of pointed or conical shape to rounded 'ball' shapes with varying degrees of densely packed leaves.

Spring
Spring cabbage traditionally have pointed heads, but there are now round-headed types. For 'spring greens', use their immature leaves or choose a leafy variety bred for this purpose.

'**Greensleeves**' is an early-cropping variety of spring greens. '**Offenham 1 Myatts Offenham Compacta**'* is a tasty, very early spring cabbage and has dark green leaves. '**Pixie**'* is another very early spring cabbage, with compact, tight hearts. It is ideal for small gardens.

Early summer/summer
Varieties which harvest in early summer usually have pointed heads.

'**Derby Day**'* is an excellent 'ball-head' cabbage for harvesting from early summer. '**Hispi**'* is reliable, with pointed heads of good quality and taste. Maturing rapidly, it is ideal for close spacing. '**First of June**'* is a dark-leaved variety with a compact head, for successional sowing in summer. '**Ruby Ball**'* is an ornamental and colourful red cabbage, very reliable and particularly excellent for use in salads.

Late summer/autumn
Late summer and autumn cabbage varieties generally have round or 'ball' heads.

'**Golden Acre**', a ball-headed variety, is compact and sweet-tasting with round grey-green heads. It tolerates close spacing, is high-yielding and grows well on poorer soils. **'Quickstep'*** is of good colour and quality. **'Stonehead'*** has a tightly packed head and is early-maturing. It is resistant to yellow and black rot.

Winter/winter storage
Winter cabbages are usually ball- or drum-headed. The white-leaved Dutch cabbage (used primarily for coleslaw) matures from mid- to late autumn and can be cut for storage or left to stand in mild conditions. The extremely hardy, tasty and attractive Savoy types with puckered green leaves mature from mid-autumn to late winter.

'Ice Queen'* is a highly-regarded Savoy cabbage. **'January King 3'** is an excellent drum-head Savoy type, which is extremely hardy and frost-resistant, maturing in mid-autumn to early winter. **'Multiton'*** is a winter-storage cabbage.

CULTIVATION

Propagation
Seeds sown in trays, modules or seedbeds will be ready for transplanting about 5 weeks

A cross-section of this red cabbage is bizarrely beautiful

after sowing. Spacings can be modified according to the size of 'head' required. Closer spacing means a smaller head while wider spacing produces slightly larger heads.

Sow spring cabbage from mid- to late summer; transplant from early to mid-autumn. Space 25–30cm (10–12in) apart in and between the rows. Protect with cloches or crop covers over winter to encourage earlier cropping. For 'spring greens', grow suitable varieties with 25cm (10in) in and between the plants, or space spring cabbage plants 10–15cm (4–6in) apart and harvest when immature.

Sow cabbages for summer and autumn harvest successively, with 'earlies' and 'lates' for an extended cropping season (see 'Varieties'). You should make the first sowings in a propagator or heated glasshouse at 13–16°C (55–60°F) from late winter to early spring, pot on and transplant in mid- to late spring. Follow these with sowings in cold frames or a seedbed under cloches or crop covers. Make further sowings without protection until late spring.

Transplant from early to mid-summer, spacing plants 35–50cm (14–20in) apart depending on the size of head you require.

Sow winter-maturing varieties successively from mid- to late spring under cover or outdoors for

transplanting from early to mid-summer. Space about 45cm (18in) apart.

Growing
Cabbages flourish at around 15–20°C (59–68°F) and should not be transplanted at temperatures above 25°C (77°F), while some overwintering varieties survive temperatures down to –10°C (14°F).

Cabbages need a rich, fertile, moisture-retentive soil with a pH of 5.5–7.0. Dig in plenty of well-rotted organic matter several weeks before planting and lime the soil if necessary. Rake the soil level before planting and ensure that it is firm but not compacted.

Do not fertilize spring cabbages after planting, as this encourages soft growth and the nutrients are washed away by winter rains. Wait until early to mid-spring and scatter a general granular fertilizer round the plants, or liquid feed.

'Stonehead', a reliable early variety

'Ruby Ball', a particularly attractive and tasty red cabbage

Summer, autumn and winter cabbages need a dressing of fertilizer after transplanting and will benefit from a further granular or liquid feed in the growing season.

To increase stability, earth up spring and winter cabbages as they grow.

Provided growing conditions are good and plants healthy, you can produce a second harvest from spring or early summer varieties. After cutting the head, cut a cross shape 13mm (½in) deep in the stump, which will sprout a cluster of smaller cabbages.

Keep cabbages moist and weed-free with regular hoeing, hand weeding or mulching. Rotate cabbages with other brassicas.

Maintenance

Spring Sow and transplant summer, autumn and winter cabbage. Harvest.
Summer Sow spring cabbage. Harvest.
Autumn Transplant spring cabbage. Harvest.
Winter Sow summer cabbages. Harvest.

Harvesting & Storing

Spring cabbages are ready to harvest from mid- to late spring. Summer and autumn varieties are ready to harvest from mid-summer to mid-autumn. Winter types can be harvested from late autumn to mid-spring.

Spring and summer varieties are eaten immediately after harvest. Dutch winter white cabbages and some red cabbages can be lifted for storing indoors. Choose those which are healthy and undamaged and dig them up before the first frosts for storage in a cool, slightly humid, frost-free place. Remove the loose outer leaves and stand the heads on a slatted shelf or a layer of straw on the shed floor. Alternatively, suspend them in nets.

They can also be stored in a spare cold frame if it is well ventilated to discourage

Spacing between cabbages directly determines the size of 'head'

rotting. They should store for up to 5 months.

Freeze only the best quality fresh crisp heads. Wash, shred coarsely, blanch for about 1 minute and pack into polythene bags or rigid plastic containers.

Wrapped in plastic cling film in a refrigerator, cabbages stay fresh for about a week.

PESTS & DISEASES

Cabbages suffer from the common brassica problems, including **cabbage root fly**, **clubroot**, **aphids** and **birds**.

COMPANION PLANTING

Cabbages thrive in the company of herbs like dill, mints, rosemary, sage, thyme and chamomile. They also grow well with many other vegetables including onions, garlic, peas, celery, potatoes, broad beans and beets.

Like all brassicas, they benefit from the nitrogen left in the soil after legumes have been grown. The belief that they do not grow well with vines, oregano and cyclamen stems from Classical times. In the sixteenth century, it was well known that 'Vineyards where Coleworts grow, doe yeeld the worser Wines'.

MEDICINAL

Eating cabbage is said to reduce the risk of colonic cancer, stimulate the immune system and kill bacteria. Drinking the juice is alleged to prevent and heal ulcers.

Some active principles are partly destroyed on cooking, so cabbage is much more nutritious eaten raw.

According to folklore, placing heated cabbage leaves on the soles of the feet reduces fever; placed on a septic wound, they draw out pus or a splinter.

CULINARY

Traditionally cabbage is cooked by boiling – preferably as briefly as possible – in a small amount of water, to preserve the nutrients. Add the cabbage to boiling water, which should not stop boiling while you place the younger leaves from the heart on top of the older leaves below. Cover, cook briefly for 3 minutes, then drain. Or steam for about 6–8 minutes.

Stir-frying is an almost equally rapid method; alternatively, bake, braise or stuff. Use as a substitute for vine leaves in dolmades.

Eat shredded white or red cabbage raw in salads. Coleslaw is a mixture of shredded cabbage, carrot, apple and celery with French dressing or a mayonnaise/sour cream blend; its name derives from *cole*, the old name for cabbage, and the Dutch *slaw*, meaning salad.

Pickle red cabbage in vinegar and white cabbage in brine (as sauerkraut).

Czerwona Kapusta
Serves 6

The Polish and Czechs are extremely keen on red cabbage. This dish combines subtle flavours to make a refreshing change from our usual ways of cooking the vegetable.

1kg (2lb) red cabbage, finely sliced
1 teaspoon salt
1 tablespoon butter
1 tablespoon plain flour
150ml (¼pt) red wine
2 teaspoons sugar
Pinch ground cloves
Pinch cinnamon
Freshly ground black pepper

Colcannon

Put the cabbage in a colander and sprinkle with salt; leave for 15 minutes and then rinse well under cold water. Transfer to a heavy pan of boiling water and simmer gently until the cabbage is just cooked. Drain and keep warm. Reserve a little of the liquid.

Heat the butter in a saucepan over a medium heat and mix in the flour to make a roux. Cook for 2 minutes without burning. Dilute with the cooking liquid to make a thick sauce and stir in the cabbage. Season and add the red wine, sugar, cloves and cinnamon. Mix well and simmer for a further 5 minutes. Serve.

Colcannon
Serves 4

Probably the most famous Irish dish, some believe this was traditionally made with kale but today it is commonly made with cabbage. Use a Savoy.

500g (1lb) potatoes, peeled & cooked
1 leek, cleaned, sliced & cooked in a little cream or milk
500g (1lb) cabbage, sliced & cooked
4 tablespoons butter
Salt & freshly ground black pepper

Mash the potatoes and season them before stirring in the slices of leek and juices in which they were cooked. Then add the cabbage and mix thoroughly over a low heat. Arrange on a warmed serving dish and make a hole in the centre. Keep warm. Partly melt the butter, season, and pour it into the cavity. Serve immediately, piping hot.

Czerwona Kapusta

Brassica oleracea Gongylodes Group. *Cruciferae*

KOHLRABI

**Biennial grown as annual for rounded, swollen roots. Hardy.
Value: rich in vitamin C, traces of minerals.**

This odd-looking vegetable with a distinctive name has a rounded, swollen stem which, with the leaves removed, looks like a sputnik! Its common name, derived from the German *Kohl* meaning cabbage and *rabi*, turnip, accurately describes its taste when boiled. Raw, it has a fresh, nutty flavour. Found in northern Europe in the fifteenth century, it may already have existed for centuries, as a similar-sounding vegetable was described by Pliny around AD70. This highly nutritious, tasty vegetable is more drought-resistant than most brassicas, succeeding where swedes and turnips fail. It deserves to be more widely grown and eaten.

VARIETIES

'**Azur Star**', a very early variety, has attractive deep blue skin and is resistant to bolting. '**Green Vienna**', an early-maturing variety, is green-skinned with white flesh. '**Lanro**' is a white-fleshed, green-skinned variety which does not deteriorate when harvested after maturity. '**Purple Vienna**' is purple-skinned with white flesh, for late sowing and winter harvesting. '**Rowel**'* is juicy and sweet, with green skin, white flesh and a crisp texture. It does not become woody if allowed to grow larger than a tennis ball. '**Trero**' is sweet, uniform, vigorous and slow to become 'woody'. '**White Vienna**' has pale green skin and is delicately flavoured. Other varieties are especially well suited to growing as 'mini vegetables'.

'Purple Vienna', bizarrely shaped

CULTIVATION

Propagation
As a general rule, green varieties are sown from mid-spring to mid-summer for summer crops and the hardier purple-skinned types from mid-summer to mid-autumn for winter use. Sow successively for a regular harvest.

Early sowings in seed or multi-purpose compost in a propagator at 10–15°C (55–65°F) can be made during mid-winter to early spring. Transplant after hardening off in mid-spring when they are no more than 5cm (2in) high; if you let them grow taller or sow seed when soil temperatures are below 10°C (50°F), they are liable to run to seed. Protect with cloches or horticultural fleece until the plants are established.

Water the drills before sowing and sow later crops thinly in drills 1cm (½in) deep in rows 30cm (12in) apart. Thin seedlings when they are about 2.5cm (1in) high and the first true leaves appear, to a final spacing 15–20cm (6–8in) apart. Prompt thinning is vital, as growth is easily checked. Alternatively, plant 3 seeds together in 'stations' 15cm (6in) apart and thin to leave the strongest seedling. Kohlrabi can also be grown successfully in modules and then transplanted at their final spacing.

Kohlrabi grown as a 'mini vegetable' is ideal for the small garden. Sow cultivars like 'Rolano', 'Logo', 'Korist' and 'Kolibra'* and thin to about 2.5cm (1in) apart between the plants and rows. Harvest after 9–10 weeks when about the size of golf balls.

Growing
The ideal situation is a sunny position on light, fertile, humus-rich, well-drained soil. Incorporate organic matter the winter before planting if necessary and lime acid soils to create a pH of 6–7. The ground must be firm before planting, as (in common with other brassicas), kohlrabi does not grow well on loose soil. Lightly fork the area, removing any debris, then gently tread down the surface or firm it with the head of a rake. Finally, rake in a general fertilizer at 90g/sq m (3oz/sq yd) and level. Kohlrabi must receive a constant supply of water throughout the season. This is because if growth is checked they can become 'woody'. During drought periods, they need up to 8 litres/sq m (2gal/sq yd) of water per week. If growth slows down, liquid feed with a high-nitrogen fertilizer. Keep crops weed-free and mulch with

compost to suppress weeds and retain moisture.

Rotate kohlrabi with brassicas.

Maintenance
Spring Prepare the seedbed and sow seed *in situ* under cloches.
Summer Sow regularly for successional cropping. Sow hardier purple varieties later in the season. Weed and water as necessary.
Autumn Sow in mid-autumn and protect with cloches for early winter harvest.
Winter From late winter, sow early crops in modules or trays. Prepare the ground for outdoor sowings.

Protected Cropping
Early and late outdoor crops should be protected with cloches or crop covers.

Container Growing
Kohlrabi are ideal for containers, particularly when grown as 'mini vegetables'. Plant in a loam-based compost with a moderate fertilizer content and maintain a regular supply of water. Feed every 2–3 weeks with a general liquid fertilizer.

Harvesting & Storing
Kohlrabi matures rapidly and is ready for harvest 2 months after sowing. Lift when plants are somewhere in size between a golf ball and a tennis ball. Larger 'bulbs' tend to become woody and unpalatable, but this is less of a problem with newer cultivars.

Harvest as required. In particularly severe weather, they can be lifted and stored in boxes of sand or sawdust. Remove the outer leaves, retaining the central tuft of leaves to keep them fresh. Some flavour tends to be lost during storage.

'Rowel' is best harvested when small

CULINARY

There is no need to peel tiny kohlrabi, but peel off the tough outer skin of older globes before cooking. Young ones can be trimmed, scrubbed and boiled whole or sliced for 20–30 minutes, then drained, peeled and served with melted butter, white sauce, or mashed.

Boiled kohlrabi can be made into fritters by frying with egg and bread-crumbs. Add kohlrabi to soups and stews, serve stuffed, cook like celeriac, or eat in a cheese sauce. It complements basil and is excellent steamed.

Kohlrabi globes can also be eaten raw, grated or sliced into salads, and the leaves are good boiled.

Kohlrabi Sautéed in Butter

PESTS & DISEASES

As it matures quickly, kohlrabi is untroubled by many of the usual brassica problems, including clubroot.

Birds can cause severe damage, particularly to young plants. You should protect crops with netting, cages, humming wire or with bird scarers.

Flea beetles – 3mm (⅛in) long and black with yellow stripes – nibble holes in leaves of seedlings, checking growth. Dust plants and the surrounding soil thoroughly with derris or insecticide when symptoms appear. They can also be controlled by brushing a yellow sticky trap or piece of wood covered in glue along the tops of the plants: the insects jump out, stick to the glue and can be disposed of.

Cabbage root fly larvae cause stunted growth, wilting and death. Protect the seedlings when transplanting with 12.5cm (5in) squares of plastic, cardboard or rubberized carpet underlay, slit from edge to centre and fitted around the stems. This stops adults from laying eggs.

COMPANION PLANTING

Kohlrabi grows well with beet and onions.

Brassica oleracea Italica Group. *Cruciferae*

BROCCOLI

(Sprouting Broccoli, Calabrese) Perennial or annual grown for immature flowerheads. Hardy or half hardy. High in beta carotene, vitamin C, folic acid and iron. Moderate levels of calcium.

Said to have originated in the eastern Mediterranean, early forms of broccoli were highly esteemed by the Romans and described by Pliny in the first century AD. It spread from Italy to northern Europe, arriving in England in the eighteenth century. Philip Miller in his *Gardener's Dictionary* of 1724 called it 'Sprout Cauliflower' or 'Italian Asparagus'.

Broccoli is an Italian word, derived from the Latin *brachium*, meaning 'arm' or 'branch'. Calabrese, a similar plant with the same botanical origin, grown for its larger immature flowerheads, also takes its name from the Italian – meaning 'from Calabria'. This delicious vegetable was introduced to France by Catherine de Medici in 1560, spreading from there to the rest of Europe. 'Green broccoli' was first mentioned in North American literature in 1806, but was certainly in cultivation long before that. It is said to have been introduced by Italian settlers and is extensively grown around New York and Boston.

Calabrese should be eaten before the buds turn yellow and flowers emerge

VARIETIES

Old varieties of perennial broccoli are still available; outstanding among them all is **'Nine Star'**, a multi-headed variety with small white heads. Cropping improves if unused heads are removed before they go to seed.

Sprouting broccoli
This excellent winter vegetable produces a succession of small flowerheads for cropping over a long season from early winter to late spring. It is an excellent crop for poor soils and cold areas. 'Purple' varieties are hardier than the 'white', which have a better taste, crop later, but tend to be less productive.

'Christmas Purple Sprouting' appears early during good weather, ready for your Christmas dinner! **'Purple Sprouting'** crops heavily from early to mid-spring. **'Purple Sprouting Early'** is easy, prolific and extremely hardy. Ready for harvesting from late winter. **'Purple Sprouting Late'** is similar, but ready for picking from mid-spring. **'White Sprouting'** is delicious, with shoots like tiny cauliflowers. **'White Sprouting Early'** is the white equivalent of **'Purple Sprouting'**. **'White Sprouting Late'** is ready to harvest from mid-spring.

Calabrese
Also known as American, Italian or green sprouting broccoli, this produces a large central flowerhead surrounded by smaller sideshoots which develop after the main head has been harvested. Maturing about 3 months after sowing, it crops from summer until the onset of the first frosts.

'Broccoletto' is quick-maturing and sweet, with a single head. **'Citation'** is an early to mid-season variety with tasty blue-green 'heads'. It is resistant to downy mildew but prone to hollow stems and tends to flower prematurely. **'Early Emerald Hybrid'** produces rich green-blue heads over a season. **'Green Comet'** is early with a large dark-green flowerhead and masses of sideshoots. **'Green Sprouting'**, an old Italian variety, matures early. **'Mercedes'*** matures rapidly, producing high-quality, blue-green stems with large flat heads. **'Ramoso'** (**'DeCicco'**), an old Italian variety for spring or autumn cropping, produces heads over a long period. Tasty, tender and freezes well. **'Romanesco'** is tender with an excellent flavour and lime-green heads. Steam and serve it like asparagus.

CULTIVATION

Propagation

Prepare the seedbed for sprouting broccoli by raking the soil to a fine texture. Sow over several weeks from mid- to late spring, planting the earlier varieties first. Sow thinly in drills in a seedbed, 30cm (12in) apart and 1cm (½in) deep, thinning to 15cm (6in) apart before transplanting at their final spacing. Alternatively, sow 2–3 seeds in 'stations' 15cm (6in) apart, thinning to leave the strongest seedling.

For early spring crops, sow early maturing cultivars indoors in trays from late summer to early autumn. Transplant seedlings when they are about 13cm (5in) tall into a unheated greenhouse or cold frame. Harden off and transplant outdoors from late winter to mid-spring. Alternatively, sow 2 seeds per module and thin to leave the stronger seedling. The final spacing for plants should be about 68–75cm (27–30in) apart in and between the rows. It is worth noting that they take up a lot of space and have a long growing season!

Calabrese can be sown successively from mid-spring to mid-summer for cropping from early summer to autumn. It does not transplant well and is better sown *in situ*. Sow 2–3 seeds at 'stations', thinning to leave the strongest seedling. Close spacing suppresses sideshoots and encourages small terminal spears to form, which are useful for

The popular and prolific 'Purple Sprouting' broccoli

Calabrese 'Romanesco' is outstanding for its unusual lime-green florets

freezing. Wider spacing means higher yields. While they can be as close as 7.5cm (3in) apart with 60cm (24in) between rows, the optimum spacing is 15cm (6in) apart with 30cm (12in) between the rows.

Growing
Sprouting broccoli thrives in a warm, sunny position. Soil should be deep, moisture-retentive and free-draining. Nitrogen levels should be moderate; excessive amounts encourage soft, leafy growth. You should avoid shallow or sandy soils and windy sites.

Sprouting broccoli tends to be top-heavy, so earth up round the stem to a depth of 7.5–13cm (3–5in) to prevent wind rock, or stake larger varieties. Firm stems loosened by wind or frost.

Keep crops weed-free with regular hoeing or mulch with a 5cm (2in) layer of organic matter. Water crops regularly before the onset of dry weather: do not let them dry out. Calabrese needs at least 22 litres/sq m (4 gal/sq yd) every 2 weeks, though a

single thorough watering 2–3 weeks before harvesting is a useful option for those under watering restrictions!

Feed with a general liquid fertilizer, or scatter and water in 15g/sq m (½oz/sq yd) of granular fertilizer after the main head has been removed to encourage the sideshoots to grow.

Maintenance
Spring Sow early broccoli indoors and later crops in seedbeds. Sow calabrese.
Summer Water crops and keep weed-free. Feed calabrese after harvesting the terminal bud.
Autumn Harvest calabrese, remove and dispose of crop debris.
Winter Harvest broccoli.

Harvesting & Storing
Cut sprouting broccoli when the heads have formed, well before the flowers open, when the stems are 15–20cm (6–8in) long. Regular harvesting is essential, as this encourages sideshoot formation and should ensure a 6–8 week harvest. Never strip the plant

completely, or let it flower, as this stops the sideshoots forming and makes existing 'spears' woody and tasteless.

Sprouting broccoli can be stored in a polythene bag in the refrigerator. It will keep for about 3 days.

To freeze, soak in salted water for 15 minutes, rinse and dry. Blanch for 3–4 minutes, cool and drain. Pack it in containers and then freeze.

Cut the mature central heads of calabrese with a sharp knife, while still firm and the buds tight. This encourages growth of sideshoots within about 2–3 weeks. Pick regularly as for sprouting broccoli.

Calabrese can be stored in the refrigerator for up to 5 days, and freezes well.

PESTS & DISEASES

Pollen beetle, **pigeons** and **mealy aphids** are frequently a problem.

Check regularly for **caterpillars**.

COMPANION PLANTING

Plant with rosemary, thyme, sage, onions, garlic, beet and chards.

Broccoli makes a magnificent plant for the potager

CULINARY

Remove any tough leaves attached to the stalks and wash florets carefully in cold water before cooking. For the best flavour cook immediately after picking in boiling salted water for 10 minutes, or steam by standing spears upright in 5cm (2in) of gently boiling water for 15 minutes with the pan covered. Drain carefully and serve hot with white, hollandaise or béarnaise sauce, melted butter, or vinaigrette. An Italian recipe book recommends braising calabrese in white wine or sautéing it in oil and sprinkling with grated Parmesan cheese. In Sicily it is braised with anchovies, olives and red wine. Broccoli fritters are dipped in batter, then deep-fried.

Stir-fried florets can be blanched for 1 minute and fried with squid and shellfish. On a more mundane (but practical) level, broccoli and calabrese can be used as a fine substitute in cauliflower cheese.

Penne with Broccoli, Mascarpone & Dolcelatte
Serves 4

500g (1lb) broccoli florets
150g (5oz) mascarpone
200g (7oz) dolcelatte
2 tablespoons crème fraîche
1 tablespoon balsamic vinegar
1 tablespoon dry white wine
450g (14oz) penne
2 tablespoons capers
4 tablespoons black olives
1 tablespoon hazelnuts, crushed
Salt & freshly ground black pepper

Steam the broccoli florets over a pan of boiling water for 2–3 minutes. Run under cold water and set aside. In a heavy pan, gently heat the mascarpone, dolcelatte, crème fraîche, vinegar and wine. Add the broccoli florets. Cook the pasta until it is just tender and drain well. Pour over the hot sauce, sprinkle with the capers, olives and hazelnuts and toss well. Adjust the seasoning and serve.

Brassica rapa Pekinensis Group. *Cruciferae*

CHINESE CABBAGE

(Chinese leaves, Celery cabbage, Pe Tsai, Peking cabbage) Annual or biennial grown as annual for edible leaves, stems and flowering shoots. Half hardy. Value: moderate levels of folic acid and vitamin C.

Chinese cabbage was first recorded in China around the fifth century AD, and has never been found in the wild. It is thought to have been a spontaneous cross in cultivation between the pak choi and the turnip. Taken to the East Indies and Malaya by Chinese traders and settlers who established communities and maintained their own culture, in the 1400s Chinese cabbage could be found in the Chinese colony in Malacca.

By 1751 European missionaries had sent seeds back home, but the vegetable was regarded as little more than a curiosity. Another attempt at introduction was made by a French seedsman in 1845, but the supply became exhausted and the seed was lost. In 1970 the first large-scale commercial crop was produced by the Israelis and distributed in Europe; about the same time it was marketed in the United States as the Napa cabbage, after the valley in California where it was grown. It has become a moderately popular vegetable in the West.

VARIETIES

There are many groups, but three have become popular: the 'tall cylindrical', the 'hearted' or 'barrel-shaped' and the 'loose-headed'.

The cylindrical type has long, upright leaves and forms a compact head, which can be loosely tied to blanch the inner leaves. It is slow-growing, takes about 70 days from sowing to harvest and is most susceptible to bolting. This type is sweet and stores well.

Hearted types have compact, barrel-shaped heads with tightly wrapped leaves and a dense heart. They mature after about 55 days and are generally slow to bolt.

Loose-headed types are lax and open-headed, often with textured leaves. The 'self-blanching' ones have creamy centres, beautifully textured leaves and look good in salads. They are less liable to bolt than headed types. **'Jade Pagoda'** is cylindrical with a firm, crisp head. It takes about 65 days to mature and is cold-tolerant. **'Kasumi'**, a barrel type, has a compact head and is resistant to bolting. **'Nerva'*** is similar, maturing quickly, and has dark green leaves with dense heads. **'Ruffles'** is delicious and early-maturing, with lax, pale green heads and a creamy white heart. Early sowings are liable to bolt. **'Santo Serrated Leaved'**, a loose-headed variety, has attractively serrated leaves and makes a good seedling crop. It has good cold resistance. **'Shantung'** has a spreading habit, with tender, light green leaves and a dense heart. **'Tip Top'** is an early variety for spring planting and can be harvested around 70 days from sowing. It is vigorous and produces good-sized heads.

Chinese cabbage ready for picking, showing its open habit

CULTIVATION

Propagation

A cool-weather crop, Chinese cabbage is more likely to bolt in late spring and summer. Use resistant varieties or sow after mid-summer. The chance of bolting increases if young plants are subjected to low temperatures or dry conditions, or suffer from transplanting check.

Sow the main crop *in situ* from mid- to late summer, 2–3 seeds per 'station', spaced 30–35cm (12–14in) apart in and between the rows. Thin to leave the strongest seedling.

Alternatively, sow sparingly in drills and thin to the final spacing.

Otherwise it can be sown in modules or pots, transplanting carefully to avoid root disturbance when there are 4–6 leaves. If the soil is dry, water thoroughly.

Broadcast or sow loose-headed types as 'cut and come again' seedlings. Make first sowings in a cold greenhouse or cold frame in early spring, sow outdoors under cloches or fleece as the weather improves and the soil becomes workable. Summer sowings tend to grow too rapidly and become 'tough', unless it is a cool summer. Make the last sowing under cover in early autumn.

Cut seedlings when they have reached a few centimetres or inches tall, leaving them to resprout.

Seeds can also be sprouted, as for Alfalfa.

Growing

Chinese cabbage needs a deep, moisture-retentive, free-draining soil with plenty of organic matter. Excessively light, heavy or poor soils should be avoided unless they are improved by incorporating organic matter or grit. Alternatively, grow in raised beds or on ridges. Dig the soil thoroughly before planting; acid soils should be limed, as the ideal pH is 6.5–7.0. Slightly more alkaline soils are advisable where there is a risk of clubroot.

Chinese cabbage prefers an open site, but tolerates some shade in mid-summer.

Water crops thoroughly throughout the growing season; do not let them dry out. They are shallow-rooted and so need water little and often. Mulching is also advisable. Erratic watering can result in damage to the developing head, encouraging rots. Scatter general fertilizer around the base of transplants or feed with a general liquid fertilizer as necessary to boost growth – this is particularly important on poorer soils. Keep crops weed-free.

In late summer, tie up the leaves of hearting varieties with soft twine or raffia. (With self-hearting varieties, this is unnecessary.)

Rotate Chinese cabbage with other brassicas.

Maintenance

Spring Sow early 'cut and come again' seedling crops under cover. Sow later crops outdoors.
Summer Sow in drills from mid- to late summer. Water a little and often, mulch and keep weed-free. Harvest.
Autumn Sow quick-maturing varieties or 'cut and come again' crops outdoors; sow later crops under cover. Harvest.
Winter Harvest 'cut and come again' crops grown under cover.

Protected Cropping

Earlier crops can be achieved by sowing bolting-resistant cultivars from late spring to early summer. They need temperatures of 20–25°C (68–77°F) for the first 3 weeks after germination to prevent bolting. Harden off,

Thai workers in evening light, harvesting crops grown on raised beds

transplant, then protect the plants with cloches or with crop covers.

Late summer-sown crops should be transplanted under cover. Space plants about 13cm (5in) apart and grow them as a semi-mature 'cut and come again' crop.

Container Growing

The fast-growing varieties give the best results. Use a 25cm (10in) pot or container and loam-based compost with added organic matter and a thick basal layer of drainage material. Sow seeds 1cm (½in) deep and 2cm (¾in) apart in shallow pots or modules in mid-spring. Transplant seedlings singly into pots when they have 3–4 leaves.

Harvesting & Storing

In autumn, cold-tolerant varieties stand outside for several weeks provided it is dry. Protect from wet and cold using cloches. Lift developing crops and replant in cold frames, or uproot and lay plants on straw, bracken or similar, covering them with the same material if temperatures fall below freezing. Ventilate on warm days.

Harvest as 'cut and come again' seedlings, semi-mature or mature plants and for the flowering shoots. Cut seedlings when they are 2.5–5cm (1–2in) tall. Semi-mature or mature plants can be cut with a sharp knife about 2.5cm (1in) above the ground and will then resprout; after several harvests they will send up a flower head. Harvest the flowering shoots when they are young, before the flowers open.

Harvest mature heads when they are firm.

Chinese cabbage keeps in the salad drawer of the fridge for several weeks. Wash thoroughly before storing. Heads can be stored in a cool, frost-free shed or cellar for up to 3 months. When storing, check plants every 3–4 weeks and remove any diseased or damaged leaves immediately.

PESTS & DISEASES

Chinese cabbage can be affected by any of the usual brassica pests and diseases. You should take precautions in particular against **flea beetle**, **slugs**, **snails**, **caterpillars**, **clubroot** and **powdery mildew**. Crops grow well under horticultural fleece or fine netting.

COMPANION PLANTING

Plant with garlic and dill to discourage caterpillars. Main crops are ideal after peas, early potatoes and broad beans; late crops are good companions for Brussels sprouts. It is good for cropping between slower-growing vegetables.

Chinese cabbages are sometimes grown as sacrificial crops so that slugs, flea beetles and aphids are attracted to them rather than other crops. In the USA they are used among maize, as they attract corn worms.

Chinese cabbage crop growing near Kanchanaburi, Thailand

WARNING

To minimize the risk of listeria, you should never store Chinese cabbage in plastic bags.

CULINARY

Cook Chinese cabbage only lightly to retain the flavour and nutrients. Steam, quickly boil, stir-fry – or eat raw. (Seedlings are better cooked.) Leaves blend well in raw salads of lettuce, green pepper, celery, mooli and tomato. They also make a delicious warm salad, stir-fried and mixed with orange. Otherwise use in soups, cook with fish, meat, poultry and use in stuffing.

Outer stalks can be shredded, cooked like celery and tossed in butter. In Korea, China and Japan heads are used to make fermented and salted pickles.

Sweet & Sour Chinese Cabbage
Serves 4

2 tablespoons olive oil
1 onion or several shallots, sliced
2 tablespoons white wine vinegar
2 teaspoons sugar
6 tablespoons chopped tomatoes in their juices
750g (1½lb) Chinese cabbage, finely shredded
Salt & freshly ground black pepper

Heat the oil in a heavy-bottomed pan and cook the onions until soft. Stir in the vinegar, sugar and tomatoes and blend well. Add the Chinese cabbage and seasoning. Cook for 10 minutes with the lid on, stirring occasionally, until the cabbage is tender. Serve hot.

Sweet and Sour Chinese Cabbage

Capsicum annuum. Solanaceae

PEPPER & CHILLI

(Sweet Pepper, Bell Pepper, Capsicum, Pimento, Chilli Pepper) Annuals and short-lived perennials grown for edible fruits. Half hardy. Value: very rich in vitamin C and beta carotene.

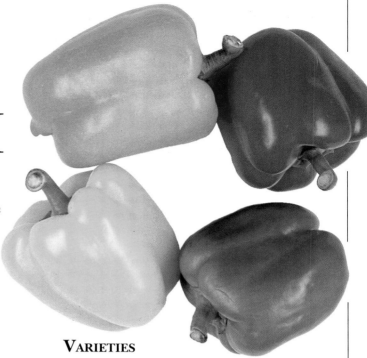

Both hot and mild peppers come from one wild species which is native to Central and South America. The name capsicum comes from the Latin *capsa,* meaning a box. It is thought that the hot types were the first to be cultivated; seeds have been found in Mexican settlements dating from 7000BC, and the Aztecs are known to have grown them extensively. They are one of the discoveries made in the New World by Columbus. He thought he had discovered black pepper, which at the time was extremely expensive, and used the name 'pepper' for this new fiery spice. Spanish and Portuguese explorers then distributed the new kinds of peppers around the world.

Sweet peppers were introduced to Spain in 1493 and were known in England by 1548 and Central Europe by 1585. The Spanish use red sweet peppers to make the spice pimentón and for stuffing green olives.

Chilli peppers are notorious for their fieriness. Their heat is caused by the alkaloid capsaicin, which is measured in Scoville Units. Mild chillies are around 600 units. Beware the 'Habanero' types, measured at between 200,000 and 350,000 units!

Peppers will keep for 14 days

VARIETIES

The larger, bell-shaped, mild-tasting sweet peppers eaten as vegetables are members of the *Capsicum annuum* Grossum Group. Green when immature, different cultivars ripen to yellow, orange, red or 'black'.

The smaller, hotter chillies used for flavouring are classed in the *C.a.* Longum Group.

Sweet peppers
'**Big Bertha**' is one of the largest bell peppers, growing to 18cm (7in) long by 10cm (4in) wide. Excellent for growing in cooler climates and for stuffing. '**Californian Wonder**' has a mild flavour, is good for stuffing and crops well over a long period. '**Calwonder Wonder Early**' grows well in short seasons. Prolific. '**Gypsy**'* is an early cropper with slightly tapered fruits. Resistant to Tobacco Mosaic Virus. '**Red Skin**' is compact and ideal for pots and growbags. '**Sweet Chocolate**' is an unusual chocolate-brown colour. Good when frozen whole.

Chilli peppers
'**Anaheim**' produces tapered, moderately hot fruits over a long period. '**Cayenne Long Slim**' is a hot pepper much used for flavouring. When kept for longer periods it becomes hotter . The moderately hot yellow fruits of '**Hungarian Yellow Wax Hot**' ripen to become crimson. Good for growing in cool areas. '**Italian White Wax**' has pointed fruits which pickle well and are mild-tasting when young. '**Jalapeno**' is extremely hot and can be harvested over a long period. '**Large Red Cherry**' is extremely hot, with flattened fruits ripening to cherry red. Good for drying and ideal in curries, pickles and sauces. '**Red Chili**' is a high-yielding extremely hot variety, for pickling or drying. Fruits are narrow and tapered. '**Ring of Fire**' is, not surprisingly, hot-fruited. Early cropping, producing short, thin cayenne-type peppers. '**Serrano**' is extremely hot with orange-red fruits. It is prolific and can be dried. '**Tabasco Habanero**' – as the name suggests – is lethal!

CULTIVATION

Propagation

Sow seed indoors from mid- to late spring in trays, modules or pots of moist seed compost at 21°C (70°F). Lower temperature gradually after germination. Transplant into 8–9cm (3–3½in) pots when 3 true leaves appear, repotting again into 10–13cm (4–5in) pots when sufficient roots have been formed. Move plants into their final position when about 10cm (4in) high and the first flowers appear. Harden off outdoor crops in cool temperate zones and transplant in late spring to early summer when the soil is warm and there is no danger of frost.

Space standard varieties 38–45cm (15–18in) apart; dwarf varieties should be spaced 30cm (12in) apart.

Growing

Sweet peppers and chillies flourish outdoors in warmer climates. More successful under cover in cooler zones, they can be grown outside in mild areas or warm micro-climates but benefit from protection with cloches or fleece. Chillies tend to be more tolerant of fluctuating temperatures and high or low rainfall and grow in

Sweet peppers are best grown under glass in cool climates

marginally less fertile soil. Blossom drops when night temperatures fall below 15°C (60°F). Soil should be moisture-retentive and free-draining on ground manured for the previous crop. Alternatively, dig in plenty of well-rotted organic matter in autumn or winter prior to planting. Rake in a granular general fertilizer at 135g/sq m (4oz/sq yd) before planting.

Keep the soil moist and weed-free; mulching is recommended. Feed with a general liquid fertilizer if plants need a boost. Excessive nitrogen can result in flower drop.

If branches are weak and thin when the plant is about 30cm (12in) tall remove the growth tips from the stems to encourage branching. Normally, they branch naturally. Support with a cane if necessary.

Maintenance

Spring Sow seeds under cover. Transplant when the danger of frost is passed or grow in an unheated greenhouse.
Summer Keep crops weed-free; damp down the glasshouse in warm weather. Harvest.
Autumn Cover outdoor crops where necessary. Harvest.
Winter Prepare the ground for outdoor crops.

Protected Cropping

Crops are better grown under glass, polythene, cold frames or cloches in cool temperate climates. In glasshouse borders, prepare the soil as for Growing. Keep it moist but not waterlogged and mist with tepid water to maintain humidity and help fruit set.

Sow mid-spring for growing in a greenhouse and in late spring for crops under cloches. Ventilate well during hot weather. If you are growing dwarf varieties on a sunny windowsill, you should turn pots daily to ensure even growth.

Peppers have the luxury of a choice of colours: here they are 'black'

Plants grown under cloches may outgrow their space: rigid cloches can be turned vertically and supported with canes. Alternatively, use polycarbonate sheeting.

Container Growing

Grow under cover or outdoors. Plant in 20–25cm (8–10in) pots of loam-based compost with moderate fertilizer levels or in growbags. Dwarf varieties can be grown successfully in pots on windowsills. Keep the compost moist but not waterlogged and mist with tepid water, particularly during flowering to assist fruit set.

Water frequently in warm weather, less at other times.

Harvesting & Storing

Harvest with scissors or secateurs when sweet peppers or chillies are green, or leave on the plant for 2–3 weeks to ripen and change colour. Picking them when they are green increases the yield.

Peppers may be stored in a cool, humid place for up to 14 days at temperatures of 13–15°C (55–58°F).

Towards the end of the season, uproot plants and hang them by the roots in a frost-free shed or green-house; fruits will continue to ripen for several months.

The heat of chillies increases with the maturity of the fruit. Fresh chillies keep for up to 3 weeks in the refrigerator in a paper bag. Or store them in an airtight jar in a dark cupboard.

Chillis can either be dried and used whole or ground into powder.

Both sweet peppers and chillies freeze successfully.

Chillies become hotter as they mature

PESTS & DISEASES

Red spider mite can be a nuisance under cover. **Slugs** can damage seedlings, stems, leaves and fruits. Remove any decaying flowers or foliage immediately.

COMPANION PLANTING

The capsicum family grows well with basil, okra and tomatoes.

MEDICINAL

Capsaicin increases the blood flow and is used in muscle liniments. It is said to help the body metabolize alcohol, acts as expectorant, and prevents and alleviates bronchitis and emphysema. 10 to 20 drops of red-hot chilli sauce in a glass of water daily (or hot spicy meals 3 times a week) can keep airways free of congestion, preventing or treating chronic bronchitis and colds. It stimulates endorphins, killing pain and inducing a sense of wellbeing.

WARNING

Ventilate the kitchen when using chillies. If you have sensitive skin, wear rubber gloves to handle them and always avoid touching your eyes or other sensitive areas after handling.

CULINARY

Sweet peppers add both colour and taste to the table. They can be eaten raw in salads, roasted or barbecued, fried or stir-fried, stuffed with rice, fish or meat mixtures, and used in countless casseroles and rice dishes.

Chillies are used in chilli con carne, curries and hotpots. Removing the internal ribs and seeds reduces the heat intensity.

Paprika is the dried and powdered fruits of sweet peppers. Cayenne pepper is dried and ground powder made from chillies.

If chilli is too strong, it can cause intestinal burning – cucumber, rice, bread and beans are a good antidote. By coating the tongue, the fat content of yoghurt and butter soothes a chilli-burnt mouth. Water only makes things worse.

If you're uninitiated at eating chilli peppers, start with small doses and build up tolerance of heat. Excessively hot peppers can cause jaloproctitis or perianal discomforture.

Mrs Krause's Pepper Hash
Serves 6

William Woys Weaver in *Pennsylvania Dutch Country Cooking* quotes this recipe from Mrs Eugene F. Krause of Bethlehem, who lived in the early part of the century and was renowned for her peppery hashes.

6 green peppers, deseeded & finely chopped
6 red peppers, deseeded & finely chopped
4 onions, finely chopped
2 small pods hot chilli peppers, deseeded & finely chopped
1½ tablespoons celery seeds
375ml (12fl oz) cider vinegar
250g (8oz) brown sugar
1½ teaspoons sea salt

Combine the peppers, onion, hot chilli peppers and celery seeds in a non-reactive preserving pan. Heat the vinegar in a non-reactive pan and dissolve the sugar and salt in it. Bring to a fast boil, then pour over the pepper mixture. Then cook over a medium heat for 15 minutes, or until the peppers begin to discolour.

Pack into hot sterilized preserving jars, seal, and place in a 15-minute water bath. Let the pepper hash mature in the jars for 2 weeks before using.

Duvec
Serves 4

This is a Croatian recipe and has subtle flavours. It makes an excellent one-dish supper and uses up leftovers as well.

Mrs Krause's Pepper Hash

1 onion, finely sliced
2 tablespoons olive oil
2 cloves garlic, crushed
3 sweet red, green or yellow peppers, deseeded & diced
500g (1lb) tomatoes, peeled & deseeded
100g (4oz) rice, cooked
500g (1lb) leftover cooked meat
450ml (¾pt) stock
Salt & freshly ground black pepper

Cook the onions in the oil in a heavy pan over medium heat until softened. Grease an ovenproof dish and put in a layer of onion and garlic, followed by one of peppers, then one of tomatoes, one of rice and bite-sized pieces of meat. Repeat the layers until all the ingredients are used up, seasoning as you go.

Pour in the stock, cover and bake in a preheated oven, 180°C, 350°F, gas 4, for about 45 minutes.

Remove the covering and continue cooking for a further 15 minutes. Serve.

Cicer arietinum. Leguminosae

CHICKPEA

(Dhall, Egyptian Pea, Garbanzo, Gram) Annual grown for seed sprouts, seeds, young shoots and leaves. Tender. Value: high in protein, phosphorus, potassium, most B vitamins, iron and dietary fibre.

Chickpeas originated in the northern regions of the fertile crescent. Evidence of their ancient use as a domesticated crop was found at a site in Jericho and dated to around 6500BC. Seeds excavated in Greece indicate that the chickpea must have been introduced to Europe with the first food crops arriving from the Near East. Today it is cultivated worldwide in sub-tropical or Mediterranean climates as a cool-season crop, needing about 4–6 months of moderately warm, dry conditions to flourish. It is the world's third most important pulse after peas and beans, and 80% of the crop is produced in India. It is eaten fresh or dried, made into flour, used as a coffee substitute and grown as a fodder crop. The plant grows about 30cm (12in) tall, with compound leaves of up to eight toothed leaflets. Its tiny white- or blue-tinged flowers are followed by a small flat pod containing one or two round seeds, each with a small 'beak' – hence the common name 'chickpea'.

in drills 6–10cm (2½–4in) deep with the rows 50cm (20in) apart, thinning to 25cm (10in) between plants after germination. Alternatively, sow 3–4 seeds in 'stations' 25cm (10in) apart and thin to leave the strongest seedling.

Growing

Dig over the area thoroughly before planting, adding organic matter to poor soils. Rake over the area to create a fine tilth and water well before sowing if the seedbed is dry. Alternatively, soak the seeds for an hour. Keep crops weed-free during the early stages; as plants mature, their spreading habit naturally stifles weed growth. Chickpeas are drought-tolerant, but watering just before flowering and as the peas begin to swell improves productivity. Rotate with other legumes and leave the roots in the ground after harvest to provide nitrogen for the following crop.

Chickpea in pod, showing the head and small 'beak'

VARIETIES

The smooth-seeded 'Kabuli' race is dominant throughout the Mediterranean and Near East and the wrinkled-seeded 'Desai' type in Ethiopia, Afghanistan and India. The following are Indian cultivars: **'Annegeri'** is a semi-spreading high-yielding variety with yellowish-brown seeds. It is deep-rooting and needs good soil, but a coarse tilth is adequate. **'Avrodhi'** has medium-sized brown seeds and is wilt-resistant. **'Bheema'**, a semi-spreading variety, has large, light brown smooth seeds and is suitable for drought-prone or low-rainfall areas.

CULTIVATION

Chickpeas need a light, fertile, well-drained soil in full sun.

Propagation

Seeds can be broadcast or sown in drills during winter in Mediterranean regions or after the rains in sub-tropical climates. Broadcasting is very simple. Prepare the soil using the 'stale seedbed' method, raking and levelling, allowing the weeds to germinate and hoeing them off before sowing. Then scatter the seed evenly, raking the soil twice – first in one direction, then again at 90° to ensure even coverage. Chickpeas can also be sown

A lilac-flowered variety, growing in the USA

Maintenance
Spring Dig over the planting area, adding organic matter where needed.
Summer Keep crops weed-free. Water in prolonged drought, just before flowering and as the peas swell.
Autumn Harvest crops.
Winter Dig over the planting area, adding organic matter where needed.

Protected Cropping
In cooler climates, sow seeds in early spring into small pots of moist seed compost in a glasshouse or on a window sill. Harden off in late spring and plant outdoors once there is no danger of frost. Growing crops in cloches or polythene tunnels increases the yield.

Container Growing
They can be grown in containers, but seed production levels do not make them a worthwhile proposition as a crop plant.

Harvesting & Storing
Crops are ready after about 4–6 months. Harvest when leaves and pods turn brown; don't leave it too late, or the seeds will be lost when the pods split. Cut the stems at the base and tie them together before drying upside down in a dry, warm place. Collect the dry seeds and store in airtight jars.

Peas can also be harvested fresh for cooking, but fresh ones deteriorate rapidly and should be used as soon as possible.

Sprouting Seeds
Always buy untreated chickpeas for sprouting, as seed sold for sowing is often treated with chemical dressings. Soak seeds overnight or for several hours in boiling water, tip into a sieve and rinse. Put several layers of moist paper towel or blotting paper in the base of a jar and cover with a layer of seed. Cut a square from a pair of tights or piece of muslin and cover the top, securing with a rubber band. Place in a bright position, away from direct sunshine, maintaining constant temperatures around 20°C (68°F). Rinse the seed 3–4 times a day by filling the jar with water and pouring off again. Harvest after 3–4 days when the 'sprouts' are about 12mm (½in) long.

Pests & Diseases
Plants can suffer from **root rot**. They turn black and finally dry up, leaves fall and the stems desiccate. Ensure the soil is well drained and destroy affected crops immediately. The acidic secretions from the glandular hairs are a good defence against most pests.
Gram pod borer caterpillars feed on the crop from seedlings to maturity, damaging seedpods and the immature seeds. Spray with pyrethrum.

MEDICINAL

The leaves are astringent and used to treat bronchitis. They are also boiled and applied to sprains and dislocated bones; the exudate is used for indigestion, diarrhoea and dysentery. The seeds are a stimulant, tonic and aphrodisiac. In Egypt they are used to gain weight, and to treat headaches, sore throat and coughs. Powdered seed is used as a facepack and also in dandruff treatment.

WARNING

The whole plant and seed pods are covered with hairs containing skin irritants. You must always wear gloves when harvesting.

CULINARY

With a protein content of 20%, chickpeas are an important meat substitute and good for children and expectant and nursing mothers. Chickpeas are used fresh or dried. They are ground into 'gram flour' (used in vegan cooking), and the ground meal is mixed with wheat and used for chapatis. Whole chickpeas are fried, roasted (to eat as a snack) and boiled. To make hommous or hummus, grind boiled chickpeas into a paste, mix with olive or sesame oil, flavour with lemon and garlic and eat on pitta bread or crackers.

Chickpeas are also used to make 'dhall' and are found in spicy side dishes, vegetable curries and soups. The young shoots and leaves are used as a vegetable and cooked like spinach – boiled in soups, added to curries or fried with spices.

Puréed Chickpeas
Serves 4

300g (10oz) dried chickpeas, soaked overnight
2 tablespoons olive oil
1 onion, sliced finely
3 garlic cloves, crushed
300g (10oz) tomatoes, peeled, deseeded & chopped
Salt & freshly ground black pepper

Drain the chickpeas, put in a heavy-bottomed saucepan, cover with fresh water and cook until tender. This will take up to 1½ hours, depending on the age of the chickpeas. Drain. Purée through a *mouli légumes*.

Heat the oil in a frying pan, sauté the onion until softened, add the garlic and cook for 30 seconds longer. Add the tomatoes and simmer for 5 minutes before adding the chickpea purée. Season well and serve immediately.

Cichorium endivia. Compositae

ENDIVE

(Escarole, Batavian Endive, Grumolo)
*Annual or biennial grown as annual for blanched
hearts and leaves. Value: rich in iron, potassium and
beta carotene; moderate vitamin A and B complex.*

The origins of this plant are obscure, but it was certainly eaten by the Egyptians long before the birth of Christ and is one of the bitter herbs used at Passover. Mentioned by Ovid, Horace, Pliny and Dioscorides, it was highly valued by the Greeks and Romans as a cultivated plant. It was introduced to England, Germany, Holland and France around 1548 and was described by several writers. The French at first used it primarily as a medicinal plant – to 'comfort the weake and feeble stomack' and to help gouty limbs and sore eyes. European colonists took it to America in 1806 and created a confusion that dogs transatlantic cookery books to this day. The French name of *chicorée frisée* – 'curly chicory' – must have travelled with it, so the USA calls the leafy green plants described here 'chicory'. (Even more confusingly, its forced 'Witloof' cousin, known as chicory in Britain, is *endive* in France and 'endive' or 'Belgian endive' in America.)

VARIETIES

There are two types. The Batavian, scarole or escarole has large, broad leaves and is an upright plant. Curly, or fringed frisée is a really pretty plant, with a low rosette of delicately serrated leaves. Curled varieties are generally used for summer cropping; the more robust broad-leaved types tolerate cold, are disease-resistant and grow well in winter.
'Broad Leaved Batavian' has tightly packed heads of broad, deep green leaves which become creamy-white when blanched. 'En Cornet de Bordeaux', an old variety, is very tasty, extremely hardy and blanches well. 'Green Curled Ruffec', a curly type, is easily blanched and makes a good garnish. Very hardy and cold resistant. 'Green Curled' ('Moss Curled') produces compact heads of dark green, fringed leaves. 'Ione' has light green finely cut leaves, with a creamy heart and mild taste. 'Limnos' is a vigorous variety which is slow to bolt with broad upright leaves and a yellow heart. 'Riccia Pancalieri' has very curly leaves with white, rose-tinged midribs. 'Salad King' is prolific and extremely hardy, with large, dark green, finely cut leaves. 'Sanda'* is vigorous and resistant to tip burn, cold and bolting. 'Scarola Verde' is broad-leaved with a large

Endive leaves are slightly bitter

Endive needs an open site

head and green and white leaves. It may bolt in heat. 'Très Fine Maraichère' ('Coquette') has finely cut curled leaves. Mild and delicious, it grows well in most soils. 'Wallone Frisée Weschelkopf' ('Wallone')* has a large, tightly packed head with finely cut leaves. Vigorous and hardy.

CULTIVATION

Propagation
Sow thinly, 1cm (½in) deep *in situ* or in a seedbed, pots or modules to transplant. Allow 30–38cm (12–15in) between plants and rows.
  Endive best germinates at 20–22°C (68–72°F). Sow early crops under cover and shade summer crops.
  Sow from early to mid-summer for autumn crops, in late summer for winter crops, using curled or hardy Batavian types. Sow all year round for 'cut and come again' seedlings or semi-mature leaves, making early and late sowings under glass.

Growing
Endive needs an open site, though summer crops tolerate a little shade. Soils should be light, moderately rich and free-draining; this is

particularly important for winter crops. If necessary, dig in plenty of well-rotted organic matter before planting. Excess nitrogen encourages lush growth and makes plants prone to fungal diseases.

Endive is a cool-season crop, flourishing between 10–20°C (50–68°F), yet it withstands light frosts; hardier cultivars withstand temperatures down to –9°C (15°F). Higher temperatures tend to encourage bitterness, though 'curled' types are heat-tolerant. Young plants tend to bolt if temperatures fall below 5°C (41°F) for long. Keep crops weed-free; mulch and water thoroughly during dry weather, as dryness at the roots can cause 'bolting'. Use a general liquid fertilizer to boost growth if necessary.

Blanch to reduce bitterness and make leaves more tender. Many newer cultivars have tight heads and some blanching occurs naturally. Damp leaves are likely to rot, so choose a dry period or dry plants under cloches for 2–3 days. Draw the outer leaves together and tie with raffia 2–3 weeks before harvest, placing a tile, piece of cardboard or dinner plate over the centre of the plant, and covering with a cloche to keep off the rain. Alternatively cover the

The more tolerant 'Batavian'

Fringed frisée is attractive

whole plant with a bucket or a flower pot with its drainage holes covered. Blanching takes about 10 days. Blanch a few at a time; they rapidly deteriorate afterwards.

Maintenance
Spring Sow early crops under glass or cloches. Harvest late crops under cover.
Summer Sow curly varieties outdoors in seedbeds for transplanting, or *in situ*. Keep early-sown crops weed-free and moist. Harvest.
Autumn Sow outdoors and under cover. Harvest.
Winter Sow under cover and harvest.

Protected Cropping
Sow hardy cultivars under cover in trays or modules at 20°C (68°F) in mid-spring for early summer crops and maintain a minimum temperature of 4°C (39°F) after germination for 3 weeks after transplanting to prevent bolting.

For winter and early spring crops, transplant in early autumn from seed trays or modules under cover. Sow 'cut and come again' crops under cover in early spring, and in early autumn.

Endive grows better than lettuce in low light and is also a useful crop for the greenhouse in winter.

Container Growing
Sow directly or transplant into large containers of loam-based compost with added well-rotted organic matter. Keep compost moist and weed-free. Use a general liquid fertilizer to boost growth if necessary.

Harvesting & Storing
Harvest endive from 7 weeks after sowing, depending on cultivar and season.

'Cut and come again' seedlings may be ready from 5 weeks. With some cultivars, only one or two cuts may be possible before they run to seed. Pick individual leaves as needed or harvest them using a sharp knife about 2cm (¾in) above the ground, leaving the root to resprout.

The whole plant can be lifted in autumn and put in a cool, dark place to blanch.

Leaves do not store well and are better eaten fresh. They last about 3 days in a polythene bag in the salad drawer of a refrigerator.

PESTS & DISEASES

Protect plants from **slugs** and control **aphids**.

Keep winter crops well watered and mulched to prevent tip burn.

COMPANION PLANTING

Endive is good for inter-sowing and intercropping.

CULINARY

Endive is used mainly in salads with – or instead of – lettuce and other greens; the slightly bitter taste and crisp texture gives it more of a 'bite' than the usual lettuce combinations. It suits strongly flavoured dressings. Crisp lardons of bacon or croutons are often included. With mature endive, use the inner leaves for salads; the outer ones can be cooked as greens. Endive can also be braised. Try serving it shredded and dressed with hot crushed garlic, anchovy fillets and a little olive oil and butter.

Warm Red & Yellow Pepper Salad
Serves 6

The slightly bitter taste of curly endive (escarole or frisée) is ideal combined with other lettuces such as lamb's lettuce or watercress in winter months. The sweetness of the peppers in this dish happily complements the endive.

1 large endive, washed & roughly chopped
Big bunch lamb's lettuce, washed
2 large red peppers
3 tablespoons olive oil
3 cloves garlic, crushed
1 tablespoon fresh herbs
Salt & freshly ground black pepper

For the dressing:
3 tablespoons extra virgin olive oil
1 tablespoon white wine vinegar
Salt & freshly ground black pepper

Arrange the lettuces in a large bowl. Core and deseed the peppers and cut them into thin strips. Heat the oil in a heavy pan and sauté the peppers, stirring constantly. Add the garlic after 5 minutes and cook for a further minute.

Add the peppers to the salad. Make the dressing and toss in the herbs and seasoning. Serve the salad alongside plain grilled fish or chicken.

Cichorium intybus. Compositae

CHICORY

(Witloof, Belgian Endive, Succory, Sugar Loaf Chicory, Radicchio) Hardy perennial grown as annual for blanched leaves or root. Extremely hardy. Value: moderate levels of potassium.

A native of Europe through to central Russia and western Asia, chicory has been cultivated for centuries. Pliny tells us that *cichorium* is a Greek adaptation of the Egyptian name; he also noted its medicinal use as a purgative and the blanching of leaves for salads.

Large-rooted varieties have long been used dried, ground and roasted as a substitute for coffee – particularly popular in England during the Napoleonic wars when a blockade of the French coast cut supplies. It has a distinctive fragrance and is often drunk by those who like the taste of coffee without caffeine. John Lindley in the nineteenth century recorded that roasted chicory was adulterated with a multitude of substances as diverse as mangolds, oak bark, mahogany sawdust and even baked horse liver!

Gibault in his *Histoire des Legumes* of 1912 tells of the accidental discovery in the 1840s that Witloof chicory could be blanched. The head gardener at Brussels Botanic Gardens wanted to bring on winter chicory in frames. He lifted several roots, chopped off the foliage and planted them. Soon small, tight shoots emerged through the soil. Next season he did the same. He kept his find a secret, but when he died his widow told her gardener, who passed it on and the technique is now widely practised. Perhaps it is due to this Brussels connection that the vegetable's American name is 'Belgian endive'.

VARIETIES

Chicory has a distinctive, slightly bitter flavour. Most varieties are hardy and make a good winter crop with colourful, attractive leaves. There are three types.

'Forcing' chicories like 'Witloof' (that is, whiteleaf) produce plump, leafy heads (known as 'chicons') when blanched. 'Red chicory' or 'radicchio' includes older cultivars which responded to the reduced daylength and lower temperatures of autumn by turning from green to red; newer cultivars are naturally red and heart earlier. 'Non-forcing' or 'sugarloaf' types produce large-hearted lettuce-like heads for autumn harvest.

'Brussels Witloof' (**'Witloof de Brussels'**) is one of the most famous forcing types which is also grown for its root. **'Grumolo Verde'** is non-forcing and very cold-hardy, with rounded leaves. **'Large Rooted Magdeburg'** (**'Magdeburg'**), like 'Brussels Witloof', is grown mainly for its root, which matures after about 17 weeks. Young leaves can be harvested. **'Palla rossa Zorzi Precoce'** is a radicchio with a tangy, delicate flavour. It colours better in cool weather. **'Rossa di Treviso'**, another radicchio, has crisp, green leaves that become deep red and veined with white in cooler conditions. Tolerates light frost. Dates back to the sixteenth century. **'Rossa di Verona'** is a radicchio with a spreading habit that withstands considerable frost. **'Sugarhat'** is a non-forcing sugarloaf variety that has sweet leaves. **'Witloof Zoom'**, a forcing chicory, produces tightly packed, high-quality leaves.

CULTIVATION

Propagation

Sow seed of forcing varieties thinly in late spring to early summer in drills 1cm (½in) deep and 23–30cm (9–12in)

'Red chicory', or 'radicchio'

Some varieties are very pretty

'Sugarloaf' (non-forcing variety)

Maintenance
Spring Sow early radicchio under cover, transplant from mid-spring. Sow sugarloaf types as 'cut and come again' crops.
Summer Harvest early radicchio and sow maincrop. Sow sugarloaf outdoors for 'cut and come again' and autumn maincrop.
Autumn Harvest radicchio crops sown early to mid-summer; sow late crops for winter. Lift forcing types or force outdoors. Sow sugarloaf indoors.
Winter Force roots indoors successively until spring. Sow sugarloaf indoors.

Protected Cropping
Non-forcing varieties can be grown under glass, for early or late crops.

In autumn, cover outdoor crops of radicchio with cloches, fleece or similar to extend the growing season.

Container Growing
All chicories can be grown in large containers or beds of loam-based compost.

Forcing
Force 'chicons' indoors if soil is heavy, if winters are severe, or for earlier crops. In mid- to late autumn when the foliage dies down, lift

apart. Thin when the first true leaves appear to 20cm (8in) apart.

Sow early radicchio under cover in seed trays and modules before hardening off and transplanting from mid-spring for summer harvest, using early maturing types first. Sow for autumn harvest from early to mid-summer, and in mid- to late summer for transplanting under cover in autumn and cropping over winter. Thin to 23–38cm (9–15in) in and between the rows.

Non-forcing or sugarloaf types can be broadcast or sown in broad drills under cover in late winter. When the soil warms and the weather improves, sow successively outdoors until late summer. Sow the final crop during early autumn under cover.

Thin to a final spacing of 23–30cm (9–12in) in and between the rows. For a semi-mature 'cut and come again' winter crop, sow seed from mid- to late summer and transplant indoors in autumn.

Growing
Chicories prefer an open, sunny site, but tolerate a little shade. Soil should be fertile and free-draining, with organic matter added for the previous crop: avoid recently manured ground, as this causes the roots to fork.

Radicchio tolerates most soils except gravel or very heavy clay. The ideal pH is 5.5–7. Rake soil to a fine texture before sowing. Apply a general balanced fertilizer at 30g/sq m (1oz/sq yd).

Keep weed-free with regular hoeing or mulching. Water thoroughly during dry weather to prevent bolting.

Force appropriate varieties *in situ* if soil is light and winters are mild. In late autumn to early winter, cut back the leaves to 2.5cm (1in) above ground level. Form a ridge of friable soil 15–20cm (6–8in) high over the stumps and cover with straw or leaf mould. After about 8–12 weeks, when the tips are appearing, remove the soil and cut the heads off at about 2.5cm (1in) above the neck. Keep the compost moist while the 'chicons' are growing.

roots carefully, discard any forked or damaged ones and keep those that are at least 3–5cm (1½–2in) in diameter at the top.

Cut off the remaining leaves to within 1cm (½in) of the crown, trim back the side and main roots to about 20–23cm (8–9in). Pack horizontally in boxes of dry sand, peat substitute or sawdust and store in a cool, frost-free place.

For forcing, remove a few roots from storage at a time.

Plant about 5 to 6 roots in a 23cm (9in) pot of sand or light soil, ensuring that 1cm (½in) of the crown is above the surface. Surround the roots with moist peat or compost, leaving the crown exposed above ground.

Water sparingly and cover with a black polythene bag, an empty flower pot with the holes blocked up, or an

empty box. Maintain temperatures of 10–15°C (50–60°F). They can also be blanched in a dark cellar or shed or under greenhouse staging (see 'Growing').

The blanched 'chicons' should be ready for cutting within 4 weeks, depending on the temperature.

Roots may resprout, producing several smaller shoots which can then be blanched.

Harvesting & Storing

Harvest chicories grown for roots after the first frost.

Cut heads of mature sugarloaf varieties with a sharp knife 2.5cm (1in) above the soil in late autumn; use immediately or store in a frost-free place.

Allow the plants to resprout as a 'cut and come again' crop under cloches.

Pick radicchio leaves as required, taking care not to over-harvest, as this weakens plants. Alternatively, cut the whole head and leave the roots to resprout.

'Chicons' can be stored in the refrigerator, wrapped in foil or paper to prevent them from becoming bitter. Non-forcing chicory will stay fresh for up to 1 month.

PESTS & DISEASES

Though seldom troubled by pests and diseases, crops can rot outdoors in cold weather

COMPANION PLANTING

The blue flowers of chicory are attractive in the ornamental border.

MEDICINAL

Chicory is said to be a digestive, diuretic and laxative, reducing inflammation. A liver and gall bladder tonic, it is used for rheumatism, gout and haemorrhoids. Culpeper suggests its use 'for swooning and passions of the heart'.

'Witloof' plants grown in the dark in stacked wooden racks to blanch for use as a vegetable

CULINARY

All types of chicory make a wonderful winter salad, particularly if you mix the colours of red, green and white. Add tomatoes or a sweet dressing to take away some of the bitter taste. Home-grown chicons stored in the dark tend to be less bitter.

. For a delicious light supper dish, pour a robust dressing (made with lemon juice rather than vinegar) over the leaves, add some anchovy fillets, crumbled hard-boiled eggs and top with a handful of kalamata olives.

As an accompaniment to cold meat and game, eat with sliced oranges, onion and chopped walnuts. With roast meats, braise chicory with butter, lemon juice and cream. Radicchio can also be braised, but loses its colour.

To make a chicory coffee substitute, dry roots immediately after harvest and grind.

Chicory with Ham & Cheese Sauce
Serves 4

4 heads chicory
8 slices smoked Bayonne ham
2 tablespoons butter
2 tablespoons plain flour
2 teaspoons Dijon mustard
150ml (¼pt) milk
Enough single cream to mix to a smooth consistency
4 tablespoons Gruyère cheese
Salt & freshly ground black pepper

Bring a pan of salted water to the boil and drop in the chicory heads. Allow to blanch for 5 minutes, drain and gently squeeze as much water as you can out of them. Cut each

Chicory with Ham & Cheese Sauce

chicory in half and wrap in a slice of the ham. Then arrange in one layer in an ovenproof dish.

Preheat the oven to 200°C, 400°F, gas 6. Make the cheese sauce: melt the butter in a heavy pan and stir in the flour. Cook for 2 minutes, then stir in the mustard. Pour in the milk gradually, stirring vigorously as the sauce thickens, then add the cream and cheese. Stir over a gentle heat for 5 minutes to let the cheese melt. Season to taste.

Pour the cheese sauce over the chicory wrapped in ham and cook in the oven for 20 minutes until nicely browned. Serve immediately.

Braised Chicory
Serves 4

The French, especially in the South-West and in Provence, braise chicory or Belgian endives and serve them with plain roasted meats such as lamb and beef.

2 tablespoons butter
1 red onion, finely chopped
2 rashers smoked bacon, diced
4 heads chicory, trimmed
150ml (¼pt) chicken stock & white wine combined

Juice of half a lemon
Salt & freshly ground black pepper

Liberally coat the sides and bottom of a heavy, lidded casserole with half the butter and heat the remaining butter in a small pan over a medium flame. Gently fry the onion and bacon, and set aside.

Arrange the endives in the casserole. Add some of the stock and white wine, season with salt and pepper and

cover. Allow to sweat over a low heat until just turning colour. Roll them over and cook on the other side.

Add a little more liquid as required. The liquid should evaporate from the endives by the end, so that they are browned and tender (you may have to remove the lid for a short while). Add the onion and bacon and quickly heat up. Drizzle over the lemon juice, season and serve immediately.

Braised Chicory

Colocasia esculenta var. esculenta. Araceae

DASHEEN

(Elephant's Ear, Arvi Leaves, West Indian Kale, Taro)
Herbaceous perennial grown for its edible leaves, shoots and tubers. Tender.
Value: tuber rich in starch; leaves high in vitamin A, good source of B2.

In cultivation for around 7,000 years, dasheen is said to have been first grown in India on terraces where rice now flourishes. The common name derives from '*de Chine*' (from China): the root was imported from South-East Asia following a competition organized by the Royal Geographical Society to find a cheap food source for the slaves on West Indian sugar plantations.

Growing in Paradise Park, Hawaii: the angle of the leaves allows accumulated water to be poured away

VARIETIES

Dasheen have a cylindrical main tuber with fibrous roots and a few side tubers. The upright stems up to 1.8m (6ft) tall are topped with large, heart-shaped leaves with prominent ribs on the underside. Cultivated types rarely flower and are grouped by the colour of their flesh, ranging from pink to yellow, and leaf stems of green, pinkish purple to almost black.

CULTIVATION

Propagation
Dasheen are propagated from 'tops' with a small section of tuber, small side tubers or 'suckers'. Plant 60cm (24in) apart with 100cm (40in) between rows, or 60–90cm (2–3ft) apart; add general fertilizer to the hole before planting.

Growing
Dasheen tolerate quite heavy, fertile, moisture-retentive soil rich in organic matter with a pH of 5.5–6.5. Dig in compost or well-rotted manure if necessary. As dasheen need plenty of water and tolerate water-logging, they are ideal for areas by streams and rivers. Where the water table is high, mound or ridge planting is advised. Irrigate heavily during dry weather.

In well-manured soil, a second crop can be planted between the rows 12 weeks before the main crop is harvested.

Maintenance
Spring Plant pre-sprouted tubers with protection.
Summer Keep crops well fed and watered and weed-free.
Autumn Harvest crops.
Winter Prepare for the following year.

Protected Cropping
Plant pre-sprouted tubers in spring into greenhouse borders. Keep temperatures around 21°C (70°F), and maintain high humidity by misting plants with soft tepid water or damping down the greenhouse floor. Do not worry about overwatering.

Feed every 3–4 weeks with a high-potash fertilizer; extra nitrogen may be needed if growth slows.

The true flowers are enclosed within the larger spath

Container Growing

Dasheen can be grown as a 'novelty' crop in 20–30cm (8–12in) pots of peat-substitute compost. Soak thoroughly after planting and stand the pot in a shallow tray of tepid water throughout the growing season. Treat as for 'Protected Cropping'.

PESTS & DISEASES

Taro leaf blight causes circular water-soaked spots on leaves followed by collapse of the plant. Those grown under glass are susceptible to aphids. Red spider mite and downy mildew can also be a problem. Take the necessary precautions.

Dasheen is an important food crop in the humid tropics – seen here in Hawaii

CULINARY

Tubers can be roasted, baked or boiled, served with spicy sauces and in stews. Larger tubers, which tend to be dry and coarse, should be braised and cooked slowly.
Leaves (with midrib removed) can be stuffed, boiled or steamed and eaten with a knob of butter. Avoid particularly large leaves; they are often tough. In the West Indies, Callaloo Soup is made from dasheen leaves, okra, crab meat and coconut milk. Young blanched shoots can be eaten like asparagus.

Palusima

This is a Western Samoan or Polynesian dish.
    Allow about 200g (7oz) dasheen per person. Peel and chop roughly, then parboil in plain salted water for 5–10 minutes. Drain, then boil until reduced in coconut milk (enough to come to half the height of the dasheen in the pan) until thickish. Mash.
    Stuff the mashed dasheen into parboiled leaves and secure with a toothpick. (Alternatively, wrap it in banana leaves, and even spinach or cabbage.) Bake for 15 minutes in a lightly greased dish in a preheated oven at 180°C, 350°F, gas 4. Serve with any good white fish such as cod.

Palusima

Harvesting & Storing
Dasheen take 7 to 11 months to mature. Harvest by lifting the main tuber, saving some of the small side tubers for eating and others for replanting. Undamaged tubers can be dried and stored for up to 4 weeks, while washed leaves keep for several days in a refrigerator.

WARNING

Although selection has, over the years, reduced calcium oxalate levels in the skin of dasheen, it is extremely important to wear gloves or to cover the hands with a layer of cooking oil. This prevents skin irritation when peeling the vegetables.
    Always make sure dasheen are cooked thoroughly before eating.

Colocasia esculenta var. *antiquorum. Araceae*

EDDOE

*Perennial grown as annual for edible tubers.
Tender. Value: rich in starch, magnesium,
potassium and vitamin C.*

This variety of taro, native of India and south-east Asia, was first recorded by the Chinese 2,000 years ago. It is now grown throughout the humid tropics. Eddoes flourish in moist soil alongside rivers and streams. The central tuber is surrounded by clusters of smaller tubers which are harvested, making it different from the single-tubered dasheen. The brown, hairy tubers can weigh up to 2.2kg (5lb), and when they are sliced reveal flesh which is usually white but can also be yellow, pink or orange. Their taste is similar to a garden potato but with an attractive nutty flavour. Tubers should never be eaten raw as all varieties contain calcium oxilate crystals which are a skin irritant.

VARIETIES

'Euchlora' has dark green leaves with violet margins and leaf stems. 'Fontanesii' produces leaf stems which are dark red-purple or violet. Its leaf blades are dark green with violet veins and margin.

CULTIVATION

Propagation
In the humid tropics, eddoes can be planted any time. In temperate climates they must be grown under glass or polythene at a minimum temperature of 21°C (70°F), and planted in spring. Plant small tubers or a tuber section containing some dormant buds in individual holes 60–75cm (25–30in) apart. Cuttings

Eddoe cultivation

consisting of the top of a tuber with several leaves and a growth point can be planted directly into the soil and will establish rapidly. Add general fertilizer to the planting hole.

Growing
Eddoes need humus-rich, slightly acid, moisture-retentive soil, in sunshine or partial shade. Cultivate the soil before planting and remove any weeds.

Maintenance
Spring Plant tubers if protected cropping.
Summer Feed every 3–4 weeks with a high potash fertilizer; additional nitrogen may be needed. During drier periods, irrigate as needed to ensure swelling of the tubers and earth up. Keep weed-free.
Autumn Harvest as required.
Winter Prepare beds for the following year's crop if growing in a greenhouse.

Protected Cropping
If you have space in a greenhouse or polythene tunnel, it is worth trying to grow eddoes. Plant pre-sprouted or chitted tubers in spring into grow-bags or 20–30cm (8–12in) pots containing peat substitute compost. Maintain heat and high humidity: damp down the glasshouse floor or mist plants with soft tepid water.

Harvesting & Storing
Eddoes take between 5 and 6 months to mature. Harvest when the stems begin to turn yellow and die back. Lift the tubers carefully with a garden fork; select some for eating and save others for replanting. If they are undamaged and dried carefully, tubers can be stored for several months.

Health
The starch grains in tubers are among the smallest found in the plant kingdom, making them easy to digest.

Eddoe Soup

CULINARY

Tubers can be boiled, baked, roasted, puréed and made into soup. They can also be fried.

PESTS & DISEASES

Eddoes grown outdoors are generally problem-free but when grown under glass they are susceptible to **aphids** and **fungal leaf spots**; **red spider mite** can also be a problem, particularly when humidity is low. **Downy mildew** can attack tubers after they have been lifted so it is important to ensure that they are dried well before being stored. Dispose of infected tubers and do not use them for propagation.

WARNING

When handling and peeling eddoes, be sure to wear gloves or cover the hands with a layer of cooking oil to prevent a nasty rash.

Cucumis sativus. Cucurbitaceae

CUCUMBER

Climbing or scrambling annual, grown for elongated or round succulent fruits. Tender. Value: moderate potassium and small amounts of beta carotene.

The smooth-skinned types can grow to well over 30cm (12in)

The wild species from central Asia is now rare in nature, yet the world-renowned salad crop has been cultivated for centuries. The first record was in Mesopotamia around 2000BC in the earliest known vegetable garden, and cucumbers were grown in India a thousand years later. The Romans in the first century AD cultivated them in baskets or raised beds mounted on wheels so they could be moved around 'as the sun moved through the heavens'. When the day cooled, they were moved back under frames or into cucumber houses glazed with oiled cloth known as *specularia*. Tiberius found them tasty and was said to have eaten them every day of the year.

Early varieties were quite bitter and were boiled and served with oil, vinegar and honey. They were a common ingredient in soups, stews and as a cooked vegetable until the nineteenth century. Eighteenth-century English recipes include cucumbers stuffed with partly cooked pigeons (with head and feathers left on: the idea was to make the head appear attached to the cucumber); the whole was then cooked in broth and the heads garnished with barberries. Cooks in Georgian England must have had a rather bizarre sense of humour!

Columbus introduced cucumbers to the New World. They are recorded as being planted in Haiti in 1494 and grown by English settlers in Virginia in 1609. About the same time, French writers Estienne and Liébault warned: 'Beware that your seed be not olde, for if it be 3 years olde, will bring forth radishes.' Obviously their soil was as fertile as their imagination.

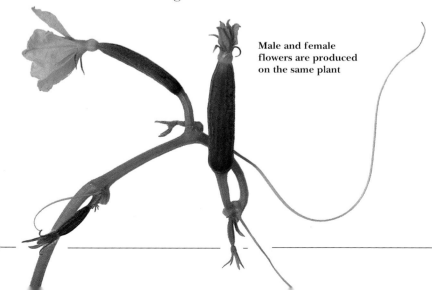

Male and female flowers are produced on the same plant

VARIETIES

Your seed catalogue will give an idea of the huge number of cultivars to choose from. There are 'greenhouse cucumbers' (though many indoor varieties can grow outdoors in a sheltered position in cooler climates and grow outdoors in warm zones); 'ridge' or outdoor types, which need protection as seedlings but can be grown outdoors in cool temperate climates; pickling cucumbers or gherkins; round varieties; Japanese climbing and bushy types.

Greenhouse or indoor cucumbers
'Crystal Apple', a small, yellow, round cucumber, is prolific and easy to grow. For the unheated greenhouse or outdoors. **'Danimas'*** is a vigorous, 'all-female' mini-cucumber for a slightly heated or cold greenhouse. **'Telegraph'** is a popular, reliable variety with smooth skin and good-sized fruits. **'Telegraph Improved'** is tasty and prolific with long fruits. **'Yamato'** produces delicious long thin fruits.

Outdoor or ridge cucumbers
'Bianco Lungo di Parigi' fruits are moderately sized and have creamy-white skin. **'Burpless Tasty Green'** is tender, tasty and crisp,

resistant to mildew and tolerant of heat. **'Chicago Pickling'** is high-yielding and disease-resistant. **'Crystal Lemon'** fruits are tangy and the size of a lemon. They are perfect for pickling, slicing or stuffing. **'Long Green Improved'** is a robust, highly productive and reliable variety with large, tasty fruits. It can be also used for pickling. **'Marketmore'** is smooth, tasty and excellent for cooler conditions. It is resistant to powdery and downy mildew. **'Boothy Blond'** has been grown for generations by the Boothby family of Maine in USA, but it is not commercially available. Many older varieties were grown from seed saved from the previous year's crop.

Pickling cucumbers or gherkins **'Arena'** is a high-yielding hybrid for outdoors that produces good-quality dark green fruits. **'Athene'*** is for outdoors or an unheated glasshouse or frame. **'Gherkin'** is fast-growing, with masses of small prickly fruits. **'Hokus'** is perfect for pickling and outdoor cultivation. **'Midget'** is a prolific and compact variety. **'National Pickling'** is short, blunt-ended with small, smooth fruits. It is vigorous and heavy-yielding. It was introduced in 1929 by the National Pickle Packers Association in Britain. **'Vert de Massy Cornichon'** is very tasty. Pickle when small, or allow to reach maturity.

CULTIVATION

Propagation

When growing outdoor cucumbers, sow 2 seeds edgeways 1–2cm (½–¾in) deep in a 5–7.5cm (2–3in) pot from mid-spring. Place in a propagator or heated greenhouse at 20°C (68°F). Retain the stronger seedling after germination, keep moist with tepid water and tie up small canes. Feed with a general liquid fertilizer to boost growth.

Give plants plenty of light and harden off before transplanting with care to avoid checks, when the danger of frost has passed. Allow 90cm (36in) between plants. Protect with cloches or horticultural fleece until established.

Sow successively to extend the cropping season. Alternatively, pregerminate or sow 2–3 seeds, 1–2cm (½–¾in) deep *in situ* under jam jars or cloches from late spring to early summer when the soil temperature is around 20°C (68°F). Thin to leave the strongest seedling.

The second method is preferable as cucumbers do not transplant well.

Growing

'Ridge' cucumbers need rich, fertile, well-drained soil in a sunny, sheltered position. A few weeks before planting, dig out holes or longer ridges at least 45cm (18in) wide and 30cm (12in) deep. Half fill with well-rotted manure or good garden compost, then return the excavated soil, mounding it to about 15cm (6in) above ground level.

Better fruits are obtained when plants are grown against supports, though traditionally they are left to trail over the ground.

Once plants have produced 5–6 leaves, pinch out growing points of the stems, allow 2 laterals to form and pinch out the growing tips again. Ridge cucumbers are insect-pollinated, so do not remove male flowers as you would with greenhouse cultivars.

Grow gherkins like ridge cucumbers, or train them up some netting.

Train Japanese cultivars up trellis, cane tripods, wire or nylon netting. Nip out the growing point when stems reach the top of the support. Water regularly; feed with a high-potash fertilizer every 2 weeks when fruits are forming.

Keep crops weed-free and the soil moist.

'Boothby Blond', from the USA

Light-shading is essential, as with these 'Telegraph' types

Maintenance

Spring Sow under cover from mid-spring.
Summer Plant ridge cucumbers outdoors once frost is past. Maintain high temperatures and humidity indoors. Train and harvest.
Autumn Harvest.
Winter Store in a cool place.

Protected Cropping

Sow under cover or in a propagator from mid-spring at 21–25°C (70–75°F). To avoid erratic germination, seeds can be pregerminated on moist kitchen towel in a covered plastic container, then placed in an airing cupboard or propagator. After about 3 days, when the seeds have germinated, sow in 7.5cm (3in) pots of seed compost.

Sow from late spring if no heat can be provided. Fill 8cm (3.5in) pots with seed compost and press the seed down edgeways into each pot about 1cm (½in) deep.

Greenhouse cucumbers need a humid atmosphere and temperatures around 20°C (70°C). Soils should be rich, moisture-retentive and free-draining, so incorporate well-rotted organic matter if you are planting in the greenhouse border. Even better, grow in 25cm (10in) pots of soil-based fertilizer with added organic matter, in growbags, or in untreated straw bales with a bed of compost in the centre.

Insert a cane at the base of the plant and tie it into the roof structure of the greenhouse. Tie in the main stem and remove the growth tip when it reaches the roof, pinching out the laterals 2 leaves beyond each fruit.

Greenhouse cucumbers should not be pollinated or they become bitter: remove male flowers. Female flowers are identified by the swelling behind each one. Or choose 'all-female' cultivars.

Mist plants regularly with tepid water and keep the compost moist with tepid water. Feed every 2 weeks with high-potash fertilizer once fruits begin to swell.

Outdoor cucumbers can be grown in cold frames or a cold greenhouse in cooler climates. They are better trained above the ground. Ventilate well on warm days and mist regularly.

Container Growing

Sow indoor types in pots or growbags (see 'Protected Cropping'). Smooth-skinned varieties can be grown in a growbag or container 30cm (12in) wide by 20cm (8in) deep in a sunny position outdoors. Sow 3 seeds 2.5cm (1in) deep in late spring or early summer.

Thin out to leave the strongest seedling; pinch out growing tips when the plant develops 6–7 leaves. Train the side shoots on netting or canes. Keep soil moist. Feed with high-potash fertilizer when fruits form. 'Bush Champion' is ideal.

Harvesting & Storing

Fruits should never be harvested until they are fully ripe, though the sixteenth-century practice of leaving fruit on until they were mottled brown and yellow with a rich flavour may not be to your taste!

Outdoor cucumbers crop mid-summer to early autumn: cut with a sharp knife when they are large enough to use. For maximum yields, you should pick fruit regularly.

Cucumbers last for several days in the salad drawer of a refrigerator. Cover the cut end with cling film and use as rapidly as possible. Or stand it stalk end down in a tall jug with a little water in the bottom. Like marrows, they can be stored in nets in a cool place.

PESTS & DISEASES

Red spider mite, **aphids**, **slugs** and **powdery mildew** can be troublesome.

Cucumber mosaic virus shows as mottled, distorted leaves. Burn young infected plants and leaves from older plants. Older plants may recover, though yields will be lower.

COMPANION PLANTING

Ridge cucumbers thrive in the shade of maize or sunflowers, and grow well with peas and beans, beet or carrots.

Climbing cucumbers flourish scrambling over sweetcorn and beans.

MEDICINAL

Cucumbers were used by the Romans against scorpion bites, bad eyesight and to scare away mice.

Wives wishing for children wore cucumbers tied around their waists, and they were carried by midwives and thrown away once the child was born.

CULINARY

Eat while the stalk end is still firm. Some people remain adamant that peeled cucumbers are best: others think the flavour and appearance of the skin enhances the vegetable.

They are frequently sliced and eaten in salads, and are good in sandwiches with salmon. Mix with yoghurt and mint as a side dish to Middle Eastern dishes or curries. Make into a delicious cold soup.

To eat them as a vegetable, peel, seed, dice and stew them in a little water and butter for 20 minutes, until soft. Thicken with cream and serve with mild- or rich-flavoured fish.

Cucumber & Cream Cheese Mousse

Cucumber & Cream Cheese Mousse
Serves 4

Half a cucumber, in chunks
275g (10oz) cream cheese
1–2 tablespoons mint leaves
2 teaspoons white wine vinegar
2½ teaspoons gelatine
150ml (¼pt) vegetable stock
Salt & freshly ground black pepper
Radicchio leaves & sprigs of mint, to serve

Put the cucumber into a blender with the cream cheese, mint and vinegar and purée until smooth. Dissolve the gelatine in a little stock over a low heat. Leave to cool, then stir in the balance of the stock. Add this to the cream cheese, season and blend.

Chill for at least 2 hours before serving, arranged individually with radicchio leaves, garnished with a few fine slices of cucumber and sprigs of mint.

Crambe maritima. Cruciferae

SEAKALE

***Perennial grown for its blanched young shoots. Hardy.
Value: an excellent source of vitamin C.***

Found on the seashores of northern Europe,
the Baltic and the Black Seas, seakale was
harvested from the wild and sold in markets
long before it came into cultivation. In
Victorian times it was seen as an aristocrat of
the vegetable garden and widely cultivated by
armies of gardeners in the enormous kitchen
gardens attached to great houses. Today it is
rarely grown, perhaps because the scale on
which it was forced for Victorian tables gave
it a reputation for being labour-intensive.
However, it is easy to grow at home, and
quite delicious; so it is high time
it experiences a revival!

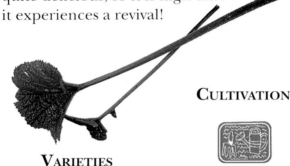

Seakale exposed to the sea breeze

VARIETIES

'Lily White' crops heavily,
has a good flavour and pale
stems. Unnamed selections
of the wild species are also
available from nurseries.

**Seakale flowers in summer and
is sweetly scented**

CULTIVATION

Propagation
Seakale can be grown from
seed, but it is usually
propagated from crowns or
root cuttings from the side
roots, taken in autumn after
the leaves have died back.
These are called 'thongs'.
Buy them from a nursery or
select roots which are pencil-
thick and 7.5–15cm (3–6in)
long. Make a straight cut
across the top of the root
and an angled cut at the
base (so the top and bottom
are distinguishable). Store
in sand until planting.

Growing
Seakale needs a sunny
position on deep, rich, well-
drained light soil with a

pH of around neutral. The
winter before planting, dig
in some well-rotted compost;
on heavier soils, add
horticultural sand or grit, or
plant on a raised bed.

Seakale should crop for
about 5–7 years before it
needs replacing, so it is vital
to prepare the ground
thoroughly. Two weeks prior
to planting, rake in a
general fertilizer. Before
planting, in early spring, rub
off all the buds to leave the
single strongest bud and
plant thongs or crowns 45cm
(18in) apart, covered with
2.5–5cm (1–2in) of soil.

Water regularly, feed
occasionally, remove flower
stems as they appear and
keep weed-free. In autumn,
cut down the yellowing
foliage. From late autumn
until mid-winter, cover the
crowns with a bucket, flower
pot (cover the drainage
holes) or seakale forcer and
surround with manure, straw
or leafmould.

Stop harvesting in late
spring, rake in a general
fertilizer and mulch with
well-rotted manure or
compost. Keep the beds
weed-free and water well in
dry periods. Delaying harvest
until the second year lets
plants become established.

Maintenance
Spring Force crops
outdoors.
Summer Water in dry
weather, feed occasionally,
keep weed-free.
Autumn Remove the
yellowing foliage.
Winter Lift crowns for
forcing.

Protected Cropping
For an early crop, lift crowns
after leaves die back, trim
the main root to 15cm (6in)
and remove the side shoots;
plant 10cm (4in) apart in
boxes or 3 per 23cm (9in)
pot filled with rich soil from
the seakale bed or loam-
based compost with a high
fertilizer content. Cover with
upturned pots, polythene or

**Seakale, after blanching, looks
like a bizarrely twisted sculpture**

anything opaque. Keep the compost moist. They should be ready in 5–6 weeks at temperatures of 10–13°C (48–55°F); from 16–21°C (60–70°F) they will be ready earlier. Keep them in a cellar, boiler house or under the greenhouse benches and maintain a constant supply by lifting crowns regularly. In frosty weather lift and store crowns in moist sand until required. Dispose of exhausted crowns after use.

Harvesting & Storing
When blanched sprouts are 7.5–20cm (3–8in) long, remove the soil from around the shoots and cut through the stems with a sharp knife, removing a tiny sliver of root. Crops forced outdoors can be harvested in late autumn to early spring. After harvesting, discard the exhausted roots of those forced indoors.

PESTS & DISEASES

Do not plant in beds infected with **club root**. **Flea beetle** make round holes in the leaves; dust seedlings with derris.

OTHER USES

Seakale is attractive in the flower border. It forms a compact rosette of large, wavy-edged, glaucous leaves, with large bunches of white, honey-scented flowers towering above the foliage in summer.

Seakale with traditional terracotta forcing jars

CULINARY

Better eaten fresh, seakale lasts for 2–3 days in the salad compartment of the refrigerator.

Wash stems and tie them into bundles using raffia and steam or lightly boil them until tender – overcooking toughens the stems and makes them less palatable.

Victorians served seakale on folded napkins or toast, drenched in white sauce or melted butter.

Seakale is also delicious served as a starter with béchamel or hollandaise sauce, or covered in lemon-flavoured melted butter.

Young flowering shoots can be eaten once they are lightly boiled.

Seakale Gratinée
Serves 4

This is excellent served with baked ham.

750g (1½lb) well-washed seakale

For the béchamel sauce:
50g (2oz) butter
2 tablespoons flour
1 teaspoon French mustard
150ml (¼pt) milk or crème fraîche
4 tablespoons good strong Cheddar cheese
Salt & freshly ground black pepper

Rinse the seakale well, tie into bundles and cook until *al dente* in boiling salted water. Drain well. Arrange in an ovenproof dish.

Make the béchamel sauce, flavouring with the Cheddar cheese. Pour the sauce over the seakale and bake in a preheated oven, 200°C, 400°F, gas 6 for 15 minutes. Serve hot.

Cucurbita maxima, Cucurbita moschata and *Cucurbita pepo. Cucurbitaceae*

PUMPKIN &
SQUASH

MARROW, COURGETTE, ZUCCHINI, POTIRON

Annuals grown for edible fruits, often colourful, which can be extremely large.
Tender. Value: high in beta carotene, moderate amounts of vitamin C and folic acid

On the coast of Coromandel
Where the early pumpkins blow
In the middle of the woods
Lived the Yonghy-Bonghy-Bo...
Edward Lear (1812–88)

The name 'pumpkin' appeared in the seventeenth century, shortly before Perrault wrote
Cinderella, the tale about a poor girl whose fairy godmother turned a pumpkin into a
golden coach which took her to a fabulous ball. 'Pumpkin' comes from the Greek word for
melon – *pepon* or 'cooked by the sun' – while one French name, *potiron*, means 'large
mushroom', from the Arabic for morel mushrooms. 'Squash' is an abbreviation of the native
North American Indian word *askutasquash*, meaning 'eaten raw or uncooked'.

The squashes originated in the Americas and are believed to have been cultivated for
between five and ten thousand years. Wild forms were originally gathered for their seeds and
were only later found to have sweet flesh. Many varieties arrived in Europe soon after the
discovery of the New World in the sixteenth century. Not only were they eaten, but the seeds
were pounded in oatmeal and applied to the face, to bleach freckles and other blemishes.
Estienne and Liébault wrote in 1570: 'To make pompions keep long and not spoiled or
rotted, you must sprinkle them with the
juice of a houseleek'. In the
seventeenth century they were
mashed to bulk up bread, or
boiled and heavily buttered.

Winter squash

This group contains a wealth
of edible and outstandingly
ornamental fruits. One of the
most beautiful sights in the
kitchen garden is pumpkins
ripening in golden sunshine
during the autumn.

'Little Gem' comes from the same group as the courgette, but grows round rather than long

VARIETIES

Members of the genus *Cucurbita* are bushy or trailing annuals – sometimes extremely vigorous plants – bearing a wide range of edible and/or ornamental fruit. The fruits from all of these species are often grouped together according to their shape or time of harvest – crookneck, summer squash, winter squash and so on; in practice categories overlap and some are multi-purpose, being served differently when young and when mature. Additional confusion arises because of local variation in what is grown and what it is called. Here they are classed according to species.

The *Cucurbita maxima* group has large, variable fruits and includes most traditional pumpkins and winter squashes, containing several ornamentals like the banana, buttercup, hubbard and turban types. They tend to have hard skins when mature, and keep well; the yellow flesh needs cooking. They flourish in low humidity from 20–27°C (68–80°F), though some tolerate cooler conditions. **'Atlantic Giant'** is not for the faint-hearted – it can

grow to 317 kg (700lb). **'Banana Pink'** is long, broad and curved, with pale pink skin. **'Big Max'** is a massive pumpkin with rough red-orange skin and bright flesh. It is excellent for pies, exhibitions and as a 'giant' vegetable. **'Buttercup'** is delicious with firm, dense, sweet flesh. The skin is dark green with pale narrow stripes. Good for soups, roasting and pumpkin pie. **'Crown Prince'** is small fruited with tender orange flesh. Tasty and keeps well.

'Queensland Blue', an attractive small variety with blue-grey skin, is very tasty. **'Turk's Turban'** (**'Turk's Cap'**), a wonderful ornamental squash, is orange with cream and green markings. The name aptly describes the shape. **'Warted Hubbard'** is a small, round fruit with extraordinary dark green warty skin, orange-yellow flesh. It keeps well. **'Whangaparoa Crown Pumpkin'**, a hard, grey-skinned variety with a pronounced crown and orange flesh, stores well.

Cucurbita pepo embraces summer squashes (including courgettes or zucchini and their larger version, the marrow), non-keeping winter pumpkins and ornamental gourds such as custard squash, plus straight and crook-necked types. The fruits are usually soft-skinned, especially when young, and may be served raw when small. One variety, **'Little Gem'**, is slow to mature, taking about 4 months. It may not be suitable for growing in cooler conditions.

'Crown of Thorns'

Summer Squash
'Early Golden Summer Crookneck' is an early cropper with bright yellow fruits, excellent for eating. Harvest when 10cm (4in) long. **'Early Prolific Straight Neck'** is lemon-yellow with finely textured thick flesh. **'Vegetable Spaghetti'** (**'Spaghetti Squash'**) is pale yellow when mature. Boil or bake fruits whole; scoop out the flesh inside and it looks like spaghetti. **'White Patty Pan'** (**'White Bush Scallop'**) has an unusual flattened shape with a scalloped edge. It is better harvested and cooked whole when about 7.5cm (3in) in diameter. It is bushy and ideal for small gardens. **'Yellow Bush Scallop'** is an old variety with coarse, pale yellow flesh and a bright yellow skin.

Marrow
This elongated type of summer squash has long been popular in Britain.
'Long Green Trailing' is a prolific, long-fruited variety which is dark green with pale stripes. **'Tiger Cross'**, an early green bush type, crops well and has good-quality fruits. Resistant to cucumber mosaic virus. **'Tender and True'** is semi-trailing and matures early. Resistant to cucumber mosaic virus, it can be used as a courgette when young.

Courgette or Zucchini
Varieties of marrow bred for picking small, the following are all bush types and ideal for the smaller garden.

'Crown Prince' looks pale beside its brighter counterparts

'**Small Sugar**' has rounded orange fruits growing to 18cm (7½in) diameter. The flesh is tender, yellow and excellent for pies. It matures from late autumn.

Cucurbita moschata includes the early butternut, butternut, Kentucky Field and crookneck squashes, harvested in autumn and winter. They are large, rounded and usually have smooth, tough skin. Possibly one of the earliest species in cultivation, they are widely cultivated and found throughout the tropics. These squashes are particularly heat-tolerant.

'**Butternut**' has pale tan, stocky, club-shaped fruits with bright orange flesh. It stores well and succeeds in cooler areas. '**Early Butternut**' is a curved, narrow fruit with a swollen tip. This bush variety matures rapidly and keeps well. '**Kentucky Field**' ('**Large Cheese**') is flattened with faintly ribbed, pale cream-coloured skin. '**Triple Treat**' is a bright orange round fruit. Its seeds are particularly good eaten raw, fried or roasted. It is easy to carve and is therefore a variety which is often grown for Halloween. '**Waltham Butternut**' has a smooth, pale tan skin, yellow-orange flesh and a nutty taste. It is very good for storing and yields extremely well.

'**Ambassador**' is high-yielding with dark green fruit and crops over a long period. '**Defender**'* produces high yields of mid-green fruits. Harvest regularly. It is resistant to cucumber mosaic virus. '**De Nice à Fruit Rond**', a round variety, should be picked when the size of a golf ball. It has a delicious flavour. '**Gold Rush**', a compact bush with yellow fruits, crops over a long period. '**Spacemiser**' is a compact,and prolific gourmet variety. '**Supremo**'* produces very tasty, dark green fruit.

Winter squash
These usually have white or pale yellow flesh, whereas pumpkins have coarse, orange flesh. '**Ebony Acorn**' ('**Table Queen**') is an ancient early-cropping variety with thin, dark green skin and pale yellow, sweet flesh. It is a semi-bush, which is good for baking. '**Jack be Little**' is a miniature pumpkin with deep ribbed fruits about 5 x 7.5cm (2x3in) in diameter and orange skin. It is edible, but is more attractive simply as an autumn decoration.

The high-yielding 'Gold Rush'

CULTIVATION

Propagation
Sow *in situ* or in pots in cooler climates as seeds do not germinate if the soil is below 13°C (56°F).

From mid- to late spring, soak the seed overnight then sow one seed edgeways, about 2.5cm (1in) deep in a 7.5cm (3in) pot or module of moist multi-purpose or seed compost and place in a propagator or on a warm window sill, preferably at 20–25°C (68–77°F). After germination transplant the seedlings when they are large enough to handle into 12.5cm (5in) pots, taking care not to damage the roots. Keep compost moist but not waterlogged. Harden off gradually and transplant from late spring to early summer when the danger of frost has passed. Protect with cloches until plants are established.

A feast of richly coloured and oddly shaped pumpkins and squashes

Alternatively, sow *in situ* when the soil is warm and workable and there is no danger of frost, from late spring to early summer.

Dig out a hole at least 30–45cm (12–18in) square and half fill with well-rotted manure 7–10 days before planting. Sow 2–3 seeds 2.5cm (1in) deep in the centre of the mound and cover with a jam jar or cut the base from a plastic bottle and use as a crop cover. After germination, thin to leave the strongest seedling, remove the cover and mark the position with a cane so you know where to water the plant among the mass of stems. Alternatively, prepare the ground as described and transplant seedlings.

Space cultivars according to their vigour. Sow bush varieties on mounds or ridges, 60–90cm (24–36in) apart with 90–120cm (36–48in) between rows. Trailing varieties should be 120–180cm (48–72in) apart with 180–360cm (6–12ft) between rows.

Growing
Pumpkins and squashes need a sunny position in rich, moisture-retentive soil with plenty of well-rotted organic matter and a pH of 5.5–6.8.

It is a good idea to plant through a black polythene mulch laid over the soil with the edges buried to hold it in place. This warms the soil, suppresses weeds, conserves moisture and protects ripening fruit.

The 'White Patty Pan' looks like a flying saucer

Outstandingly strange-looking, 'Turk's Turban' will store for several months

A thick layer of straw or horticultural fleece are useful alternatives, or you can lay the ripening fruit on a roof tile, a piece of board or similar to protect it from the soil and prevent rotting.

Hand pollination is recommended, particularly in cold weather when insect activity is reduced. Female flowers have a small swelling, the embryonic squash, immediately behind the petals, while male flowers have only a thin stalk.

When the weather is dry, remove a mature male flower, fold back or remove the petals and dust pollen on to the stigma of the female flowers. Alternatively, transfer the pollen with a fine paintbrush. Periods of hot weather can reduce the ratio of female to male flowers.

Plants need copious amounts of food and water, particularly when flowers and fruits are forming, up to 11 litres (2 gal) of water per week, but they should never be allowed to become waterlogged.

Feed with a liquid general fertilizer every 2 weeks. Plants grown with a black plastic mulch also need an occasional foliar feed to boost growth.

Pinch out tips of main shoots of trailing varieties when they reach 60cm (2ft) to encourage branching and trim back those which outgrow their position.

Trailing types can also be trained over trellis or supports. Where space is limited, you can push a circle of pegs into the soil and trail the stems around the pegs.

To guarantee large fruits, allow only 2–3 to develop on each plant.

Keep crops weed-free.

Maintenance
Spring Sow seeds under glass or outdoors.
Summer Feed and water copiously; keep crops weed-free. Harvest courgettes and marrows.
Autumn Harvest pumpkins and winter squashes, allow to ripen and protect from frost.
Winter Store winter squashes until mid-winter or later.

Protected Cropping
In cooler climates or to advance growth, sow seed indoors and transplant. Protect with cloches or crop covers until they are well established. Use bush varieties for earlier crops.

Container Growing
Courgettes, marrows, bush varieties of other squashes and those which are moderately vigorous can be grown in growbags or

containers which are at least 35cm (14in) by 30cm (12in) deep. Use a loam-based compost with additional well-rotted organic matter. Sow indoors to transplant later or sow directly outdoors. Keep plants well watered and do not allow the compost to dry out.

Plants can be grown up strong canes 2m (6½ft) tall. Pinch out growing points when stems reach the top; tie the main stem and sideshoots firmly to the supporting canes.

Hand pollinate for successful cropping.

Harvesting & Storing
Pick courgettes or zucchini and summer squashes when they are about 10cm (4in) long and still young and tender. Marrows are harvested when they have reached full size. Push your thumbnail gently into the skin near the stalk; if it goes in easily then the marrow is ready for harvest. Cut them from the stem leaving a short stalk on the fruit and handle with care to avoid bruising. Harvest regularly for continual cropping. They can be stored in a cool place for about 8 weeks.

Courgettes can be kept in a polythene bag in the refrigerator and will stay fresh for about a week.

Courgettes are suitable for freezing. Cut into 1cm (½in) slices, blanch for 2 minutes, cool, drain and dry. Freeze in polythene bags. Flesh of winter squashes and pumpkins can be cooked then frozen, without any loss of flavour.

Towards the end of the growing season, remove any foliage which shades the fruits. Harvest pumpkins and winter squashes from late summer to autumn, though they must be brought into storage before the first heavy frosts. On maturity, the foliage rapidly dies, the skin hardens and stem starts to crack.

After harvest, leave them outdoors for about 14 days as cold weather improves the taste and sugar content, hardening the skin and sealing the stem. Protect from heavy frost with hessian, straw or similar.

In cooler areas they can be ripened in a greenhouse or on a sunny windowsill. Pumpkins will last until mid-winter when stored in a frost-free shed.

Store winter squashes at a minimum temperature of 10°C (50°F); they last for up to 6 months, but may deteriorate earlier. Some Japanese varieties will last even longer.

Marrows are traditionally allowed to trail, but can also be grown on frames

The edible flowers of the marrow

COMPANION PLANTING

Grow courgette and marrow alongside sweetcorn for support and shade, and with legumes, which provide essential nitrogen.

PESTS & DISEASES

If fruits show signs of withering, water and feed more often.

Aphids, **powdery** and **downy mildew** and **slugs** can be a problem.

Cucumber mosaic virus causes yellow mottling and puckering of the leaves and rotting of the fruit. Destroy infected plants immediately and control aphids which transmit this virus.

CULINARY

Flowers of all varieties can be used in salads or stuffed with rice or minced meat and fried in batter. Prepare the meat, rice and batter before picking the flowers as they wilt quickly. They can also be puréed and made into soup. Young shoots are steamed or boiled. Pumpkin flesh is used for pies; their seeds are deep-fried in oil, salted and are known as 'pepitos'.

The fruits can be stuffed, steamed, stir-fried, added to curries, made into jam or pickles.

Courgette Omelette
Serves 2

A particularly pretty omelette can be made with young courgettes; use a mixture of yellow and green ones to good effect.

5 eggs
300g (10oz) courgettes
4 tablespoons olive oil
1 tablespoon fresh basil leaves
* (purple for preference)*
1 tablespoon fresh thyme leaves
Salt & freshly ground black
* pepper*

Whisk the eggs with salt and pepper and set aside. Dice the courgettes coarsely. Heat half the oil and sauté them for a couple of minutes. Then remove from the heat.

In an omelette pan, heat the balance of the oil and pour in the eggs, courgettes and herbs. Stir gently over a low heat while the omelette sets. Turn it on to a plate and slide back into the pan to cook the second side for a minute or so until it is nicely browned.

Serve as a refreshing Sunday supper dish.

Pumpkin Kibbeh
Serves 4

A centre piece of many Middle Eastern meals, these 'balls' should be served warm, rather than hot. This recipe was given to me by Arto der Haroutunian.

200g (7oz) freshly boiled
* pumpkin flesh*
400g (14oz) bulgar wheat
150g (6oz) plain flour
1 onion, finely chopped
Salt & freshly ground black
* pepper*

For the filling:
2 shallots, finely chopped
250g (8oz) spinach, washed
150g (6oz) cooked chickpeas,
* drained*
50g (2oz) chopped walnuts
50g (2oz) dried apricots
¼ teaspoon sumac
* (from Cypriot delis)*
1 tablespoon lemon juice
Salt & freshly ground black
* pepper*
Oil for frying

In a large bowl, purée the pumpkin using a fork. Sieve the bulgar and flour into the bowl and mix in the onion and seasoning. Leave in a cool place for 10–15 minutes. If the dough is too hard to handle, you may need to add a tablespoon of water and knead well.

To make the filling, sauté the shallots in the oil until they just turn brown. Mix in the spinach and allow to wilt, stirring constantly, for a couple of minutes. Then add the rest of the ingredients, mixing well.

Make the kibbehs with wet hands to prevent the mixture from sticking. Form the bulgar and pumpkin mixture into oval patties – they should be about 8cm (3in) long and just big enough to stuff. Create an opening at one end and fill each kibbeh with the spinach and apricot stuffing. Using your fingers, seal up the ends.

Fry the kibbehs in hot oil for a couple of minutes on each side and drain on kitchen paper. There should be enough to make between 20 and 24 kibbehs.

Courgette Omelette

Acorn Squash with Balsamic Vinegar

Allow 100g (4oz) of acorn squash per person. Cut in half and remove the seeds and fibres. Place in a buttered, ovenproof dish and pour over 1 tablespoon balsamic vinegar, 2 tablespoons runny honey and 1 tablespoon lemon juice for each serving. Cook in a preheated oven, 180°C, 350°F, gas 4 for 40 minutes, turning over halfway.

Custard Marrow with Bacon & Cheese

500g (1lb) custard marrow
2 tablespoons butter
1 small onion, finely sliced
75g (3oz) smoked back bacon, diced
150ml (¼pt) crème fraîche
4 tablespoons grated mature Cheddar
Salt & freshly ground black pepper

Cut the custard marrow into a rough dice and steam it until just tender. Remove from the heat and keep warm. Make a sauce by heating the butter and cooking the onion until softened. Add the bacon and continue cooking for 5 minutes, stirring from time to time. Mix in the crème fraîche, the custard marrow and seasoning and pour into a greased ovenproof dish. Top with the cheese and cook in a preheated oven, 225°C, 425°F, gas 7, for 15 minutes.

Traditional Hallowe'en lanterns

OTHER USES

Pumpkins are hollowed out and made into Hallowe'en 'Jack o'Lanterns'. Mature marrows can be used for wine making.

MEDICINAL

In Ethiopia seeds from squashes are used as laxatives and purgatives; they are used worldwide to expel intestinal worms. Eating winter squash and pumpkin is said to reduce the risk of cancer.

WARNING

Be careful when lifting large squashes: bend from the knees, not the back!

Cynara cardunculus. Compositae

CARDOON

*(Cardon) Perennial grown as annual for 'heart' and
blanched leaf midribs.
Half hardy. Value: rich in potassium.*

This close relative of the globe artichoke is found in the wild through much of the Mediterranean and North Africa. Cultivated versions are valued as a vegetable and in the ornamental garden. When grown as a food crop, the stems are blanched during autumn in a similar manner to celery. Its delights have been enjoyed for centuries; it was grown before the birth of Christ and was esteemed by the Romans, who paid high prices for it in their markets as an ingredient for stews and salads. Cardoons reached England by 1658 and North America by the following century, but never established themselves as a major crop despite their popularity in Europe. Today they are more likely to be found in the herbaceous border, where the bold angular foliage and tall candelabras of thistle-like purple flowers are outstanding.

VARIETIES

'Gigante di Romagna' is a reliable variety with long stalks. 'Plein Blanc Inerma Ameliora' grows to 120cm (4ft) tall, with white ribs that are well textured and tasty. 'Tours' is a large and vigorous variety. Beware of the large spines and protect yourself accordingly!

Cardoons make fine ornamentals

CULTIVATION

Cardoons need a sunny, sheltered site on light, fertile, well-drained soil.

Propagation

Sow *in situ* in mid-spring, planting 3–4 seeds 2.5cm (1in) deep in 'stations' 50cm (20in) apart with 1.5m (5ft) between rows. Thin after germination to retain the strongest seedling. In cooler areas or if spring is late and the soil is yet to warm up, sow indoors. Place 3 seeds in 7.5cm (3in) pots or modules of moist seed compost in a propagator or glasshouse at 13°C (55°F). Thin, leaving the strongest seedling, then harden off before planting outdoors in mid- to late spring, when there is no danger of frost. Water well after planting and protect from scorching sunshine until they have established.

Growing

The autumn or early spring before seed sowing or planting out seedlings, double dig the site, adding well-rotted organic matter. Alternatively, plant in trenches 38–50cm (15–20in) wide and 30cm (12in) deep; dig these in late autumn or early spring, incorporating plenty of rotted manure or compost into the base and refilling to 7.5–10cm (3–4in) below the surface. Leave the remaining soil alongside for earthing up. Before planting, rake in general fertilizer at 60g/sq m (2oz/sq yd).

In late summer to early autumn, on a day when the leaves and hearts are dry, begin blanching: pull stems into a large bunch (wear long sleeves and gloves for protection), and tie with raffia or soft string just below the leaves. Wrap cardoons with 'collars' of newspaper, corrugated cardboard, brown wrapping paper or black polythene tied firmly around the stems.

Tile drainpipes and plastic guttering are just as effective at excluding the light. Support collars with a stake, particularly on exposed sites. Alternatively, cardoons can be earthed up. Cover stems with dry hay, bracken or straw held firmly at several points with twine and cover with soil, banked at an angle of 45°. The first method is easier, cleaner and quicker.

Cardoons need a regular water supply from early summer through to early autumn, and liquid general fertilizer every 2 weeks. Keep weed-free by hand weeding, hoeing or, preferably, mulching with a 5cm (2in) layer of organic matter once plants are established.

Maintenance

Spring Sow seeds *in situ* or under glass.
Summer Feed and water regularly. Keep weed-free.
Autumn Harvest crops using a sharp knife. Prepare the planting bed.
Winter Store in a cool, dry place until required.

The flower heads are similar to those of globe artichokes

Protected Cropping
Protect transplants or seedlings under cloches or horticultural fleece if late spring frosts are forecast.

Container Growing
Grow in large containers of loam-based compost with added organic matter or in free-draining, moisture-retentive soil. Allow plenty of room for leaves to grow. Water and feed regularly: do not let the compost dry out. Blanch using 'collars'.

Harvesting & Storing
Blanching takes about 3–4 weeks. When ready to harvest, lift plants with a garden fork, trim off roots and remove outer leaves. Cardoons can remain in the ground until needed, but protect with bracken, straw or other insulating material in moderate frosts. If hard frosts are forecast, lift and store in a cool shed or cellar

Pests & Diseases
Cardoons are robust and have few problems. They can be affected by **powdery mildew**, which is worse when plants are dry at the roots and if nights are cold and days warm and dry.
  Mice will eat the seeds. An old remedy is to dip the seeds in paraffin; otherwise buy humane traps or a cat!

CULINARY

The leaf midribs and thinly sliced hearts are eaten raw in salads, in soups and stews or as an alternative to fennel or celery. They can be boiled in salted water with a squeeze of lemon juice for about 30 minutes until tender. Once cardoons are cut, drop them into water with a squeeze of lemon juice as the cut surfaces do tend to blacken.
  The dried flowers are used as a substitute for rennet in Spain and some parts of South America.

Lamb Tangine with Cardoons
Serves 4

Tangines (or stews) are popular in northern Africa. Cardoons give this traditional Moroccan dish a rich flavour.

750g (1½lb) chunks lamb
3 cloves garlic, crushed
1 teaspoon ground ginger
Pinch saffron
¼ teaspoon turmeric
2–3 tablespoons vegetable oil
2 tablespoons coriander
1 onion, peeled and sliced
750g–1kg (1½–2lb) cardoons
2 preserved lemons, quartered
4 tablespoons black olives
Juice of 2 lemons
Salt & freshly ground black pepper

Put the lamb, garlic, ginger, saffron, turmeric, oil, chopped coriander and onion in a heavy pan and mix well. Pour over a cup or two of water and bring to the boil.
  Skim if needs be and then simmer, covered, for 1 hour, adding more water if necessary, to just cook the lamb. Then add the cleaned cardoons and enough water to cover them (this is important), and continue cooking for a further 30–40 minutes.
  Stir in the preserved lemon quarters and the olives and enough lemon juice to taste, and ensure the tangine is well mixed. Taste and adjust the seasoning before serving piping hot.

Lamb Tangine with Cardoons

Cynara scolymus. Compositae

GLOBE ARTICHOKE

(French artichoke, Green artichoke) Tall, upright perennial grown for edible flower buds.
Half hardy. Value: 85% water; half carbohydrate indigestible inulin, turning to fructose in storage;
moderate iodine and iron content.

Originating in the Mediterranean, globe artichokes were grown by the Greeks and Romans, who regarded them as a delicacy. The common name comes from the Italian *articoclos*, deriving from *cocali*, or pine cone – an apt description of the appearance of the flower bud. Artichokes waned in popularity in the Dark Ages, but were restored to favour when Catherine de Medici introduced them to France in the sixteenth century. From there they spread around the world. Globe artichokes reached the United States in 1806, travelling with French and Spanish settlers.

In Italy its bitter principle flavours the aperitif *cynar*, which is popular as a vermouth and definitely an acquired taste!

Growing to about 1.2–1.5m (4–5ft) tall, with a 90cm (3ft) spread, attractive leaves and large thistle-like flowers, globe artichokes always look wonderful in the flower border and make excellent dual-purpose plants.

VARIETIES

'Green Globe' has large green heads with thick, fleshy scales. It needs winter protection in cooler climates. 'Gros Camus de Bretagne' is only suitable for warmer climates, but is worth growing for its large, well-flavoured heads. 'Purple Globe' is hardier than the green form, but is not as tasty. 'Purple Sicilian' has small, deep purple-coloured artichokes which are excellent for eating raw when they are very young. This variety is not frost-hardy. 'Vert de Laon' is hardy with an excellent flavour. 'Violetta di Chioggia', a purple-headed variety, is excellent in the flower border.

CULTIVATION

Artichokes need an open, sheltered site on light, fertile, well-drained soil.

Propagation
Artichokes can be grown from seed or divided, but are usually propagated from rooted 'suckers' – shoots arising from the plant's root system. Suckers are bought or removed from established plants in mid-spring. They should be healthy, about 20–23cm (8–9in) long and

An immature flower head, just before harvesting

well rooted, with at least 2 shoots. Clear soil from around the roots of the parent plant and remove them with a sharp knife, cutting close to the main stem between the sucker and parent plant. Alternatively, divide established plants in spring by lifting the roots and easing them apart with 2 garden forks, a spade or an old knife and replanting the sections; these too should have at least 2 shoots and a good root system. To keep your stocks vigorous and productive, renew the oldest one-third of your plants every year. This extends the cropping season, too, as mature plants are ready for harvest in late spring to early summer and young plants in late summer.

You can grow from seed and select the best plants, but this is time-consuming, uses valuable space and is not recommended; it is far better to grow proven, named cultivars. If you have the time and inclination, then sow seed in trays of moist seed compost in an unheated glasshouse during late winter or outdoors in early spring. Thin to leave the strongest seedlings and harden off before planting out at their final spacing in late spring. Once flower buds have been produced, retain the best plants for harvest and for future propagation, discarding the rest.

Growing

If necessary, improve the soil by digging in plenty of well-rotted organic matter in spring or autumn before planting. This prevents summer drought and winter waterlogging, conditions which globe artichokes dislike. Before planting, rake in general fertilizer at 60g/ sq m (2oz/sq yd).

Plant suckers or divisions 60cm (2ft) apart with 60–75cm (2–2½ft) between each row, trimming the leaves back to 12.5cm (5in), which helps to reduce water loss, and shading them from full sun until they are established. Water thoroughly after planting and during periods of dry weather, applying a high-potash liquid fertilizer every 2 weeks when the plants are actively growing.

Keep the beds weed-free and mulch with organic matter in spring. During autumn and winter, if heavy frosts are forecast, protect plants by earthing up with soil, then covering them with a thick layer of straw, bracken or other organic insulation. Remove the covering in spring.

Maintenance

Spring Divide or remove suckers from existing plants and replant. .
Summer Keep weed-free and water thoroughly during drought.
Autumn In areas with moderate temperatures, retain leaves and stems as frost protection.
Winter If severe frost is forecast, remove the decayed leaves, earth up, and protect plants with insulating material. Remove the materials in spring before growth begins.

Harvesting & Storing

Each flowering stem normally produces one large artichoke at the tip and several smaller ones below. A few flower heads will be produced in the first year; these are best removed so that the energy goes into establishing the plant, but if you cannot resist the

Globe artichoke flowers, which are closely related to the cotton thistle, are attractive to pollinating insects

temptation, harvest in late summer. In the second and third years more stems will be produced and are ready for cutting in mid-summer. Harvest when the scales are tightly closed, removing the terminal bud first with 5 or 7.5cm (2 or 3in) of stem, then the remaining side buds as they grow large enough. Alternatively, remove the lower artichokes for eating when they are about 4cm (1½in) long.

Once the scales begin to open, globe artichokes become inedible.

Pests & Diseases

Slugs attack young shoots and in leaves – the problem is worse in damp conditions. Keep the area free of plant debris, use biological controls, scatter aluminium sulphate based slug pellets around plants or make traps from plastic cartons half-buried in the ground and filled with milk or beer. Lay rooftiles, newspaper, old lettuce leaves or other tempting vegetation on the ground and hand pick

regularly from the underneath. Or put a barrier of grit around plants, or attract natural predators such as birds to the garden. **Lettuce root aphid** can be a problem. Creamy yellow aphids appear on the roots during summer, sucking sap and weakening plants. Water well in dry weather; apply systemic insecticide.

MEDICINAL

Artichokes are highly nutritious and are especially good for the liver, aiding detoxification and regeneration. They reduce blood sugar and cholesterol levels, stimulating the gall bladder and helping the metabolism of fat. Artichoke is also a diuretic and used to treat hepatitis and jaundice. It was used in folk medicine as a contraceptive and aphrodisiac, but its potency is not recorded!

Globe artichokes grow to 1.5m (5ft) high

CULINARY

Artichokes can be stored for up to a week in a polythene bag in a refrigerator.

The edible parts are the fleshy base of the outer scales, the central 'heart' and the bottom of the artichoke itself. Wash the artichoke thoroughly before use and sprinkle any cut parts with lemon juice to prevent them from turning black. Boil artichokes in a non-metallic pan of salted water with lemon juice for 30–45 minutes until soft. Check if they are ready by pushing a knife through the heart, or try a basal leaf to check it for tenderness.

Eat artichokes by hand, pulling off the leaves one by one and dipping the base in mayonnaise, hollandaise, lemon sauce, melted butter or plain yoghurt before scraping off the fleshy leaf base between your teeth. Pull off the hairy central 'choke', or remove it with a spoon, and then eat the fleshy heart.

Bottoms can be a garnish for roasts, filled with vegetables or sauces. Cook 'Cypriot-style' with oil, red wine and coriander seeds, or toss in oil and lemon dressing as hors-d'oeuvre. Make a salad of cubed artichoke bottoms and new potatoes (leftovers are suitable) and season well. Toss in mayonnaise and crumble over finely chopped hard-boiled egg and good-quality black olives. Sprinkle with chives and flat-leaved parsley. Whole baby artichokes can be battered and deep-fried or cooked in oil. Eat them cold with vinaigrette.

A seventeenth-century herbalist and apothecary wrote that even the youngest housewife knew how to cook artichokes and serve them with melted butter, seasoned with vinegar and pepper. Florence White, a founder of the English Folk Cookery Association and member of the American Home Economics Association, gives a recipe in *Good Things in England* (1929) for a recipe from the time of Queen Anne:

A Tart of Artichoke Bottoms
'Line a dish with fine pastry. Put in the artichoke bottoms, with a little finely minced onion and some finely minced sweet herbs. Season with salt, pepper and nutmeg. Add some butter in tiny pieces. Cover with pastry and bake in a quick oven. When cooked, put into the tart a little white sauce thickened with yolk of egg and sharpened with tarragon vinegar.'

Risotto with Artichokes
Serves 6

Rose Gray and Ruth Rogers give this recipe in their wonderful *River Café Cookbook*:

8 small globe artichokes, prepared & trimmed (chokes removed if at all prickly)
2 garlic cloves, peeled & finely chopped
3 tablespoons olive oil
Sea salt & freshly ground black pepper
1litre (1¾pt) chicken stock
150g (5oz) butter
1 medium red onion, very finely chopped
300g (10oz) risotto rice
75ml (2½fl oz) extra dry white vermouth
175g (6oz) Parmesan, freshly grated

Cut the artichokes in half and slice as thinly as possible. Fry gently with the garlic in 1 tablespoon of the olive oil for 5 minutes, stirring continuously, then add 120ml (4fl oz) water, salt and pepper and simmer until the water has evaporated. Set aside.

Heat the chicken stock and check for seasoning. Melt 90g (3oz) of the butter in the remaining oil in a large heavy-bottomed saucepan and gently fry the onion until soft, about 15–20 minutes. Add the rice and, off the heat, stir for a minute until the rice becomes totally coated. Return to the heat, add 2 or so ladlefuls of hot stock or just enough to cover the rice, and simmer, stirring, until the rice has absorbed nearly all the liquid. Add more stock as the previous addition is absorbed. After about 15–20 minutes, nearly all the stock will have been absorbed by the rice; each grain will have a creamy coating, but will remain *al dente*.

Add the remaining butter in small pieces, then gently mix in the vermouth, Parmesan and artichokes, being careful not to overstir.

Risotto with Artichokes

Eruca vesicaria subsp. *sativa. Cruciferae*

ROCKET

(Rocket Salad, Roquette, Italian Cress, Rucola, Arugula) Annual grown for tender edible leaves. Hardy. Value: high in potassium and vitamin C.

Rocket has been cultivated since Roman times and is native to the Mediterranean and Eastern Asia, though it grows in many areas after 'escaping' from gardens. *Eruca* means 'downy-stemmed'; *vesicaria*, 'bladder-like', describes the slender seed pods. Introduced to North America by Italian settlers, the spicy leaves were particularly popular in Elizabethan England.

Flowering rocket in the herb garden

SPECIES

Eruca vesicaria subsp. *sativa*, an erect plant growing to 1m (36in), has hairy stems, broadly toothed leaves and cross-shaped, creamy flowers with attractive purple veins. Cultivated plants, a separate subspecies, are larger than their wild counterparts and have paler flowers.

CULTIVATION

Propagation
Sow seed successively every 2–3 weeks, from mid-spring to early summer, in drills 12mm (½in) deep and 30cm (12in) apart. Thin when large enough to handle until 15cm (6in) apart. Rocket germinates at fairly low temperatures. In warmer climates sow in winter or early spring.

Growing
Rocket needs rich, moisture-retentive soil in partial shade. It may need extra shading in hot weather, otherwise it produces less palatable leaves. Keep weed-free and water regularly.

Maintenance
Spring Sow seeds from mid-spring; thin when large enough to handle.
Summer Continue sowing until mid-summer. Water and feed as necessary. Harvest regularly to encourage tender growth and keep from 'bolting'.
Autumn Harvest, prepare the ground for the following year's sowing and sow seeds for protected crops.
Winter Harvest winter crops.

Protected Cropping
Although hardy, protect against severe frosts with cloches. Sow autumn/winter crops from late summer in a cool greenhouse, cold frame, or under cloches.

Container Growing
Rocket is not the perfect plant for pots, but it can be grown in a soil-based compost with low fertilizer levels with added peat-substitute compost. Sow seed *in situ*. Water thoroughly.

Harvesting
Plants are ready to harvest after 6–8 weeks. Pick frequently to encourage a regular supply of good-quality leaves and to prevent plants from running to seed in hot weather. Discard any damaged leaves. Either pull leaves as required or treat as a 'cut and come again' crop, cutting the plant 2.5cm (1in) above the ground.

Pests & Diseases
Rocket is usually trouble-free, but **black flea beetle** can damage seedlings. Treat and protect accordingly.

MEDICINAL

Young leaves are said to be a good tonic and are used in cough medicine. Dioscorides described rocket as 'a digest-ive and good for ye belly'.

CULINARY

The increasingly popular leaves are delicious in salads – younger leaves are milder. They can be lightly boiled or steamed, added to sauces, stir-fried, sautéed in olive oil and tossed with pasta. The flowers are edible and can decorate salads.

Penne with Merguez & Rocket
Serves 4

400g (14oz) penne
2 tablespoons olive oil
300g (10oz) merguez sausages, cut into bite-size pieces
1 red onion, thinly sliced
2 tablespoons dry white wine
12 cherry tomatoes, halved
85g (3oz) rocket leaves, washed & shredded
Salt & freshly ground black pepper
50g (2oz) Parmesan, freshly grated

Bring a pan of salted water to the boil and cook the penne. Meanwhile, heat the oil in a large frying pan, add the merguez and onion and fry for 2–3 minutes. Add the wine and simmer for 10 minutes. Then add the tomatoes. When the pasta is cooked, drain well and toss in the sauce with the rocket. Mix well, season and serve at once with Parmesan.

Cyphomandra betacea (syn. *C. crassicaulis*). *Solanaceae*

TAMARILLO

(Tree Tomato) Woody perennial grown as annual shrub or tree for fruit. Half hardy. Value: rich in beta carotene, vitamin E; moderate levels of vitamin C.

This fast-growing small evergreen tree has large, heart-shaped leaves, clusters of caramel-scented white flowers and attractive fruits. The fruits are also delicious, with a distinctive, intense flavour. Native to the foothills of the Andes in Peru and surrounding countries, it was introduced to several tropical and sub-tropical countries as a garden fruit tree during the nineteenth century. In the 1960s commercial production began in New Zealand, but already in the 1920s they had developed cultivars with large, attractive crimson fruits and given it the name 'tamarillo'.

VARIETIES

Most so-called 'cultivars' have arisen as a result of grower selection. As plants are easy to grow from seed, any with different characteristics are often named. Because of this they do not have official cultivar status. Yellow-skinned types do not have dark pigment around the seeds and the flesh retains its yellow pigmentation after cooking. **Amberlea Gold**, a medium-sized, yellow-skinned variety, is moderately tasty. **Bold Gold** is a large yellow variety of inferior taste. **Goldmine**, with golden skin sometimes blushed red, is an exceptionally sweet type. **Oratia Red** has large fruit with deep red skin enclosing moderately sweet, well-flavoured flesh. **Red Beau** is oval-shaped, with red skin and an excellent flavour. **Red Delight** is a large, round red-skinned type with moderate flavour.

CULTIVATION

Tamarillo is an excellent fruit tree for small gardens in warm temperate zones. It can also be grown under glass in colder areas.

Propagation

Take stem cuttings in late summer, each with 2 leaves, from the current season's growth; trim below the bottom leaf joint, dip in rooting compound and insert in a gritty, open compost. Place in a propagator or bright, warm position away from direct sunlight at 20°C (68°F). Cuttings root after 3 to 4 weeks; pot them individually using a loam-based compost with added perlite or sharp sand to improve drainage. Overwinter under glass or indoors in a light, frost-free position at 7° (45°F). Pinch out the growing point early to encourage development of 4–6 side branches from the base.

A well-grown tamarillo can crop very heavily. Mature fruit on tree in New Zealand

Growing

Tamarillo flourishes in moisture-retentive, free-draining soil and benefits from mulching in spring. Water during dry periods.

Maintenance

Spring Pot on before the compost becomes congested with roots.
Summer Water and feed; place containerized plants outdoors.
Autumn Bring indoors before the first frosts.
Winter Water sparingly.

Protected Cropping

Tamarillos need bright, frost-free conditions in a conservatory or glasshouse, or can be overwintered by the window in a cool room at 7°C (45°F).

Indoors, restrict ventilation and maintain high temperatures and humidity; tapping fully open flowers ensures pollination. By late summer, first-year plants are about 1m (3ft) and should produce 5 to 8 fruits. At the same time remove cuttings to provide the following season's plants. During the growing season feed every 2 weeks with a high-potash fertilizer.

To keep the plants for the next season, after harvest, cut the main branches back to a single bud. Flowers are carried on the current season's growth, so maintaining a large, woody framework of branches is unnecessary. Alternatively, repropagate annually from cuttings.

In spring, prune larger trees back to a bud to keep them within their allotted space, and remove and replace the top 7.5cm (3in) of compost.

Reduce watering in cool winter conditions and keep the compost slightly moist.

Container Growing

Tamarillos are ideal for growing in containers. They grow rapidly, so pot on regularly, using loam-based compost with moderate

Tree tomatoes are a common feature in gardens in parts of South America. This one grows in Columbia

fertilizer levels. If you intend keeping the plant for several years, add a third part of perlite or sharp sand to the compost to improve drainage. Stand plants outdoors in a sheltered, sunny position once the danger of frost has past. If leaf scorch occurs in direct sunshine, move the plant into dappled shade.

Outdoors, the self-fertile flowers are pollinated by bees. Bring plants indoors before the first frosts and place in a sunny position for the fruits to ripen.

Harvesting & Storing

In autumn, fruits continue to swell and are ready for picking when brightly coloured, but may not be fully ripe until mid-winter. Pick them at the point where the stem naturally breaks, about 5cm (2in) above the fruit. The crop ripens over several weeks.

Pests & Diseases

Tamarillos are very prone to **whitefly**. Use the predatory wasp *Encarsia formosa*, sticky traps or spray with soft soap.

Control **aphids** with soft soap and **red spider mite** by maintaining humidity.

Companion Planting

Plant French marigolds alongside to deter whitefly.

CULINARY

Tamarillos are ripe when soft to the touch. Blanch in boiling water for 3 minutes, then plunge into cold water. The skins peel off easily if you start at the stem. Do not eat without removing the skin – it is very bitter.

Use them in salads. Puréed, they make a cheesecake topping or can be used in pies. Eat with chicken, lettuce, cottage cheese, cold meat and fish. Add to pasta or make jams. They can be kept in a refrigerator for about 2 weeks or can be cooked and frozen.

Tamarillo Chutney
Makes about 2 jars

Serve this garlic-flavoured, deep purple, hot relish with fried foods, roast duck or pork or ham. Its lush texture and intense taste make a little go a long way.

4 large tamarillos, peeled
50g (2oz) sugar
½ teaspoon cinnamon
⅛ teaspoon cloves
1 tablespoon peanut or corn oil
4 large garlic cloves, chopped
2 small jalapeño or serrano chilli peppers, seeded & minced
2 medium onions, roughly diced

1 large tart apple, peeled & diced
½ teaspoon salt
2 tablespoons cider vinegar

Slice the tamarillos lengthwise, then across into half-rounds. Combine them in a bowl together with the sugar, cinnamon and cloves.

Heat the oil in a flame-proof casserole, then stir in the garlic, chillies and onions and cook over a low heat for about five minutes. Add the apple, tamarillo mixture and salt and vinegar and stir over a moderate heat for about 15 minutes. The mixture should thicken slightly and the apples should be tender.

Cool, then cover and chill. This keeps for up to two weeks and freezes well.

Banana & Tamarillo Purée
Makes about 2 jars

This is a simple, all-purpose recipe which can be used in a variety of ways: spooned over fresh or cooked fruit, vanilla pudding or rice pudding; spread in sandwiches or between cake layers; layered with whipped cream or crème fraîche as a *parfait*; or blended with light cream cheese for a delicious brunch.

2 large tamarillos, peeled
75ml (3fl oz) lemon juice
2 medium bananas peeled & sliced
75g (3oz) sugar

Slice the tamarillos, then toss them in a bowl with the lemon juice, bananas and sugar. Allow to stand for 30 minutes. Purée the fruit in a processor or blender until smooth. Scrape the mixture into a small pot, then bring to the boil, stirring. Cool, then cover and refrigerate.

Daucus carota complex *sativus. Umbelliferae*

CARROT

**Swollen-rooted biennial grown as annual for edible orange-red roots.
Hardy/half hardy. Value: extremely rich in beta carotene (vitamin A),
small amounts of vitamin E.**

Though there are white, yellow, purple and violet carrots, most of us are more familiar with orange carrots, which have been known only since the eighteenth century. Domestication is thought to have occurred around the Mediterranean, Iran and the Balkans. The Greeks cultivated them for medicinal uses, valuing them as a stomach tonic. In Roman and early medieval times, carrots were branched, like the roots of wild types; the conical-rooted varieties seem to have originated in Asia Minor around AD1000. Moorish invaders took them to Spain in the twelfth century; they reached North-West Europe by the fourteenth and England in the fifteenth century. Gerard mentions only one yellow variety, purple ones being most popular – even though when cooked they turned into a nasty brown colour.

The Elizabethans and early Stuarts used flowers, fruit and leaves as fashion accessories for hats and dresses and carrot tops were highly valued as a substitute for feathers, particularly when they coloured up in autumn.

European explorers took the carrot across the Atlantic soon after the discovery of the New World and it was growing on Margarita Island, off the coast of Venezuela, in 1565, arriving in Brazil before the middle of the seventeenth century. The Pilgrim Fathers took it to North America and it was grown by early colonists in Jamestown, Virginia in 1609. Said to make you see well in the dark and to make your hair curly, it is now highly valued as a rich source of vitamin A.

'Chanterey'

'Sweetheart' produces good, uniform roots and is ideal for early cropping.

VARIETIES

There are several groups of carrots and the names indicate the root shape and time of maturity. With successional sowing it is possible to harvest carrots for up to 9 months of the year and still have supplies in store.

Paris Market types
These have small round or square roots and are ideal for difficult shallow, heavy or stony soils. Fast-maturing for early crops. **'Early French Frame'** is round-rooted, tasty and quick-maturing, ideal for forcing or sowing in succession outdoors. **'Little Finger'** is blunt-tipped with extremely sweet, bright orange round roots. **'Parmex'**, an early-maturing round carrot, is excellent for heavy, stony or shallow soil.

Amsterdam types
These varieties have small, stumpy, cylindrical roots. **'Amsterdam Forcing–3'** is early, slender-rooted and tasty. Ideal for freezing. **'Sweetheart'** has good colour and taste. Good for early crops and forcing.

Nantes types
These carrots are broader and longer. Mainly for forcing and early crops. **'Nantes Express'***, an early maincrop, is suitable for early sowing in frames. **'Navarre'** is tasty, sweet and well coloured. Crops heavily. **'Newmarket'** are good-quality, sweet-tasting, tender carrots.

Chantenay types
This group is stump-rooted and slightly tapered. A maincrop for summer. **'Red Cored Supreme'**, a smooth-skinned early maincrop, can be sown successively from spring to late summer. **'Red Cored-2'** is a richly coloured carrot with an excellent flavour and small core. **'Babycan'** is ideal for small carrots.

Berlicum types
These are cylindrical and stump-rooted, a late crop for storing. **'Camberly'** produces a high-quality, deep orange root with a smooth skin. **'Ingot'** is extremely tasty. Particularly high in beta carotene and vitamin C.

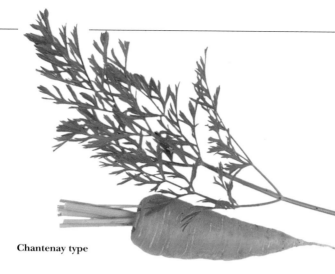

Chantenay type

Autumn King types
These are large and late-maturing. For winter use and storing. **'Autumn King'** is robust, substantial and well coloured. **'2 Vita Longa'** is late-harvesting, heavy-cropping and keeps well.

Three other carrots worth growing are **'Flyaway'** and **'Sytan'*** (both show considerable resistance to carrot fly) and **'Juared'**, also known as **'Juwarot'**. This is a medium to late variety, is extremely rich in vitamin A and is ideal for winter storage.

'Juared' has approximately double the quantity of vitamin A in regular varieties, and is ideal for juicing

CULTIVATION

Propagation
Germination is poor at soil temperatures below 7.5°C (45°F): warm the soil before sowing early crops. Another option is available for the small Paris Market varieties – sow 3–4 seeds per module and plant out after hardening off in mid-spring.

Carrot seed is very small and is easier to sow when mixed with sand or 'fluid sown'. Sow sparingly to reduce thinning and associated problems with carrot fly.

Seeds should be in drills 2cm (¾in) deep in rows 15cm (6in) apart; allow 10cm (4in) between plants in the rows for early crops and 4–6cm (1½–2¼in) apart for maincrops, depending on the size of roots you require.

Sow all but the Berlicum and Autumn King types from mid- to late spring for cropping from late summer to early autumn.

Sow Chantenay, Autumn King and Berlicum types from mid- to late spring for mid- to late autumn crops.

Sow Autumn King and Berlicum types in late spring for mid- to late winter harvesting.

Growing
Early carrots need an open, sheltered position; maincrops are less fussy. Soils should be deep, light and free-draining, warming early in spring, and with a pH of 6.5–7.5. Carrots are the ideal crop for light sandy soils – you should be able to push your index finger right down into the seedbed. Avoid walking on prepared ground to ensure maximum root growth.

Dig in plenty of well-rotted organic matter in the autumn before planting. On heavy or stony soils, grow round or short-rooted varieties, or plant in raised beds or containers.

Rake the seedbed to a fine texture about 3 weeks before sowing and use the 'stale seedbed' method, allowing the weeds to germinate and hoeing off before sowing.

Keep crops weed-free at first by mulching, hand weeding or careful hoeing to avoid damaging the roots. In later stages of growth the foliage canopy will suppress weed growth.

Keep the soil moist to avoid root splitting and bolting. Water at a rate of 14–22 litres/sq m (3–5 gal/sq yd) every 2–3 weeks, taking particular care with beds surrounded by barriers as a protection against carrot fly, as these create an artificial rain-shadow.

Maintenance
Spring Sow crops successively from mid-spring when the soil is workable.
Summer Harvest early crops, sow maincrops. Keep well watered.
Autumn Sow under cover for a mid-spring crop. Harvest.
Winter Harvest and store.

'Autumn King' ready for lifting

Protected Cropping
Sow Nantes types in an unheated greenhouse, under cloches or fleece in mid-autumn for a mid-spring crop. Sow Paris Market, Nantes and Amsterdam Forcing in mid-spring for early to mid-summer crops.

Container Growing
Choose short-rooted or round varieties for containers, windowboxes or growbags. Sow in loam-based compost; keep moist throughout the growing season.

Harvesting & Storing
Early cultivars are ready to harvest after around 8 weeks, maincrops from 10 weeks. In light soils, roots can be pulled straight from

'Early Nantes' to the left; Autumn King' centre and right

the ground, but on heavier soils they should be eased out with a garden fork. Water the soil beforehand if it is dry.

On good soils, maincrop carrots can be left in the ground until required. Cover with a thick layer of straw, bracken or similar material before the onset of inclement weather to make lifting easier.

Alternatively, lift roots, cut or twist off foliage and store healthy roots in boxes of sand in a cool, dry, frost-free place for up to 5 months. Check regularly and remove any which are damaged.

Freeze finger-sized carrots in polythene bags. Top and tail, wash and blanch for 5 minutes. Cool and rub off the skins.

Carrots will stay fresh for about 2 weeks in a cool room or in a polythene bag in the refrigerator.

PESTS & DISEASES

Carrot fly is the most serious problem. Attracted by the smell of the juice from the root, their larvae tunnel into the roots making them

inedible. Leaves turn bronze: Sow resistant cultivars, sow sparingly to avoid thinning, thin on a damp overcast day (or water before and after), pinch off the tops of thinnings just above the soil level and dispose of them in the compost heap. Lift and dispose of affected roots immediately. Lift 'earlies' by early autumn and maincrops by mid-autumn.

Since these pests do not fly very high, grow carrots under fleece or film, or surround with a barrier of fine netting or fleece 60cm (24in) high, or grow in raised beds or boxes.

Root and **leaf aphids** can also be a problem.

COMPANION PLANTING

Intercropping carrots with onions reduces carrot fly

attacks; leeks and salsify have also been used with some success.

Mixing with seeds of annual flowers also seems to discourage carrot fly.

Carrots grow well with lettuce, radishes and tomatoes and encourage peas to grow. They dislike anise and dill.

If left to flower, carrots attract hoverflies and other beneficial predatory insects to the garden.

MEDICINAL

Reputed to be therapeutic against asthma, general nervousness, dropsy, and skin disorders.

Recent research suggests that high intake of beta carotene slows cancerous growths. Beetroot and carrot juice is reported to prevent diarrhoea.

A bunch of carrots just waiting for Peter Rabbit to swipe them!

Carrot Juice

CULINARY

For eating raw, harvest young for maximum sweetness. Older carrots need to be peeled and the hard core discarded. Grated, they can be made into salads and are especially good mixed with raisins and a little chopped onion and then tossed in a good French dressing or mayonnaise thinned with a little virgin olive oil.

Try freshly plucked baby carrots, rinsed under the tap, topped and tailed, very lightly boiled in as little water as possible, then sprinkled with chopped parsley, a little sugar and freshly ground black pepper, or just a knob of butter. Add a sprinkling of sugar, a tablespoon of butter and a pinch of salt, cover and gently steam until tender. Cook in a cream sauce seasoned with tarragon, nutmeg and dill, or steam with mint leaves.

Cut into sticks as raw snacks, slice for stews and casseroles, pickle, stir-fry, use for jams, wine and carrot cake. Carrots are an essential ingredient in stocks, soups and many sauces.

Balkali Havuçi
Serves 4

Serve this Armenian-Turkish dish with pilav and salad; it can be topped with a dollop of yoghurt.

500g (1lb) broad beans, shelled
300ml (½pt) water
1 onion, chopped
2 cloves garlic, finely chopped
2 carrots, cut into rings 2.5cm (1in) thick
2 tablespoons dill or mint, chopped
1 teaspoon salt
Freshly ground black pepper
Pinch sugar
3 tablespoons virgin olive oil

Rinse the beans. Put the water into a large saucepan and bring to the boil; add the onion and beans, bring to the boil, cover and simmer until tender.

Stir in the remaining ingredients and cook until the vegetables are just tender, about 20 minutes more. Serve hot with chunks of good bread as a starter.

Carrot and Raisin Cookies

Carrot & Raisin Cake

This spicy dough mixture can equally be used to make cookies, in which case drop heaped tablespoonfuls of dough on to a lightly greased baking sheet 5cm (2in) apart and bake for 12–15 minutes until golden. Cool on a rack and store in tins in the refrigerator.

150g (6oz) plain flour
2 teaspoons baking powder
1 teaspoon cinnamon
Pinch mace
Pinch salt
2 heaped tablespoons seedless raisins
100g (4oz) carrots, grated
Grated zest of half an orange
2 tablespoons orange juice
100g (4oz) butter
125g (5oz) brown sugar
2 large eggs

Sift the flour, baking powder, spices and salt into a large bowl and set aside. Mix the raisins, carrots, orange zest and juice and set aside. Cream the butter and sugar thoroughly in a mixer and beat until light. Add the eggs, one at a time, with the blender on slow. Combine the batter with the flour and carrot mixtures and blend well.

Pour into a greased and lined 20cm (8in) tin and bake in a preheated oven (180°C, 350°F, gas mark 4) for 40–60 minutes. Test with a skewer to ensure the cake is cooked and allow to cool in the tin for 15 minutes before turning out on a wire rack.

Balkali Havuçi

Dioscorea alata. Dioscoreaceae

YAM

(Greater Yam, Asiatic Yam, White Yam, Winged Yam, Water Yam)
Twining climber grown for large edible tubers. Tender. Value: rich in carbohydrate and potassium, small amounts of B vitamins.

Yams maturing in paddy fields in Luazon, Philippines

The 'greater yam' is believed to have originated in east Asia and is widely cultivated as a staple crop throughout the humid tropics. It was said to have reached Madagascar by AD1000 and by the sixteenth century Portuguese and Spanish traders had taken it to West Africa and the New World, often as a food on slave-trading ships. Christopher Columbus knew of the plant as *nyame* and the tubers were regularly used for ships' supplies because they stored for several months without deteriorating and were easy to handle. There are hundreds of different forms producing tubers with an average weight of 5–10kg (8–22lb), although specimens with massive tubers up to 62kg (136lb) have been recorded.

VARIETIES

Dioscorea alata has square, 4-winged or angled twining stems with pointed, heart-shaped, leaves. Small bulbils are often produced on the stems. The tubers are brown on the outside with white flesh, vary in size and are usually produced singly. There is a great number of cultivars which vary in the colour and shape of the stems, leaves and tubers.
  'White Lisbon', one of the most widely grown, is high-yielding, shallow-rooted and tasty; it will store for up to 6 months. **'Belep'**, **'Lupias'**, **'Kinbayo'**, and **'Pyramid'** are also high-yielding.

Propagation
Yams are usually planted on banks, mounds or ridges at the end of the dry season while they are still dormant, as they need the long rainy season to develop. Small tubers, bulbils or sections with 2–3 buds or 'eyes' taken from the tops of larger tubers are used for propagation. The latter are preferable, as they sprout quickly and produce higher-yielding plants. They can be 'sprouted' in a shady position before planting 15cm (6in) deep and 30–90cm (12–36in) apart on mounds 120cm (48in) across or ridges 120cm (48in) apart. Spacing depends on the site, soil and the variety.

Growing
Yams need a humid, tropical climate, 150–175cm (60–70in) of rain in a 6–12 month growing season and a site in sun or partial shade. Soils must be rich, moisture-retentive and free-draining, as yams can survive drought but not waterlogging.
  Dig in plenty of well-rotted organic matter before planting and grow plants up trellising, arbours, poles or netting at least 180cm (72in) high, or allow them to grow into surrounding trees.
  Keep crops weed-free.
  Tropical crops do not grow well below 20°C (68°F). Growth increases with temperature and the crucial time for rain is 14 to 20 weeks after planting, when food reserves are nearly depleted and the shoots are growing rapidly.

Maintenance
Spring Increase watering as new shoots appear when growing under cover.
Summer Maintain high temperatures and humidity.
Autumn Reduce watering as stems turn yellow.
Winter Keep compost slightly moist.

Protected Cropping
If you are able to provide an environment and cultural conditions similar to those described under 'Growing', yams can be grown indoors. The minimum temperature for active growth is 20°C

Yams drying in the sun

(68°F); damp down greenhouse paths and mist with tepid water during summer, and reduce watering during the resting season as the stems die back, gradually increasing the amount in spring when plants resume active growth.

Harvesting & Storing
Depending on the variety and weather conditions, tubers are ready to harvest from 7–12 months after planting as the leaves and stems die back. Lift them carefully, as damaged tubers cannot be stored.

Tubers are normally dried on a shaded vertical frame or in an open-sided shed before being stored in a dark, cool, airy place where they can last for several months. Do not store yams at temperatures below 10°C (50°F).

PESTS & DISEASES

Leaf spot appears as brown or black spots on stems and leaves. **Storage rot** can be a serious problem and **yam beetles** feed on tubers and damage the shoots of newly planted sets. **Scale insect** also causes problems.

Yams need to be well spaced to flourish

COMPANION PLANTING

Grows well with taro, ginger, maize, okra and cucurbits.

MEDICINAL

Yams have been used as a diuretic and expectorant.

WARNING

All yams except *Dioscorea esculenta* contain a toxin, dioscorine, which is destroyed by thorough cooking.

CULINARY

Yam can be peeled and then boiled, mashed, roasted and fried in oil. In West Africa, they are pounded into *fufu* in a similar way to manioc, and are added to a thick soup made of spices, meat, oil, fish and vegetables. Yams are tasty cooked with palm oil, candied, casseroled with orange juice or curried.

They can be peeled and boiled in water with a pinch of salt, then brushed with melted butter and grilled or barbecued until brown; serve with more butter.

In China they are mashed with lotus root, wrapped in lotus leaves and steamed.

They can also be peeled, rubbed with oil and baked at 180°C (350°F) for 1½ hours, then slit like a baked potato and eaten with seasoned butter or a similar filling.

Yellow Yam Salad
Serves 6

1.5kg (3lb) yellow yams
1 large onion, sliced
3 tablespoons chopped chives
1 sweet green pepper, deseeded & diced
8 tablespoons mayonnaise
½ teaspoon cayenne pepper
Salt & freshly ground black pepper
4 hard-boiled eggs, chopped
1 tablespoon black olives, stoned & sliced

Clean the yams and cook in boiling salted water until tender but firm. Drain and allow to cool slightly, then cut into cubes. Add the onions, chives and pepper and mix well.

Season the mayonnaise with the cayenne, salt and pepper and stir into the yam mixture, folding in the eggs and olives carefully.

Check the seasoning. Chill for an hour before serving.

Foeniculum vulgare var. *azoricum* (syn. *Foeniculum dulce*). *Umbelliferae*

FLORENCE FENNEL

(Sweet Fennel, Finocchio)
Biennial or perennial grown as annual for pungent swollen leafbases, leaves and seeds. Half hardy. Value: good source of potassium; small amounts of beta carotene.

This outstanding vegetable with a strong aniseed flavour, swollen leafbases (known as 'bulbs') the texture of tender celery and delicate feathery leaves has been cultivated for centuries as an ornamental vegetable. Its close relative, wild fennel, which lacks the swollen base, is used as a herb. When Portuguese explorers first landed on Madeira in 1418, they found the air fragrant with the aroma of wild fennel, so the city of Funchal was named after *funcho*, the Portuguese name for the plant. Florence fennel was popular with the Greeks and Romans, whose soldiers ate it to maintain good health – while the ladies used it to ward off obesity. In medieval times, seeds were eaten during Lent to alleviate hunger, and dieters still chew raw stalks to suppress their appetite. The first records of its cultivation in England date from the early eighteenth century, when the 3rd Earl of Peterborough cultivated and ate it as a dessert.

In 1824 Thomas Jefferson received seeds from the American consul in Livorno and sowed them in his garden in Virginia. He enthused: 'Fennel is beyond every other vegetable, delicious ... perfectly white. No vegetable equals it in flavour.' However, it has become a weed in those countries where conditions are particularly favourable.

VARIETIES

'Cantino' is ready to harvest from late summer and is resistant to bolting. 'Fino' ('Zefa Fino') is particularly vigorous and ornamental, looking good in the flower border. It is resistant to bolting. 'Herald', an old Italian variety, forms plump, sweet bulbs, is resistant to

bolting and ideal for early and successional sowing. 'Perfection', a French variety, has medium-sized bulbs and a delicate aniseed flavour. Resistant to bolting, it is ideal for early sowing. 'Sirio', again from Italy, is compact with large, sweet white bulbs, and matures rapidly. 'Sweet Florence' is moderately sized and should be sown from mid-spring to late summer. 'Tardo' ('Zefa Tardo') is an early cropping, bolting-resistant variety.

'Sweet Florence', showing its developing bulbs and light, feathery foliage

CULTIVATION

Propagation
Fennel thrives in a warm climate and is inclined to bolt prematurely if growth is checked by cold, drought or transplanting. For early sowings choose cultivars which bolting-resistant.

Grow successively from late spring to late summer for summer and autumn crops. Sow thinly in drills 1.5cm (½in) deep and 45–50cm (18–20in) apart, thinning when seedlings are large enough to handle to a final spacing of 23–30cm (9–12in) apart.

Where possible, fennel is better sown *in situ* to reduce problems with bolting. Modules are preferred for plants started under cover. Growing in trays is fine if transplants are treated carefully enough.

Growing
Fennel flourishes in temperate to sub-tropical climates, though mature plants can withstand light frosts. The largest bulbs are formed during warm, sunny summers. Plants should be grown as rapidly as possible, so incorporate a slow-release general fertilizer into the soil before planting at

0–60g/sq m (1–2oz/sq yd). Plants need a sunny, warm, sheltered position and well-drained, moisture-retentive, slightly alkaline soil. A light, sandy soil with well-rotted organic matter dug in the winter before planting is ideal. Stony soils and heavy clays should be avoided. Never allow the soil to dry out; mulch in spring and hand weed around bulbs to avoid damage.

When the stem bases start to swell, earth up to half their height to blanch and sweeten the bulbs. Or tie cardboard 'collars' round the base.

Maintenance

Spring Sow early crops under cover. Warm the soil with cloches before sowing early crops outdoors.
Summer Keep the soil constantly moist and weed-free. Harvest mature bulbs.
Autumn Cover later crops to prolong the growing season.
Winter Transplant later sowings for an early winter crop.

Protected Cropping

Cover early outdoor crops with cloches. Sow from mid-spring, in modules or trays of seed compost at 16°C (60°F). Pot on seedlings grown in trays when very small, with a maximum of 4 leaves, into 7.5cm (3in) peat

Mature plant ready for harvest

pots. Transplant in the pots a month after hardening off.

Harden off and plant out those grown in modules at a similar size. Late sowings can be made for transplanting under cover in early winter. Plants do not always produce 'bulbs', but leaves and stems can be used in cooking.

Container Growing

Grow single plants in a container at least 25cm (10in) wide by 30cm (12in) deep containing loam-based compost with added sharp sand. Apply a general liquid fertilizer monthly from late spring to late summer.

Harvesting & Storing

Harvest about 15 weeks after sowing or 2–4 weeks after earthing up, when the bulbs are plump, about 5–7.5cm (2–3in) across and slightly larger than a tennis ball. Cut the bulb with a sharp knife, just above the ground, and the stump should resprout producing small sprigs of ferny foliage. Bulbs do not store and should be eaten when they are fresh.

Leaves can be harvested throughout summer and used fresh in salads, or deep-frozen.

Pests & Diseases

Slugs can damage young plants. Lack of water, fluctuating temperatures and transplanting check can cause bolting.

The bulb is made up of swollen, overlapping leaf bases

Companion Planting

Allow a few plants to flower; they are extremely attractive to a large number of beneficial insects which prey on garden pests.

Fennel has a detrimental effect on beans, kohlrabi and on tomatoes.

Medicinal

An infusion aids wind, colic, urinary disorders and constipation. Recent research indicates that fennel reduces the effects of alcohol.

Use in an eye bath or as a compress to reduce inflammation.

Chew to sweeten breath or infuse as a mouthwash or gargle for gum disease and sore throats, to alleviate hunger and ease indigestion.

Warning

Do not take excessive doses of the oil; nor should it be given to pregnant women.

Culinary

Use bulbs like celery, removing green stalks and outer leaves. For salads, slice inner leaf stalks and chill before serving. (To ensure that bulbs are crisp, slice and place in a bowl of water and ice cubes in the fridge for an hour.)

Fennel can be parboiled with leeks and is suitable for egg and fish dishes. Steam, grill or boil and serve with cheese sauce or butter. Infuse fresh leaves in oil or vinegar, add to a bouquet garni or snip as a garnish over soups or salads. Gives characteristic flavour to *finocchiona*, an Italian salami, and the French liqueur, *fenouillette*.

Fennel Sautéed with Peas & Red Peppers
Serves 4

2 tablespoons olive oil
2 sweet red peppers, deseeded & cut into thin strips
500g (1lb) fennel, trimmed & finely sliced
2 cloves garlic, crushed
250g (8oz) peas, shelled
Salt & freshly ground black pepper

In a wok or heavy-based frying pan heat the oil, add the peppers and fennel and cook for 10–15 minutes over a moderate heat until crunchy, stirring occasionally. Add the garlic and peas and continue cooking for 2 minutes. Season and serve.

Glycine max (syn. *Glycine soja*). *Leguminosae*

SOYA BEAN

(Soy Bean) Annual grown for seed sprouts and seeds. Half hardy.
Value: rich in potassium, protein, fibre, vitamins E, B and iron.
Seed sprouts are rich in vitamin C.

One of the most nutritious of all vegetables, this native of Asia is thought to have been the plant that the Chinese emperor Shen Nung used to introduce people to the art of cultivation. It is mentioned in his *Materia Medica* from around 2,900BC. Soya beans were first known in Europe through Engelbert Kaempfer, physician to the governor of the Dutch East India company on an island off Japan in 1690–92. The Japanese guarded their culture, but, by bribing the guards and picking plants along the route, Kaempfer was able to get his botanical specimens. Benjamin Franklin sent seeds back from France to North America in the late eighteenth century. In 1829 it was being grown at Cambridge, Massachusetts, where it was considered a luxury. One of the first Americans to be interested in soya beans was Henry Ford, who saw their potential for manufactured goods and is said to have eaten soya beans at every meal, had a suit made from 'soy fabric' and sponsored a 16-course soya bean dinner at the 1934 'Century of Progress' show in Chicago.

VARIETIES

Glycine max is a herb, usually with trilobed leaves and white to pale violet flowers. The pods containing 2–4 seeds are mainly on the lower parts of the stem. **'Black Jet'** is early-maturing; the seeds have a good flavour and it is ideal for a short growing season. **'Fiskeby V'** has yellow beans and is very hardy. **'Hakucho Early'**, an early dwarf Japanese variety, produces 3 small seeds per pod but is high-yielding. **'Lammer's Black'** is the best bean for short seasons, producing heavy crops of thin-skinned,

tasty seeds. **'Maple Arrow'** is yellow, hardy and used in processed products. **'Prize'** is widely planted and good for sprouting.

Immature soya bean pods on plant, USA

CULTIVATION

Propagation
Sow when danger of frost has passed and the soil has warmed. Sow 2–3 seeds 2.5cm (1in) deep in heavy soil and 3cm (1½in) deep in lighter soils in 'stations' 7.5–10cm (3–4in) apart with 45–60cm (18–24in) between rows. After germination, thin, leaving the strongest seedling. Alternatively, sow thinly and thin to the final spacing when large enough.

Sprouting Seed
Seeds can also be sprouted. Use untreated seed and remove any which are

damaged or mouldy. Soak overnight in cold water. The following morning rinse then thoroughly. Put a layer of moist kitchen roll over the base of a flat-bottomed bowl, tray or 'seed sprouter'. Sprea over a layer of soya beans 1cm (½in) deep and cover with clingfilm. Exclude light by putting the bowl in a dark cupboard or wrapping it in newspaper or tinfoil. Temperatures should be 20–25°C (68–75°F). Check regularly that the absorbent layer stays damp, rinsing morning and night. They should be ready to harvest in 4–10 days when shoots are 2.5–5cm (1–2in) long. Remove sprouts from the shell, and rinse thoroughly before eating.

Growing
Soya beans flourish in an open site with rich, free-draining soil and a pH of 5.7–6.2, although there are now cultivars to suit most soils. Where necessary, lime soils and dig in well-rotted organic matter before planting. They are not frost hardy; they prefer 20–25°C (68–75°F); exceeding 38°C (100°F) may retard growth.
Keep plants well watered during drought and early stages of growth. Remove weeds regularly, or suppress by mulching in spring.

Maintenance
Spring Sow seeds under cove or outdoors when there is nc danger of frost.
Summer Keep crops weed-free. Water during drought.
Autumn Harvest before the pods are completely ripe.
Winter Hang in bunches in a cool shed and collect seed when the pods open.

Protected Cropping
In cooler climates, sow seeds in pots, modules or trays of seed compost, planting out when the soil is warm. Harde off before transplanting and protect under cloches until established. In cooler climates, sow crops in a heated glasshouse.

Looking onto soya bean crop planted to match the field contours, Kansas, USA

Container Growing

This is only worth growing in containers as a 'novelty' crop. Use 20–25cm (8–10in) pots and loam-based compost with moderate fertilizer levels, adding well-rotted organic matter. Keep well watered and weed-free.

Harvesting & Storing

Soya needs a hot summer and fine autumn for the seeds to ripen. Harvesting should be carefully timed so that the seeds are ripe but the pods have not yet split. If conditions are unfavourable, pull up plants when the pods turn yellow and hang up to ripen in a dry place.

Do not harvest when plants are wet, as the seeds are easily bruised. Harvest for green beans as soon as pods are plump and the seeds are almost full size.

PESTS & DISEASES

Fungal diseases can be a problem if plants are harvested when wet and pods are bruised or broken.

OTHER USES

Soya oil is used in a range of products including ice cream, margarine, soaps and paint; milk substitute is made from the crushed beans, and fermented they make soy sauce and tofu, and also Worcestershire sauce. Also firefighting foam and meat substitute. A valuable plant indeed!

MEDICINAL

Said to control blood sugar levels, lower cholesterol, regulate the bowels and relieve constipation.

WARNING

Soya beans should be cooked before drying; they can cause stomach upset.

CULINARY

Used mainly when green or sprouted for salads or stir-fries. Remove the shell by plunging into boiling salted water for 5 minutes, then allow to cool and squeeze out the seeds. Cook for 15 minutes, then sauté with butter. Juvenile pods can be cooked and eaten whole.

Soak dried beans before eating. A short-cut is to cover with water in a kettle, boil for 2 minutes, allow to stand for one hour, then cook until tender.

Soya Bean & Walnut Croquettes
Serves 4

112g (4oz) soya beans, soaked & well rinsed
1 onion, finely chopped
1 clove garlic, crushed
28g (1oz) butter
112g (4oz) walnuts, pulverized in the liquidizer
½ teaspoon dried thyme
56g (2oz) wholewheat breadcrumbs
1 tablespoon tomato purée
2 tablespoons chopped parsley
½ teaspoon grand mace
1 egg
Salt & freshly ground black pepper
Wholewheat flour
1 beaten egg
Dried breadcrumbs
Oil for shallow frying

Cook the beans until very tender, drain, then mash with a fork, enough to break them up. Fry the onion and garlic in the butter for 10 minutes, then remove from the heat and stir in the beans. Add the walnuts and thyme, together with the breadcrumbs, tomato purée, parsley, mace and egg. (You may need to add more liquid; otherwise use fewer breadcrumbs.) Mix well and season to taste.

Using your hands, shape into small croquettes, then roll in the flour, dip into the egg and roll in the crumbs. Fry in hot oil until crisp and drain on kitchen paper. Serve hot. These go particularly well with a spicy tomato sauce.

Helianthus tuberosus. Compositae

JERUSALEM ARTICHOKE

(Girasole, Sunchoke) Tall perennial grown as annual for edible tubers. Hardy.
Value: high in carbohydrate but mostly inulin, turning to fructose in storage;
moderate vitamin B1, B5, low in calories.

This vegetable is not from Jerusalem, nor is it any relative of the globe artichoke. 'Jerusalem' is said to be a corruption of the Italian *girasole* or 'sunflower' – a close relative; the nutty-flavoured tubers were thought to taste similar to globe artichokes, hence the adoption of that name. Frost-hardy, these tall, upright perennials are native to North America, where they grow in damp places. The tubers contain a carbohydrate which causes flatulence; in 1621 John Goodyear wrote that 'they stirre and cause a filthie loathsome wind within the bodie'. In the 1920s they were a commercial source of fructose and were expected to replace beet and cane as a source of sugar.

VARIETIES

'**Boston Red**' has large, knobbly tubers with rose-red skin. '**Dwarf Sunray**' is a short-stemmed, crisp, tender variety which does not need peeling. It flowers freely and is good for the ornamental border. '**Fuseau**' has long, smooth, white tubers. Plants are compact, reaching 1.5–1.8m (5–6ft). It is a traditional French variety. '**Golden Nugget**' has tapering, carrot-shaped tubers. '**Stampede**' is a quick-maturing variety with large tubers. '**Jacks Copperclad**' has dark coppery-purple tubers and small pretty sunflowers. Plants are tall, reaching 300cm (10ft). It is high yielding and has an excellent taste. '**Mulles Rose**' has large white tubers with rose-purple fleshed eyes. It is easy to grow and extremely tolerant of cold conditions. The tubers of '**Sun Choke**' have a fresh nutty flavour, and are excellent raw in salads, cooked or creamed.

CULTIVATION

Jerusalem artichokes prefer a sunny position, but will grow in shade. They tolerate most soils, though tubers are small on poor ground; the best are grown on sandy, moisture-retentive soil.

They will grow in heavy clay provided it is not extremely acid or subject to winter waterlogging. The fibrous root system makes them useful for breaking up uncultivated ground. The tall stems make excellent temporary screens or windbreaks in sheltered areas, but need staking in more exposed sites.

Propagation

Tubers bought from the greengrocer's can be used for planting. Choose tubers the size of hen's eggs, plant from early to late spring, when the soil becomes workable, 10–15cm (4–6in) deep, 30cm (12in) apart and 90cm (3ft) between rows; cover the tubers carefully. During harvest, save a few tubers to replant or leave some in the soil for the following year.

Growing

Incorporate organic matter in autumn or early winter before planting. Earth up the base of stems to improve stability when plants are 30cm (12in) high. Water during dry weather.

Remove flower buds as they appear. Shorten stems to 1.5–1.8m (5–6ft) in late summer to stop them from being blown over; on windy sites they may also need staking. On poor soil, feed with liquid general fertilizer every 2–3 weeks.

Maintenance

Spring Plant tubers.
Summer Keep weed-free, water and stake if necessary. Remove flower buds.

Jerusalem artichoke stems can make effective windbreaks

Autumn Cut back stems and begin harvesting.
Winter Save tubers for next year's crop.

Harvesting & Storing

In autumn, as the foliage turns yellow, cut back stems to within 7.5–15cm (3–6in) of the ground. Use the cut stems as a mulch to protect the soil from frost, making lifting easier; alternatively, cover with straw. Lift tubers from late autumn to mid-winter. They keep better in the ground, but in cold climates or on heavy ground, lift in early winter and store for up to 5 months in a cool cellar in moist peat substitute or sand.

Pests & Diseases

Slugs tend to hollow out tubers. Set traps, aluminium sulphate pellets, pick off manually.

Sclerotinia **rot** causes stem bases to become covered with fluffy white mould. Lift and burn diseased plants; water healthy plants with fungicide.

Cutworms eat stems at ground level; damaged plants wilt. Keep crops weed-free, cultivate well or scatter an appropriate insecticide in the soil before planting.

MEDICINAL

The carbohydrate inulin is difficult to digest; tubers are low calorie and suitable for diabetics.

WARNING

Jerusalem artichokes can become an invasive weed. After harvesting, lift even the smallest tuber from the ground.

Artichoke Soup

CULINARY

Artichokes are versatile vegetables when the weather is cold; they can be kept in the ground until you want to cook them and then dug up root by root. Fresh tubers have a better flavour, but they become more digestible if stored; they will keep in a polythene bag in the salad drawer of the fridge for anything up to 2 weeks.

There is no need to peel them painstakingly unless you want a very smooth, creamy-white purée – the vitamins are, after all, just below the skin. (If you do want them peeled, steaming or boiling knobbly varieties makes the job easier.) To serve as a vegetable, scrub tubers immediately after lifting, boil for 20–25 minutes in their skins in water with a teaspoon of vinegar; peel before serving if desired. The addition of a little grated nutmeg always does wonders in bringing out the unusual flavour.

To make rissoles, form boiled, mashed artichokes into flat cakes and deep-fry. Jerusalem artichokes can also be fried, baked, roasted or stewed – or eaten raw.

Artichokes gratinéed in a sauce made with good, strong Cheddar make an excellent accompaniment to plain meat dishes such as baked ham or roast lamb. Parboil the artichokes and drain when they are just tender. Roughly slice and layer into a dish. Pour over a béchamel sauce flavoured with French mustard and well-matured cheese and bake in a hot oven (200°C, 400°F, gas 6) until browned.

Artichoke Soup
Serves 4

500g (1lb) Jerusalem artichokes
2 tablespoons olive oil
2 large onions, sliced
1 large garlic clove, crushed
600ml (1pt) chicken stock
Strip of orange peel
Salt & finely ground black
  pepper
4 tablespoons thick cream

Scrub the artichokes, discard any hard knobs and roughly chop. Heat the oil in a heavy-based pan and add the onions. Cook until translucent, add the garlic, continue cooking for a couple of minutes and add the artichokes. Toss well to coat with oil and pour in the chicken stock. Bring to the boil, add the orange peel and season. Cover and simmer for 15–20 minutes, until cooked. Remove from the heat, discard the peel and blend in a food processor. Return to the pan, adjust the seasoning, stir in the cream and serve.

Hibiscus esculentus (syn. *Abelmoschus esculentus*). *Malvaceae*

OKRA

**(Lady's Fingers, Bhindi, Gumbo) Annual grown for its edible pods. Tender.
Value: rich in calcium, iron, potassium, vitamin C and fibre.**

The okra, a close relative of the ornamental hibiscus, with slender edible pods, has been cultivated for centuries. It is thought to have originated in northern Africa around the upper Nile and Ethiopia, spreading eastwards to Saudi Arabia and to India. One of the earliest records of it – growing in Egypt – describes the plant, its cultivation and uses. It was introduced to the Caribbean and southern North America by slaves who brought the crop from Africa; the name 'gumbo' comes from a Portuguese corruption of the plant's Angolan common name.

The red forms lose their strong coloration when cooked

VARIETIES

'**Artist**', with purple-red pods, crops early and turns green when cooked. '**Burgundy**' grows about 1.5m (5ft) tall, with wonderful rich red pods which are excellent in salads. The colour, however, is lost on cooking. This tolerates cooler growing conditions than most. '**Clemson Spineless**' is a popular, reliable variety with high yields of dark, fleshy pods over a long period. It grows well under cover. '**Dwarf Green Long Pod**' is only about 90cm (3ft) tall, but crops well, producing dark green, spineless pods. '**Mammoth Spineless Long Pod**' is vigorous and high-yielding with pods that stay tender for a long time. It is excellent fresh or bottled.

'**Pure Luck**', in spite of the name, is one of the best varieties for growing under cover in cooler climates. Harvest when the pods are about 5cm (2in) long. '**Red Velvet**', another spectacular red variety, is vigorous, reaching 1.2–1.5m (4–5ft). '**Star of David Heirloom**' is

A defoliated plant with several upward-pointing fruits

an Israeli variety growing to 1.8–2.5m (6–8ft) tall, well flavoured and high-yielding. The pods grow to 23cm (9in) long, but are better eaten when small.

CULTIVATION

A garden plant for the tropics and warm temperate climates, okra can be tried outdoors in cooler climates during hot summers, though success is better guaranteed if they are sown under cover.

Propagation
Soak the seeds in warm water for 24 hours before planting. My friend Robert Fleming, who gardens in Memphis, Tennessee, has been successful with several other methods which reduce germination time from 15

down to 5 days: soak the seed in bleach for 45–60 minutes, rinse, then plant; pour boiling water over seed, soak overnight, then plant, or place 3 seeds in each section of an ice-cube tray, allow to freeze for a few hours, then plant.

When soil temperatures are about 16°C (60°F), sow seeds in rows about 60cm (24in) apart, leaving the same distance between plants. Alternatively, sow in 'stations 20–30cm (8–12in) apart, thinning to leave the strongest seedling. Plant seedlings grown in trays or modules into 7.5cm (3in) pots when they are large enough to handle and later harden them off ready for transplanting when they are about 10–15cm (4–6in) tall.

Growing
Okra needs a rich, fertile, well-drained soil, so incorporate organic matter several weeks before sowing. Put a stake in place before transplanting and tie in the plant as it grows, pinching out the growing tip on the main stems when plants are around 23–30cm (9–12in) tall to encourage bushy growth. Apply a general liquid fertilizer until plants become established, then change to a liquid high-potash feed every 2 weeks or scatter sulphate of potash around the plant base.

In cool temperate conditions, warm the soil for several days before planting outdoors, spacing plants 60cm (24in) apart once the danger of frost has passed.

Maintenance

Spring Sow seeds under cover or outdoors in warmer climates when the soil is warm enough. Pinch out the growth tips as they appear. *Summer* Water, feed and tie in plants to their supporting stakes. Keep crops weed-free. Harvest young pods. *Autumn* Protect outdoor crops in cooler climates to extend the cropping season. *Winter* Prepare the ground for the following season.

Protected Cropping

In cooler climates, plant okra in heated greenhouses or polythene tunnels from early spring, waiting until mid-spring if heat is not provided. Plant them about 60cm (24in) apart in beds or borders. Insert a supporting cane before planting.

Temperatures should be a minimum of 21°C (70°F) with moderate humidity. Feed plants every 2 weeks with a liquid general fertilizer, changing to a high-potash fertilizer once they are established.

Container Growing

Okra can be grown in 25cm (10in) pots or growbags in peat-substitute compost, under cover or outdoors. Water regularly and feed every 2 weeks with a high-potash liquid fertilizer during the growing season.

Harvesting & Storing

Harvest with a sharp knife or scissors while seed pods are young, picking regularly for a constant supply of new pods. Handle gently: the soft skin marks easily. Pods keep for up to 10 days wrapped in a polythene bag in the salad drawer of the fridge.

Pests & Diseases

Precautions should be taken against heavy infestations of **aphids**, which weaken and distort growth, and **powdery mildew**, which stunts growth and, in severe cases, causes death. This is more of a problem when plants are underwatered. **Whitefly** can cause yellowing, stickiness and mould formation on the leaves. They form clusters on the leaf undersides and fly into the air when the foliage is disturbed.

COMPANION PLANTING

Okra flourishes when it is grown with melons and cucumbers, as it enjoys the same conditions.

Growing in Brazil; bright yellow flowers are followed by the developing pods

CULINARY

Okra is used in soups, stews and curries, can be sautéed or fried and eaten to accompany meat or poultry. To deep-fry, remove the stalks, trim round the 'cone' near the base, simmer for about 10 minutes, drain and dry each pod, then deep-fry until crisp. In the Middle East pods are soaked in lemon juice and salt, then fried and eaten as a vegetable. In Indian cooking, bhindi is used as a vegetable or as a bhagee to accompany curries.

Okra should not be cooked in iron, brass or copper pans, otherwise it will discolour.

Overcooked, the pods become very slimy. Any 'gluey' texture can be overcome by adding a little lemon juice to the pan and the fine, velvety covering over the pod can easily be removed by scrubbing the pod gently under running water.

Okra can also be eaten raw in salads or used as a 'dip'. Wash pods, carefully trimming off the ends. To reduce stickiness, soak them for about 30 minutes in water with a dash of lemon juice, then drain, rinse and dry.

Okra seed oil is also used in cookery.

Gumbo
Serves 4
This spicy Creole dish is known for its good use of okra.

500g (18oz) okra
1 tablespoon olive oil
250g (8oz) home-cooked ham, cubed
175g (6oz) onion, finely sliced
175g (6oz) celery, chopped
1 red pepper, deseeded & chopped
½ tablespoon tomato purée
500g (18oz) tomatoes, skinned & chopped
1 dried chilli, chopped small
Salt & freshly ground black pepper

Trim the stalk ends of the okra to expose the seeds, then soak for 30 minutes in acidulated water.

In the meantime, heat the oil and gently cook the ham, onion, celery and pepper until the onion begins to colour. Add the tomato purée and the tomatoes, mix in well, and cook over a high heat for a minute or so.

Stir in the drained okra and season well. Cover and cook gently until stewed. Add a little water if the mixture gets dry.

Serve with plain grilled chicken.

MEDICINAL

The mucilage from okra is effectively used as a demulcent, soothing inflammation.

In India, infusions of the pods are used to treat urino-genital problems as well as chest infections.

Okra is also added to artificial blood plasma products.

Gumbo

Ipomea batatas. Convolvulaceae

SWEET POTATO

(Kumara, Louisiana Yam, Yellow Yam) Trailing perennials grown as annuals for starchy tubers and leaves. Tender. Value: excellent source of beta carotene, rich in carbohydrates, moderate potassium and vitamins B and C. Yellow and orange types rich in vitamin A.

The 'sweet potato' is unrelated to the 'Irish' potato but is a relative of the bindweed, in the morning glory family. It was cultivated in prehistoric Peru and is now found throughout the tropics; it is also a 'staple' crop in Polynesia. Its arrival there is a mystery; some suggest it was taken there by Polynesians who visited South America, others think it arrived on vines clinging to logs swept out to sea. It was cultivated in Polynesia before 1250 and reached New Zealand by the fourteenth century. Captain Cook and Sir Joseph Banks found the Maoris of the North Island growing it when they landed in 1769. It was grown in Virginia by 1648. Columbus introduced it to Spain and it was widely cultivated by the mid sixteenth century, pre-dating the 'Irish' potato by nearly half a century. It reached England via the Canary Islands about the same time and was the 'common potato' in Elizabethan times, some even holding it to be an aphrodisiac.

VARIETIES

There are hundreds of sweet potato varieties worldwide. They are classified under three groups: dry and mealy-fleshed, soft and moist-fleshed, and coarse-fleshed types used as animal feed. White or pale types are floury with a chestnut-caramel flavour, while yellow and orange varieties are sweet and watery.

'Centennial' is vigorous, to 5m (16ft), with bright copper-orange skin and deep orange flesh. Prolific with high-quality tubers, it grows well in short seasons. 'Jewel', a vigorous, high-yielding variety, has excellent quality copper-coloured tubers with moist white flesh. Stores well and disease-resistant. 'Porto Rico Bush' has deep orange, sweet flesh. Excellent for baking. Does not need much space. 'Tokatoka Gold' is large, rounded and smooth-textured. Popular in New Zealand. 'Vardaman' does not 'vine', has golden-yellow skin and deep red-orange flesh. High-yielding.

CULTIVATION

Propagation

Take cuttings from healthy shoots 20–25cm (8–10in) long. Cut just below a leaf joint, remove basal leaves.

Alternatively, pack several healthy tubers in a tray of moist and sharp sand, vermiculite or perlite in a warm greenhouse, or plant into hotbeds. When shoots reach 23–30cm (9–12in), cut them off 5cm (2in) above the soil and take the cuttings as described above. Three potatoes should produce about 24 cuttings, enough for a 10m (25ft) row.

In the humid tropics and sub-tropics, cuttings are rooted *in situ* at the start of the rainy season. Plant on ridges 15–30cm (6–12in) high and 1–1.5m (3–4½ft) apart. Just below the ridge top, insert cuttings 23–30cm (9–12in) apart, leaving half of the stem exposed.

Or, instead of cuttings, plant small tubers 7.5–10cm (3–4in) deep along the top of the ridge. On sandy, free-draining soil plant cuttings and tubers on level ground.

Growing

Sweet potatoes thrive in a tropical or sub-tropical climate with an annual temperature of 21–26°C (70–77°F). Light frost kills leaves and damages tubers.

Ideal annual rainfall is 750–1200mm (30–50in), with wet weather in the growing period and dry conditions for the tubers to ripen. Tuber production is

Large-scale sweet potato crop in North Carolina, USA

fastest and sugar production highest when daylengths exceed 14 hours.

Soils should be moisture-retentive and free-draining with a pH of 5.5–6.5. If necessary, dig in well-rotted organic matter before planting. Watering is rarely needed if planted at the start of the rainy season.

Excessive nitrogen encourages stems to develop rather than tubers. Once established, scatter a high-potash granular fertilizer around plants. Occasionally lift vines from the ground to prevent rooting at the leaf joints. Rotate crops.

Maintenance

Spring Take cuttings under cover, keep warm and moist.
Summer Keep cuttings weed-free, water well and feed. Prune as necessary.
Autumn Harvest. Save some tubers for the next crop.
Winter Keep compost slightly moist.

Protected Cropping

Grow under cover in cool temperate climates at a minimum temperature of 26°C (77°F).

Take cuttings as normal from healthy shoots of mature plants, and insert about 4 cuttings round the outside of a 15cm (6in) pot filled with cuttings compost. Keep moist with tepid water. Transplant into a green-house border once a good root system has formed. Mist regularly. Prune stems longer than 60cm (24in) to encourage sideshoots and also from late winter to thin out congested growth.

Container Growing

Grow in pots or containers 30cm (12in) deep and 37.5cm (15in) wide using loam-based compost with moderate fertilizer levels. Provide supports.

Harvesting & Storing

In good conditions, tubers ripen in 4–5 months. Lift when slightly immature; otherwise wait until vines

The flower is similar to that of the Morning Glory

begin to yellow. Lift carefully to avoid bruising. Use fresh or store once dried in a cool dark place for up to a week.

PESTS & DISEASES

Leaves can suffer from **leaf spot** and **sooty mould**. **Black rot** appears at the base of the stem and **brown rots** on the tuber. Check stored tubers regularly. Also susceptible to **white fly** or **red spider mite** under cover.

MEDICINAL

Sweet potatoes and their leaves contain antibacterial and fungicidal substances and are used in folk medicine. In Shakespeare's day they were sold in crystallized slices with sea holly ('eringo') as an aphrodisiac. In *The Merry Wives of Windsor*, Falstaff cries: 'Let the sky rain potatoes...hail kissing-comforts and snow eringoes'. The Empress Josephine introduced sweet potatoes to her companions, who were soon serving them to stimulate the passion of their lovers. The results are not recorded!

CULINARY

A sweet potato contains roughly one and a half times the calories and vitamin C of the 'Irish' potato. Before cooking, wash carefully and peel or cook whole. Parboil and cut into 'chips', grate raw and make into fritters or roast with a joint of meat.

Glazed with butter, brown sugar and orange juice, sweet potatoes accompany Thanksgiving dinner. In Latin America and the Caribbean they are used in spiced puddings, casseroles, soufflés and sweetmeats. The leaves can be steamed.

Tzimmes
Serves 4

This one-pot meal is based on Olga Phklebin's recipe from *Russian Cooking* but adapted to our ingredients.

1–2 sweet potatoes, depending on size
2 large potatoes
Olive oil
1kg (2lb) stewing steak, cubed
1 large onion, chopped
2 carrots, chopped
750ml (1¼pt) vegetable stock
3 tablespoons honey
½ teaspoon cinnamon powder
1 tablespoon plain flour
Chopped parsley, to garnish
Salt & freshly ground black pepper

Peel both sorts of potato and cut roughly. Heat the oil in a heavy pan and sauté the meat well to brown it on all sides. Remove from the pan and keep warm. Brown the onion, adding the carrots and the meat and sufficient stock to cover. Season with salt and pepper and bring to the boil, then simmer for 45 minutes.

Stir in the potatoes, the honey, cinnamon and more seasoning if required. Bring back to the boil and simmer for a further 45 minutes, covered. If the stew is too liquid, allow it to boil fast at this stage. Remove 5 tablespoons of the stock and mix with the flour. Pour this back into the pot, bring to the boil and cook for a further 30 minutes or until the meat is tender and the potatoes are cooked. Sprinkle with parsley and serve with a green salad.

Lactuca sativa. Compositae

LETTUCE

Annual grown for edible leaves. Half hardy to hardy.
Value: rich in beta carotene, particularly outer leaves.

The garden lettuce is believed to be a selected form of the bitter-leaved wild species *Lactuca serriola*, which is found throughout Europe, Asia and North Africa. The ancient Egyptians were said to have been the first to cultivate lettuces and there are examples of tomb wall paintings depicting a form of Cos lettuce, which is said to have originated on the Greek island of the same name. They believed it was an aphrodisiac and also used its white sap and leaves in a concoction alongside fresh beef, frankincense and juniper berries as a remedy for stomach ache. The Romans, too, attributed medicinal properties to the lettuce and the Emperor Augustus erected an altar and statue in its honour; they believed that it upheld morals, temperance and chastity. The Romans were said to have introduced it to Britain with their conquering armies and even after many centuries it is still regarded as the foundation of a good salad.

'Lollo Rossa'

VARIETIES

The many cultivars are divided into three main categories – cabbage, leaf and Cos types. They can be grown all year round, and many modern cultivars are disease-resistant.

Cabbage Lettuce
More tolerant of drought and drier soils than the other kinds, this group includes Butterhead types, with soft buttery-textured leaves which are usually grown in summer, and Crisphead types, which have crisp leaves forming compact hearts.

Butterhead: **'Action'** has thick, pale green leaves and is resistant to mosaic virus and downy mildew. **'All Year Round'** is tasty and compact with pale green leaves. It is slow to bolt and hardy. **'Avondefiance'** is an excellent, high-yielding, dark green lettuce which withstands drought and high temperatures. It is ideal for summer crops, particularly those sown from mid- to late

summer, and is resistant to root aphid and downy mildew. **'Buttercrunch'** has compact, crisp, dark green heads and a beautiful 'buttery' heart. Slow to 'bolt' and heat-resistant. **'Dolly'** is a large lettuce for mid-summer to mid-autumn cropping. It has good resistance to downy mildew and lettuce mosaic virus. **'Kwiek'**, a large-headed variety for winter cropping, is downy mildew-resistant. Sow in late summer for harvesting in mid-winter or force as an early spring crop. **'Musette'** has dark green, succulent leaves and is resistant to root aphid, lettuce mosaic virus and downy mildew. **'Sabine'** is

'Lobjoits Green' combines well with sorrel and can be made into soups

Cos lettuce

'Oak Leaf', an old variety, has several different colour forms

'Premier Great Lakes' is large, crisp and rapidly maturing. Heat- and 'tip-burn'-resistant. **'Saladin'** is excellent for summer cropping and is resistant to 'tip burn'. **'Webb's Wonderful'** is extremely popular, and rightly so. It is a good-quality lettuce which lasts well at maturity.

Salad Bowl or Leaf lettuce
These are loose-leaved varieties which sometimes form an insignificant heart. Cut to resprout, or remove single leaves as needed. They stand longer before bolting than other types and can be grown at any time of year; however, growth is slower in winter.
   'Grand Rapids' has crinkled pale green leaves

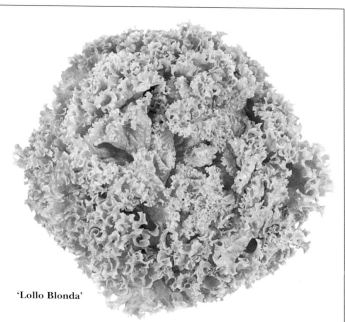

'Lollo Blonda'

resistant to root aphid and downy mildew. The outer leaves of **'Sangria'** are tinged red, the inner a pale green. Has some resistance to mildew and mosaic virus. **'Soraya'** also has some resistance to downy mildew and lettuce mosaic virus. **'Valdor'**, which has firm, dark green hearts, is a

'Rosa Pablo', showing its tightly packed habit

hardy lettuce for overwintering outdoors.

Crisphead: **'Avoncrisp'** has some resistance to mildew and root aphid, but can suffer from 'tip burn'. **'Iceberg'** has very crisp tender leaves with large ice-white hearts, ideal for spring or summer sowing. The heart has the best-quality leaves. **'Malika'** grows very rapidly and should be harvested soon after it matures. It has some resistance to 'tip burn' and lettuce mosaic virus.

and is resistant to 'tip burn'. **'Lollo Blonda'** is similar to 'Lollo Rossa', but with fresh pale green leaves and some resistance to lettuce root aphid. **'Lollo Rossa'** adds colour to salads. The leaves are tinged red with serrated, wavy margins. Good mixed with Cos or Iceberg lettuces and attractive as an edging plant in the flower border or vegetable plot. **'Oak Leaf'** has several different colour forms, from pale green to brown. It dates from the late eighteenth century and is tasty and ornamental. **'Red Salad Bowl'**

has bronze-green to crimson leaves. **'Ruby'** is crinkled and pale green with deep red tints. Has good heat resistance. **'Salad Bowl'** was one of the first leaf lettuces with masses of green, deeply lobed leaves which are crisp but tender. Good resistance to bolting.

Cos or Romaine
These flourish in humus-rich, moist soil, take longer to mature than other varieties and are better in cooler weather. Some can overwinter outdoors or be grown as leaf lettuce if closely spaced. They are generally very tasty.
   'Bubbles' is similar to 'Little Gem', with crisp, crinkly leaves and a good

flavour. It is ideal for the small garden. **'Lobjoits Green'** is a large, good-quality, tasty old variety which is deep green and crisp. It can be grown as closely as leaf lettuce. Subject to 'tip burn'. **'Little Gem'** is a compact, quick-maturing, semi-Cos with a firm, sweet heart. Good as a catch crop, for early crops under cover and for small gardens. It has remained a popular variety since the late nineteenth century. **'Valmaine'** is good for growing as a 'cut and come again' or for close planting and use as leaf lettuce. **'Winter Density'** is very sweet-tasting and good for overwintering outdoors or for sowings under cover.

'Webb's Wonderful'

CULTIVATION

Propagation

Germination is poor, particularly with Butterhead types, if soil temperatures exceed 25°C (77°F), with the critical period being a few hours after planting. During hot weather sow in late afternoon or evening when soil temperatures are lower, water after sowing to reduce soil temperature, shade before and after sowing, germinate in trays or modules in a cool place and transplant, or fluid sow. Lettuces do not transplant well in dry soil and hot weather; where possible, summer sowings are better made *in situ* or in modules.

Sow thinly in drills 1–1.5cm (½–¾in) deep; seeds sown too deeply are slow or fail to germinate. Thin to the final spacing when plants are large enough to handle (overcrowding checks growth and can cause bolting). In cool weather, thinnings can be transplanted if lifted with care to avoid root damage.

Sow those grown in trays or modules in loam-based

potting compost to maintain strong growth and harden off before transplanting when they have 4 to 5 true leaves. Do not transplant when the weather is hot and dry, unless shading can be provided, and do not plant them too deeply.

Sow summer crops from mid-spring to mid-summer. Sow winter-hardy varieties from late summer to early autumn, thinning to the final spacing in spring.

As they do not last long after maturity, maintain a continuous supply of lettuce by sowing successionally, about every 2 weeks, just as the seedlings from the previous sowing appear.

Thin when the seedlings are large enough to handle, where possible staggering them in a triangular pattern to make optimum use of the area.

Space small lettuces 20cm (8in) apart in and between the rows, Butterheads with about 28cm (11in) in and between the rows, or 25cm (10in) apart in rows 30cm (12in) apart. Crispheads should be planted 38cm (15in) apart or 30cm (12in) apart with the rows 38cm (15in) apart. Plant Salad Bowl or Cos about 35cm (14in) apart in and between the rows.

Leaf lettuce can also be grown as 'cut and come

'All Year Round' – ironically, for sowing only from spring to autumn

again' seedlings providing 2 or 3 harvests before bolting: summer crops tend to run to seed more rapidly. Make sure you sow thinly.

Cos varieties like 'Lobjoits Green' can be grown as leaf lettuce. Sow in rows 13cm (5in) apart, thinning to 2.5cm (1in). Sow weekly from late spring to early summer and again in 3 consecutive weeks from late summer. This technique was developed at Horticulture Research International, Wellesbourne, UK.

Growing

Lettuce prefer cool growing conditions, from 10–20°C (50–68°F), and need an open, sunny site on light, rich, moisture-retentive soil, with a pH of around neutral.

They struggle on dry or impoverished soil, so dig in plenty of well-rotted organic matter the autumn before sowing or grow on ground manured for the previous crop. Lightly fork in a base dressing of general fertiliser at 60g/sq m (2oz/sq yd) about 10 days before sowing and create a seedbed by raking to a fine tilth.

Hoe and hand weed regularly to remove weeds. A constant supply of moisture is vital for success. Lettuce

need 22 litres/sq m (4 gal/ sq yd) per week in dry weather. Water in the mornings on sunny days so that the water on the leaves evaporates quickly, reducing the risk of disease. If water is scarce, apply only on the last 7–10 days before harvest.

Boost growth of winter-hardy outdoor crops with a liquid general fertilizer in mid-spring and use the same treatment for slow-growing crops at any time of year.

Rotate crops every 2 years to avoid the build up of pests and diseases.

Maintenance

Spring Sow crops under glass or outdoors under cloches in early spring. Sow later crops outdoors. Harvest early crops.
Summer Sow successionally and harvest overwintered crops. Keep crops weed-free, water as needed. Harvest.
Autumn Sow and protect crops under cloches. Harvest.
Winter Sow crops under cover. Harvest.

Protected Cropping

Sow from late winter to early spring in modules or trays for transplanting under cloches or cold frames from mid- to late spring.

It is worth growing the attractive 'Sangria' in ornamental borders

Alternatively, they can be sown *in situ* in cold frames or under cloches for growing on or transplanting outdoors in a protected part of the garden and covered with floating cloches.

Protect late spring and summer transplants under cloches until they become established and protect late summer sowings under cloches to maintain the quality of autumn crops.

Grow hardier varieties under floating cloches or in a glasshouse or a cold frame over winter, ideally with a gentle heat around 7°C (45°F).

Sow from late summer to mid-autumn for transplanting. Earlier sowings can be made outdoors in a seedbed for transplanting; others can be sown in modules or seed trays. Ventilate well to avoid disease problems.

Harvest from late autumn to mid-spring. Cover outdoor winter-hardy crops with glass or floating cloches to ensure a good-quality crop and provide protection during severe weather.

Sow early crops of 'cut and come again' seedlings under cover in late winter or spring, and also from mid-autumn.

Container Growing

Compact varieties are suitable for growing in pots, containers and window boxes. Use a soil-based compost, mix in a slow-release granular fertilizer and water regularly. Sow either *in situ* or in modules for transplanting.

Harvesting & Storing

Summer maincrop lettuce are ready to harvest from early summer to mid-autumn, around 12 weeks after sowing. Cos stand for quite a time in cool weather but Butterheads deteriorate within a few days of maturity. Crispheads last for about 10 days before deteriorating. Leaf lettuces can be picked over a long period. Harvest hardy overwintered outdoor crops from late spring to early summer.

Harvest 'cut and come again' seedlings about 4 weeks after sowing and Cos types grown as leaf lettuce about 2.5cm (1in) above the ground when they are 7.5–12.5cm (3–5in) high. A second crop can be harvested from 3 to 8 weeks later, depending on the growing conditions.

Cut mature lettuces at the base just below the lower leaves. Do not squeeze hearting lettuces to check if they are ready for harvesting as this can damage the leaves: press them gently but firmly with the back of your hand. Pull single leaves from leaf lettuce as required or cut 2.5cm (1in) above the base and allow to resprout.

Growing lettuce under black plastic sheeting warms the soil, suppresses weeds and conserves moisture

Store lettuce in the refrigerator in the salad drawer or a polythene bag for up to 6 days. Cos lettuce stores the longest.

PESTS & DISEASES

Root aphids appear in clusters on the roots and are usually covered in a white powdery wax. The symptoms are stunted growth and yellowing leaves; plants may collapse in hot weather. They are less of a problem in cool, damp conditions. Pick and destroy affected plants or grow resistant varieties.

Aphids can also be a problem.

Leaf tips become brown and dry when affected by **'tip burn'**, caused by sudden water loss in warm weather. Water well and shade if necessary; do not allow lettuces to grow excessively large; grow resistant varieties where possible.

Botrytis or **grey mould** can be a problem in cool, damp conditions. Do not plant seedlings too deeply, handle transplants carefully to avoid damage, thin early, remove diseased material, improve ventilation, spray with systemic or copper-based fungicide. Grow resistant varieties.

Bolting or **running to seed** is caused by check during transplanting, drought, temperatures over 21°C (70°F), or long days; otherwise lettuces will only bolt after hearting. Grow resistant varieties or leaf lettuce.

Pigeons and sparrows can damage seedlings. Grow under horticultural fleece, tie thread between bamboo canes, use humming line or other deterrents.

Lettuce mosaic virus causes the leaves to become puckered and mottled, veins become transparent and growth is stunted. More of a problem on overwintering crops. Destroy those which are affected, control aphids, grow resistant varieties.

'Webb's Wonderful', a large-hearted lettuce, grows well in hot summers

COMPANION PLANTING

Lettuce grow well with cucumbers, onions, radishes and carrots. Dill and chervil protect them from aphids.

MEDICINAL

Lettuce is used as a mild sedative and narcotic, and lettuce soup is reported to be effective in treating nervous tension and insomnia. Lettuce sap dissolved in wine is said to make a good painkiller.

Lettuce soothes inflammation – lotions for the treatment of sunburn and rough skin are made from its extracts.

It can also be used as a poultice on bruises or taken internally for stomach ulcers and for irritable bowel syndrome.

It is also anti-spasmodic and can be used to soothe coughs and bronchial problems; it is reputed to cool the ardour.

CULINARY

Wash leaves thoroughly before use. Use fresh or wilted in salads, braise with butter and flavour with nutmeg or braise with peas and shallots and serve with butter. Stir-fry with onions and mushrooms, steam and add to chicken soup or make cream of lettuce soup and garnish with hard-boiled eggs and a sprinkling of curry powder. Stalks can be sliced and steamed.

Braised Lettuce
Serves 4

Cos lettuces all seem to bolt at the same time, and braising them is an excellent way of ringing the changes from salads.

4–5 lettuce, trimmed
A little oil or butter
50g (2oz) bacon, roughly diced
1 carrot, roughly diced
1 red onion, sliced
300ml (½pt) well-flavoured vegetable stock
2 tablespoons chopped thyme & parsley
Salt & freshly ground black pepper

In a saucepan of salted water, cook the lettuces for 5 minutes. Drain and refresh in cold water. Drain again and remove as much liquid as possible.

Grease an ovenproof dish and sprinkle the base with the bacon, carrot, onion and seasoning. Arrange the lettuces neatly in the dish and pour in the stock. Cover with buttered paper and braise in a preheated oven, 180°C, 350°F, gas 4, for 30–40 minutes.

Remove the lettuces and other ingredients and keep hot. Then reduce the cooking liquid and pour it over the vegetables. Sprinkle with the fresh herbs and serve very hot.

Braised Lettuce

Lettuce-wrapped Minced Prawns
Serves 6–8, with other dishes

Yan-Kit So gives this recipe in her *Classic Food of China* (published by Macmillan).

30 raw prawns, shelled
 & deveined
¼ teaspoon salt
2 teaspoons cornflour
2 tablespoons egg white
1 crisp lettuce (Webb's or
 Iceberg)
4 tablespoons peanut or
 vegetable oil
50g (2oz) Sichuan zhacai,
 trimmed & finely chopped
1 teaspoon garlic, finely
 crushed

Mince the prawns coarsely and put in a large mixing bowl. Season with salt. Add the cornflour and egg white and stir in the same direction until the egg white is absorbed and the mixture is elastic. Refrigerate, covered, for 1 hour.

Arrange the separated lettuce leaves, preferably cup-shaped, on a plate on the dining table.

Heat a wok until hot. Add 1 tablespoon of oil and the Sichuan zhacai and cook for a few seconds, stirring. Scoop on to a dish and keep near by. Wipe the wok clean.

Reheat the wok until the smoke rises. Add the rest of the oil and coat the wok with it. Add the garlic and the prawns, stirring to break up the mixture as much as possible. Add the Sichuan preserved vegetables and continue cooking until the prawns turn pink and are cooked. Then place on a plate next to the lettuce.

To serve, each person takes a lettuce leaf, spoons some prawn mixture into the centre and wraps the lettuce around it: perfect finger-food.

Lactuca sativa var. *augustana. Compositae*

CELTUCE

(Stem Lettuce, Asparagus Lettuce, Chinese Lettuce)
Annual grown for edible leaves. Value: little nutritive value;
low in carbohydrate and calories; a source of potassium.

Introduced from China, where it has been grown for centuries, this 'oriental vegetable' consists of a short-stemmed mutation lettuce. It has been listed in European catalogues since 1885, but the name 'celtuce' was adopted by an American seed company who first offered seeds in 1942. It aptly describes its characteristics: the stems are used like celery; the leaves make a lettuce substitute.

VARIETIES

'Zulu' is a new variety for cooler climates, with narrow, dull-textured leaves. Others are sold in seed mixes of broad, dull, glossy or red-leaved varieties.

CULTIVATION

Celtuce needs well-drained, rich, fertile soil, with a pH of 6.5–7.5, around neutral. Celtuce tolerates a range of temperatures from light frosts to over 27°C (80°F). It tends to bolt prematurely in extremely hot conditions, but is still more heat-resistant than lettuce. Grow celtuce as a winter crop in mild areas.

Propagation
For successional cropping, sow every 2 weeks from mid-spring until mid-summer in drills 1cm (½in) deep and 30cm (12in) apart. When large enough to handle, thin to 9cm (3½in).

Germination is poor in temperatures above 27°C (80°F). In hot summers, sow in seed trays or modules in a cool, partially shaded position. Modules tend to produce better plants than seed trays; weak seedlings rarely produce good stems. Transplant when 3–4 leaves have been produced, generally after 3–4 weeks. Mulch after planting to conserve moisture and suppress weeds; the shallow roots are very easily damaged by hoeing.

Growing
In poor soils add copious amounts of organic matter the winter before planting. Celtuce grows well on light soil, but develops a stronger root system and more robust plants on heavier soils.

Water well as leaves develop to keep them tender; as the stems develop, reduce watering, but take care to keep the supply steady: if the soil becomes too wet or too dry, the stems may crack. Feed with a liquid general fertilizer every 3 weeks.

Maintenance
Spring Sow seed.
Summer Water and remove weeds.
Autumn Transplant seedlings for winter crops.
Winter Grow under cover; harvest mature crops.

Narrow-leaved celtuce

Protected Cropping

Grow in cloches, unheated glasshouses, tunnels or under horticultural fleece to extend the season. Raise early crops by sowing and planting under cover in early spring and late crops by transplanting summer-sown seedlings under cover in autumn.

Container Growing

Sow in containers or pots in a loam-based compost with moderate levels of added fertilizer.

Harvesting & Storing

Harvest 3–4 months after sowing, when 30cm (12in) high and 2.5cm (1in) diameter. Cut the stalks, pull up the plant or cut it off at ground level. Trim the leaves from the stem but do not touch the top rosette of leaves in order to keep the stem fresh.

Celtuce stems can be kept for a few weeks in cool conditions.

PESTS & DISEASES

Celtuce is susceptible to the same problems as lettuce. Pick off **slugs**, set traps or use aluminium sulphate pellets. **Downy mildew** is worse in cool, damp conditions: treat with fungicide, and remove infected plants and debris at the end of the season.

COMPANION PLANTING

Plant with chervil and dill to protect from aphids. Interplant between slower-growing crops such as cauliflower, self-blanching celery or Chinese chives.

CULINARY

Celtuce is excellent raw and cooked. Prepare the stems by peeling off the outer layer. Cut into thin slices for salads, or into larger pieces for cooking. In salads, it can either be eaten raw or cooked and cooled, served with a spicy dressing.

Cook lightly, for 4 minutes at the most. Stir-fry with white meat, poultry, fish, other vegetables, or on its own seasoned with garlic, chilli, pepper, soy or oyster sauce. It is also delicious served with a creamed sauce or baked *au gratin*.

Young leaves can be cooked like 'greens'.

Crispy Spring Rolls
Serves 4–6

225g (8oz) fresh beansprouts, washed & husked
225g (8oz) celtuce stems
115g (4oz) bamboo shoots
115g (4oz) white mushrooms
115g (4oz) carrots
Oil for frying & deep frying
1 teaspoon sugar
1 tablespoon light soya sauce
1 tablespoon rice wine
1 pack 20 frozen spring roll skins, defrosted
Salt & freshly ground black pepper
1 tablespoon plain flour mixed with 1 tablespoon water

Prepare the beansprouts and roughly chop all the other vegetables to the same size. Heat a little oil in a wok until smoking and stir-fry the vegetables for 1 minute, then add the sugar, soya sauce, rice wine and seasoning, and cook for a further 1–2 minutes. Set aside to cool.

Cut the spring roll skins diagonally in half. Place a teaspoon of the vegetable mixture in the centre of each and roll up neatly, folding in all the corners. Place on a lightly floured plate and brush the upper edge with a little flour/water paste to seal.

Heat enough oil to deep-fry until steaming and drop in the spring rolls for 3–4 minutes, until crispy, cooking in batches. Drain and serve with chilli sauce.

Crispy Spring Rolls

Alpinia galanga (syn. *Languas galanga*). *Zingiberaceae*

GREATER GALANGAL

(Galangal languas, Siamese Ginger) Herbaceous perennial; rhizomatous rootstock used as flavouring. Tender. Value: negligible nutritive value.

Two species, greater and lesser galangal, have been grown for centuries for their pungent, aromatic roots, which are used as spices and medicinally. The earliest records date from around AD550, while Marco Polo noted its cultivation in southern China and Java in the thirteenth century. In the Middle Ages it was known as 'galangale', a name also used for the roots of sweet sedge, whose violet-scented rhizomes are used in perfumery.

The word galangal came from the Chinese, meaning 'a mild ginger from Ko', a region of the Canton province. It is an essential ingredient of many Malaysian and Thai dishes. The spicy rhizomes have a somewhat different use in the Middle East, where they have been used to 'spike' horses!

CULTIVATION

The plant is a herbaceous perennial with pale orange-flushed cream bulbous rhizomes. Stems grow to 2m (6ft) tall, with dark green lance-shaped leaves to 50cm (20in) long. Flowers are pale green and white with pink markings; the fruit a round red capsule. There are many different races in cultivation, including types with red and white rhizomes. Lesser galangal is regarded as superior as it is more pungent and aromatic, but is uncommon in cultivation.

Propagation
Sow fresh seed in pots of peat-substitute compost at 20°C (68°F). Keep the compost moist using tepid water and transplant seedlings when they are large enough to handle. In tropical and sub-tropical regions they can be sown outdoors in a seedbed (for ground preparation, see 'Growing').

Divide rhizomes in spring when the young shoots are about 2.5cm (1in) long. Remove young, vigorous sections from the perimeter of the clump using a sharp knife, dust the cuts with fungicide and transplant just below the soil or compost surface. Soak thoroughly with tepid water and maintain high humidity and temperatures.

Growing
Galangal grows outdoors in tropical or sub-tropical climates, thriving in sunshine or partial shade. It needs a rich, free-draining soil, so dig in plenty of well-rotted compost and allow the ground to settle for a few weeks before planting. Allow 90cm (36in) between plants. Keep crops weed-free and water during dry periods. Mulch with well-rotted compost when plants are well established.

Container growing
Plants can be grown in containers under cover in a compost mix of 2 parts each of loam and leafmould, 1 part horticultural grit or sharp sand and 3 parts medium-grade bark. Repot and divide in spring when the rhizomes outgrow their allotted space.

Protected Cropping
In temperate zones, plants can be grown in a heated polythene tunnel or greenhouse in bright filtered light, with a minimum temperature of 15°C (58°F). Maintain high humidity by misting plants with tepid water and 'damping down' paths. Prepare borders as for 'Growing' and allow 90cm (36in) between plants. Keep the compost constantly moist with tepid water and reduce watering in lower temperatures. After flowering reduce watering as the foliage gradually becomes yellow and dies back. The compost should remain slightly moist throughout the dormant period. Increase watering when new shoots emerge the following spring.

Feed regularly with a liquid general fertilizer every 2 weeks while the plant is actively growing. Mulch plants grown in borders annually in spring with well-rotted manure.

Harvesting & Storing

Rhizomes are ready to harvest after 3–4 years. Lift plants towards the end of the growing season and remove mature rhizomes, retaining younger ones for transplanting. It is a good idea to divide and replant a few each year to ensure a constant supply.

Galangal are better used immediately after harvest but will keep for at least a week in a cool place. Alternatively, they can be frozen whole in a polythene bag and segments removed as required. Keep dried roots in airtight containers in a cool dark place.

PESTS & DISEASES

Red spider mite can be a problem under glass. Check plants regularly, as small infestations are easily controlled. Speckling, mottling and bronzing of the leaf surface are the usual symptoms; in later stages, fine webbing appears on leaves and stems. They prefer hot, dry conditions. Control by maintaining high humidity or spray with derris or a similar insecticide.

MEDICINAL

Plants contain cineol, an aromatic, antiseptic substance. The essential oil acts as a decongestant and respiratory germicide and digestive aid. In India it is used as a breath purifier and deodorant, and a paste is made from the rhizomes to treat skin infections. It is also said to be an aphrodisiac. Infusions are taken after childbirth.

CULINARY

Before use scrape or peel off the skin. The raw chopped or minced root is used in Malaysian and Indonesian dishes with bean curd, meat, poultry, fish, curries and sauces. It is also used as a marinade to flavour barbecued chicken. The fruits are a substitute for cardamon, the buds can be pickled and the flowers are eaten raw with vegetables or pickles in parts of Java. In Thai cooking it is preferred to ginger. In medieval England a sauce was made from bread crusts, galangal, cinnamon and ginger pulverized and moistened with stock. It was heated with a dash of vinegar and strained over fish or meat.

Galangal Soup
Serves 4
There are many variations on this soup, the recipe for which comes from Vietnam.

First, make a stock from the following:
1 litre (1¾pt water)
1 chicken carcass
4 bulbs lemon grass, bruised
12cm (5in) galangal, peeled & sliced
1 onion, roughly sliced
2 red dried chillies
6 kaffir lime leaves
Salt & freshly ground black pepper

Then strain the stock through some fine muslin. Reheat in a heavy saucepan, adding the meat from the chicken carcass, chopped finely, together with 1 tablespoon of fish sauce and 4 tablespoons of lime juice. Simmer for 5 minutes and then add 125g (4oz) shi-itake mushrooms, left whole. Simmer for a further 3 minutes before stirring in 125ml (¼pt) thick coconut milk. Do not allow to reboil, and check the seasoning. Serve hot.

OTHER USES

Roots of lesser galangal are used in Russia for flavouring tea and a liqueur called Nastoika. The rhizomes produce a yellow or yellow/green dye.

Kaempferia galanga
(Chinese keys)

The rhizomes, common in the markets of South-East Asia, produce a distinctive cluster of finger-like roots which are pale brown with bright yellow flesh and a pungent aroma. They have a very strong taste and should be used sparingly in green curry paste, sauces, soups and curries.

The rhizomes may be eaten raw when young, or steamed and eaten as a vegetable. Young shoots are cooked as a vegetable, pickled or eaten raw.

Chinese keys are used as a carminative, stomachic, expectorant, analgesic, and to treat dandruff and sore throats.

Lagenaria siceraria. Cucurbitaceae

DOODHI

(Bottle Gourd, Calabash Gourd, White-flowered Gourd, Trumpet Gourd)
Vigorous annual climber grown for edible young fruits, shoots and seeds.
Tender. Value: little nutritive value; a moderate source of vitamin C,
small quantities of B vitamins and protein.

Early evidence for the cultivation of this versatile tropical gourd comes from South America around 7000BC, though it is thought to have originated in Africa south of the Sahara or India. Some sources suggest that it may have dispersed naturally by floating on oceanic currents from one continent to another: experiments have found that seed will germinate after surviving over seven months in seawater. One of the earliest crops cultivated in the tropics, these gourds with their narrow necks have developed in many shapes and sizes, some reaching up to 2m (6ft) long. The young fruits are edible, but mature shells become extremely hard when dried and have been used to make bottles, kitchen utensils, musical instruments, floats for fishing nets and even gunpowder flasks. In the past *lagenaria* leaves were used as a protective charm when elephant hunting.

VARIETIES

Lagenaria siceraria is a vigorous annual, climbing or scrambling by means of tendrils to more than 10m (30ft). The leaves are broad and oval with wavy margins. Its solitary, fragrant, white flowers open in the evenings. Its fruits are pale green to cream or yellow, with a narrow 'neck', and contain white, spongy flesh and flat creamy-coloured seeds. The names of selected forms (like 'bottle', 'trumpet', 'club' or 'powder-horn' gourd) relate to their use and appearance.

CULTIVATION

They flourish in warm conditions, around 20–30°C (68–86°F) and plenty of sunshine, but will grow outdoors in warm temperate climates where humidity levels are moderate to high. Plants need to be trained over supporting structures.

Propagation
Soak seeds overnight in tepid water before sowing on mounds of soil about 30cm (12in) apart, containing copious amounts of well-rotted manure. Plant 3 seeds, edgeways, and thin to leave the strongest seedling. Seeds can be sown in a nursery bed and transplanted when they have 2 to 3 leaves. Seeds are usually sown at the start of the rainy season.

Growing
Doodhi needs fertile, well-drained soil, preferably with a pH of 7. Add a granular general fertilizer to the planting hole or scatter it around the germinated seedling. Train the stems into trees, or over fences, arbours or frames covered with 15cm (6in) mesh netting. Erect stakes or trellis on the beds or among the groups of mounds. Alternatively, grow plants in beds 120–180cm (48–72in) square, planting a seedling at each corner and training towards the centre. Pinch out the terminal shoots when they are 3–4cm (1¼–1½in) long to encourage branching. The best yields are obtained in warm-climate areas with rainfall around 80–120cm (28–48in) per annum, but they grow well in drier regions if they are kept well watered. Feed with a high-nitrogen fertilizer every 3 weeks during the growing season, keep crops weed-free and mulch with a layer of organic matter.

Plants can grow extremely rapidly in hot weather: 60cm (2ft) in 24 hours has been recorded. Where conditions are suitable they can be grown all year round. To grow outdoors in cooler climates, harden off under cloches or cold frames and plant in a sheltered, sunny position when the danger of frost has passed.

The chance of success is greater in hot summers; they should reach edible size, though they rarely have a long enough season to mature fully.

Maintenance

Spring Sow seeds under glass in warm conditions.
Summer Train vines over trellis or netting. Water regularly, feed as necessary. Damp down the greenhouse to maintain humidity and harvest young fruits.
Autumn In cooler climates harvest mature gourds for preserving, before the onset of the first frosts.

Protected Cropping

In cool temperate climates, sow seeds 6–8 weeks before the anticipated planting out time. Sow 2–3 seeds in a 15cm (6in) pot of peat-substitute compost in late winter or early spring at 21–25°C (70–75°F).

Germination takes 3–5 days. If the ideal temperatures cannot be achieved and maintained, delay sowing until mid- to late spring. Transplant when seedlings are 10–15cm (4–6in) high. They will grow at temperatures down to 10°C (50°F), but flourish at high temperatures and in humid conditions in bright filtered light.

Damp down the greenhouse floor at least twice a day, depending on outside weather conditions. Dig in plenty of well-rotted manure and horticultural grit or sharp sand into the glasshouse border, or grow in containers. Keep the compost constantly moist using tepid water and feed with a liquid general fertilizer every 2 weeks.

Train up a trellis, wires or netting. Flowers will appear from early summer and only 1 or 2 should be allowed to grow to maturity.

Doodhi growing in a Cypriot village garden

Container Growing

Pot on as plants grow until they are in 30cm (12in) pots, or grow in large containers of loam-based compost with added organic matter and horticultural grit or sharp sand to improve drainage. Keep the compost moist, with tepid water. Growth is better restricted when they are grown in pots and is preferable in the greenhouse border, increasing the chance of successful fruiting.

Stop the shoot tips when the stems are 1.5m (5ft) long and train the side stems along a wire. (It is worth noting that even with this method, plants still need a considerable amount of space.) Hand pollination ensures a good crop. (Male and female flowers are on the same plant: females are recognized by the ovary at the back of the flower, covered in glandular hairs.) Once a flower has formed, allow 2 more leaves to appear, then pinch out the growing tip. If it is a male flower or a fruit is not going to form, cut the stem back to the first leaf. A replacement will be formed.

Harvesting & Storing

Vines begin to fruit 3–4 months after planting. Harvest immature fruits when a few centimetres (inches) long, 70–90 days after sowing. Mature fruits can be harvested and dried slowly as ornaments.

Pests & Diseases

This very robust plant is rarely troubled by disease. **Whitefly** can occasionally be a problem when plants are grown under cover. In warm, humid climates, **anthracnose** appears as pinhead-sized, water-soaked lesions on the fruits, combining to form a small black mass. **Fruit rot** can also be a problem. Spray with Bordeaux or Cheshunt compound and remove badly affected leaves. Harvest fruits carefully to avoid damage.

MEDICINAL USES

The fruit pulp around seeds is emetic and purgative and is sometimes given to horses! Juice from the fruit treats baldness; mixed with lime juice, it is used for pimples; boiled with oil, it is used for rheumatism. Seeds and roots are used to treat dropsy and the seed oil used externally for headaches.

CULINARY

Young fruits, which are rich in pectin, are popular in tropical Africa and Asia. They have a mild, somewhat bland taste, are peeled before eating and any large seeds removed. They can be cubed or sliced, sautéed with spices to accompany curries and other Indian dishes and added to stews or curries. Young shoots and leaves can be steamed or lightly boiled. Seeds are used in soups in Africa and are boiled in salt water and eaten as an appetizer in India. The seed oil is used for cooking.

Lens culinaris. Leguminosae

LENTIL

(Split Pea, Masur)
Annual herb grown for edible flattened seeds. Tender.
Value: rich in protein, fibre, iron, carbohydrate, zinc
and B vitamins.

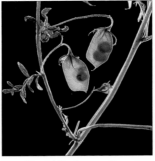

'Lentille du Puy', a small seed French variety, in unripe pod

'Lentille du Puy', ready for harvest

Presumed to be native to south-west Europe and temperate Asia, lentils are one of the oldest cultivated crop plants. Carbonized seeds found in Neolithic villages in the Middle East have been dated at 7–6000BC, and it is believed that they were domesticated long before that. By 2200BC plants appeared in Egyptian tombs; they are referred to in the Bible as the 'mess of pottage' for which Esau traded his birthright (Genesis 25: 30, 34). The English 'lens', describing the glass in optical instruments, comes from their Latin name – its cross-section resembles a lentil seed. Christian Lent has the same origin, as it was traditionally eaten during the fast.

Grown throughout the world, it has become naturalized in drier areas of the tropics. Because of its relatively high drought tolerance, it is suitable for semi-arid regions. The quick-maturing plant is rarely more than 45cm (18in) tall and has branched stems forming a small bush. The white to rose and violet flowers lead to 2–3 seeded pods.

VARIETIES

Lentils have been selected over many centuries for their size and colour. Today many different races and cultivars exist. Two main races predominate, the larger, round-seeded types usually grown in Europe and North America, and the smaller, flatter-seeded types common in the East.

Frequently encountered is the **split red** or **Persian lentil**, which is extremely tender and quick to cook.

Among round-seeded types grown in Europe, the **'Lentille du Puy'**, a tiny green form, is the tastiest and tenderest. Similar but coarser is the **lentille blonde** or **yellow lentil** commonly grown in northern France, while **German** or **brown lentils** are coarser still and need lengthy cooking to make them tender. Of varieties grown in North America, **'O'Odham'** has flat grey-brown to tan-coloured seeds and **'Tarahumara Pinks'** from Mexico has mottled seeds and thrives well in semi-arid conditions.

CULTIVATION

Propagation

Prepare the seedbed by removing any debris from the soil surface and raking to a moderate texture. Sow in spring when the soil is warm in drills 2.5cm (1in) deep, thinning seedlings to 20–30cm (8–12in) apart with 45cm (18in) between rows. They can also be broadcast and then thinned after germination to 20–30cm (8–12in) apart.

Growing

Lentils are not frost-hardy but flourish in a range of climatic conditions. They prefer a warm, sunny, sheltered position on light, free-draining, moisture-retentive soil. Sandy soils with added well-rotted organic matter are ideal, though equally good crops are grown on silty soil. Keep crops weed-free and irrigate if necessary during periods of prolonged drought. Excessive watering can lead to over-production of leaves and poor cropping.

Lentils can be grown as a 'novelty' crop in cool temperate climates, but yields are not high enough to make it worthwhile on a large scale.

Growing in Idaho, USA

Maintenance

Spring Prepare the seedbed and sow when soil is warm.
Summer Keep crops weed-free and irrigate if necessary.
Autumn Harvest before the seeds split.
Winter Store seeds or pods in a cool dry place, for use as required.

Protected Cropping

In cool temperate climates sow seeds in spring in trays, pots or modules of seed compost. Keep compost moist and pot on when seedlings are large enough to handle. Harden off before planting outdoors when the soil is warm and workable and there is no danger of frosts. Protect plants under cloches until they are properly established.

Container Growing

Grow in containers of soil-based compost with moderate fertilizer levels. Water well and keep weed-free. To avoid the need for transplanting, seeds can be sown in a container which is then moved outdoors into a sunny spot after they have germinated.

Harvesting & Storing

Lentils take about 90 days to reach maturity. Harvest as foliage begins to yellow, before the pods split and the seeds are shed. Lift the whole plant and lay on trays or mats in the sunshine to air-dry or put them in an airy shed. When the pods dry and split, remove the seed and store in a cool, dry place.

CULINARY

As their protein content is about 25%, lentils are an important meat substitute. They also have the lowest fat content of any protein-rich food.

Soak overnight, drain and replace the water. Boil rapidly for 10 minutes, then simmer for 25 minutes until tender. Use in soups, thick broth or grind into flour.

Lentils are commonly used for 'dhal'. Seeds are moistened with water and oil and dried before milling 2–3 times, each time separating the 'chaff' from the meal.

Puy Lentils with Roasted Red Peppers & Goat's Cheese
Serves 4

3 red peppers
175g (6oz) lentilles du Puy
1 red onion
1 carrot
Sprig each of parsley, marjoram & thyme
2 tablespoons sun dried tomatoes, chopped
100g (4oz) crumbled goat's cheese
1 tablespoon freshly chopped herbs

for the dressing:
4 tablespoons extra-virgin olive oil
1½ tablespoons lemon juice
Salt & freshly ground black pepper

Roast the peppers on a baking tray in a pre-heated oven, 250°C, 475°F, gas 9, for 30 minutes. Put them into a polythene bag in the fridge. When cooled, deseed and peel the peppers, then cut into strips. Set aside.

Wash the Puy lentils thoroughly and cook them, covered, with the whole onion, carrot and herbs. These lentils cook faster than other types and should be done in 15 minutes. Drain. Roughly chop the onion and add back into the lentils. Discard the carrot and herbs. While still warm, add the tomatoes and goat's cheese and stir gently. Season.

Make the dressing and toss the lentil mixture in it. Arrange the lentils with the slices of red pepper on individual plates. Sprinkle with the herbs and serve.

PESTS & DISEASES

Lentils suffer from few pests and diseases. **Leaf rust** can occur; burn plants after harvest and use treated seed.

COMPANION PLANTING

Lentils can be grown as a 'green manure'.

OTHER USES

Dried leaves and stems are used as forage crops.

Lentils have also been used as a source of commercial starch in the textile and printing industries, the by-products being used as cattle feed. Plants are used fresh or dried as hay and fodder.

WARNING

Never eat lentils raw.

Lycopersicon esculentum. Solanaceae

TOMATO

(Love Apple) Short-lived perennial herb grown as annual for fleshy, succulent berry. Half hardy. Value: rich in beta carotene and vitamin C; some vitamin B.

'Tigerella' is unusual but worth growing for its flavour

The wild species is believed to have originated in the Andean regions of north and central South America, spreading to Central and North America along with maize during human migrations over 2,000 years ago. The fruits had been cultivated in Mexico for centuries when European explorers found them growing under local names including *tomati*, *tomatl*, *tumatle* and *tomatas*. When they were first brought to Europe around 1523, tomatoes were considered to be poisonous, due to their strong odour and bright white, red and yellow berries, and were grown only as ornamentals. Dodoens in his *Historie of Plants* of 1578 records, 'This is a strange plant and not found in this country, except in the gardens of some herborists...and is dangerous to be used.'

In Europe, it was first used for food in Italy. Like many vegetable introductions from the New World, it was considered to be an aphrodisiac. The Italian name *pommi dei mori* was corrupted during translation to the French *pomme d'amour* or 'apple of love', as it was thought to excite the passions. Not all believed it to have this effect. Estienne and Liébault wrote that tomatoes were boiled or fried, but gave rise to wind, choler and 'infinite obstructions' – hardly an inducement to romance!

The use of tomatoes by North American settlers was not recorded until after Independence, but they were regularly used as food by Italian immigrants to New England and French settlers living in New Orleans, who were making ketchup by 1779. Thomas Jefferson was certainly growing them in his garden in 1781 and they were introduced to Philadelphia eight years later.

VARIETIES

Most greenhouse varieties are 'indeterminate', with a main stem which can become several metres or yards long – these are usually grown as 'cordons'. Most of those grown outdoors are bush types which do not need supporting and can be grown under crop covers or cloches. Low-yielding, dwarf varieties are good for pots or window boxes.

As you will see from any seed catalogue, there are hundreds of tomato varieties. Those for cultivation under cover in a cold greenhouse and outdoor varieties are generally interchangeable. They range in size from the large ribbed, 'beefsteak' types to small 'cherry', 'pear-shaped' and 'currant' tomatoes in a great range of colours including mottled, dark skinned, pink and yellow.

'Ailsa Craig' grows well indoors/outdoors. It is a reliable, tasty, heavy-cropping variety. **'Alicante'**, another indoor/outdoor variety, crops heavily, producing smooth tasty fruit. Early maturing, it

'Brandy Wine' can weigh up to 0.4kg (1lb) each

grows well in grow-bags. **'Black Plum'** is a Russian variety found in specialist lists. The fruit are elongated, about 7.5cm (3in) long and are deep mahogany to brown. **'Brandywine'** is a delicious old variety; the fruit can become quite sizeable. The skin is rosy pink or tinged slightly purplish-red. Better in cooler climates. **'Cherry Belle'**, a tasty little 'cherry' tomato, is of good quality and high yielding. It has resistance to tobacco mosaic virus. **'Delicious'** is a large 'beefsteak' variety with fruits weighing up to 0.4kg (1lb). They are tasty, succulent and store well. **'Dombito'**, another 'beefsteak', is delicious, crops well and has resistance to tobacco mosaic virus and fusarium wilt. **'Gardener's Delight'*** is extremely popular, producing long trusses of delicious, sweet, 'cherry' tomatoes over a long period. Grows indoors/outdoors, is ideal for containers and generally trouble-free. **'Green Zebra'** is a tasty tomato with unusual green fruits and yellow stripes. **'Marmande Super'** is a delicious outdoor variety with deep red ribbed fruits. Early cropping and resistant to fusarium and verticillium wilt. **'Marvel Striped Traditional'** is an old Mexican variety with large, tasty, juicy striped fruits. **'Minibel'** is a bush tomato

with tiny, tasty fruit. It grows well in pots and window boxes. **'Moneymaker'** is a famous old variety for indoors/outdoors. The succulent scarlet fruits are full of flavour. **'Oaxacan Pink'** has small, flattened, pink fruits. **'Red Alert'** is an early bush variety for the greenhouse or outdoors with small, sweet, oval fruits. **'Roma VF'** is an outdoor bush 'plum' tomato for paste, ketchup, bottling, soups or juice. It crops heavily and has high resistance to fusarium and verticillium wilt. It sometimes needs supporting. **'San Marzano'**, another Italian tomato, is good for soups, sauces or garnishing salads. Crops heavily. **'Shirley'*** is grown commercially and has good quality, tender, tasty fruit. Withstanding lower temperatures than most types, it does not suffer from 'greenback', is highly resistant to tobacco mosaic virus, leaf mould and fusarium. An ideal tomato for organic growers. **'Siberia Tomato'** crops extremely early, around seven weeks from transplanting. This bush variety sets fruit at temperatures down to 5°C (38°F), producing clusters of bright red berries. **'Super Beefsteak'** is a huge old fleshy variety whose fruits are at least 0.4kg (1lb) in weight. Has resistance to wilt and root knot nematodes.

'Tigerella'* produces tasty, small orange-red fruits with pale stripes. Crops well over a long period. **'Tiny Tim'** is compact, bushy and ideal for pots, window boxes and hanging baskets. Fruits are cherry-sized and tasty. **'Tumbler'** was bred for hanging baskets. It has flexible, hanging stems, the bright red fruits ripen quickly and are sweet to the taste. **'Yellow Cocktail'** produces large trusses of tiny, pear-shaped, golden-yellow fruits. Grow under glass. **'Yellow Pearshaped'** are well described by their name. The dense clusters of fruit are sweet-tasting and have few seeds. Plants are vigorous and high-yielding. **'Yellow Perfection'*** is prolific with bright yellow fruits, early cropping and tasty. An excellent tomato.

CULTIVATION

Propagation

A minimum temperature of 16°C (60°F) is needed for germination, but seedlings can tolerate lower night temperatures if those during the day are above this level.

In cool climates, for growing in heated glasshouses, sow from mid-winter. For growing outdoors or in an unheated greenhouse, sow seed indoors 2cm (¾in) deep in trays of seed compost, 6–8 weeks before the last frost is due or sow 2–3 seeds in 7.5cm (3in) pots or modules, thinning to leave the strongest seedling.

The popular and prolific 'Gardener's Delight'

Transplant tray- or module-grown seedlings into 7.5cm (3in) pots when 2–3 leaves have formed, keeping the plants in a light, well ventilated position. Harden off carefully and plant out when there is no danger of frost and air temperatures are at least 7°C (45°F) with soil temperatures at a minimum of 10°C (50°F).

Transplant, with the first true leaves just above the soil level, when the flowers on the first truss appear. Do not worry if your plants have become spindly; planting them deeply stimulates the formation of roots on the buried stems, making the plants more stable.

Tomatoes can also be fluid-sown from mid-spring *in situ* or in a cold frame for transplanting after warming the soil. Germinate on moist kitchen towel at 21°C (70°F), sowing when the rootlets are a maximum of 5mm (¼in) long (see advice on fluid sowing). Sow outdoors in drills and thin to leave the strongest seedling or in 'stations' at their final spacing. Cover the drills with compost and protect them with cloches until the first flowers appear.

When sowing in cold frames, sow seed in rows 12.5–15cm (5–6in) apart, thinning to 10–12.5cm (4–5in) apart in the rows. Transplant carefully when the plants are 15–20cm (6–8in) tall.

Alternatively, buy plants grown individually in pots rather than packed in boxes or trays, using a reliable supplier.

Plant 'cordon' types 38–45cm (15–18in) apart, or in double rows with 90cm (36in) between each pair of rows. Plant bush types should be planted 45–60cm (18–24in) apart and dwarf cultivars 25–30cm (10–12in) apart, depending on the variety.

Closer spacing produces earlier crops; wider spacing generally produces slightly higher yields.

Growing

Outdoor tomatoes need a warm, sheltered position, preferably against a sunny wall, in a moisture-retentive, well-drained soil. Add well-rotted organic matter where necessary and lime acid soils to create a pH of 5.5–7. If tomatoes are grown in very rich soil or are fed with too much nitrogen they produce excessive leaf growth at the expense of flowers and fruit.

Fruit will not set at night temperatures below 12°C (55°F) and day temperatures above 33°C (90°F). Night temperatures around 25°C (76°F) may well cause blossom to drop.

Tomatoes should be fed with a liquid general fertilizer until established, then with a high-potash fertilizer to encourage flowering and fruiting. Excessive feeding and watering spoils the flavour.

Keep crops weed-free by hoeing and hand weeding, taking care not to damage the stems, or mulch with a layer of organic matter.

Keep them constantly moist but not waterlogged;

Plum tomatoes, grown primarily for cooking and tomato paste because of their fuller flavour

erratic watering causes the fruits to split and also encourages 'blossom end rot', particularly when plants are grown in containers or grow-bags. Use tepid water. In dry conditions or when the first flowers appear they need about 11 litres (2 gal) water each week.

Careful watering and feeding is essential, particularly near harvest time to ensure that the fruits are not excessively watery and have a good flavour. Feed with tomato fertilizer according to the manufacturer's instructions.

Cordons need supporting with canes, strings or a frame. Using a sharp knife or by pinching between the finger and thumb, remove sideshoots when they appear and 'stop' plants by removing the growing tip 2–3 leaves above the top truss when 3–5 trusses have been formed or when the plant has reached the top of the support. The number of trusses on each plant depends on the growing season: in shorter growing seasons, leave fewer trusses. Remove any leaves below the lowest truss to encourage good air circulation.

In seasons when ripening is slow, remove some of the leaves near to the trusses with a sharp knife, exposing fruits to the sunshine.

To keep the fruit clean and stop fruit from rotting, grow bush tomatoes on a mulch of straw, felt or crop covers laid over the soil. Black polythene or even a split bin liner (with the edges anchored by burying them in the soil) absorbs heat, warms the soil, conserves moisture and helps fruit to ripen.

Rotate crops annually.

Maintenance
Spring Sow crops under cover and, later, outdoors.
Summer Keep crops watered, fed and weed-free. Shade and ventilate as necessary. Remove sideshoots. Harvest.
Autumn Ripen later outdoor

'Pearshaped' and currant tomatoes

crops under cloches or indoors.
Winter Harvest crops in mid-winter from cuttings taken in late summer.

Protected Cropping
In cooler climates, more reliable harvests can be achieved by growing tomatoes in an unheated greenhouse or polythene tunnels. Rotate crops to avoid the build-up of pests and diseases and sterilize or replace the soil every 2–3 years. Or use containers.

To assist pollination and fruit set, particularly of plants grown indoors, mist occasionally and tap the trusses once the flowers have formed; do this around midday if possible. (It is not so important for outdoor crops, as wind movement assists pollination.) Shade glasshouses before the heat of summer and ventilate well in warm conditions.

A fairly recent innovation is the 'Wall-o-Water', a series of connected plastic tubes filled with water which absorbs heat during the day and warms by radiated heat at night. This is reusable and

offers protection down to –8°C (16°F), extending the growing season and warming the soil. Adding roughly 1 part bleach to 500 parts water will prevent the formation of algae on the inside of the tubes.

For tomatoes at Christmas, take cuttings in mid-summer from sideshoots 13cm (5in) long and root them in a container of sharp sand or perlite and water. When roots appear they can be potted into 10cm (4in) pots and grown on under cover.

Protect newly planted outdoor tomatoes with cloches or floating crop covers until they become established. Once the first flowers are pushing against the cover, make slits along the centre; about 7–10 days later slit the remainder of the cover and leave as a shelter alongside the plants. 'Indeterminate' varieties can then be tied to canes.

Container Growing
Tomatoes are excellent for containers, pots or growbags, indoors or outside where they can be included in 'edible' displays in

window boxes, pots and hanging baskets.

Grow in 23cm (9in) pots of loam-based compost with high fertilizer levels. For requirements see 'Growing' and 'Protected Cropping'. Bushy varieties are ideal.

Plants in containers dry out rapidly, so careful feeding and watering is essential. Water regularly and remember to label your plants.

Harvesting & Storing
Harvest fruits as they ripen, about 7–8 weeks after planting for bush types and 10–12 weeks for cordon varieties. Lift and break the stem at the 'joint' just above the fruit. Outdoor crops should be harvested before the first frosts. Towards the end of the season, 'cordon' varieties with unripe fruit can be lifted by the roots and hung upside down in a frost-free shed to ripen. Alternatively, they can be detached from their support, laid on straw and covered with cloches or put in a drawer or a paper bag with a ripe banana or apple (the ethylene these produce

ripens the fruit). Bush and dwarf types can be ripened under cloches.

Tomatoes can be cooked and bottled in airtight jars. To freeze, skin and core when ripe, simmer for 5 minutes then sieve, cool and pack in a rigid container.

Tomatoes stay fresh for about 1 week in a polythene bag or the salad drawer of a refrigerator. To retain flavour they are better stored at 15°C (60°F).

Dry large 'meaty' tomatoes in the sun or the oven. Cut into halves or thirds and put skin side down on a tray and cover with a gauze frame as a protection from insects. Ideal drying conditions are in warm, dry windy weather, but they should be brought indoors at night if dew is likely to form. Humid conditions are not suitable for outdoor drying. Oven-dry just below 65°C (145°F) until tomatoes are dried but flexible. Stored in airtight containers in a cool place, they can last for up to 9 months. Before use put the tomatoes in boiling water or a 50:50 mix of boiling water and vinegar and allow them to stand until soft. Drain and marinate for several hours in olive oil with added garlic to suit your taste. They last in the marinade for about a month and are excellent with pasta and tomato sauce.

Pests & Diseases
Blossom end rot appears as a hard, dark flattened patch at the end of the fruit away from the stalk. This indicates a deficiency in calcium, usually caused by erratic watering. It is often a problem with plants grown in growbags. Water and feed regularly, particularly during hot weather. Erratic watering causes fruit to split, which may also happen with sudden growth after overcast weather. Pick and use split fruits immediately.

'Greenback', hard, green patches appearing near the stalk, caused by sun scorch and overheating, is more of a problem with plants growing under glass. Sometimes this becomes an internal condition known as 'whitewall'. Shade and ventilate well, water regularly and feed with a high-potash liquid fertilizer.

Curled leaves are caused by extreme temperature fluctuations between day and night. It is often a problem in greenhouses: shade, ventilate and damp down. Close ventilation before temperatures drop.

Whitefly, **aphids** and **red spider mite** can be a problem, as can **potato blight** in wet summers: dark blotches with lighter margins appear on the leaves. Spray with a copper fungicide before fruit set.

Plants with **verticillium wilt** droop during the day and usually recover overnight. Lower leaves turn yellow and cut stems have brown markings on the inside. Do not plant when the soil is cold, drench with a spray-strength solution of systemic fungicide, mist regularly and shade. Mounding moist compost round the stem encourages the formation of a secondary root system. The symptoms and control of **fusarium wilt** are similar.

Tobacco mosaic and other viruses show as mottling on the leaves, some of which may be misshapen; inside the fruit is browned and pitted and growth is stunted. Dispose of affected plants, wash your hands and sterilize tools by passing them through a flame. Grow the following year's plants in sterilized compost or in growbags.

Tomato moth caterpillars eat the fruit. They are about 4cm (1½in) long and green or brown with a pale lemon line along the body. They appear from late spring to early summer. Check the underside of leaves and squash the eggs. Also hand pick or spray plants with a biological control.

The symptoms of **magnesium deficiency** are yellowing between the leaf veins, older leaves being affected first. Spray, drench or scatter magnesium sulphate around the base.

Where possible, grow disease-resistant varieties.

COMPANION PLANTING

Grow with French marigolds to deter whitefly.

Tomatoes grow well with basil, parsley, alliums, nasturtiums and asparagus.

MEDICINAL

Tomatoes are believed to reduce the risk of cancer and appendicitis.

In American herbal medicine tomatoes have been used to treat dyspepsia, liver and kidney complaints and are also said to cure constipation.

WARNING

Some doctors believe that tomatoes aggravate arthritis and may be responsible for food allergies. The leaves and stems are poisonous.

Cherry tomatoes underplanted with thyme

CULINARY

In salads, tomatoes are particularly good with mozzarella, basil, olive oil and seasoning. They are also good with chives. Some people prefer to peel them first, by immersing in boiled water for 1 minute to loosen the skins. Use in soups, stews, sauces, pasta and omelettes. Gazpacho is a spicy cold soup of tomatoes, peppers, cucumbers and onions and is delicious.

Tomatoes are wonderful grilled: cut them in half and cover the cut surface with olive oil, pepper and sugar. Grill for 5 minutes. Alternatively, glaze them with wine and brown sugar and grill.

Try a 'BLT' – a cold bacon, lettuce and tomato sandwich. Eat 'currant' and 'cherry' varieties as a snack.

Use larger 'beefsteak' varieties as a garnish with steak or hollow out and stuff with shrimps, potato salad, cold salmon, cottage cheese or mashed curried egg. Serve hot or cold.

Green tomatoes can be sliced, dipped in batter and then breadcrumbs, and fried in hot oil, or made into chutney or jam. They can also be added to orange marmalade.

Tomato & Red Onion Salad

Stuffed Tomatoes
Serves 4

In times gone by Catholics all over Europe ate these on fast days, when meat was not allowed.

4 large ripe tomatoes
350g (12oz) white breadcrumbs
  (day-old bread)
150ml (¼pt) milk
2 eggs, lightly beaten
2 tablespoons chopped basil
2 tablespoons finely chopped
  parsley
2 cloves garlic, finely crushed
1 onion, finely chopped
2 tablespoons toasted breadcrumbs
5–6 tablespoons grated Gruyère
Olive oil
Salt & freshly ground black
  pepper

Remove a slice from the top of each tomato and scoop out the pulp. Season the insides of the tomatoes with salt and pepper, and arrange in a greased baking dish.

Preheat the oven to 180°C, 350°F, gas 4. To make the stuffing, combine the white breadcrumbs with the milk and eggs in a bowl and add the garlic, herbs and onions. Season with salt and pepper and fill the tomatoes.

Sprinkle over the toasted breadcrumbs and Gruyère and drizzle over a little olive oil to prevent burning. Bake until the tomatoes are tender, about 30 minutes.

Manihot esculenta (syn. M. utilissima). Euphorbiaceae

CASSAVA

(Tapioca, Yucca, Manioc)
Tall herbaceous perennial grown for edible tubers and leaves. Tender.
Value: mainly starch; small amounts of vitamin B, C and protein.

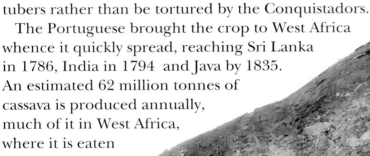

Mature cassava plants, Thailand

One of the most important food crops in the humid tropics, cassava is believed to have been cultivated since at least 2500BC. Unknown as a wild plant, it may have originated in equatorial South America in the Andean foothills, the Amazon basin or regions of savannah vegetation. The earliest archaeological records, from coastal Peru, date from 1000BC. Tubers contain highly toxic cyanide, which is removed by cooking; accounts tell of starving European explorers eating raw manioc and dying at the moment they thought sustenance had been found. The indigenous Indians tipped their arrows and blowpipe darts with its toxic sap; Arawak Indians committed suicide by biting into uncooked tubers rather than be tortured by the Conquistadors.

The Portuguese brought the crop to West Africa whence it quickly spread, reaching Sri Lanka in 1786, India in 1794 and Java by 1835. An estimated 62 million tonnes of cassava is produced annually, much of it in West Africa, where it is eaten as 'fufu'.

VARIETIES

Manihot esculenta is tall and branched, its stems becoming woody with age. The leaves are long-stalked, with 5–9 lobes; toxic latex is present in all parts of the plant. The swollen tubers are cylindrical or tapering, forming a cluster just below the soil surface, and weigh 5–10kg (11–22lb).

There are two types. **'White cassava'** is sweet, soft and used as a source of starch; **'yellow'** varieties are bitter and usually grown as a vegetable. The more primitive bitter varieties contain larger quantities of cyanide, which is washed out by boiling in several changes of water before cooking. In recent selections of 'sweet' varieties, most of the toxin is in the skin, and tubers are edible after simple cooking.

There are well over 100 different forms with local names. **'Nandeeba'**, quick to mature, and **'Macapera'**, used for boiling, are both from Brazil.

Propagation
Take cuttings from mature stems 15–30cm (6–12in) long; plant 1.2m (4ft) apart in rows 1m (3ft) apart or 'pits' 90–105cm (3–3 ½ft) square in a grid pattern. Planting cuttings upright, leaving the top 5cm (2in) exposed, gives best results. Plant cuttings at the start of the rainy season.

Growing
Cassava flourishes where the warm rainy season is followed by a dry period. It has good resistance to drought; in a constantly wet climate, there is excessive

Heaps of harvested cassava roots for sale in an Indian market

stem growth and tuber formation is poor. Soils should be deep, rich and free-draining. It is often grown on ridges or mounds as it dislikes waterlogging. Dig deeply before planting, adding well-rotted organic matter. Earth up as necessary. Cassava is a heavy feeder and cannot usually be grown for more than 3 years on the same ground.

Maintenance
Spring Dig in organic matter before planting.
Summer Plant cuttings at the start of the rainy season.
Autumn Keep weed-free.
Winter Harvest at maturity.

Protected cropping
In cool temperate zones, plants can be grown as a 'novelty crop' in a hothouse. Prepare the borders and cultivate as for 'Growing'. Water well during the growing season and reduce watering during winter.

Harvesting & Storing
Varieties are harvested from 8 months to 2 years after planting, depending on the locality and variety. Harvest when plants have flowered and the leaves are yellow. Lift the whole plant and carefully remove the tubers. They store for up to 2 years in the ground, but should be used within 4–5 days of lifting.

PESTS & DISEASES

White fly and **fungal diseases** can be a problem. **Bacterial diseases**, **scale** and **cassava mosaic** are a severe problem in Africa.

Plants are highly resistant to locusts.

OTHER USES

Cassava is also a source of starch for the manufacture of plywood, textiles, adhesives and paper.

WARNING

All parts of the plant contain toxic latex. Prepare tubers thoroughly before eating. Inhabitants of Guyana take chillies steeped in rum as an antidote to yucca poisoning, but do not rely on it!

Harvesting cassava plants, Indonesia

CULINARY

The fresh root is equivalent in starch to 33.3% of its weight in rice and 50% in bread, but its nutritional value is unbalanced and high consumption often leads to protein deficiency.

Wash thoroughly and remove the skin and rind with a sharp knife or potato peeler. Boil in several changes of water and allow to dry before cooking.

It can be eaten mashed or boiled as a vegetable or made into dumplings and cakes. Mix with coconut and sugar to make biscuits. The juice from grated cassava is boiled down and flavoured with cinnamon, cloves and brown sugar to make 'cassareep', a powerful antiseptic and essential to the West Indian dish, Pepperpot. Tapioca flour is made from ground chips.

In Africa the fresh root is washed, peeled, boiled and pounded with a wooden pestle to make 'fufu'. Cook cassava chunks in boiling water for 45–50 minutes, drain, cool, pound into dough and shape into egg-sized balls to add to soups and stews as a traditional African accompaniment.

Roots of 'sweet' forms can be roasted like sweet potato, baked or fried in slices.

Young leaves can be boiled or steamed and eaten with a knob of butter.

Cassava Chips (Singkong)

These thin, crispy wafers are perfect served as a snack or as a garnish. Allow 300g (10oz) per person to accompany a plain meat course.

Slice the cassava very thinly and leave to dry. Heat some peanut or vegetable oil (do not allow it to smoke) in a wok or a deep pan. Deep fry 1–3 slices at a time by immediately submerging each below the surface of the oil. Remove quickly from the heat and drain well on layers of paper towels.

Cooked Singkong can be stored in an airtight container for several weeks, but is best served at once.

Medicago sativa. Leguminosae

ALFALFA

(Lucerne, Purple Medick) Grown as annual or short-lived perennial for seed sprouts and young leaf shoots. Hardy. Value: good source of iron, higher in protein than most vegetables.

'Medick' comes from the Latin *Herba medica*, the Median or Persian herb, imported to Greece after Darius found it in the kingdom of the Medes. It was a vital fodder crop of ancient civilizations in the Near East and Mediterranean, and known in Britain by 1757. Today, alfalfa is valued by gardeners as a green manure as well as a nutritious vegetable. Its blooms in the wildflower meadow are rich in nectar, while the leaves are a commercial source of chlorophyll.

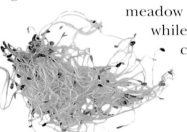

VARIETIES

The species *Medicago sativa* is a fast-growing evergreen legume with clover-like leaves; growing ultimately to 1m (3.5ft), it has spikes of violet and blue flowers. It produces quality crops on poor soils, as it is highly effective at fixing nitrogen in the root nodules.

Penetrating up to 6m (20ft) into the ground, the roots draw up nutrients and aerate the soil. Agricultural varieties are available. If you want to sprout alfalfa seeds, buy untreated seed; that sold for sowing as a crop is usually chemically treated.

CULTIVATION

Alfalfa can be grown as a short-lived perennial, a 'cut and come again' crop or as seedsprouts. It tolerates low rainfall and can be grown in any soil, in temperate to sub-tropical conditions or at altitude in the tropics.

Propagation

Sow in spring or from late summer to autumn. Thin those grown as perennials to 25cm (10in) apart when large enough to handle. Sow 'cut and come again' crops, spaced evenly, by broadcasting or in shallow drills 10–12.5cm (4–5in) wide.

Growing

Prepare seedbeds in winter, fork the area, remove debris and stones, rake level. Keep weed-free until established. Cut perennials to within a few inches of the base after flowering and renew every 3–4 years, as old plants become straggly.

Maintenance

Spring Sow seed outdoors.
Summer Harvest young shoots from perennials.
Autumn Sow protected crops.
Winter Prepare seedbed.

Protected Cropping

Sow under cloches, horticultural fleece or glass in late summer to autumn for winter cropping.

Container Growing

Sow 'cut and come again' crops in a bright open position in a loam-based compost with low fertilizer levels; water pots regularly.

Harvesting

Harvest 'cut and come again' crops when about 5cm (2in) long a few weeks after sowing. Cut back plants regularly to encourage new growth; they provide young growths for 4–5 years.

Sprouting Seeds

To sprout alfalfa, soak seeds overnight or for several hours, tip seeds into a sieve and rinse. Put several layers of moist paper towel or blotting paper in the base of a jar and cover with a 5mm (¼in) layer of seed. Cut a square from a pair of tights or piece of muslin to cover the top, securing with a band. Place in a bright position, away from direct sun, maintaining constant temperatures around 20°C (68°F). Rinse seed daily by filling the jar with water and pouring off again. Harvest shoots after 3–7 days, when they have nearly filled the jar. Wash and dry sprouts and use as required; do not store more than 2 days.

Pests & Diseases

Rabbits can be a problem.

CULINARY

Young shoot tips and sprouted seeds can be used raw in salads or cooked lightly.

For a tasty salad, try it with hard-boiled eggs (1 per person), anchovies and capers served on a bed of endive and radicchio leaves. To stir-fry, pour a little oil in a pan, add the alfalfa, stir briskly for 2 minutes; serve immediately.

COMPANION PLANTING

Alfalfa accumulates phosphorus, potassium, iron and magnesium; it keeps grass green longer in drought.

MEDICINAL

An infusion of young leaves in water is used to increase vitality, appetite and weight. The young shoots, rich in minerals and vitamin B, are highly nutritious and the seeds appear to reduce cholesterol levels.

Momordica charantia. Cucurbitaceae

KARELA

(Bitter Gourd, Balsam Pear, Bitter Cucumber, Momordica) Annual climber grown for edible fruits and leaves. Tender. Value: fruit a good source of iron, ascorbic acid and vitamin C; leaves and young shoots contain traces of minerals.

The odd-looking, slender fruit have a blistered, puckered skin

This strange-looking fruit with skin the texture of a crocodile has been grown throughout the humid tropics for centuries. Rudyard Kipling's description in Mowgli's 'Song Against People' conveys the plant's vigour as it climbs to 4m (12ft) with the aid of tendrils:

I will let loose against you the fleet-footed vines,
I will call in the Jungle to stamp out your lines.
The roofs shall fade before it, the house-beams
*   shall fall;*
And the Karela shall cover it all.

The strongly vanilla-scented flowers are followed by the elongated fruit. When ripe, it splits at the tip into three sections, exposing brown or white flattened seeds surrounded by blood-red pulp. The fruits are better eaten young.

CULTIVATION

Male and female flowers are borne on the same plant. Male flowers are 5–10cm (2–4in) long; females are similar, but with a slender basal bract. The fruit can grow up to 25cm (10in) – which ripens to become orange-yellow, though a white variety is grown in India and eastern Asia.

Propagation
In humid tropical climates sow at the start of the rainy season, placing 2–3 seeds outdoors in 'stations' 90cm (36in) apart, in and between the rows. Thin after germination, leaving the strongest seedling. Water plants as necessary.

The first flowers appear 30 to 35 days after sowing. In temperate zones, sow seed in early spring under glass at 20°C (68°F) in peat-substitute compost. Keep the compost moist with tepid water and repot as necessary when the roots become visible through the drainage holes.

Growing
Karela flourish in moderate to high temperatures with sunshine and high humidity. Plant in beds or mounds of rich, moisture-retentive, free-draining soil. Dig in plenty of well-rotted manure or similar organic matter before sowing.

Pinch out the terminal shoots when they are 3–4cm (1¼–1½in) long to encourage branching, then train the stems into trees, or over fences, arbours, trellis or frames covered with 15cm (6in) mesh netting. Keep plants constantly moist and weed-free throughout the growing season.

Maintenance

Spring Sow seed under glass in peat-substitute compost.
Summer Keep plants well fed and watered.
Autumn When cropping finishes add leaves and stems to your compost heap
Winter Prepare the greenhouse border for the following year's crop.

Container Growing

Plants can be grown indoors in containers containing a rich, well-drained potting mixture of equal parts loam-based compost and well-rotted organic matter with added peat and grit.

Keep the compost moist with tepid water and feed every 2 weeks with a liquid general fertilizer.

Protected Cropping

Grow under cover in temperate zones. Plants need hot, humid conditions in bright light. When growing plants in the greenhouse border, prepare the soil as for 'Growing'.

Growth is better restricted in borders and containers. Stop the shoot tips when the main stems are 1.5m (5ft) long, training the lateral stems along wires or trellis.

Once a flower has formed, allow 2 more leaves to appear, then pinch out the growing tip. If it is a male flower or a flower does not form, cut the stem back to the first leaf to allow a replacement to form. Flowers should be hand pollinated.

You should damp down the greenhouse floor regularly during hot weather.

Harvesting & Storing

The first fruits appear about 2 months after sowing and should be harvested when they are about 2cm (1in) long and are yellow-green in colour. They can be eaten when longer.

Fruits can be kept in a cool dark place for several days or stored in the salad drawer of a refrigerator for 4 weeks. Karela can also be sliced and dried for use out of season.

Ripe fruit showing crimson seeds

PESTS & DISEASES

Fruit fly is common; spray with contact insecticide or protect the fruits with a piece of paper wrapped round the fruit and tied with string round the stalk. **Red spider mite** is a common pest under cover. Leaves become mottled and bronzed. Check plants regularly; small infestations are easily controlled – isolate young plants. The mite prefer hot, dry conditions, so keep humidity high. Spray with derris.

MEDICINAL

The fruits are said to be tonic, stomachic and carminative and are a herbal remedy for rheumatism, gout, and diseases of the liver and spleen. In Brazil, the seeds are used as an anthelmintic. Its fruits, leaves and roots are used in India and Puerto Rico for diabetes. In India, leaves are applied to burns and as a poultice for headaches and the roots used to treat haemorrhoids. In Malaya they are used as a poultice for elephants with sore eyes.

CULINARY

Remove the seeds from mature fruit, and remove any bitterness by salting. Young fruits do not need to be salted.

Karela are ideal diced in curries, Chop Suey or pickles, stuffed with meat, shrimps, spices and onions and fried or added to meat and fish dishes. Mature fruits can be parboiled before adding to a dish or cooked like courgettes and eaten as a vegetable.

Young shoots and leaves are cooked like spinach.

Pelecing Peria
Serves 4

Sri Owen gives this recipe in her marvellous book, *Indonesian Food and Cookery*. Some of the ingredients need determination to track down, but it is worth the trouble.

3-4 karela (peria)
Salt
6 cabé rawit (or hot red chillies)
3 candlenuts
2 cloves garlic
1 piece terasi (shrimp paste, available at Thai shops)
1 tablespoon vegetable oil
Juice of 1 lime

Cut the karela lengthwise in half, take out the seeds, then slice like cucumbers. Put the slices into a colander, sprinkle liberally with salt and leave for at least 30 minutes. Wash under cold running water before boiling for 3 minutes with a little salt.

Pound the cabé rawit, candlenuts, garlic and terasi in a mortar until smooth. Heat the oil in a wok or frying pan and fry for about 1 minute. Add the karela and stir-fry for 2 minutes; season with salt and lime juice. Serve hot or cold.

Rorippa nasturtium-aquaticum. Brassicaceae (syn. Nasturtium officinale. Cruciferae)

WATERCRESS

**(Summer Watercress) Usually aquatic perennial grown for pungent, edible leaves and stems. Hardy.
Value: excellent source of beta carotene, vitamins C and E, calcium, iron and iodine.**

This highly nutritious aquatic herb, a native of Europe, North Africa and Asia, has been cultivated as a salad plant since Roman times and is grown throughout the world's temperate zones. It has become a weed in North America and New Zealand. Pliny records the Latin derivation of its original generic name as *Nasus tortus*, meaning 'writhing nose' – referring to its spicy taste and pungent odour; *officinale* is often applied to plants with medicinal uses. Watercress was listed as an aphrodisiac in Dioscorides' *Materia Medica* of AD77.

It was mentioned in early Irish poetry around the twelfth century – 'Well of Traigh Dha Bhan, Lovely is your pure-topped cress' and, 'Watercress, little green-topped one, on the brink of the blackbirds' well...' Early references to the shamrock are believed to be watercress. Evidence to support this comes from Ireland's County Meath and Shamrock Well, whose watercress was still remembered in the 1940s as 'the finest in the district'. Watercress was also known in Ireland as 'St Patrick's Cabbage'. The first records of commercial cultivation are from Germany around 1750, France between 1800 and 1811 and near Gravesend in England, around 1808.

CULTIVATION

Found in and alongside fast-flowing rivers and streams, watercress has fleshy, glossy leaves on long stalks with 5 to 10 leaflets. Its long stems creep or float on the surface and root easily. Small whitish-green flowers appear in flat-topped clusters from mid-spring to early autumn.

The best watercress is grown in pure, fast-flowing chalk or limestone streams with slightly alkaline water. This avoids the risk of contamination from pollution, which can cause stomach upsets.

Propagation
The easiest way to propagate watercress is from shop-bought material. Cuttings 10cm (4in) long take only about a week to root when placed in a glass of water.

If you live by a fast-flowing stream, plant rooted cuttings 15cm (6in) apart in the banks. Firm well to prevent them from being dislodged.

To grow watercress in the garden, dig a trench 60cm (2ft) wide and 30cm (12in) deep, put a 15cm (6in) layer of well-rotted farmyard manure or compost into the base, mix in a little ground limestone if your soil is not alkaline, then cover with 7.5–10cm (3–4in) of soil. Plant cuttings 15cm (6in) apart in mid-spring. (Do not use sheep manure as it can carry dangerous liver fluke.)

Alternatively, in spring, mark out an area and dig in well-rotted organic matter and ground limestone, firm and soak with water before scattering seed thinly on the surface. Water daily.

Seeds can also be sown indoors from mid- to late spring, in a propagator or trays of peat-substitute seed compost on a window sill. Cover the seeds with 3mm (⅛in) of compost, keep it constantly moist at around 10–15°C (50–60°F).

Transplant 3–4 seedlings into a 7.5cm (3in) pot when large enough to handle, then plant out 10–15cm (4–6in) apart from mid-spring onwards. When plants deteriorate replace them with fresh cuttings.

Growing
Plants grown in the garden need a bright, sheltered position away from direct sunshine; never allow it to dry out, or plants run to seed. As a cool-season crop, watercress grows most actively in spring and autumn, and during the winter in warmer climates.

Occasional feeding with a dilute high-nitrogen liquid fertilizer or liquid seaweed may be needed. Do not grow in stagnant or still water.

Maintenance
Spring Take cuttings or sow seed mid- to late spring.
Summer Do not let compost-grown plants dry out. Keep weed-free. Harvest as needed. Remove flower heads as they appear.
Autumn Continue to harvest.
Winter Protect with cloches for continuous growth.

Protected Cropping
Cover plants with cloches, fleece or polythene tunnels before the first frosts. Make a watercress bed in an unheated greenhouse over winter, or grow in pots.

Container Growing
Grow in large pots or containers of moist

Wild watercress by a fast-flowing stream, Guernsey

eat-substitute compost, ith a layer of gravel in the ase, spacing 10–15cm (4–6in) apart. Keep compost moist by standing the pot in bowl of water which is eplaced daily. Grow plants n a bright window sill, but way from direct sunshine.

Harvesting & Storing

Older leaves near the stem ips have the best flavour. Harvest lightly during the first season and annually towards autumn if plants are to be overwintered, cutting regularly for a constant supply of bushy shoots.

Use leaves fresh or store in the salad compartment of a refrigerator for 2–3 days.

PESTS & DISEASES

Watercress is rarely troubled, but caterpillars of **cabbage white butterfly** may cause problems.

MEDICINAL

Watercress has been valued for its medicinal qualities since antiquity. It has been eaten to cure rheumatism, and used as a diuretic and as an expectorant for catarrh, colds and bronchitis; it is a stimulant, a digestive and a tonic to promote appetite, counteract anaemia and also to lower blood-sugar levels in diabetes.

Externally it is a hair tonic. Rubbed on the skin it is said to remove rashes. Culpeper recommended the bruised leaves or juice for clearing spots and freckles and a poultice was said to heal glandular tumours and lymphatic swellings.

Traditionally it was taken as a spring tonic. In the past,

in isolated parts of the British Isles where the diet was predominantly shellfish and salt meat, it was often grown to prevent scurvy, and was so mentioned by Philip Miller in his *Gardener's Dictionary* of 1731.

Unless harvested regularly, watercress develops small white flowers. Once flowered, the leaves are less tender

CULINARY

As with its relative the radish, the hot, spicy taste of watercress comes from mustard oil. Remove discoloured leaves and wash thoroughly, shaking off excess water. Eat in salads and stir-fries, or liquidize to make chilled soup. It makes a perfect garnish for sandwiches. Chop finely and add to butter, mashed potatoes, dumplings or a white sauce. Also sauté in butter for 10 minutes and serve as a vegetable.

Among her many tastebud-tingling recipes, Jane Grigson suggests cutting orange segments into quarters and mixing with watercress, olive oil vinaigrette and black pepper; add walnuts or black olives and eat as a salad with ham, duck or veal.

Salmon with Watercress Sauce
Serves 6

6 salmon fillets, trimmed
4 tablespoons butter
4 tablespoons finely chopped shallots
2 large bunches watercress, plus sprigs to garnish
150ml (¼pt) double cream
Salt & freshly ground black pepper

WARNING

Gathering from streams is not recommended if sheep are grazing near by, as there is a risk of liver fluke. Fluke can be destroyed by thorough cooking.

Steam the salmon fillets, covered, on a steamer rack over boiling water until cooked; this should take 10 minutes or so.

Meanwhile, prepare the sauce by melting the butter in a heavy frying pan and sautéing the shallots until softened. Add the watercress and, constantly stirring, allow the watercress to wilt for about 2 minutes; it should retain its bright green colour. Stir in the cream and seasoning and bring to the boil. Remove from the heat and blend in a liquidizer until smooth. Then reheat gently.

Arrange the salmon fillets in the centre of individual plates and spoon sauce over each, garnishing with a little fresh watercress.

Oxalis tuberosa. Oxalidaceae

OCA

(Iribia, cuiba, New Zealand yam) Perennial grown for tubers. Half hardy. Value: about 85% water with some carbohydrates and small amounts of protein.

This is common in the high-altitude Andes from Venezuela to northern Argentina, where it is second only to the potato in popularity. At the northern end of Lake Titicaca, more than 150 steep terraces dating from the Incas are still cultivated. Oca is grown in New Zealand, where it was introduced from Chile in 1869. Today it is rarely found in European or American gardens, though it was once grown as a potato substitute. Tubers form in autumn when day lengths are less than 9 hours.

VARIETIES

Oxalis tuberosa is bushy to 25cm (10in) tall, with tri-lobed leaves and orange-yellow flowers. It produces small tubers 5–10cm (2–4in) long which are yellow, white, pink, black or piebald.

CULTIVATION

Propagation
Plant single tubers or slice into several sections, each with an 'eye' or dormant bud and dust the cut surfaces with fungicide.

Plant 12.5cm (5in) deep and 30cm (1ft) apart with 30cm (1ft) between rows. In frost-free climates plant in mid-spring; in cooler areas propagate undercover in 12.5–20cm (5–8in) pots of compost before planting out once frosts have passed.

Growing
Oca flourish in deep fertile soils, so incorporate organic matter before planting. Earthing up before planting increases the yield.

Maintenance
Spring Plant tubers.
Summer Water as necessary.

Exposed tubers, New Zealand

Autumn Tubers can be lifted when needed.
Winter Store tubers in sand.

Protected Cropping
Where early or late frosts are likely, grow under cover to extend the harvest season. Plant in mid-spring in greenhouse borders. Harvest from mid-autumn to early winter. Extend outdoor cropping by protecting with horticultural fleece or cloches.

Container Growing
Oca grow well in containers, although yields are lower. Tubers should be planted in spring in 30cm (12in) pots in loam-based compost with moderate fertilizer levels, with added organic matter.

Regular watering is vital, particularly as tubers begin to form. Allow the compost surface to dry out before rewatering. An occasional feed with liquid fertilizer helps to boost growth.

Harvesting & Storing
About 8 months after planting, check to see if the tubers are mature, then lift carefully. Undamaged tubers can be stored in boxes of sand in a dry frost-free place.

Pests & Diseases
Slugs are often a problem.

COMPANION PLANTING

Oca grow well with potatoes and can be grown under runner beans, maize or crops of a similar height.

WARNING

Prepare tubers correctly before eating to remove calcium oxalate crystals.

CULINARY

Tubers have been selected over the centuries for flavour and reduced levels of calcium oxalate crystals, which otherwise render them inedible. Leave them for a few days to become soft before eating. In South America they are dried in the sun until floury and less acid. If dried for several weeks, they become sweet, tasting similar to dried figs.

The acidity can be removed by boiling in several changes of water. The flavour of tubers even improves once frozen.

Oca can be eaten raw, roasted, boiled, candied like sweet potato and added to soups and stews. Use leaves and young shoots in salads or cook them like sorrel.

Oca & Bacon

Clean 500g (1lb) oca and cut into cubes. Boil in salted water until just tender; drain and combine with 250g (½lb) smoked bacon which has been diced and fried. Coat with mayonnaise, sprinkle over fresh chives and season. Serve warm.

Pastinaca sativa. Umbelliferae

PARSNIP

*Biennial grown as annual for edible root. Hardy.
Value: some carbohydrate, moderate vitamin E,
smaller amounts of vitamins C and B.*

This ancient vegetable is thought to have originated around the eastern Mediterranean. Exactly when it was introduced into cultivation is uncertain as references to parsnips and carrots seem interchangeable in Greek and Roman literature: Pliny used the word *pastinaca* in the first century AD when referring to both. Tiberius Caesar was said to have imported parsnips from Germany, where they flourished along the Rhine – though it is possible that the Celts brought them back from their forays to the east long before that. In the Middle Ages, the roots were valued medicinally for treating problems as diverse as toothache, swollen testicles and stomach ache. In sixteenth-century Europe parsnips were used as animal fodder, and the country name of 'madneps' or 'madde neaps' reflects the fear that delirium and madness would be brought about by eating the roots.

Introduced to North America by early settlers, they were grown in Virginia by 1609 and were soon accepted by the American Indians, who readily took up parsnip growing. They were used as a sweetener until the development of sugar beet in the nineteenth century; the juices were evaporated and the brown residue used as honey. Parsnip wine was considered by some to be equal in quality to Malmsey and parsnip beer was often drunk in Ireland. In Italy pigs bred for the best-quality Parma ham are fed on parsnips.

VARIETIES

Roots are 'bulbous' (stocky, with rounded shoulders), 'wedge' types (broad and long-rooted) or 'bayonet' (similar, but long and narrow in shape).

'**Alba**' has small, thin wedge- and bayonet-shaped roots and good canker resistance. '**All American**' has wedge-shaped roots and is sweet-tasting. '**Avonresister**' is small with bulbous roots, and excellent resistance to canker and bruising. It is sweet-tasting, performs well on poorer soil and grows rapidly. '**Cobham Improved Marrow**'* is wedge-shaped, medium in size and well-flavoured. Resistant to canker. '**Exhibition Long**' is extra-long, with an excellent flavour. '**Gladiator**' produces large, vigorous, well-shaped and fine-flavoured roots with good canker resistance. '**Javelin**'* is wedge- or bayonet-shaped, high-yielding and canker-resistant; 'fanging' rarely occurs. '**Hollow Crown**' has fine, mild, tender flesh and crops well. '**New White Skin**' has uniform, wedge-shaped roots and a pure white skin. Good canker resistance. '**Student**' has long slender roots and is very tasty. It originated around 1810 from a wild parsnip found in the grounds of the Royal Agricultural College, Cirencester, England. '**Tender and True**'* is an old variety. Very tasty, tender and sweet, it has very little core. '**White Gem**' has wedge-shaped to bulbous smooth roots, with delicious flesh and good canker resistance. It is ideal for heavier soils.

Parsnips cultivated commercially are also rotated; seen growing here in Devon, England

CULTIVATION

Propagation

Parsnip seed must always be sown fresh, as it rapidly loses the ability to germinate. Seeds are also renowned for erratic, slow germination in the cold, wet conditions which often prevail early in the year when they are traditionally sown.

To avoid poor germination, sow later, from mid- to late spring, depending on the weather and soil conditions, when the ground is workable and temperatures are over 7°C (45°F).

Warm the soil with cloches or horticultural fleece a few weeks before sowing. Rake in a granular general fertilizer at 60g/sq m (2oz/sq yd) 1–2 weeks before sowing. Rake the seedbed to a fine texture before sowing.

Sow *in situ* on a still day so the light, papery seeds are not blown away. In dry conditions, water drills before sowing 2–3 seeds at the recommended final spacing in 'stations', thinning to leave the strongest seedling after germination. Sow radishes between the stations to act as a marker crop indicating where slower-germinating parsnip seeds are sown.

Alternatively, sow thinly in drills 5mm to 1cm (¼ to

'Hollow Crown Improved' lifted and washed, ready for use

½in) deep, sowing shorter-rooted varieties in rows 15–20cm (6–8in) apart, thinning to 5–10cm (2–4in), and larger types in rows 30cm (12in) apart, thinning to 13–20cm (5–8in).

In stony soil make a hole up to 90 x 15cm (36 x 6in) with a crowbar, fill with finely sieved soil or compost, sow 2–3 seeds in the centre of the hole and thin to leave the strongest seedling. Grow short-rooted varieties in shallow soils.

Growing

Parsnips thrive in an open or lightly shaded site on light, free-draining, stone-free soil which was manured the previous year.

Traditionally, parsnips are not grown on freshly manured soil as this causes 'fanging', or forking of the roots; however, recent research has not supported this. Dig the plot and add plenty of well-rotted organic matter in autumn or early winter the previous year. Deep digging is particularly important when growing long-rooted varieties.

The ideal pH is 6.5–7.0; lime where necessary, as roots grown in acid soil are prone to canker. Rotate with other roots.

Keep crops weed-free, by hoeing or hand weeding carefully to avoid damaging the roots, or by mulching with well-rotted organic matter. Do not let the soil dry out, as erratic watering causes roots to split. Water at 16–22 litres/sq m (3–4 gal/sq yd) every 2 weeks during dry weather when the roots are swelling.

Maintenance

Spring Rake the seedbed to a fine tilth, apply general fertilizer, sow seed in modules, 'fluid sow', or sow *in situ* when the soil is warm. *Summer* Keep crops weed-free by mulching, hand weeding or careful hoeing. *Autumn* Harvest crops. *Winter* Cover crops with straw or bracken before the

Wild parsnip bears little resemblance to its cultivated counterparts and is less tasty

onset of inclement weather. Dig the soil for the following year's crop.

Protected Cropping

Possible germination problems can be avoided by pre-germinating and fluid-sowing seed, or by sowing in modules under cover and transplanting before the tap root starts to develop.

Container Growing

Shorter-rooted varieties can be grown in large containers of loam-based compost. Longer types are grown in large barrels, making a deep hole in the compost as described above for stony soil. Make sure that containers are well drained.

Harvesting & Storing

Parsnips are a long-term crop and occupy the ground for around 8 months – a factor worth bearing in mind if your garden is small. Roots are extremely hardy and can remain in the ground until required.

Harvest from mid-autumn onwards, covering plants with straw, bracken or hessian for ease of lifting in frosty weather. Make sure you lift them carefully with a fork to avoid root damage.

Lift all your roots by late winter and store them in boxes of moist sand, peat substitute or wood shavings in a cool shed.

Parsnips have a better flavour when they have been

exposed for a few weeks to temperatures around freezing point. (This changes stored starch to sugar, increasing sweetness and improving the flavour.) Stored in a polythene bag in the refrigerator, they remain fresh for up to 2 weeks.

Wash, trim and peel roots, then cube and blanch in boiling water for 5 minutes before freezing them in polythene bags.

PESTS & DISEASES

Parsnip canker is a black, purple or orange-brown rot, often starting in the crown, which can be a problem during drought, when the crown is damaged or the soil is too rich. There is no chemical control. Sow crops later, improve drainage, keep the pH around neutral, rotate crops and sow canker-resistant varieties. **Carrot fly** can also be a problem.

COMPANION PLANTING

Sow rapidly germinating radish and lettuces between rows. Parsnips grow well alongside peas and lettuce, providing they are not in the shade.

Plant next to carrots and leave a few to flower the following year as they attract beneficial insects.

MEDICINAL

In Roman times, parsnip seeds and roots were regarded as an aphrodisiac.

CULINARY

In seventeenth-century England there are records of parsnip bread and 'sweet and delicate parsnip cakes'. They were often eaten with salt fish and were a staple during Lent.

Scrub rather than peel parsnips, and use boiled, baked, mashed or roasted with beef, pork or chicken. They combine particularly well with carrots.

Parsnips can be lightly cooked and eaten cold. Parboil and fry like chips or slice into rings, dip in batter and eat as fritters. Grate into salads, add chopped and peeled to casseroles or soups. Or parboil, drain, then stew in butter and garnish with parsley. They are also good parboiled, then grilled with a sprinkling of Parmesan. Try steaming them whole, slicing them lengthways and pan-glazing with butter, brown sugar and nutmeg, or garnishing them with chopped walnuts and a dash of sweet sherry.

Purée of Parsnips

Boil some parsnips and mix them with an equal quantity of mashed potatoes, plenty of salt and freshly ground black pepper, a little grated orange rind, a splash of thick cream and enough butter to make a smooth dish. Sprinkle with chopped flat-leaf parsley and serve piping hot. (Puréed parsnips are also wonderful combined with carrots and seasoned with nutmeg.)

Curried Parsnip Soup
Serves 4–6

1kg (2lb) parsnips
1 large onion, sliced
1 tablespoon butter
2 cloves garlic, crushed
1 good teaspoon curry powder
1 x 400g (14oz) tin chopped tomatoes
1 litre (1¾pt) vegetable stock
1 bay leaf
Sprig each of thyme & parsley
4–6 teaspoons yoghurt
Salt & freshly ground black pepper
Chopped parsley, to garnish

Clean the parsnips and peel if old. Chop them roughly. Add the onion to a large soup pot with the butter and garlic and sauté over a medium heat until lightly browned (this helps to give the flavour of Indian cuisine). Stir in the curry powder and continue to cook for 1 minute, stirring constantly.

Then add the parsnips and stir, coating them well in the curry and onion mixture, and add the tomatoes, stock and herbs. Stir thoroughly. Season, bring to the boil and simmer, covered, for about 15–20 minutes, until the parsnips are tender.

Remove the herbs. Then liquidize the soup, adjust the seasoning and garnish with yoghurt and parsley. This is delicious served with crusty bread.

Curried Parsnip Soup

Petroselinum crispum var. *tuberosum. Umbelliferae*

HAMBURG PARSLEY

The leaves look similar to those of flat-leaved parsley

(Parsley Root, Turnip-rooted Parsley) Swollen-rooted biennial, usually grown as annual for roots and leaves. Hardy. Value: root contains starch and sugar; leaves high in beta carotene, vitamin C and iron.

Hamburg parsley is an excellent dual-purpose vegetable. The tapering white root looks and tastes similar to parsnip and can be eaten cooked or raw. The finely cut, flat, dark green leaves resemble parsley; they are coarser in texture, but contribute a parsley flavour and can be used as garnish. As an added bonus it grows in partial shade, is very hardy and an ideal winter vegetable.

Popular in Central Europe and in Germany, it is one of several vegetables and herbs known as *Suppengrun* or 'soup greens' which are added to the water when beef or poultry is boiled and later used for making sauce or soup. Introduced from Holland to England in the eighteenth century, this versatile vegetable enjoyed only a relatively brief period of popularity, but should certainly be more widely grown by Britain's gardeners.

CULTIVATION

Hamburg parsley needs a long growing season to develop good-sized roots. Grow it in moisture-retentive soil in an open or semi-shaded position.

Propagation
As seeds are sown early in the year, it may be necessary to cover the bed with cloches or polythene before sowing to warm up the soil. Sow from early to mid-spring in drills 1cm (½in) deep and 25–30cm (10–12in) apart, thinning seedlings to a final spacing of 20cm (9in).

They can also be sown in 'stations', planting 3–4 seeds in clusters 23cm (9in) apart. Thin to leave the strongest seedling when they are large enough to handle.

Seeds can also be sown in modules, but should be planted in their final position before the tap root begins to form.

To extend the harvesting season, make a second sowing in mid-summer, which will provide crops early the following year.

Growing
Dig in plenty of well-rotted organic matter the autumn before planting or plant in an area where the soil has been manured for the previous crop.

Rake the soil finely before sowing. Germination is often slow and it is important that the seedbed is kept free of weeds, particularly in the early stages.

Use a hoe with care as the plants become established to avoid damaging the roots. Mulching established plants is a sensible option as this stifles weed growth and conserves moisture. A 2.5cm (1in) layer of well-rotted compost will perform the task perfectly. Root splitting can occur if plants are watered after the soil has dried out, so water thoroughly and regularly during dry periods to maintain steady growth.

Maintenance
Spring Sow seeds outdoors, warming the soil if necessary. Seeds can also be sown in modules.
Summer Keep crops weed-free, water during drought and make a second sowing in mid-summer for early crops the following year.
Autumn Harvest as required.
Winter Cover crops with bracken or similar protection to make lifting easier in severe weather.

Container Growing
Hamburg parsley can be grown in containers if they are deep enough not to dry out rapidly and provide sufficient space for the roots to form. Regular watering is vital and plants should also be kept out of scorching, bright sunshine.

Harvesting & Storing
This is such a hardy vegetable that it can remain in the ground until required

any time from early autumn to mid-spring. When frosts are forecast, cover with straw, bracken or a similar material to make lifting easier. After removing the foliage, store in a box of sand or peat substitute in a cool shed or garage; some of the flavour is lost when roots are stored in this way, so they are better left in the ground if possible.

PESTS & DISEASES

This tough vegetable is generally trouble-free, but it can suffer from **parsnip canker**. This appears as dark patches on the root. Control is impossible, but the following measures will help. Dig up and dispose of affected plants immediately, ensure that the soil is well drained, rotate crops and maintain the soil at a pH around neutral.

COMPANION PLANTING

When 'station sowing', fill the spaces by planting 'Tom Thumb' or a similar lettuce variety. Sowing radishes between 'stations' is also useful because their rapid germination indicates the position of the Hamburg parsley and prevents your accidentally removing any newly germinated seedlings when weeding.

WARNING

Hamburg parsley should not be eaten in large amounts by expectant mothers or those with kidney problems.

Hamburg parsley, showing its small parsnip-like roots – rarely seen in greengrocers in the UK

CULINARY

The flavour reminiscent of celeriac, Hamburg parsley is frequently used in Eastern European cooking.

Prepare for cooking by removing the leaves and fine roots, then gently scrubbing to remove the soil: don't peel or scrape. Try Hamburg parsley sliced, cubed and cooked like parsnips (sprinkle cut areas with lemon juice to prevent discoloration). It is delicious roasted, sautéed or fried like chips as well as boiled, steamed or added to soups and stews. It can also be grated raw in winter salads.

Dried roots can be used as a flavouring. Dry them on a shallow baking tray in an oven heated to 80°C (170°F); allow to cool before storing in an airtight jar, in a dark place. Wash the leaves and used as flavouring or garnish.

Croatian Hamburg Parsley Soup
Serves 8

500g (1lb) Hamburg parsley
1 turnip, peeled
1 large onion, peeled
1 good sized leek, cleaned
50g (2oz) butter
2½ litres (4pt) vegetable stock
Salt & freshly ground black pepper
4 tablespoons, sour cream
2 tablespoons each chives & dill
4 tablespoons croûtons

Chop all the vegetables coarsely. Heat the butter in a heavy-bottomed pan and sauté the vegetables until softened. Stir to prevent burning. Pour over the stock, season with salt and pepper and simmer until the vegetables are tender.

Put through a *mouli légumes* or liquidize and return to the pan. Stir in the sour cream and the herbs, allow to heat through again and adjust the seasoning. Do not allow to boil. Serve piping hot, with croûtons.

MEDICINAL

The leaves are a good source of vitamins A and C and contain similar properties to traditional garnishing parsley. They reduce inflammation, are used for urological conditions like cystitis and kidney stones, and help indigestion, arthritis and rheumatism. After childbirth the leaves encourage lactation; the roots and seeds promote uterine contractions. The leaves are also an excellent breath freshener – powerful enough to counter the effects of garlic!

Persea americana. Lauraceae

AVOCADO PEAR

(Butter pear) Evergreen tree or shrub grown for fruit. Tender. Value: very rich in vitamin E, average fat content, high in monounsaturated fatty acids.

This sub-tropical tree from Central America was originally introduced to Europe by the Conquistadors and has since been planted in many parts of the world. Its anglicized name is a corruption of the Aztec word *ahuacatl*, which was used to describe both its fruit and the testicle. There are three main races: Guatemalan fruits are large with a warty skin; Mexican ones are small, and large, smooth-skinned types come from the West Indies. All have been hybridized, producing hundreds of cultivars suitable for Mediterranean to tropical climates.

VARIETIES

'Ettinger' (Mexican x Guatemalan) produces oblong fruit with bright green, shiny skin. 'Fuerte' (Mexican x Guatemalan) is the most common cultivar, producing large fruit with green, textured skin. 'Hass' (Guatemalan) is self-fertile, the skin dark purple when it is mature.

CULTIVATION

Avocados flourish in shelter and sunshine.

Propagation

Avocados are propagated from seed, although the seedling may not come true (more reliable results are obtained professionally by grafting named cultivars on to disease-resistant rootstocks). Choose healthy seeds, cut 1cm (½in) from the pointed end and dip the wound in fungicide. Sow in a 15cm (6in) pot of moist seed compost, with the cut end just above the surface. Germinate in a glasshouse, propagator or place the pot in a clear polythene bag, lightly knot the end and put in a bright position away from direct sunshine at 21–27°C (70–80°F).

When the fourth leaf appears, remove the bag and leave the plant for 2 weeks to acclimatize. Do not force the stone from the roots; allow it to rot away. Pot on as the compost becomes congested with roots; when they outgrow 30–40cm (12–16in) pots, plant out into their final positions.

Growing

The ideal soil is a slightly acid, moisture-retentive, free-draining loam. Improve sandy or clay soils by adding organic matter.

Temperatures should be between 20–28°C (68–82°F) with humidity greater than 60 per cent all year round. Some can withstand temperatures down to 10–15°C (48–58°F). Allow 6m (20ft) between the trees and the rows. In exposed areas, plant windbreaks to prevent damage.

During the growing season, apply 1.5–2kg (3lb 4oz–4lb 6oz) of general fertilizer in 2 or 3 doses. Mulch round the base to suppress weeds. Water during times of drought until trees are established.

Shape young trees to ensure a balanced crown. Remove diseased, damaged or crossing branches after fruiting. They withstand hard pruning. Plant several cultivars with overlapping or simultaneous flowering periods to produce fruit.

Maintenance

Spring Repot containerized plants.
Summer Feed, harvest and water as necessary.
Autumn Bring containerized plants indoors in cool temperate zones.

A cluster of fruits in South Africa, ripe and ready for harvest and the increasingly demanding export market

An avocado orchard in Transvaal, South Africa

Winter Reduce watering and stop feeding avocados grown under glass.

Protected Cropping
Grow in a greenhouse or conservatory, maintaining moderate temperatures and humidity according to the origin of the cultivar.

Flowers and fruit are rarely produced in cool temperate zones due to low light intensity and reduced daylight hours.

Container Growing
Repot young plants as the compost becomes congested with roots. Every 2–3 years repot established plants into a pot one size larger, using a loam-based compost with moderate fertilizer levels. Top-dress in the intervening years by removing and replacing the top 5–7.5cm (2–3in) of compost in spring. Apply a general fertilizer every 2–3 weeks when plants are actively growing.

Water as the compost surface dries out. Reduce watering in winter and do not feed.

In spring, prune side branches to encourage bushy growth. Containerized plants can be placed outdoors in summer in a warm, sheltered position when there is no danger of frost. During winter, they need a light, cool position with temperatures no lower than 16°C (60°F).

Harvesting & Storing
Seed-raised trees fruit after 5 to 7 years; grafted plants take 3 to 5 years.

Remove fruit carefully using secateurs. Discard damaged fruit. They are ready for eating if slightly soft when pressed. If unripe, store for a few days.

PESTS & DISEASES

Use resistant rootstocks against **avocado root rot**. Those grown indoors may be attacked by **whitefly**: use sticky traps, the predator *Encarsia formosa* or soft soap. Control **red spider mite** by maintaining humidity and

Avocados for sale, Costa Rica

remove **mealybug** by dabbing them with a paintbrush dipped in methylated spirits.

OTHER USES

The pulp of avocados makes an ideal natural ingredient for face masks and for skin moisturisers.

CULINARY

Coat cut surfaces with lemon or lime juice to prevent discoloration. Avocado is delicious simply with olive oil and vinaigrette. The flavour also blends well with prawns, crabmeat and other seafood or grapefruit and pineapple. Try it with bacon in a sandwich, or made into a fine salad. To create the Mexican dip, *Guacamole*, bake and then mash avocados with chillies, onions and garlic and serve with tortillas.

Cold Avocado Soup
Serves 2

This is a welcome alternative to vichyssoise.

Purée 2 avocados, peeled and stoned, with 300ml (½pt) crème fraîche or low-fat yoghurt combined with double cream. Gently heat 1 litre (1¾pt) well-flavoured chicken stock and stir in the avocado purée, gently heating: do not boil.

Season with salt and freshly ground black pepper and a judicious squeeze or two of lemon juice to accent the flavour. Decorate with a dollop of yoghurt and sprinkle with fresh chives.

Avocado Mousse
Serves 4

Oded Schwartz gives this unusual dessert recipe in Reader's Digest *Fast & Fresh Cooking*.

225ml (8fl oz) double cream
1 tablespoon sugar
1 teaspoon orange-blossom water
2 avocados
2 tablespoons runny honey
3 tablespoons Grand Marnier
Grated rind & juice of 2 limes
Mint, to garnish

Whip the cream until stiff and add the sugar and orange blossom water. Chill well. Meantime, scoop the pulp from the avocado shells and purée with all the remaining ingredients bar half the lime rind.

Transfer to a mixing bowl and stir in the cream. Serve in individual glass bowls and decorate with the remaining rind and a sprig of mint.

Nutrition
Avocados are high in protein, vitamin B complex and vitamin E, have low carbohydrate levels and no cholesterol.

Avocado Mousse

Phaseolus aureus. Leguminosae

MUNG BEAN

(Green gram, golden gram) Annual grown for its seed sprouts and seeds. Tender. Value: sprouts: rich in vitamins, iron, iodine, potassium, calcium; seeds: rich in minerals, protein and vitamins.

VARIETIES

Phaseolus aureus is a sparsely leaved annual to about 90cm (3ft) with yellow flowers and small, slender pods containing up to 15 olive, brown or mottled seeds.

CULTIVATION

Propagation

Rake in a general fertilizer at 60g/sq m (2oz/sq yd) about 10 days before sowing. Seeds can be broadcast or sown in drills on a well-prepared seedbed, thinning to 20–30cm (8–12in) apart with 40–50cm (16–20in) between the rows.

Growing

Mung beans flourish on rich, deep, well-drained soils and dislike clay. Add organic matter if necessary and lime to create a pH of 5.5–7.0. Water well throughout the growing season. Ideal growing conditions are between 30–36°C (86–97°F) and with moderate rainfall.

Sprouting Seeds

Use untreated seeds for sprouting, as those treated with fungicide are poisonous. Remove any which are discoloured, mouldy or damaged. Soak them overnight in cold water and the following morning, rinse in a colander. Place a layer of moist kitchen roll or damp flannel over the base of a flat-bottomed tray or 'seed sprouter', then spread a layer of mung beans about 1cm (½in) deep over the surface. Cover the container with polythene and put the bowl in a dark cupboard, or wrap it to exclude light.

Temperatures of 13–21°C (55–70°F) should be maintained for rapid growth: an airing cupboard is ideal. Rinse the sprouts daily, morning and night.

Make a 'seed sprouter' from a large yoghurt pot or a plastic ice cream tub with holes punched in the bottom and use the lid as a drip tray. This makes for

This major Indian pulse crop was introduced to Indonesia and southern China many centuries ago and is grown throughout the tropics and subtropics, being sown towards the end of the wet season to ripen during the dry season. The leaves and stems are used to make hay and silage and the seeds are used for cattle feed. Mung beans came to prominence in the West with an increased interest in Oriental cuisine: bean sprouts are an easy-to-grow major crop. Among other uses, their flour is a soap substitute and they serve as a replacement for soya beans in the manufacture of ketchup.

Young crop growing in a field in Thailand

Seed sprouts make great stir-fries

easier daily rinsing of the seedlings.

Maintenance
Outdoors Broadcast or sow seed in drills, water when needed, as the soil dries out. Harvest before the pods split. *Sprouting* Keep seeds moist. Harvest regularly.

Harvesting & Storing
Harvest shoots from 3 days onwards when they are about 2.5–5cm (1–2in) long. If the seed coats remain attached to the sprouts, soak them in water, then 'top-and-tailed', removing the seed and shoot tip. Store in the fridge.

When growing for seed, gather before they split to prevent the seeds being lost.

Pests & Diseases
Powdery mildew is a problem when plants are dry at the roots. Mulch and water regularly, remove diseased leaves immediately, spray with a systemic fungicide or bicarbonate of soda and destroy plant debris at the end of the season.

MEDICINAL

The seeds are said to have a cooling and astringent effect on fever and an infusion is used as a diuretic when treating beriberi. In Malaya it is prescribed for vertigo.

WARNING

Do not let bean sprouts become waterlogged, as they rapidly become mouldy.

Dried beans just before soaking

CULINARY

Bean sprouts can be eaten raw, in salads, with a suitable dressing or lightly cooked for about 2 minutes only in slightly salted water. (Be warned: overcooked shoots lose their taste.)

To stir-fry, use only a little oil, stirring briskly for about 2 minutes. In Oriental cooking, bean sprouts combine well with other vegetables, eggs, red meat, chicken and fish and can be used to stuff savoury pancakes, egg rolls and tortillas.

Stir-fried Mung Beans
Serves 2

1 bag mung beans
Groundnut oil, for frying
2 cloves garlic, crushed
250ml (8fl oz) chicken stock
1 tablespoon light soy sauce
1 heaped teaspoon cornflour
2–3 spring onions

Rinse the mung beans well. Heat the oil and the garlic in a wok, then add the mung beans. Fry for 1 minute, stirring constantly.

Cover with chicken stock and cook until tender and the liquid has evaporated. Then stir in the soy sauce and the cornflour. Cook for 2 minutes more.

Garnish with roughly chopped spring onions and serve with rice.

Phaseolus coccineus. Leguminosae

RUNNER BEAN

(Scarlet Runner) Perennial climber grown as annual in temperate climates for edible pods and seeds.
Half hardy. Value: moderate levels of iron, vitamin C and beta carotene.

A native of Mexico, the runner bean has been known as a food crop for more than 2,200 years. In the early seventeenth century, Gerard's *Herball* mentions it as an ornamental introduced by the plant collector John Tradescant the Elder: 'Ladies did not . . . disdain to put the flowers in their nosegays and garlands', and in the garden it was grown around gazebos and arbours. Vilmorin Andrieux commented in 1885: 'In small gardens they are often trained over wire or woodwork, so as to form summer houses or coverings for walks.' Philip Miller, keeper of Chelsea Physic Garden, is credited with being the first gardener to cook them.

It was the fashion in seventeenth-century England to experiment with soaking seeds. Mr Gifford, minister of Montacute in Somerset, noted in his diary: 'May 10th 1679, I steep'd runner beans in sack five days, then I put them in sallet-oyle five days, then in brandy four days and about noon set them in an hot bed against a south wall casting all liquor wherein they had been infused negligently about the holes, within three hours space, eight of the nine came up, and were a foot high with all their leaves, and on the morrow a foot more in height . . . and in a week were podded and full ripe.' You could try this for yourself – or perhaps you would prefer to stick to today's more conventional methods!

VARIETIES

Older cultivars were rather stringy unless eaten young; newer varieties are 'stringless'. Besides the traditional tall-growing climbers, there is also a choice of dwarf varieties which do not need supporting and are ideal for smaller gardens, early crops under cloches and in exposed sites.

Non–stringless types
'Bokki' has wonderful red flowers and pods. **'Enorma'*** is equally ornamental, with red flowers. It has long pods and is very tasty. **'Liberty'*** has good-quality pods to 45–50cm (18–20in) long.

'Painted Lady', a variety grown since the nineteenth century, has delicate red and white flowers and long pods.

Stringless types
'Butler' is vigorous and prolific, with tender pods. **'Desiree'** has white flowers and seeds, and is high-yielding and tasty. **'Kelvedon Marvel'*** is tasty, matures early and crops heavily. It can also be grown along the ground. **'Polestar'** crops heavily with long, well-flavoured pods. **'Red Knight'**, with red flowers, crops heavily and is excellent for freezing; it is disease-resistant. **'Red Rum'** is very early, high-yielding, tasty and resistant to halo blight. It can also grow along the ground. **'Scarlet Emperor'** is a traditional variety with scarlet flowers and tasty pods.

Supports must be strong to take the weight of the heavy vines

Dwarf varieties
'Hammonds Dwarf Scarlet'
is ideal for the small garden.
Pods are easy to harvest.
Tops may need to be
pinched out. **'Pickwick'** is
red-flowered, producing
early heavy crops of juicy
pods. No support needed.

CULTIVATION

Propagation
Runner beans are not frost-
tolerant and need a
minimum soil temperature
of 10°C (50°F) to germinate.
Sow from late spring to early
summer 5–7.5cm (2–3in)
deep, 15cm (6in) apart in
double rows 60cm (24in)
apart. To shelter pollinating
insects they are better grown
in blocks or several short
rows rather than a single
long one. Allow 1–1.75m
(3–5ft) between rows for ease
of harvesting, depending on
the cultivar.

Climbing types can be
encouraged to bush by
pinching out the main stems
when they are around 25cm
(10in); the sideshoots can be
pinched out at the second
leaf joint for a bushy plant
that does not need staking.

Seed sown outdoors crops
in about 14–16 weeks,
depending on climatic and
cultural conditions.

Growing
Runner beans are not frost-
hardy and are less successful
in cooler areas unless you
have a suitable micro-
climate. They flourish
between 14–29°C (57–85°F),
needing a warm, sheltered
position to minimize wind
damage and encourage
pollinating insects.

Soil should be deep,
fertile and moisture-
retentive. Dig a trench at
least 30cm (12in) deep and
60cm (24in) wide in late
autumn to early winter
before planting, adding
plenty of well-rotted organic
matter to the backfill. Before
sowing, rake in 60–90g/sq m
(2–3oz/sq yd) of granular
general fertilizer.

Keep crops weed-free
during early stages of
growth. Mulch after
germination or after
transplanting. Watering is
essential for good bud set:
the traditional method of
spraying flowers has little
effect. As the first buds are
forming and again as the
first flowers are fully open
plants need 5–11 litres/sq m
(1–2gal/sq yd). Crops
should be rotated.

Climbers can be up to 3m
(120in) or more tall and a
good sturdy support should
be in place before sowing or
transplanting. Traditionally,
a 'wigwam' of canes, or a
longer row of crossed canes,
were used; these may need
supporting strings at the end
of each row, like tent guy
ropes. Do improvise: I once
saw a wonderful structure
like a V-shaped frame
designed so the beans would
hang down and make
picking easier. Use canes,
strong wooden stakes, steel
tubes, or make frameworks
of netting. There should be
one cane or length of strong
twine for each plant.

Maintenance
Spring Sow crops under
cover or outdoors in late
spring. Erect supports.
Summer Keep crops weed-
free and well watered.
Harvest regularly.

'Pickwick' is stringless

Autumn Continue
harvesting until the first
frosts.
Winter Prepare the soil for
the following year's crop.

Protected Cropping
For earlier crops and in
cooler climates, sow in boxes
or pots of seed compost
under cover from mid-
spring, harden off and plant
out from late spring. Protect
indoor and outdoor crops
with cloches or horticultural
fleece until they are
established.

Container Growing
Runner beans can be grown
in containers at least 20cm
(8in) wide by 25cm (10in)
deep, depending on the
vigour of the cultivar.

Sow seeds 5cm (2in) deep
and 10–13cm (4–5in) apart
indoors in late spring,
moving the container
outdoors into a sunny site.
Water frequently in warm
weather, less often at other
times. Feed with liquid
general fertilizer if plants
need a boost.

Stake tall varieties,
pinching out growing points
when plants reach top of
supports. Otherwise use
dwarf varieties.

Harvesting & Storing
Harvest from mid-summer
to mid-autumn. Regular
picking is essential to ensure
regular cropping, high yields
and to avoid 'stringiness'.

Runner beans freeze well.

The seeds of 'Painted Lady' are a pink/brown colour

Beans growing over a frame

PESTS & DISEASES

Slugs, **black bean aphid** and **red spider mite** may be troublesome.

Grey mould (*botrytis*) and **halo blight** may cause problems in wet or humid weather. **Mice** may eat seeds.

Root rots may kill plants in wet or poorly drained soils. Rotate.

COMPANION PLANTING

Runner beans are compatible with all but the Allium family.

Grow with maize to protect the latter from corn army worms. Nitrogen-fixing bacteria in the roots improve soil fertility. After harvesting, cut off tops, leave roots in the soil or add to compost heaps. They thrive with brassicas; Brussels sprout transplants are sheltered and grow on once beans die back.

Late in the season, their shade can benefit celery and salad crops if enough water is available.

CULINARY

Wash, 'top and tail', pull off stringy edges, slice diagonally and boil for 5–7 minutes. Drain and serve with a knob of butter. Alternatively, cook whole and slice after cooking.

Runner Bean Chutney
Makes 1.5kg (3lb)

Clare Walker and Gill Coleman give this recipe in *The Home Gardener's Cookbook*:

1kg (2lb) runner beans
500g (1lb) onions
300ml (½ pt) water
1 level tablespoon salt
1 level tablespoon mustard seeds
75g (3oz) sultanas
1½ level teaspoons ground ginger
1 level teaspoon turmeric
6 dried red chillies, left whole
600ml (1pt) spiced vinegar
500g (1lb) demerara sugar

Wipe, top, tail and string the beans and cut them into small slices. Place in a preserving pan with the peeled and finely chopped onions. Add the water, salt and mustard seeds and simmer gently for 20–25 minutes until the beans are just tender.

Then add the sultanas, ginger, turmeric, chillies and spiced vinegar, bring back to the boil and simmer for a further 30 minutes, or until the mixture is fairly thick.

Stir in the sugar, allow to dissolve, then boil steadily for about 20 minutes until the chutney is thick. Pour into warm, dry jars, cover with thick polythene and seal with a lid, if available. Label and store in a cool, dry place for at least 3 months before using. The chillies can be removed before potting.

Runner Bean Chutney

Phaseolus vulgaris. Leguminosae

FRENCH BEAN

(Common, Kidney, Bush, Pole, Snap, String, Green, Wax Bean; Haricot;
Baked Bean; Flageolet; Haricot Vert)
Annual grown for edible pods and beans. Half hardy.
Value: moderate potassium, folic acid and beta carotene. Very rich in protein.

Evidence of the wild form, found in Mexico, Guatemala and parts of the Andes, has been discovered in Peruvian settlements from 8000BC. Both bush and climbing varieties were introduced to Europe during the Spanish conquest in the early sixteenth century, though the dwarf varieties did not become popular for two more centuries. They were first referred to as 'kidney beans' by the English in 1551, alluding to the shape of their seeds.

Gerard in his *Herball* calls them 'sperage' beans and 'long peason', while Parkinson wrote: 'Kidney beans boiled in water and stewed with butter were esteemed more savory...than the common broad bean and were a dish more oftentimes at rich men's tables than at the poor.' Another writer commented in 1681: 'It is a plant lately brought into use among us and not yet sufficiently known.'

In Europe, 'haricot vert' was used in ships' stores in voyages of exploration during the early 1500s. When European colonists first explored the Americas, they found climbing beans planted with maize, providing starch and protein for indigenous tribes.

Beans are self-pollinating, so close spacing provides higher yields

VARIETIES

This group of beans contains considerable variety. Plants are dwarf (ideal for the smaller garden or containers) or climbing, pods are flat, oval or round in cross-section and are green, yellow (waxpods) or purple, or marbled.

The seeds are colourful and often mottled. As well as being grown for the immature pods, eaten whole, the seeds may be allowed to swell and ripen; seeds are eaten fresh as 'flageolets', or dried and known as 'haricots'.

Climbing types
'Borlotto Lingua di Fuoco' is an ornamental 'fire tongue' form, with red-marked green pods. **'Corona d'Oro'** is high-yielding with rounded,

tender, golden-yellow pods. **'Hunter'*** is flat-podded, and crops heavily over a long period. **'Kwintus'*** produces tender, tasty pods. **'Musica'*** can be sown early and is full of flavour. **'Or du Rhin'** is a yellow-podded, late maincrop type. It is delicious picked young. **'Romano'**, an old variety, is tender, tasty and prolific. Excellent for freezing.

Dwarf or bush types
'Annabel'* is high-yielding, round and tasty – perfect for the patio. **'Chevrier Vert'**: this classic French flageolet from 1880 is tasty and tender. **'Forum'** is cold-tolerant. Yields high-quality beans. Resistant to halo blight and anthracnose. **'Masai'*** has long thin pods, is robust, early and high-yielding, with good disease and cold tolerance. **'Purple Queen'** is delicious, producing heavy yields of glossy purple pods. **'Royal Burgundy'** germinates well

'Royalty', ideal for the 'potager'

in cold soil and has tasty, dark green pods. Resistant to pea and bean weevil. Freezes well. **'Royalty'** crops heavily. Delicately flavoured dark purple pods which turn green when cooked. The dark green pods of **'Sprite'*** freeze well. **'Vibel'*** is high-yielding, crops over a long period and is very tasty. A gourmet bean.

CULTIVATION

Propagation
French beans dislike cold wet soils and are inclined to rot; for successful germination, do not sow until the soil is a minimum of 10°C (50°F). For early sowings or in cold weather warm the soil first with cloches or black polythene 3–4 weeks before sowing.

Sow successively from mid-spring to early summer in staggered drills 4–5cm (1½–2in) deep with 22cm (9in) between the rows and plants for optimum yields.

Climbing varieties should be in double rows 15cm (6in) apart with 60cm (2ft) between rows.

Growing
French beans flourish in a sheltered, sunny site on a light, free-draining, fertile soil where organic matter was added for the previous

crop. Alternatively, dig in plenty of well-rotted organic matter in late autumn or winter before planting.

The plants need a pH of 6.5–7.0; lime acid soils if necessary. Rake the soil to a medium tilth about 10–14 days before sowing, incorporating a balanced granular fertilizer at 30–60g/sq m (1–2oz/sq yd).

Keep crops weed-free or mulch when the soil is moist. Earth up round the base of the stems for added support and push twigs under mature bush varieties to keep pods off the soil, or support plants with pea sticks. Support climbing varieties in the same way as runner beans.

Keep well watered during drought; plants are particularly sensitive to water stress when the flowers start to open and as pods swell. Apply 13–18 litres/sq m (3–4 gal/sq yd) per week.

Maintenance
Spring Sow early crops under cover or outdoors in late spring. Support climbers. Transplant when 5–7.5cm (2–3in) tall.
Summer Keep crops weed-free, mulch, water in drought. Harvest regularly.
Autumn Continue harvesting until the first frosts. Protect later crops with cloches or fleece.
Winter Prepare the soil for the following year's crop.

Protected Cropping
For earlier crops and in cooler climates, sow in boxes, modules or pots of seed compost under cover from mid-spring. Warm the soil before transplanting. Harden off and plant out from late spring, depending on the weather and soil conditions. Protect crops sown indoors or *in situ* with cloches, polytunnels or with horticultural fleece until established.

For very early harvest, sow in pots in a heated greenhouse at 15°C (60°F)

from late winter. Sow 4 seeds near the edge of a 23–25cm (9–10in) pot containing loam-based compost with moderate fertilizer levels.

Seeds can also be pregerminated on moist kitchen towel in an airing cupboard or similar. Keep moist with tepid water, ventilate in warm weather, harvest in late spring.

Container Growing
French beans can be grown in containers which are at least 20cm (8in) wide by 25cm (10in) deep.

Sow seeds 4–5cm (1½–2in) deep indoors in mid-spring, moving the container outdoors into a sheltered, sunny site. Feed with liquid general fertilizer if necessary.

Stake climbing varieties; pinch out growing points when plants reach the top of supports.

Harvesting & Storing
Plants are self-pollinating, so expect a good harvest. Pick when pods are about 10cm (4in) long, when they snap easily, before the seeds are visible. Pick regularly for maximum yields. Cut them with a pair of scissors or hold the stems as you pull the pods to avoid uprooting the plant.

For dried or haricot beans, leave pods until they mature, sever the plant at the base and dry indoors. When pods begin to split, shell the beans and dry on paper for several days. Store in an airtight container.

French beans freeze well. Wash and trim young pods, blanch for 3 minutes, freeze in polythene bags or rigid

Climbing French beans

containers. You should use within 12 months.

They keep in a polythene bag in the refrigerator for up to a week and last about 4 days in a cool kitchen.

PESTS & DISEASES

Slugs, **black bean aphid** and **red spider mite** can be troublesome. **Grey mould** (**Botrytis**) and **halo blight** may be problems in wet or humid weather. **Mice** may eat seeds. **Root rots** can kill plants in wet or poorly drained soils. Rotate crops.

COMPANION PLANTING

French beans do well with celery, maize, cucurbits, sweet corn and melons. Intercrop with brassicas.

MEDICINAL

One cup of beans per day is said to lower cholesterol by about 12%

French Bean, Roquefort & Walnut Salad

CULINARY

French beans, fresh from the garden, have such a delicate flavour that they hardly need more than boiling in water and serving as an accompaniment to meat and other dishes. Wash, 'top and tail' pods and cook whole in boiling salted water for 5–7 minutes, preferably within an hour of harvesting. Cut large flat-podded types into 2.5cm (1in) slices.

Alternatively, serve cold in salads or try them stir-fried with other vegetables.

For haricot beans, place fresh beans in cold water, bring to the boil, remove from the heat and allow to stand for an hour. Drain and serve as a hot vegetable, or in vinaigrette as a salad.

French Bean, Roquefort & Walnut Salad
Serves 4

300g (10oz) French beans, topped & tailed
250g (8oz) Roquefort cheese
125g (4oz) walnuts
1 small radicchio
2 little gem lettuces
3 tablespoons extra virgin olive oil
1 tablespoon balsamic vinegar
1 clove garlic, crushed
Salt & freshly ground black pepper

Wash the beans and steam them over a pan of boiling water until just crunchy. Keep warm. Crumble the Roquefort and lightly crush the walnuts. Wash the lettuces. Make a dressing with the remaining ingredients.

Arrange the lettuces in a large bowl, top with the beans, walnuts and cheese, and pour over the dressing. Toss and serve while the beans are still warm.

Red Chilli Beef
Serves 4

3 or 4 ancho chillies
1–2 small red chillies, dried
1 tablespoon ground cumin
3 tablespoons vegetable oil
2 onions, finely sliced
3 cloves garlic, finely crushed
750g (1½lb) minced beef
300g (10oz) cooked red kidney beans
2 tablespoons tomato purée
Salt & freshly ground black pepper
300ml (½pt) good stock

Infuse the ancho chillies in hot water to soften them. Remove the stems and push the flesh through a fine sieve. Set aside. Then finely chop and deseed the dried chillies.

Put the cumin into a heavy frying pan over a medium heat and toast until the fragrance comes out, taking care not to burn it. Set aside.

Heat the oil in a large, heavy saucepan and cook the onions and garlic until just coloured. Add the meat and brown well. Add both sorts of chilli, the kidney beans, tomato purée and salt and pepper. Mix well.

Pour in the stock and cook for 40 minutes, covered, adding a little extra liquid if necessary. Serve hot with plainly cooked rice.

'Mangetout'

Pisum sativum. Leguminosae

PEA

(Garden Pea, English Pea) Climbing or scrambling annual grown for seeds, pods and shoot tips. Half hardy. Value: good source of protein, carbohydrates, fibre, iron and vitamin C.

'Early Onward', a robust, prolific variety

Like many legumes, peas are an ancient food crop. The earliest records are of smooth-skinned types, found in Mediterranean and European excavations dating from 7000BC. The Greeks and Romans cultivated and ate peas in abundance and it was the Romans who were said to have introduced them to Britain. In classical Greece they were known as *pison*, which was translated in English to 'peason'; by the reign of Charles I they became 'pease' and this was shortened to 'pea' in the eighteenth century. During the reign of Elizabeth I types seen as 'fit dainties for ladies, they come so far, and cost so dear' were imported from Holland.

In England 'pease pudding', made from dried peas, butter and eggs, was traditionally eaten with pork and boiled bacon. It was obviously quite versatile, hence the nursery rhyme beginning, 'Pease pudding hot, pease pudding cold, pease pudding in the pot nine days old'. Peas were eaten dried or ground until the sixteenth century, when Italian gardeners developed tender varieties for cooking and eating when fresh. It took until the following century before this practice was accepted by the wealthy and fashionable in England.

They were the favourite vegetable of Thomas Jefferson, who held an annual competition among his friends to grow the first peas. The winner had the privilege of inviting others in the group to dinner celebrating their arrival. Invitations were issued saying, 'Come tonight, the peas are ready!'

A row of peas sitting snugly in the pod

VARIETIES

Peas are usually listed according to the timing of the crop – early, second early (or early maincrop) and maincrop types – but

some descriptions refer to the pea itself, or to the pod.

Earlier varieties are lower-growing than later types, which are taller and consequently higher-yielding. Smooth-seeded types are hardy and are used for early and late crops. Wrinkle-seeded varieties are less hardy and generally sweeter. 'Petit pois' are small and well flavoured. 'Semi-leafless' peas have more tendrils than leaves, becoming intertwined and self supporting as they grow.

'Sugar peas' or 'mangetout' – varieties of *Pisum sativum* var. *macrocarpon* – are grown for their edible immature pods; of these, the 'Sugar Snap' type are particularly succulent and sweet. Some varieties can be allowed to mature and the peas eaten.

Early peas
'Early Onward'* is a heavy cropper, with large blunt pods and wrinkled seeds. 'Feltham First' is an excellent early round-seeded variety with large, well-filled pods. 'Prince Albert' is early and vigorous, producing bumper crops.

Maincrop peas
'Cavalier'* produces huge crops and is highly resistant to mildew. Easy to harvest, with wrinkled seeds and fusarium resistance. 'Daisy' is low-growing, to 60cm (2ft), producing good yields of excellent-quality peas.

'Feltham First', an early type, can be grown up pea sticks or netting

'Darfon' is a high-yielding 'petit pois' type, its pods packed with small peas. It resists downy mildew and fusarium. **'Hurst Green Shaft'*** is sweet-tasting and heavy-cropping, maturing over a long period. Wrinkle-seeded. Downy mildew and fusarium resistant. **'Bikini'** is a high-yielding semi-leafless type, which is good for freezing. Fusarium-resistant.

Sugar peas
'Oregon Sugar Pod' is sweet and tasty; harvest as the peas form. Fusarium-resistant. **'Reuzensuiker'*** is a compact plant, needing little support. Its pods are wide and fleshy, and very sweet. **'Sugar Snap'*** produces succulent, sweet edible pods or can be grown on for peas. Very sweet. Fusarium-resistant.

CULTIVATION

Propagation
Germination is erratic and poor on cold soils; do not sow outdoors when soil temperatures are below 10°C (50°F).

Sow earlies or second earlies successively every 14–28 days from mid-spring to mid-summer. Avoid excessively hot times; these can effect germination.

According to the growing conditions, earlies mature after about 12 weeks, second earlies (or early maincrop) take 1–2 weeks longer, and maincrops take another 1–2 weeks longer again. As an alternative option, sow groups of earlies, second earlies and maincrops in mid- to late spring; the length of time taken for each type to reach maturity will give you a harvest over several weeks.

In mid-summer, with at least 12 weeks before the first frosts are expected, sow an early cultivar for harvesting in autumn, and where winters are mild, sow earlies in mid- to late autumn for overwintering. Cloche protection may be necessary later in the season.

Peas can be sown in single V-shaped rows 2.5–5cm (1–2in) deep and 5cm (2in) apart, double rows 23cm (9in) apart or broad or flat drills 25cm (10in) wide.

The distance between the rows or pairs of rows should equal the ultimate height of the plant.

Peas can also be sown in strips 3 rows wide with the seeds 11cm (4½in) apart in and between the rows and with 45cm (18in) between the strips.

They can also be sown in blocks 90–120cm (36–48in) wide with seeds 5–7.5cm (2–3in) apart.

Yields are higher when plants are supported. Use pea sticks made from brushwood or netting. Place supports down one side of a single row, on either side or down the centre of wide drills and around the outside of blocks of plants.

Growing
Peas are a cool-season crop flourishing at 13–18°C (55–65°F), so crops will be higher in cooler summer temperatures. They do not tolerate drought, excessive temperatures or waterlogged soil. Peas should be grown in an open, sheltered position on moisture-retentive, deep, free-draining soil with a pH of 5.5–7.0.

Incorporate plenty of organic matter in the autumn or winter prior to sowing or plant where the ground was manured for the previous year's crop.

Keep crops weed-free by hoeing, hand weeding or mulching (which also keeps the roots cool and moist). Earth up overwintering and early crops to provide extra support.

Unless there are drought conditions, established plants do not need watering until the flowers appear, then, for a good harvest, they will need 22 litres/sq m (4gal/sq yd) each week until the harvest is complete.

Maintenance
Spring Sow early maincrops. *Summer* Sow maincrops early in the season. Harvest, keep weed-free and water. Sow earlies for autumn harvest. *Autumn* Sow early overwintering crops under cover. Prepare the ground for the following year. *Winter* Sow early crops under cover.

Protected Cropping
Warm the soil before sowing treated seed in spring. Sow the seed of dwarf cultivars under cover in early spring, removing the covers when the plants need supporting.

Early spring and late autumn sowings can be made under cover, as flowers and pods cannot withstand frost.

Container Growing
Sow early dwarf varieties successively through the season in large containers of loam-based compost with moderate fertilizer levels. Provide support, keep weed-free and well watered.

Harvesting & Storing
Harvest early types from late spring to early summer and maincrops from mid-summer to early autumn. Pick regularly to ensure a high yield when the pods are swollen. Harvest those grown for their pods when the peas are just forming.

If peas are to be dried, leave them on the plant as long as possible, lifting just before the seeds are shed; hang in a cool airy place or spread the pods out on trays to dry until they split and the peas can be harvested. Store in airtight containers.

Freeze young peas of any variety. Shell and blanch for 1 minute. Allow to drain, cool and freeze in polythene bags or containers. Use within 12 months.

Peas in a polythene bag in the refrigerator stay fresh for up to 3 days.

Evening light illuminating the foliage of young peas

Peas are one of the most popular frozen vegetables

Pests & Diseases
Birds and **mice** can be a problem: net and trap.

Pea moths are common, their larvae eating the peas. Protect with crop covers at flower bud stage. Autumn, early and mid-summer sowings often avoid problems; spray with pyrethrin-based insecticide 10 days after flowers open.

Pea thrips attack developing pods, making pods distorted and silvery; peas do not develop. Spray with derris or pyrethrum.

Mice may also be troublesome, eating seeds, particularly with overwintered crops.

Powdery mildew, **downy mildew** and **fusarium wilt** can be a problem: sow resistant varieties.

COMPANION PLANTING

Peas grow well with other legumes, root crops, potatoes, cucurbits and sweetcorn.

MEDICINAL

Peas are said to reduce fertility, prevent appendicitis, lower blood cholesterol and control blood sugar levels.

CULINARY

Garden peas are eaten fresh or dried. When small and tender, they can be eaten raw in salads.

Peas are traditionally boiled or steamed with a sprig of mint. Eat with butter, salt and pepper or herbs. Serve in a cream sauce with pearl onions, with celery, orange, carrots, wine or lemon sauce.

Mangetout should be boiled for 3 minutes (or steamed), tossed in butter and served.

Young shoot tips can be cooked and eaten.

Pea & Pear Soup
Serves 4

An unusual combination and very refreshing in summertime when there is a glut of peas.

500g (1lb) peas, shelled weight
6–7 pears, very ripe, unpeeled
900ml (1½pt) chicken stock

Pea & Pear Soup

Pinch cayenne pepper
2 tablespoons finely chopped fresh mint
Salt & freshly ground black pepper

Cook the peas in lightly salted water for 5 minutes or so. Drain. Quarter and core the pears. Liquidize them in a blender and, with the peas, the stock and the cayenne. Pour into a saucepan and stir in the mint and seasoning. Heat through and serve.

Pasta and Mangetout Salad

Pasta & Mangetout Salad
Serves 4

Mangetout or sugar peas from the garden are completely different from the tired beasts bought in the greengrocers. The quicker they are cooked, the better they taste.

500g (1lb) pasta – penne or fusilli
4 tablespoons olive oil
300g (10oz) mangetout, topped & tailed
1 small onion, finely sliced
2 cloves garlic, crushed
250g (8oz) tuna, drained & flaked
2 tablespoons thick cream
2 tablespoons flat-leaf parsley
Salt & freshly ground black pepper

Cook the pasta in boiling salted water for 10 minutes, or until *al dente*, and drain. Drizzle over 1 tablespoon of the oil and toss well. Allow to cool.

Meanwhile, cook the mangetout in a steamer for 2–3 minutes; they should remain crunchy. In a separate pan, heat the oil and sauté the onion for a couple of minutes, then add the garlic and continue cooking for 1 minute. Remove from the heat and allow to cool.

Put the pasta into a large serving bowl and mix in all the ingredients. Taste for seasoning and serve.

Portulaca oleracea subsp. *sativa. Portulacaceae*

PURSLANE

(Summer Purslane) Annual grown for succulent shoot tips, stems and leaves. Half hardy. Value: rich in beta carotene, folic acid, vitamin C; contains useful amounts of essential fatty acids.

Purslane has been grown for centuries in China, India and Egypt, and is now widespread in the warm temperate and tropical regions of the world. It was once believed to protect against evil spirits and 'blastings by lightning or planets and burning of gunpowder'. Its name in Malawi translates as 'buttocks of the wife of a chief', referring to the plant's succulent, rounded leaves and juicy stems! The cultivated form has an erect habit and larger leaves than the wild species.

VARIETIES

Portulaca oleracea var. sativa is a vigorous, upright annual growing to 45cm (18in) tall with thick, succulent stems, spoon-shaped leaves and bright yellow flowers.

P. o. var. aurea is a yellow-leaved, less hardy form. It is more succulent, but has less flavour. Attractive in salads and as an ornamental.

CULTIVATION

Propagation
Sow in seed trays indoors in late spring and transplant seedlings into modules when large enough to handle. Harden off and plant when there is no danger of frost, 15cm (6in) apart. In frost-free climates or for later crops, sow directly, thinning to 15cm (6in) apart. Sow in late spring for a summer crop and in late summer for autumn cropping.

Mature purslane plant in flower

Growing
Easily cultivated, purslane thrives in a sunny, warm, sheltered site on light, well-drained soil. Add organic matter and sand to improve drainage if needed. Remove flowers as they appear.

Maintenance
Spring Sow protected crops, or *in situ* once the danger of frost is passed.
Summer Keep plants weed-free and water as necessary. Harvest regularly.
Autumn Cut back mature plants to allow regrowth.
Winter In late winter sow early crops under glass.

Protected Cropping
To extend the season, sow in early to mid-spring and early to mid-autumn under cover. Make earlier and late summer sowings under cover as a 'cut and come again' crop.

Container Growing
Plant seedlings or sow seed in pots or containers when there is no danger of frost, using a soil-based compost with a low fertilizer content. Continue to water regularly.

Harvesting
Pick young shoot tips, stems and leaves when about 3–5cm (1½–2in) long. 'Cut and come again' crops are ready to harvest after about 5 weeks. Regular picking encourages young growth. As older plants deteriorate towards the end of the growing season, cut them back to within 5cm (2in) of the ground, water well and they should resprout.

Pests & Diseases
Purslane is prone to **slug** damage, particularly when young. **Damping off** can be a problem if sown at low temperatures or in cold soil.

Medicinal
A traditional remedy for dry coughs, swollen gums and, infused in water, for blood disorders. Research indicates that its high levels of fatty acids can prevent heart attacks and stimulate the body's immune system.

CULINARY

Wash thoroughly; growing close to the ground, leaves can be gritty. It can be lightly cooked, although the taste is not memorable. Older leaves can be pickled.

Purslane Salad
Serves 4

Use young buds and stems as well as the leaves.

4 ripe nectarines or peaches
Hazelnut oil
Handful of purslane
15 hazelnuts, toasted
½ teaspoon of coriander seeds, freshly crushed

Slice the nectarines or peaches and arrange on a salad plate brushed with hazelnut oil. Add the purslane leaves. Trickle over a little more oil, sprinkle with the chopped nuts and season with crushed coriander.

WARNING

Expectant mothers and those with digestive disorders should not eat purslane in large quantities.

Rumex acetosa. Polygonaceae

SORREL

(Bread and Cheese) Perennial often grown as annual for young leaves. Hardy. Value: rich in vitamin C.

Sorrel comes from the old French *surele* meaning 'sour', describing its taste. It was popular in England until the eighteenth century. John Evelyn wrote that 'Sorrel imparts a grateful quickness to the rest as supplying the want of oranges and lemons.'

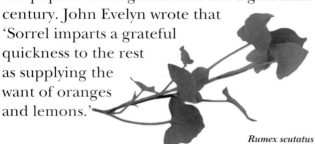

Rumex scutatus

VARIETIES

Rumex acetosa, upright, hardy, deep-rooted, grows to 120cm (4ft). Its broad, lance-shaped leaves have backward-pointing basal lobes. Less acidic is *Rumex scutatus*, buckler-leaf or French sorrel, a low-growing ground-cover plant with oblong shield-shaped leaves.

CULTIVATION

Grow in a bright or lightly shaded position on fertile, moist soil. Its presence often indicates iron in the soil.

Propagation
In late spring, sow seeds in drills 5mm (¼in) deep and 45cm (18in) apart, thinning to 23cm (9in) when large enough to handle. Or sow in modules or seed trays and plant out in spring. Divide mature plants in spring or early autumn, while still dormant. Alternatively, leave a few to self-seed, then transplant into rows, or broadcast several seedheads.

Growing
Before planting enrich poor soils with organic matter. Mulch in spring with well-rotted manure or compost. Remove flowers as they appear. Renew plants after 3–5 years. Sorrel can also be grown as an annual. Sow in early spring, thin to 10cm (4in) apart and lift plants with sufficient young leaves.

Rumex acetosa **growing: a healthy plant crops over a long period**

Maintenance
Spring Sow seed in beds, trays or modules.
Summer Mulch early and water well in dry weather.
Autumn Remove and compost dead leaves.
Winter Lift protected crops.

Protected Cropping
Overwinter under cloches or fleece by sowing seeds in trays or pots in late summer. Or transplant existing specimens into greenhouse borders, pots, or cold frames.

Container Growing
This is advisable on chalk soils. Use large containers of loam-based compost with moderate levels of fertilizer and added organic matter. Keep the compost moist but not waterlogged and feed every 3 weeks with a dilute liquid general fertilizer.

Harvesting
Harvest lightly until plants are established. Pick a few leaves from each; smaller leaves are tender, less bitter.

CULINARY

Sorrel withers rapidly and should be used quickly. Add to salads; its tanginess is refreshing. Use in soup and stews, as a garnish, or cook like spinach.

Sorrel Tart
Serves 4

250g (8oz) sorrel, washed
50g (2oz) butter
1 onion, finely sliced
1 tablespoon flour
1 teaspoon French mustard
300ml (½pt) milk
250g (8oz) Cheddar, grated
Salt & freshly ground pepper
20cm (8in) tart tin, lined
*   with shortcrust pastry*

Gently cook the sorrel with half the butter, until dark green. Remove from the heat and chop finely. Add the rest of the butter to the pan and cook the onion until soft. Stir in the flour and cook for 2 minutes. Add the mustard, then the milk and bring to the boil, stirring. Add the cheese and cook gently until melted.

Mix in the sorrel and season. Pour into the tin and cook in a preheated oven, 200°C, 400°F, gas 6, for 20–30 minutes, until the top is golden. Turn off the heat and leave on the bottom shelf for 5 minutes. Serve with a green salad.

The red haze of sorrel in flower

MEDICINAL

Sorrel was added to ale as a treatment for fever and is said to increase the haemoglobin content of blood.

WARNING

Sorrel contains high levels of oxalic acid, which in large doses causes kidney damage.

Raphanus sativus. Cruciferae

RADISH

nnual or biennial grown for edible swollen roots, seed pods and leaves. Hardy. Value: low in calories, oderate vitamin C, small amounts of iron and protein.

Thought to be native to Asia, yet domesticated in the Mediterranean, his reliable little salad vegetable has been in ultivation for centuries. Depicted in the yramid of Cheops, it was cultivated by the gyptians in 2780BC and Herodotus noted hat labourers working on the pyramids eceived 'radishes, onions and garlic' as their ations. By 500BC it was grown in China, eaching Japan 200 years later. Pliny records hat 'models of turnips, beetroots and adishes were dedicated to Apollo in the emple at Delphi, turnips made of lead, beets of silver and radishes of gold,' while Horace vrote of 'lettuces and radishes such as excite he languid stomach.' John Evelyn, too, vrote: 'Radishes are eaten alone with salt only, as conveying their pepper in them.' The fiery flavour is due to the presence of nustard oil. Although radishes are usually ed, there are also black, purple, yellow and green-skinned types.

VARIETIES

The fast-growing salad types are ready to harvest in about 4 weeks. Larger, slow-growing types, often with long cylindrical roots, include large overwintering varieties and the Oriental varieties known as 'mooli' or 'daikon'.

Salad and overwintering radishes
'Cherry Belle' is round, with crisp, white, mild flesh. Tolerant of poorer soils, it is slow to go woody and keeps well. Harvest 3 weeks after sowing. **'China Rose'** is a well-flavoured winter variety with bright red roots and white flesh. **'D'Avignon'** is rose-coloured with a white tip, crunchy and extremely hot. **'18 Day'** is a fast-growing French Breakfast type, crisp and mild. **'French Breakfast 3'*** is long, mild, sweet and tender. Harvest at maturity or they become hot and woody. **'Scarlet Globe'** is justifiably popular for its mild flavour and good quality. Can be sown early under cover. **'Long Black Spanish'**, a winter variety, has wonderful dark skin and is extremely hot. **'Munchen Bier'** is grown for its tasty green pods, which are eaten raw or stir-fried. **'Round**

'Round Black Spanish'

Black Spanish'** is similar to 'Long Black Spanish', but globe-shaped. **'Short Top Forcing'*** is a bright red variety, excellent for winter sowing under cover.

Mooli or daikon
'Mooli' and **'daikon'** are general terms for a group of long, white radishes (*Raphanus sativus* var. *longipinnatus*) which need cool temperatures and short daylength to flourish.
'April Cross' is crisp, juicy and mild. **'Long White Icicle'** is tender with a pungent, almost nutty taste. **'Minowasa Summer'**, a Japanese variety, is long and mild. **'Mino Early'** is a large Japanese variety. **'Summer Cross Hybrid'** is fast-growing and ready to harvest when 15cm (6in) long.

CULTIVATION

Propagation
Radishes are one of the easiest and quickest vegetables to grow. Sow successively every 2 weeks from when the soil becomes workable in early to mid-spring to early autumn. Sow thinly in drills 1cm (½in) deep and 15cm (6in) apart, thinning to 2.5cm (1in) apart about 10 days after they appear. Alternatively, broadcast seed and thin to 2.5cm (1in) apart. Radishes dislike being overcrowded.

Sow overwintering radishes in summer, 2cm (¾in) deep in rows 23–30cm (9–12in) apart; depending on the cultivar, thin to 15–23cm (6–9in). Sow mooli/daikon from mid- to late summer.

Small radishes can be grown as 'cut and come again' seedlings. Harvest when seedlings are 5–7.5cm (2–3in) tall; if you allow them to grow to 20–22.5cm (8–9in), the leaves can be cooked like spinach.

Growing
As radishes are a cool-weather crop, grow earlier and later crops in an open site, but plant summer crops in light shade, surrounded by taller plants. They flourish in a light, moisture-retentive, free-draining soil which was manured for the previous crop, with a pH of 6.5–7.5. Dig the ground thoroughly before preparing the seedbed and remove any stones, particularly when growing longer-rooted varieties.

Rake a slow-release granular fertilizer into the seedbed at 30g/sq m (1oz/sq yd) before sowing the first crops and before planting winter varieties.

Rapid growth is essential for tasty, tender roots, so supply plenty of water and do not let the seedbed dry out. Overwatering encourages the production of leaves rather than roots and erratic watering causes roots to become woody or split. During drought, water weekly at 11 litres/sq m (2 gal/sq yd). Hoe and hand weed regularly.

Radishes' pretty exterior belies their fiery taste

Maintenance
Spring Sow crops outdoors when soil conditions allow.
Summer Sow successionally; keep crops well watered and weed-free. Sow winter crops.
Autumn Grow later crops under cover.
Winter Harvest over-wintering crops. Sow early crops under cover.

Protected Cropping
Grow early and late crops of summer varieties under cloches to extend the cropping season. Ventilate and water thoroughly.

Grow summer crops under floating cloches to protect them.

Container Growing
Radishes are easily grown in containers. These should be 15–30cm (6–12in) wide by 20cm (8in) deep. Use a loam-based compost or free-draining, moisture-retentive garden soil. Water well and liquid feed with general fertilizer if necessary. They can also be sown in grow-bags, thinning until they are 2.5–5cm (1–2in) apart.

Harvesting & Storing
Pull immediately they mature after 8 to 10 weeks, otherwise they will become woody or run to seed.

Later crops can be stored. Twist off leaves and store in boxes of dry sand or sawdust in a frost-free place. Overwintering types can be left in the ground and lifted as needed. Protect with straw or bracken. For ease of lifting, these can be allowed to grow over 35cm (15in) long without being coarse.

Kept in a polythene bag in the refrigerator, radishes stay fresh for about a week.

Pests & Diseases
Flea beetle, **cabbage fly** and **slugs** can be a problem.

COMPANION PLANTING

Radishes grow well with chervil, peas and lettuce and thrive with nasturtium and with mustard.

Because of their rapid growth, radishes make an excellent 'indicator crop'. Sown in the same row as slow-germinating crops like parsnips or parsley, they mark where the maincrop has been sown, make weeding easier, and can be harvested without disturbing the developing plants.

MEDICINAL

Radishes can be eaten to relieve indigestion and flatulence as well as being taken as a tonic herb as an expectorant.

'Long Spanish Black'

'Cherry Belle', picked and packed

Radish & Scallop Soup

CULINARY

Radishes are usually eaten raw, whole, grated or sliced into salads. Alternatively wash and trim the root, remove the leaves and all but the bottom 2.5cm (1in) of stalk to use as a 'handle' and enjoy it with rough bread, creamy butter, salt, cheese and a pint of good ale! (In Germany, you'll find them on the bar instead of peanuts.) They can also be sliced and used instead of onions in hamburgers.

Seedling leaves are eaten raw and older leaves are cooked like spinach.

Long white summer radishes and winter radishes can be eaten raw but are usually cooked and added to casseroles, stews or curries.

Winter varieties are also pickled. Peel, then cube or slice in slightly salted water for about 10 minutes. Drain thoroughly and serve tossed in butter.

Thin slices of winter varieties or larger summer types can be stir-fried.

For extra crispness, put them into a bowl of water with a few ice cubes for a couple of hours.

Slice radishes and tangerines, mandarins or oranges into small pieces, sprinkle lightly with salt, chopped fennel leaves and lemon juice. This interesting recipe is an acquired taste!

To make a 'radish rose', remove the stalk and make a number of vertical cuts from the stalk almost to the root. Place in iced water for 30 minutes; the petals open.

Immature green seed pods can be eaten raw, cooked or pickled. Pick when crisp and green.

Scrape or peel and 'top and tail' mooli or daikon before use. In India they are eaten cooked or raw. In Japan shredded mooli is a traditional accompaniment to 'sashimi' (raw fish) and is eaten with 'sushi'.

As with summer radishes, a thin slice makes an excellent mustard substitute with a roast beef sandwich.

Radish & Scallop Soup
Serves 4

2 bunches radishes, topped
  & tailed
10 scallops, trimmed
2 spring onions, chopped
2 tablespoons butter
600ml (1pt) fish stock & milk
  combined
2 bay leaves
Pinch cayenne pepper
1 tablespoon parsley
4 tablespoons double cream

First wash the radishes thoroughly and cut them into small dice. Then cut the scallops in half and set to one side.

In a soup pot, cook the onions in the butter until soft, and then add the scallops. Cook them for 30 seconds on each side over a gentle heat and then add the radishes.

Pour over the stock and milk mixture. Add the bay leaves, cayenne and parsley and cook for 15 minutes over a gentle heat, just simmering.

Remove the soup from the heat. Take the scallops out of the soup with a slotted spoon; cut them into slivers and return them to the pan.

Lastly, stir in the parsley and the cream and serve immediately.

Rheum x hybridum (syn. *R. x cultorum*). *Polygonaceae*

RHUBARB

**(Pieplant) Large perennial herb grown for pink edible stems. Half hardy.
Value: very low in calories, contains small amounts of vitamins.**

The earliest records of rhubarb date from China in 2700BC, and there are references to its cultivation in Europe in the early 1700s. It was originally grown for its medicinal use as a powerful purgative; the annual value of imports to England for this purpose was once estimated to be £200,000. It was first mentioned as a food plant in 1778 by the French, for making tarts and pies. Rhubarb was introduced to Maine from Europe around 1790; from there it spread to market gardeners in New England and Massachusetts. Forcing and blanching were discovered by chance at the Chelsea Physic Garden in 1817 after crowns were covered in debris when a ditch was cleared!

VARIETIES

A greater range of cultivars is to be found in specialist nurseries. **'Crimson Red'** has a distinctive sweet yet sharp flavour. **'Early Champagne'** (**'Early Red'**) produces long, delicious scarlet stalks which are excellent for wine-making and early forcing. **'Glaskin's Perpetual'** is vigorous and tasty, and crops over a long period. **'The Sutton'**, introduced by Suttons Seeds in 1893, is tasty and good for forcing. **'Timperley Early'** is very early, vigorous and suitable for forcing. **'Valentine'** is hardy and vigorous with tender, rose-coloured stalks. Perfect for pies and jams, it has a wonderful flavour. **'Victoria'**, a reliable old variety, is variable in size. Harvest from late spring. **'Zwolle Seedling'** has good flavour and fragrance and stays firm when cooked.

Rhubarb forced using traditional terracotta jars

CULTIVATION

Propagation

Rhubarb can be grown from seed, but the results are invariably poor. It is better to lift and divide mature crowns of known varieties or buy virus-free plants from a reputable nursery.

Plants should be divided every 2 or 3 years; if plants are any older, take divisions from the outer margins. Lift dormant crowns in winter after the leaves have died back and divide with a spade or knife. Each 'set' should be about 10cm (4in) across with plenty of fibrous roots and at least one bud.

Plants tend to establish more rapidly if transplanted into 25cm (10in) pots of multi-purpose compost for 3 months prior to planting out. Transplant, 75–90cm (2½–3ft) apart, from late autumn (the best time) to early spring, with the bud tip covered by 2.5cm (1in) of soil. Plant cultivars which have large buds with the buds slightly above ground to prevent rotting. Plants remain productive for several seasons, their decline is marked by the production of masses of thin stalks.

Alternatively, sow in drills about 2.5cm (1in) deep and 30cm (12in) apart, thinning to 15cm (6in). Plant out the strongest in autumn or the following spring.

Growing

Rhubarb flourishes in an open, sunny position in deep, fertile, well-drained soil with a pH of 5.0–6.0. It is ideal for cool temperate climates. It is very hungry, with deep roots, so ensure that the soil contains well-rotted manure or compost. On very heavy soils, plant on ridges or raised beds.

Mulch plants every winter with a good thick layer of well-rotted compost or manure. Do not allow them to flower unless you wish to save the seed, as this affects cropping the following year. Keep weed-free and watered removing dead leaves instantly. In early spring, scatter a balanced general fertilizer around the crowns.

Maintenance

Spring Force early crops under a bucket or similar. *Summer* Harvest stems. *Autumn* When stems die back remove all plant debris *Winter* Mulch with well-rotted compost or manure.

'Timperley Early', a popular variety for gardeners

Protected Cropping

For early crops lift a few crowns in late autumn, leave them above ground and let them be frosted, then bring indoors into a cool place for forcing. Put in a large container packed with soil or plant under greenhouse staging. Exclude light with an upturned box or bucket 38–45cm (15–18in) high to allow for stem growth. They can also be forced in bin liners. Keep compost moist. Dispose of exhausted forced crowns after harvest.

Alternatively, from late winter, cover *in situ* with a 15cm (6in) layer of straw or leaves or with an upturned bin, bucket or blanching pot covered with straw or strawy manure. Harvest in early to mid-spring. Do not harvest from a crown for at least 2 years after forcing.

Harvesting & Storing

Do not harvest until 12–18 months after planting, taking only a few 'sticks' in the second season and more in later years. Cropping can last from early spring to mid-summer. To harvest, hold the stems near the base and twist off. Avoid breaking the stems, as it can cause fungal problems. Do not over-pick; it can weaken the plant.

To freeze, chop the stems into sections and place on an open tray, freeze for 1 hour before packing into polythene bags. This prevents the sections from sticking together. They can be stored for up to a year.

PESTS & DISEASES

Honey fungus may appear as white streaks in dead crown tissue; orange toadstools appear round base. Dig out and burn diseased roots.

Crown rot damages terminal buds and makes stems spindly. Dig out and burn badly infected plants. Do not replant in the area.

Virus disease has no cure. Dig up and burn.

COMPANION PLANTING

Rhubarb is reported to control red spider mite. A traditional remedy suggests putting rhubarb in planting

CULINARY

Forced rhubarb is tender and needs less sugar. Cook stems slowly with sugar. Very little or no water is required; do not overcook them. Avoid using aluminium pans.

Rhubarb can be stewed for fruit pies, bottling or preserving, fools, mousses and rhubarb crumble, which is delicious. The flavour can be improved by adding orange juice, marmalade or cinnamon. It can also be puréed with apple. Claudia Roden's *Middle Eastern Food* demonstrates that it is unexpectedly wonderful stewed with beef or lamb in Persian *khoresh*.

Preserved Rhubarb

3.5kg (7lb) rhubarb
3.5kg (7lb) preserving sugar
Juice & grated peel of 2 lemons
50g (2oz) blanched almonds

Cut the rhubarb into 2.5cm (1in) lengths and cook gently in a preserving pan until the juices start to run. Add the sugar, lemon juice and peel and the almonds. Stir until the

sugar dissolves, then boil until a good colour and thickened. Pot up into sterilized jars and seal.

Rhubarb Sorbet
Serves 4

400g (14oz) rhubarb
150g (5oz) caster sugar
Juice of half a lemon

Cut the rhubarb into 2.5cm (1in) lengths and put into a heavy-bottomed pan. Add 50ml (2fl oz) water. Warm gently until the juices run, then stir in the sugar and lemon juice and simmer, covered, until tender. Freeze, whisking several times as it freezes to break up the ice crystals. If you use a sorbetière, churn until smooth. Remove from the freezer 15 minutes before serving and leave in the fridge.

Rhubarb Sorbet

holes to control clubroot. An infusion of leaves is effective as an aphicide and to check blackspot on roses.

MEDICINAL USES

Rhubarb is an astringent, stomachic and potent laxative. Dioscorides recommended it for chest, stomach and liver

complaints, and ringworm. By the sixteenth century, in western Europe, it was taken as an infusion with parsley as a cure for venereal disease.

WARNING

Do not eat the leaves, which are extremely poisonous!

Crithmum maritimum. Apiaceae

SAMPHIRE

(Rock Samphire, Sea Fennel, Sea Samphire) Low-growing maritime perennial.
Half hardy. Value: good source of iron and vitamin C with moderate iodine.

Rock samphire is found on the shores and cliffs of Europe. Its name comes from 'sampiere', a contraction of the French *herbe de St Pierre* – the fisherman Saint's herb. Collected from the wild for centuries, by the English Tudor period it was widely cultivated in gardens. William Turner wrote: 'Creta marina groweth much in rockes and cliffes beside Dover.' This precarious habitat is mentioned in *King Lear*, where harvesters dangle over the cliffs from a rope. Robert Turner in 1664 described similar dangerous activities on the 200m (600ft) cliffs of the Isle of Wight, 'yet many adventure it though they buy their sauce with the price of their lives'. Samphire harvests were sent in casks of seawater to London, where wholesalers paid four shillings a bushell, but for the privilege of collecting it and gulls' eggs the Lord of the Manor exacted an annual rent.

VARIETIES

Crithmum maritimum has a woody base, with stems to 60cm (2ft) and lobed grey-green leaflets. The white/cream flowers, in flat clusters, are followed by small oval fruits. The leaves have an aromatic odour which has been likened to the smell of furniture polish!

CULTIVATION

Propagation
Plants are propagated from fresh seed sown in autumn or spring in a sheltered position. Transplant when large enough to handle, or divide plants in spring.

Growing
Its natural habitat is in sand; if you create a satisfactory habitat in a coastal garden, natural colonies may form. Plants often inhabit dry stone walls. They flourish in well-drained, sandy or gritty soil, which is constantly

Samphire flourishes in sea spray

moist and protected from full heat. An open east- or south-facing position is ideal. Mulch with seaweed, or burn seaweed and scatter with the sodium-rich debris. If possible, water with seawater or sea salt solution.

Maintenance
Spring Sow seed in gritty compost or in shallow drills. *Summer* Keep soil moist with a saline solution. Harvest. *Autumn*: Harvest. Protect crops during colder weather. *Winter* Mulch with straw or leaves.

Protected Cropping
As a succulent plant, rock samphire needs frost protection. Cover with leaves, straw or cloches.

Container Growing
Grow in containers of gritty, loam-based compost. Water regularly in summer; in cooler climates, bring plant indoors during the winter.

Harvesting & Storing
Harvest young shoots and leaves by cutting or pulling. Young spring growth is the most tender. Do not harvest excessively from each plant. It is best eaten immediately after harvesting, but will last for up to 2 days in a fridge.

Pests & Diseases
Usually trouble-free.

CULINARY

Wash thoroughly in running water before use.

Tender young shoots and leaves can be eaten fresh or cooked as a vegetable. They are added raw to salads or dressed with oil and lemon juice as an hors-d'oeuvre.

Pickle young shoots, leaves and stems by filling a jar with samphire cut into 2.5cm (1in) lengths, add peppercorns and a little grated horseradish, pour over a boiling mixture of equal parts dry cider and vinegar, and infuse for an hour before sealing. Pickled it is used as a garnish and as a caper substitute.

In Italy it is known as 'Roscano'.

MEDICINAL

John Evelyn noted 'its excellent vertues and effect against the Spleen. Cleansing the Passages and sharpning appetite.' It was also recommended as a kidney, bladder and general tonic and as a treatment for 'stones'. It is said to be a diuretic, to improve digestion and has been used to encourage weight loss.

Sechium edule. Cucurbitaceae

CHAYOTE

(Choko, Chow Chow, Christophine) Vigorous, scrambling, tuberous-rooted perennial, grown for edible fruit and seed. Tender. Value: 90% water; low in calories; some vitamin C.

In good conditions, this climber spreads to 15m (50ft) and produces huge tubers. It originated in central America; 'chayote' comes from the Aztec *chayotl*, while in the West Indies it is called 'christophine' after Columbus, who reputedly introduced it to the islands. The pear-shaped fruits contain a single nutty-flavoured seed, much prized by cooks.

VARIETIES

'Ivory White' is a small, pale-skinned variety.

CULTIVATION

Chayote needs rich, fertile, well-drained soil.

Propagation

Propagate cultivars from soft tip cuttings in spring at 18°C (65°F). Alternatively, plant the whole fruit laid on its side, at a slight angle, with the narrow end protruding from the soil.

Growing

Grow on mounds 30–40cm (12–14in) high and 90 x 90cm (3 x 3ft) apart; cover a shovel full of well-rotted manure with 15cm (6in) of soil. Lightly mulch.

Alternatively, grow on beds 3m (9ft) square; dig in organic matter, plant seeds in the corners and grow vines towards the centre. Or, plant in 90cm (3ft) wide ridges. Train the stems into trees, over trellising, fences, or 15cm (6in) mesh netting. Water regularly in dry weather; optimum growth is during the wet season. A day length of just over 12 hours is required for flowering.

In the humid tropics, it grows better in moderate temperatures at altitude.

Maintenance

Spring Sow seed or take cuttings.
Summer Feed and water.
Autumn Harvest.
Winter Store fruit for next year's crop.

Protected Cropping

In cool temperate regions, grow under glass in bright light with moderate temperatures and humidity. In warmer areas, start off indoors and plant when the danger of frost has passed. Grow in the greenhouse border or in containers.

Container Growing

Propagate in spring from seed or cuttings. Pot on into loam-based compost with a high fertilizer content, add well-rotted manure and grit to improve drainage. Water thoroughly, feed fortnightly with general liquid fertilizer and, once established, with a high-potash fertilizer. Train the growth on to a trellis.

Harvesting & Storing

In tropical climates, plants last for several years, fruiting from 3 to 4 months after sowing, all year round. Harvest by cutting the stalk above the fruit with a knife. Fruit reaches its maximum size 25–30 days after fruit set. It will keep up to 3 months in a cool place.

Pests & Diseases

Root knot nematode causes wilting; **powdery mildew** can appear on leaves and stems; and **red spider mite** affects plants grown under glass.

MEDICINAL

Chayote is good for stomach ulcers. It contains some trace elements.

CULINARY

This versatile vegetable can be made into soups, boiled, candied, puréed (spiced with chilli powder) or added to stews, curries and chutneys. Its seeds can be cooked in butter, the young leaves cooked like spinach, and the tuber eaten when young. Its flesh stays firm after cooking. It makes a good substitute for avocado in a salad and is ideal for those on a diet.

For a stuffing, try a well-flavoured bolognese sauce; add boiled chayote flesh and stuff back into halved chayote shells. Sprinkle with Cheddar and bake in an oven preheated to 180°C, 350°F, gas 4, for 30 minutes.

Chayote in Red Wine
Serves 6

Jane Grigson gives a recipe for this pudding.

6 pear-sized chayotes, peeled & left whole
150g (5oz) sugar
300ml (½pt) water
150ml (¼pt) red wine
5cm (2in) cinnamon stick
4 cloves
Lemon juice
Whipped cream & icing sugar

Use a pan that will hold the chayote in a single layer. Put the sugar and water on to dissolve and simmer for 2 minutes. Carefully add the chayote, then the wine and spices.

Cover and simmer until tender. Remove the chayote to a bowl and arrange upright like pears. Reduce the liquid until syrupy and add a little lemon juice to bring out the flavour. Strain the juice over the chayote and serve with whipped cream lightly sweetened with icing sugar.

Chayote in Red Wine

Scorzonera hispanica. Compositae

SCORZONERA

(False Salsify, Spanish Salsify)
Grown as biennial for shoots, flower buds and flowers; annual for cylindrical tapering roots. Hardy. Value: contains indigestible carbohydrate inulin, which, when converted to fructose in storage, increases calorific content (27 calories per 100g); small amounts of vitamins and minerals.

Scorzonera is very similar to salsify, though scorzonera is perennial, not biennial, its skin is darker, the roots narrower and the flavour is not as strong. The name scorzonera may have come from the French '*scorzon*' or serpent, as the root was used in Spain to cure snake bites. Another interpretation suggests it comes from the Italian '*scorza*', bark, and '*nera*', black, describing the roots. Native to central and southern Europe through to Russia and Siberia, scorzonera was known by the Greeks and Romans, who took little interest in its cultivation; it arrived in England by 1560 and in North America by 1806. It is widely grown in Europe as an excellent winter vegetable. The leaves have been used as food for silkworms.

If allowed to grow, the bright yellow flowers make ideal ornamentals

VARIETIES

'**Duplex**' produces long tasty roots. '**Flandria Scorzonera**' has long roots, growing to 30cm (12in), with strongly flavoured flesh. '**Habil**' is long-rooted with a delicious flavour. '**Lange Jan**' ('**Long John**') has long, tapering, dark brown roots. '**Long Black**' is similar, but with black roots. '**Russian Giant**' lives up to its name, with long roots and a subtle, delicate flavour.

CULTIVATION

Propagation
Sow fresh seed *in situ* from mid- to late spring, in drills 1–2cm (½–¾in) deep with rows 15cm (6in) apart. Alternatively, sow 2 or 3 seeds in 'stations' 15cm (6in) apart, thinning to leave the strongest seedling when large enough to handle. Or sow in late summer for use early the following autumn.

Growing
It flourishes in a sunny position on a deep, light, well-drained soil which should have been manured for a previous crop. Do not grow on freshly manured or stony ground, as this causes 'forking'. A pH of 6.0–7.5 is ideal, so lime the soil if necessary. On heavy or stony soils, fill a narrow trench about 30cm (12in) deep with finely sieved soil or free draining compost so that the roots grow straight. Dig the soil deeply and rake in 60–90g/sq m (2–3oz/sq yd) general balanced fertilizer 10 days before sowing.

Remove weeds around the plants by hand, as roots bleed easily when damaged by a hoe. Mulching once the roots have established helps to smother weeds, conserves moisture and reduces the risk of bolting during dry weather. Water at a rate of 16–22 litres/sq m (3–5 gal/sq yd) per week.

'Russian Giant', one of the more commonly grown varieties

Scorzonera tends to be neglected by English gardeners, but is often found growing in Mediterranean countries

PESTS & DISEASES

Scorzonera rarely suffers from problems but may develop 'white blister', which looks like glistening paint splashes. Affected plants become distorted.

COMPANION PLANTING

Scorzonera repels carrot root fly and the flowers attract beneficial insects.

MEDICINAL

The name derived from the Spanish reflects its reputation as an antidote to snake venom, '...and especially to cure the bitings of vipers (of which there may be very many in Spaine and other hot countries),' wrote Gerard in his *Herball* of 1597. This has not been proven.

Roots can be left in the ground to produce 'chards' (edible shoots) the following spring. In autumn cut off old leaves, leaving 1–2.5cm (½–1in) above the soil. Earth up the roots to a depth of about 15cm (6in) so the developing shoots are blanched during the winter. In late spring, scrape away the soil and harvest when the shoots are 12–15cm (5–6in) long. They can also be blanched by covering to a similar depth with straw or leaves in early spring. Roots too small to harvest in the first year can be left to mature the following year.

Maintenance
Spring Sow thinly, from mid- to late spring. Thin when large enough to handle.
Summer Keep crops weed-free and water thoroughly as needed to keep soil moist.
Autumn Leave roots in the ground and lift carefully with a fork as needed.
Winter Continue harvesting. Prepare the ground for the next crop.

Protected Cropping
Scorzonera is hardy, but protection with straw or cloches before the onset of severe weather makes lifting much easier.

Container Growing
In shallow or stony soils plants can be grown in deep containers of loam-based compost. Water regularly.

Harvesting & Storing
Plants need at least 4 months to reach maturity and are ready to harvest from mid-autumn to mid-spring. In a good year the roots may grow to 40cm (16in), but are more usually about 20cm (8in) long.
Roots can either be left in the ground until needed or lifted – with care, as they are easily damaged. Clean and store in boxes of sand or sawdust in a cool place. They last up to 1 week in a fridge.
Mature plants flower in spring or summer of the second year. The buds can be harvested with about 8cm (3in) of stem.
If, while lifting, you see that your crop has many forked roots, the remaining plants can be kept for their young shoots and buds.

CULINARY

Roots can be baked, puréed, dipped in batter, sautéed and made into croquettes and fritters, deep-fried or served *au gratin* with cheese and breadcrumbs.
Boiling allows you to appreciate the flavour fully. They discolour when cut, so drop into water with a dash of lemon juice, then boil for 25 minutes in salted water with a tablespoon of flour added. Peel after boiling as you would a hard-boiled egg.

Toss with melted butter and chopped parsley. Young 'chards' can be served raw in salads. The flower stalks are considered tastier than those of salsify.

Sautéed Scorzonera
Allow 150–175g (5–6oz) per person of cleaned scorzonera; it should not be peeled. Chop roughly and cook in a heavy frying pan in a little extra-virgin olive oil until *al dente*, turning to cook every side. Drain on kitchen paper and sprinkle with lemon juice mixed with 1 crushed garlic clove and 1 tablespoon finely chopped flat-leaf parsley.

Sautéed Scorzonera

Solanum melongena. Solanaceae

AUBERGINE

(Brinjal, Garden Egg, Eggplant, Guinea Squash, Pea Aubergine) Short-lived perennial grown as annual for fruits. Tender. Value: small amounts of most vitamins and minerals; very low in calories, containing 3% carbohydrates and 1% protein.

Aubergine flowers reveal the family likeness to the potato

This glossy-skinned fruit was known to sixteenth-century Spaniards as the 'apple of love'. In contrast, many botanists of the time called it *mala insana* or 'mad apple', because of its alleged effects. The Chinese first cultivated aubergines in the fifth century BC and they have been grown in India for centuries, yet they were unknown to the Greeks and Romans. Moorish invaders introduced them to Spain and the Spaniards later took them to the New World. 'Aubergine' is a corruption of the Arabic name *al–badingan*.

VARIETIES

Fruits vary in shape from large, purple-skinned types to small, rounded white fruits 5cm (2in) diameter. Most modern F1 hybrids are bushy and grow about 1m (3ft) tall. Unlike older varieties, they are almost spineless. **'Bambino'** is a small variety, grown as a 'mini vegetable'. **'Black Beauty'** produces dark purple fruits of good quality over a long period. It is high-yielding. **'Black Enorma'** has monstrous, dark, almost spherical fruit. Regular harvesting is advisable and a stout supporting stake is recommended, too! **'Easter Egg'**, despite its name, is not chocolate-coloured and sweet, but white, about the size of a large hen's egg. It should be harvested when it is about 12.5cm (5in) long. It ripens after 2 months in good growing conditions. **'Florida Market'** is oval, glossy purple-black and ideal for warm climates. Cropping over a long period, the fruits are rot-resistant and tasty. **'Long Purple'** produces good yields of dark purple fruits about 15cm (6in) long. **'Moneymaker'*** is a superb early variety with tasty fruits. Tolerant of lower temperatures, it can be grown indoors as well as outside. **'Ova'** is delightful, producing masses of small, white-skinned fruits. It is decorative and ideal for unheated greenhouses. **'Short Tom'** is a small, early cropping variety. The fruits can be harvested when they are small or allowed to grow larger. It is ideal for containers. **'Violette di Firenze'** needs warmth to ripen fully. The unusual yet very attractive dark mauve fruits make this an ideal plant for growing in a 'potager'.

CULTIVATION

Aubergines need long, hot summers, and are the ideal crop for warm climates. In cooler regions, they will grow outside, but better harvests come from those protected indoors. Constant temperatures between 25–30°C (75–86°F) with moderate to high humidity are needed for optimum flower and fruit production. Below 20°C (68°F) growth is often stalled.

Propagation

Temperatures of 15–21°C (58–70°F) are needed for good germination. Sow seed in early spring, in trays, pots or modules of moist seed compost in a propagator or warm glasshouse or on a window sill. Soaking seed in warm water for 24 hours before sowing helps germination. When 3 leaves appear, pot on plants grown in seed trays into 5–7.5cm (2–3in) pots, repotting as required until they are ready to plant outdoors or under cover. If you are growing aubergines outdoors, sow seeds 10–12 weeks before the last frosts are expected.

Growing

Aubergines flourish in a sunny, sheltered position on fertile, well-drained soil. Before planting, fork in a slow-release general fertilize at 30–60g/sq m (1–2oz/sq yd), improve the soil with the addition of organic matter and, in cooler climates, warm the soil before planting and leave the cloches in place until the plants are established for 2–3 weeks, allowing them to 'harden off' before removing the cloches.

Space plants 50–60cm (20–24in) apart. 'Pinch out' the growth tip when plants are 40cm (16in) tall, or 23–30cm (9–12in) for smaller varieties. Stake the main stem or support branches with string if necessary as fruit begins to mature. Mulch outdoor plants to conserve moisture and suppress weeds.

Feed plants with a liquid general fertilizer until they are established, then water with a high-potash liquid feed every 10 days once the first fruits are formed. When the flowers begin to open a light spray with tepid water helps pollination; for large, high-quality fruits, allow only 4–5 to form on each plant, after which any new side shoots should be removed.

Maintenance

Spring Sow seeds under glass.
Summer Once frosts are over, transplant outdoors. Retain 4–6 fruits per plant, harvesting as they mature.
Autumn Protect outdoor crops from early frosts.
Winter Order seed for the following growing season.

Protected Cropping

When growing plants indoors, mist them regularly with tepid water or 'damp down' the paths on hot days. Keep the compost moist throughout the growing season but take care to avoid waterlogging.

Container Growing

Aubergines can be grown in 20–30cm (8–12in) pots or in growbags. Keep temperatures around 15–18°C (58–65°F); water regularly, keep the compost moist and feed with a half-strength high-potash fertilizer every other watering.

Harvesting & Storing

Harvest when the skin is shiny: overripe fruits have dull skin and are horribly bitter. Using a knife, cut the fruit stalks close to the stem. They will keep for 2 weeks in a cool, humid place or in a refrigerator.

PESTS & DISEASES

Aubergines are susceptible to the typical problems of crops grown under glass.
Check plants for **aphids**, **whitefly** and **red spider mite**. **Powdery mildew** can stunt growth, and in severe cases leaves become yellow and die. **Verticillium wilt** turns lower leaves yellow; plants wilt but recover overnight.

COMPANION PLANTING

Aubergines flourish alongside thyme, tarragon and peas.

MEDICINAL

In Indian herbal medicine white varieties are used to treat diabetes and as a carminative. The Sanskrit *vatin–ganah* means 'anti–wind vegetable'. *Kama Sutra* prescribes it in a concoction for 'enlarging the male organ for a period of 1 month'. Neither claim has been proven!

WARNING

Always remove the fruit's bitter principle as it irritates the mucous membranes.

'Violette di Firenze', beautiful and unusual

CULINARY

The large 'berries' contain a bitter principle in the flesh. Slice large varieties, sprinkle with salt and leave for 30 minutes to leach out the bitterness, before rinsing. Small and newer varieties do not need this treatment. Rub cut surfaces with lemon juice to prevent discoloration.

Aubergines can be made into soups, puréed, stewed, stuffed, fried and pickled. Slices can be dipped in batter to make fritters, or drizzled with olive oil and grilled or roasted. In the Middle East the skin is burned off over a naked flame, giving the flesh a smoky flavour.

In Provence the vegetable stew *ratatouille* is made from aubergines, garlic, peppers, courgettes, onions and coriander seeds, all cooked in olive oil. The Greek *moussaka* contains minced meat and aubergines.

In the Caribbean small white varieties are stewed in coconut milk and sweet spices. Oriental aubergines have a sweetness that does not suit European cooking; use them in stir-fries.

Sautéed Aubergines with Mozzarella
Serves 4

This dish goes well with plain meats.

4 small, long, thin aubergines
1 clove garlic, crushed
1 tablespoon chopped parsley
Salt & freshly ground black pepper
50g (2oz) toasted breadcrumbs
3 tablespoons olive oil
100g (4oz) buffalo mozzarella, cut into 5mm (¼in) slices

Cut the aubergines in half lengthwise. Score the flesh deeply, but do not cut the skin. Arrange in a shallow pan, skin side down. Mix the garlic, parsley, salt and pepper, the breadcrumbs and half the olive oil and press this into the scored aubergines. Drizzle over the rest of the oil and place in a preheated oven (180°C, 350°F, gas 4) until tender, about 20 minutes.

Raise the heat to 200°C, 400°F, gas 6 and, as the oven warms, arrange the mozzarella on top of the aubergines. Return to the oven for 5 minutes. Serve this dish immediately the mozzarella melts.

Solanum tuberosum. Solanaceae

POTATO

(Common Potato, Irish Potato) Perennial, grown as annual for edible starchy tubers. Half hardy. Value: rich in carbohydrates, magnesium, potassium; moderate amounts of vitamins B and C.

Then a sentimental passion of a vegetable fashion must excite your languid spleen.
An attachment à la Plato for a bashful young potato or a not too French French bean.
Sir William Gilbert (1836–1911)

The world's fourth most important food crop after wheat, maize and rice, the potato is a nutritious starchy staple grown throughout temperate zones. Hundreds of varieties have been developed since 5000BC, when potatoes were first cultivated in Chile and Peru. The name derives from *batatas*, the Carib Indian name for the sweet potato, or from *papa* or *patata*, as it was called by South American Indians.

The Spaniards introduced potatoes to Europe in the sixteenth century and Sir John Hawkins is reputed to have brought them to England in 1563. Extensive cultivation did not start until Sir Francis Drake brought more back in 1586, after battling with the Spaniards in the Caribbean. Sir Walter Raleigh introduced them to Ireland and later presented some to Elizabeth I. Her cook is said to have discarded the tubers and cooked the leaves, which did not help its popularity!

In England and Germany potatoes were considered a curiosity; in France they were believed to cause leprosy and fever. However, in 1773 the French scientist Antoine Parmentier wrote a thesis extolling the potato's virtues as a famine food after eating them while a prisoner of war in Prussia. He established soup kitchens to feed the malnourished; potato soup is now known as *Potage*

Parmentier, and there is also *Omelette Parmentier*. He created 'French fries', which were served at a dinner honouring Benjamin Franklin, who was unimpressed; it was Thomas Jefferson who introduced French fries to America at a White House dinner.

Parmentier presented a bouquet of potato flowers to Louis XVI, who is said to have worn one in his buttonhole. Marie Antoinette wore them in her hair, which made it highly fashionable. By the early nineteenth century, the potato had become a staple in France.

Ireland's climate and plentiful rain produced large crops. Potatoes were propagated from small tubers which were passed from one household to another, so the whole crop came from a few original plants. These were susceptible to potato blight, and devastating crop failure in the 1840s caused the death of more than 1.5 million people. Almost a million others emigrated to North America. Without the potato famine, John Kennedy and Ronald Reagan may never have been presidents of the United States.

During the American Civil War, potatoes were sent to the prisons and front lines. By eating the potatoes in their skins, soldiers received adequate supplies of vitamin C. The common name 'spud' came from a tool which was once used to weed the potato patch.

VARIETIES

Potatoes are classified as 'first early', 'second early' (or 'mid-crop') and 'maincrop' varieties. Early and second early varieties grow rapidly, taking up less space for a shorter time than maincrops, so are better for small gardens. Yields are usually lower. They are also unaffected by some of the diseases afflicting maincrops. Second earlies are planted about a month after earlies. Maincrop are for immediate consumption or winter storage.

Potatoes come in a huge range of shapes, sizes, colours and textures. The skin may be red, yellow, purple or white and the flesh pale cream or yellow, mottled or blue. Their texture may be waxy or floury and shapes variously knobbly, round and oval. Because of Government legislation, some old varieties are only available from specialist societies, though many suppliers have a good range for sale. Choose varieties recommended for your area.

'Avalanche'* can be grown as a second early or a maincrop. The round to oval white tubers have white flesh. They are uniform, productive and excellent for baking. 'Belle de Fontenay' is a very old, rare, French early variety which is excellent for salads. The yellow tubers are small and kidney-shaped, with a waxy texture and fine flavour. 'Concorde'* is heavy-cropping and very early. The tubers are large and oval with pale yellow flesh, a waxy texture and excellent flavour. Suitable for most soils, showing resistance to late frosts. 'Desirée' is a popular maincrop with pink skin and pale yellow flesh. Crops well on most soils, but prefers medium to heavy. Good for chips and baking. Susceptible to mosaic and common scab. 'Famosa'*, a maincrop, has white-skinned long to oval tubers and pale yellow flesh. It has an excellent flavour and texture. 'Golden Wonder' is a variety well known to crisp eaters. This is a late maincrop with floury, yellow flesh, is good for baking and ideal for crisps, but usually disintegrates when boiled. It grows well in moist, humid climates, is resistant to scab but susceptible to slug

'King Edward', a variety which is nearing its centenary

damage and drought. 'Kennebec', a second early to maincrop, is smooth and white-skinned, with white flesh. A heavy cropper, it is easy to peel, good for boiling and keeps well. Resistant to blight and mosaic virus. 'King Edward', another famous high-yielding, good-quality maincrop, is good for

large, tasty tubers which are good for French fries. 'Navan'* is a white-skinned, oval, high-yielding maincrop. First early 'Pentland Javelin' produces high yields of oval, white-skinned tubers with white waxy flesh. Resistant to common scab and golden eelworm. 'Pink Fir Apple' is a wonderful old late maincrop. The unusual elongated tubers are pink-skinned with

'Pink Fir Apple'

baking. Susceptible to blight, wart disease and drought. 'Maris Bard' is a very early 'first early', with white skin and white waxy flesh. It is high-yielding and good under cover. Excellent quality and good virus resistance. 'Maris Peer' is a second early. Its moderate yields of small white tubers are used for canning. It is scab- and skin spot-resistant, but susceptible to drought. 'Maris Piper' **is a prolific second early with waxy flesh when cooked**. 'Maxine'* is a maincrop with round, smooth, red-skinned tubers. The white waxy flesh remains firm when cooked. It produces heavy crops of

pale yellow flesh. They are good in salads, remaining firm when cold, and make good chips. 'Red Norland' is an extra-early round potato with smooth red skin and white flesh. High-yielding, hardy, tasty and excellent for cooking. Good resistance to scab. 'Stroma'* can be used as a second early or maincrop. It is oval with pink to red skin and pale yellow flesh. It is well flavoured and slug-resistant. 'Wilja' is a high-yielding second early with long white tubers and pale yellow waxy flesh. Good for salads and excellent for cooking. Resistant to blight, it has some resistance to scab and blackleg.

Sprouting seed potatoes, 'Maris Piper'

Potato crop in Oregon, USA

CULTIVATION

Propagation

Potatoes are normally grown from small tubers known as 'seed potatoes'. Buy 'certified' virus-free stock from a reputable supplier to be certain of obtaining a good-quality crop.

These are 'sprouted' (or 'chitted') about 6 weeks before planting to extend the growing season, which is particularly useful for early cultivars and in cooler climates. It is worth chitting second earlies and maincrops if they are to be planted late. Put a single layer of potatoes in a shallow tray or egg box with the 'rose end' (where most of the 'eyes' or dormant buds are concentrated) upwards, then put the tray in a light, cool, frost-free place to encourage growth. At 7°C (45°F) it takes about 6 weeks for shoots around 2.5cm (1in) long to form. At this stage, they are ready for planting. They can be planted when the shoots are longer, but need handling with care, as they are easily broken off. For a smaller crop but larger potatoes, leave 3 shoots per tuber on earlies; otherwise leave all of the shoots for a higher yield.

Plant earlies from mid-spring and maincrops from late spring, when there is no longer any danger of hard frosts and soil temperatures are 7°C (45°F).

Make trenches or individual holes 7–15cm (3–6in) deep, depending on the size of the tuber. Plant them upright with the shoots at the top and cover with at least 2.5cm (1in) of soil. Take care not to damage the shoots. Earlies can be planted a little deeper to give more protection from cooler weather. Ideally the rows should face north-south so that both sides of the row receive sunshine.

Plant earlies 30–38cm (12–15in) apart with 38–50cm (15–20in) between the rows and maincrops 38cm (15in) apart with 75cm (30in) between the rows. Alternatively, plant earlies 35cm (14in) apart and second earlies and maincrops 30–38cm (12–15in) apart in and between the rows. Spacing can be varied according to the size of the tubers and also to their subsequent cropping potential.

While the traditional method of propagation is very common, seed is also available, which is easy to handle and produces healthy crops. Seeds are sown indoors before potting on, hardening off and transplanting. 'Plantlets' produced by tissue culture are also available; these are healthy, virus-free and vigorous. These, too, will need growing on before hardening off and then transplanting.

Cutting large potatoes in half is not recommended; nor is the method I once saw being used – hollowing the tubers to leave a thin layer of flesh, then planting the skins only!

Growing

Potatoes flourish in an open, sunny, frost-free site on deep, rich, fertile, well-drained soil. They grow better in cool seasons, when temperatures are between 16–18°C (61–64°F), and are tolerant of most soils. Lighter soils are better for growing earlies. Add organic matter to sandy soils. Alkaline soils or heavy liming encourages scab. Grow resistant varieties and lime acid soils gradually to create a pH of 5–6, or cultivate in raised beds or containers. If necessary, dig in plenty of well-rotted organic matter in autumn, then rake to a rough tilth 10 days before planting, adding a general granular fertilizer at 90–120g/sq m (3–4oz/sq yd).

Potatoes are an excellent crop for new or neglected gardens; while the crop may not be large, the root system breaks up the soil and improves its structure. Keep crops weed-free until they are established, when the dense canopy of foliage suppresses weeds.

Potatoes are 'earthed up'; this prevents exposure to light, which makes them green and inedible, and also disturbs germinating weeds. When the plants are about 20–23cm (8–9in) tall, use a rake or spade to draw loose soil carefully around the stems to a depth of 10–15cm (4–6in). Alternatively, begin earthing up in stages when the plants are about 10cm (4in) tall, adding soil every 2–3 weeks.

To avoid having to earth up, plant small tubers about 12.5cm (5in) deep and 23–25cm (9–10in) apart on level ground. Wide spacing means tubers are not forced to the surface, yet still produce a moderate crop.

Potatoes need at least 500mm (20in) of rainfall over the growing season for a good crop. During dry weather water earlies every 12–14 days at 16–22 litres/sq m (3–4 gal/sq yd). Except when there are drought

Planting 'Baillie'

conditions, do not water maincrops until the tubers are the size of marbles (check their development by scraping back the soil below a plant). At this point, a single, thorough soaking with at least 22 litres/sq m (5 gal/sq yd) encourages the tubers to swell, increases the yield and makes them less prone to scab.

Potatoes need a constant supply of water; erratic watering causes malformed, hollow or split potatoes.

An organic liquid feed or nitrogenous top dressing helps plants to become established during the early stages of growth.

Early potatoes can be grown under black polythene, which also makes earthing up unnecessary. Prepare the soil, lay a sheet of black polythene over the area, anchor the edges by covering with soil and plant your potatoes through rosses cut in the polythene. Alternatively, plant the potatoes, cover them with plastic and when the foliage appears, make a cut in the polythene and pull through.

Where early frosts and windy conditions do not occur and the ground is excessively weedy or eelworm is a problem, potatoes can be grown in a bed of compost and straw. Clear the ground and cover the soil with a good layer of well-rotted manure or compost. Space the potatoes as required and cover them with a 5–7.5cm (2–3in) layer of straw or hay, adding more as the potatoes grow, to a maximum of 15cm (6in). At this point, spread a 7–4in layer of lawn mowings over the area to exclude light from the developing tubers.

Rotate earlies every 3 years and maincrops every 5 years.

Maintenance
Spring Chit potatoes before planting.
Summer Keep crops weed-free and water as necessary. Harvest and use or store.
Autumn Plant winter crops under cover. Prepare the soil for the following year.
Winter Harvest winter crops.

Protected Cropping
To advance early crops and protect them from frost, cover early potatoes with cloches or floating crop covers, anchored by burying the edges under the soil. When the shoots appear, cut holes in the plastic and pull the foliage through. After 3–4 weeks cut the cover, leaving it in place to allow the potatoes to become acclimatized.

Protect the foliage and stems ('haulm') from heavy frosts by covering them at night with a layer of straw, bracken or newspaper, or a thin layer of soil. Light frosts do not generally cause problems.

For winter crops of new potatoes, in warm areas, plant earlies in mid-summer and cover with cloches in autumn. Alternatively, grow them in the borders of a frost-free greenhouse at 7–10°C (45–50°F). Provide warmth if necessary.

Container Growing
Potatoes can be grown in any container if it is at least 30cm (12in) wide and deep and has drainage holes. It is possible to buy a potato barrel for this purpose – some models have sliding panels for ease of harvesting – but an old dustbin, flower pot or similar is just as good. Potatoes can also be grown in black bin-liners! Wider containers can of course hold more potatoes.

Potatoes growing in a compost heap

Place a 10–12.5cm (4–5in) layer of compost or good garden soil in a container, stand 2–3 chitted potatoes on the surface and cover with a layer of compost about 10–15cm (4–6in) high. When the shoots are about 15cm (6in) tall, cover with another 10–15 (4–6in) layer of compost, leaving the tips showing. Continue earthing up until the shoots are within 5–7.5cm (2–3in) of the rim of the container.

Winter crops of first earlies can also be grown in containers. Plant in mid-summer for harvesting at Christmas. Cover the 'haulms' in frosty weather or grow under glass.

Be sure to keep crops well fed and watered.

Harvesting & Storing
Earlies are ready to harvest from early to mid-summer, second earlies from late summer to early autumn and maincrops mature from early to mid-autumn.

Harvest earlies when they are about the size of a hen's egg: their readiness is often indicated by the flowers opening. Remove some soil from the side of a ridge and check them for size before lifting the root. Insert a flat-tined fork into the base of the ridge and lift the whole plant, bringing the new potatoes up to the surface.

Harvest those grown under black polythene by folding back the sheeting: the crop of potatoes will be lying on the surface. Collect as required.

Scrape away compost from those grown in containers to check their size before harvesting them.

Leave healthy maincrop potatoes in the soil for as long as possible, but beware of slugs! In early autumn cut back the haulm to about 5cm (2in) above the soil, or wait until the foliage dies down naturally; leave the tubers in the ground for 2 weeks for the skins to harden before lifting.

Cut back the haulm and work along the side of each ridge, lifting the potatoes with a fork. Harvest on a dry sunny day when the soil is moderately moist, leave in the sun for a few hours to dry, then brush off the soil. If the weather is poor, dry them under cloches or on trays indoors. Store healthy tubers in paper or hessian sacks or boxes in a dark, cool, frost-free place. They should keep until spring. Check tubers weekly, removing those which are damaged or diseased.

When harvesting, ensure that all potatoes, however small, are removed from the soil to prevent future problems occurring with pests and diseases.

New potatoes do not store, but can be frozen. Blanch whole in boiling water for 3 minutes. Cool, drain, pack into rigid containers and freeze. Chips and French fries can also be frozen.

Digging up potatoes, Devon, England

PESTS & DISEASES

Common potato scab shows as raised, corky scabs on the surface of the tuber. It does not usually affect the whole potato and can be removed by peeling. It is common in hot, dry summers, on light, free-draining and alkaline soils. Water well in dry conditions, add plenty of organic matter to the soil before planting, avoid excessive liming, or rotating after the soil has been limed for brassicas. Do not put infected potatoes or peelings on the compost heap. Grow resistant cultivars.

Potato blight appears on the leaves as brown patches, often with paler margins. The infection can spread to the stems and through the tuber, making it inedible. The disease spreads rapidly in warm, humid conditions and maincrops are more susceptible. Grow resistant cultivars, avoid overhead watering; before the problem appears apply a systemic fungicide every 2 weeks from mid-summer. Alternatively use copper sulphate sprays such as 'Bordeaux mixture'. Earthing up creates a protective barrier, slowing the infection of tubers. Lift early potatoes as soon as possible and in late summer, cut back the 'haulms' of infected plants just above the ground and burn the infected material or put it in the dustbin. Leave tubers in the ground for 2 weeks before lifting.

Potato cyst eelworm ('golden nematode' or 'pale eelworm'). Growth is checked and yields can be severely reduced; badly affected plants turn yellow and die. Lift and burn infected plants, rotate crops, and do not grow potatoes or tomatoes in the soil for at least 6 years. Try to grow resistant varieties.

Wireworms are about 2.5cm (1in) long and golden brown in colour. They tunnel into the tubers, making them inedible. They are fairly easy to control. Cultivate the soil thoroughly over winter to expose to the weather and birds, keep crops weed-free, and lift 'maincrops' as early as possible. Also rake in a soil insecticide.

Blackleg shows when the upper leaves roll and wilt and the stem becomes black and rotten at the base. The tubers may be rotten. It is more severe in wet seasons; do not plant on waterlogged land. Remove affected plants immediately, burn or put in the dustbin. Do not store damaged tubers.

Slugs can tunnel into the tubers; damage is more severe the longer they remain in the ground.

COMPANION PLANTING

Growing horseradish in large sunken pots near to potatoes controls some diseases. Plant with sweetcorn, cabbage, beans and marigolds. Grow with aubergines, which are a greater attraction to colorado beetle.
Protect against scab by putting grass clippings and comfrey leaves in the planting hole or trench.

OTHER USES

Potatoes are made into flour and turned into bread. They can be boiled and the starch turned to glucose, which can be fermented to produce strong alcohol, like the poteen made in Ireland. In the past, they have also

Riddling and sorting potato crop under artificial lights

been a source of starch powder for whitening wigs. The juice of mature potatoes is particularly excellent for cleaning silks, cotton, wool and even furniture.

MEDICINAL

Potatoes are said to be good for rheumatism. One traditional cure for sciatica and lumbago is to carry a potato in your pocket.

The juice from a raw potato or the water in which potatoes have been boiled is said to relieve gout, rheumatism, lumbago, sprains and bruises.

Uncooked peeled and pounded potatoes are said

to make a soothing plaster to scalds or burns when applied cold.

Potatoes contain little fat and provide more potassium pro rata than bananas, while the average potato contains as many kilojoules as most apples or a glass of orange juice and can be eaten by those on a diet.

WARNING

Green potatoes contain the toxic alkaloid solanine, which can cause vomiting and stomach upsets. Do not eat green potatoes. Beware that the tomato-like fruits and leaves of the plant are also poisonous.

CULINARY

There are more than 500 ways of serving potatoes. They can be boiled, steamed, baked, roasted, mashed, sautéed, fried and cooked *au gratin*.

In the past potatoes have been preserved and candied or mashed with butter, sherry, egg yolks, nutmeg and a little sugar and baked until brown.

Rub the skin from new potatoes under running water and boil for 12 minutes with a sprig of mint. Drain and toss in butter, then eat hot or cold in salads.

Scrape old potatoes; peeling removes much of the vitamin C just below the surface.

Cut potatoes into 1cm (½in) strips, wash in ice-cold water, drain and dry thoroughly. Fry until golden in a shallow frying basket in a pan one third full of oil at 125°C (250°F).

The difference between 'French fries' and 'chips' is their size and the method of cooking. French fries are very thinly sliced and deep-fried in oil. Chips are sliced thickly and were originally cooked in animal fat. Nowadays the only difference is the size.

Microwaving generally retains the flesh colour in unusual potatoes.

Mashed Potatoes with Olive Oil

For those on a diet, this at least has less calories than the traditional dish!

1kg (2lb) potatoes, peeled
8–10 cloves garlic, unpeeled
8 tablespoons olive oil, preferably extra-virgin
Salt & freshly ground black pepper

Put the potatoes and garlic cloves in a pan, cover with water and add salt. Bring to the boil and cook until tender, about 20 minutes, and then drain, reserving the potato cooking liquid. Boil this separately in the pan to reduce to roughly 250ml (8fl oz). Meanwhile peel the garlic cloves.

Mash the potatoes and garlic. Return the pan to a gentle heat and beat in the olive oil and enough potato liquid to give the potatoes the right texture. Season with salt and pepper.

To make the Irish champ, add 115–175g (4–6oz) of cooked and roughly chopped cabbage or spring greens to the above.

Rösti
Serves 4

750g (1½lb) waxy potatoes
1 small onion, finely chopped
50g (2oz) smoked bacon, diced
6–8 tablespoons goosefat or olive oil
Salt & freshly ground black pepper

Clean the potatoes and boil them in lightly salted water until just tender. Drain and, when cool enough to handle, peel. Grate coarsely.

In a heavy pan, gently sauté the onion and bacon in half the fat. Fold this into the potatoes with the seasoning. Form the potatoes into one big 'cake'. In the same pan heat the balance of the fat and gently slide the potatoes into the pan. Cook over a high heat until the first side is browned. Place a plate over the pan and turn the potatoes onto the plate; then gently slide the 'cake' back into the pan to allow the second side to cook. Serve piping hot.

This classic Swiss dish can be eaten with Emmenthal melted on top (put the browned potatoes, covered with cheese slices, under the grill for a few minutes).

Rösti

Potato Salad with Goat's Cheese dressing
Serves 4

The South Americans have excellent ways of cooking potatoes, including this rich salad which makes a good summer first course.

750g (1½lb) potatoes, fairly small
½ red pepper, deseeded & diced
1 small onion, peeled & finely chopped
2 hard-boiled eggs, peeled & diced
Handful black olives, stoned
2 tablespoons flat-leaf parsley, chopped

For the dressing:
175g (6oz) well flavoured goat's cheese
2 cloves garlic, peeled
2 tablespoons yoghurt
2 tablespoons lemon juice
1 jalapeño pepper, de-seeded
¼ teaspoon turmeric
½ teaspoon ground cumin

Potato Salad with Goat's Cheese Dressing

Cook the potatoes in their skins in boiling water until tender, drain and peel.

Cut into generous dice and put into a serving dish.

While the potatoes cook, mix the dressing ingredients in a blender, puréeing until smooth.

Combine the potatoes with the red pepper and onion. Add the dressing and toss. Decorate the top with the crumbled eggs, olives and parsley.

Spinacia oleracea. Chenopodiaceae

SPINACH

Fast-growing annual, grown for highly nutritious leaves. Hardy. Value: high in iron, beta carotene and folic acid; rich in vitamins A and C.

Spinach is thought to be native to South-West Asia. Unknown to the Greeks and Romans, it was first cultivated by the Persians, was grown in China by the seventh century AD and reached Europe around 1100, after its introduction to Spain by the Moors. The prickly-seeded form was known in thirteenth-century Germany and by the following century it was commonly grown by European monastery gardens. Smooth-seeded spinach was first described in 1522. Its first mention in England comes in William Turner's *New Herball*, in the sixteenth century: 'An herbe lately found and not long in use.' The name comes from Old French *espinache*, derived from its Arabic and Persian name.

Children were encouraged to eat spinach because of its effect on Popeye the Sailor. The idea that it contains exceptional levels of iron originated from Dr E. von Wolf in 1870. His figures went unchecked until 1937, when it was discovered that the iron content was one-tenth that claimed by him as a result of a misplaced decimal point!

Harvest spinach regularly

VARIETIES

Traditionally there are two main groups. Prickly-seeded varieties, which have lobed leaves, are regarded as hardier than the round, smooth-seeded types, which cope better with higher temperatures and are used for summer cropping. Modern cultivars are generally more adaptable.

'America' has thick deep green leaves for spring sowing. It does not overwinter well. 'Bloomsdale' ('Bloomsdale Long Standing') is a savoy-leaved spinach with fleshy, tasty leaves. It is cold-tolerant, slow to bolt and crops over a long period. 'Dominant'* is a good all-rounder for spring or autumn sowing; it is thick-leaved, prolific and resistant to bolting. 'Giant Winter'*, a robust late autumn and winter variety, withstands some frost and is highly disease-resistant. 'Medania' is for summer cropping. It withstands hot, dry weather and is resistant to downy mildew. 'Sigmaleaf'* is vigorous and tasty. Suitable for spring or autumn sowing. 'Space' has smooth, dark green leaves and is resistant to downy mildew. Ideal for any season. 'Trinidad', for summer and autumn, has dark green leaves, is slow to bolt and shows good resistance to downy mildew.

CULTIVATION

Spinach grows best in cool conditions, at temperatures around 16–18°C (60–65°F). It thrives in a bright position, but is better in light shade and moist ground if your garden is hot and sunny.

Propagation
Soak seed overnight to speed up germination. My friend Robert Fleming wraps seed in a wet paper towel and places it in a sealed container in the fridge for 5 days before planting. Germination usually takes 5 days. As a cool-season plant, it will not germinate above 30°C (86°F).

Sow summer crops every 2–3 weeks from early to late spring for a summer harvest.

Sow in late summer, for cropping in winter until early summer. Sow *in situ* 2.5cm (1in) apart and 1–2cm (½–¾in) deep in rows 30cm (12in) apart. Thin when large enough to handle to 15–25cm (6–10in). It also works as a 'cut and come again' crop.

In colder areas it is better to sow in seed trays or modules for transplanting.

Sow thinly in broad drills the width of a hoe or in rows 10cm (4in) apart. Leave unthinned unless growth is slow, when they can be thinned to 5cm (2in) apart. Plants can be thinned to 10–12.5cm (4–5in) apart for larger leaves, though they are more inclined to bolt.

Growing
Spinach needs a rich, fertile, moisture-retentive soil, so where necessary, dig in well-rotted organic matter before planting. On poor soils leaves are stunted, bitter and prone to bolt. The ideal pH is 6.5–7.5; lime acid soils.

Never allow the soil to dry out. Water regularly before

the onset of dry weather and grow bolting-resistant cultivars. Water every 2 weeks with a high-nitrogen liquid fertilizer.

Maintenance

Spring Sow early crops successively.
Summer Keep the soil moist and weed-free. Sow winter crops from late summer.
Autumn Protect late crops under cloches, sow 'cut and come again' crops under glass.
Winter Protect winter crops under cloches or fleece or sow in cold frames.

Protected Cropping

Hardy varieties for winter and early spring cropping are better protected in cold frames, cloches or under horticultural fleece.

Container Growing

Spinach is ideal for containers 20–45cm (8–18in) wide and 30cm (12in) deep. Water regularly in dry weather. Avoid scorching sunshine.

Harvesting & Storing

Harvest from 5 weeks after sowing, cutting the outer leaves first. To harvest as a 'cut and come again' crop, remove the heads 2.5cm (1in) above the ground and allow them to resprout. Pick off the leaves carefully; the stems and roots are easily damaged. Alternatively, pull up whole plants and resow. Use the leaves fresh, or freeze. They can be washed and stored for up to 2 days in the refrigerator.

The leaves of 'Medania' are particularly thick

Pests & Diseases

Aphids and **slugs** can be troublesome, especially among seedlings. **Downy mildew** appears as yellow patches with fluffy mould on the underside of the leaf. **Bolting** caused by drying out or hot weather is most common cause of failure.

COMPANION PLANTING

Good with beans, peas, sweetcorn and strawberries.

MEDICINAL

Spinach is said to be good for anaemia, problems of the heart and kidney and in low vitality and general debility. Iron is in a soluble form, so any water left after cooking can be left to cool before drinking.

Research has shown that those who eat spinach daily are less likely to develop lung cancer. Of all the vegetable juices, spinach juice is said to be the most potent for the prevention of cancer cell formation.

OTHER USES

The water drained from spinach after cooking is said to make good matchpaper. It was used to make touchpaper for eighteenth- and nineteenth-century fire-works, as paper soaked in it smouldered well.

Spinach is packed with goodness

CULINARY

Wash leaves thoroughly. Eat immediately after harvesting. Use young leaves raw in salads, lightly cooked or steamed. Place spinach in a pan without adding water, cover and stand on moderate heat so the leaves do not scorch.

After 5 minutes, stir and cook over high heat for 1 minute. Drain in a colander and cut with a knife or fish-slice.

Spinach can also be cooked with olive oil, cheese, cream, yoghurt, ham, bacon and anchovies, besides being seasoned with nutmeg, pepper and sugar. All will bring out the flavour.

Scrambled Eggs with Raw & Cooked Spinach
Serves 6

1kg (2lb) young spinach
2 tablespoons olive oil
Pinch grated nutmeg
2 tablespoons butter
12 eggs, lightly beaten with
*   1 tablespoon thick cream*
1 tablespoon chopped chives
Salt & freshly ground black
*   pepper*

Wash the spinach and remove any tough stalks. Heat the oil in a heavy pan and then wilt most of the spinach, keeping back a couple of handfuls for decoration. Season with nutmeg, salt and pepper. Set aside and keep warm.

In the same pan, melt the butter and allow to just brown. Over a low flame, pour in the eggs and season. Stir constantly until just set (overcooked scrambled eggs are bad news!). Mound the eggs in the centre of individual plates and sprinkle with chopped chives. Arrange the cooked spinach around the outside, and then make a further ring from the raw spinach leaves. Serve hot.

Scrambled Eggs with Spinach

Stachys affinis. Labiatae

CHINESE ARTICHOKE

(Japanese Artichoke, Crosne) Dwarf herbaceous perennial grown as annual for edible tubers. Hardy. Value: very high in potassium.

From the same family as mint, lavender and many other herbs, Chinese artichokes are not grown for their aromatic foliage but for the small, ridged tubers at the tips of creeping underground stems.

A native of Japan and China, it has rough, oval leaves and white to pale pink flowers that appear in small spikes. It was introduced from Peking to France by a physician in the late nineteenth century. It has never been hugely popular, probably because a large area is needed for decent quantities, but it is worth trying, if only as a 'novelty' crop.

CULTIVATION

Chinese artichokes flourish in an open, sunny site on light, fertile yet moisture-retentive soil.

Propagation

For early crops, sprout the tubers in shallow trays or pots of potting compost in a moderately warm room, then plant out when soil is warm. Increase your stock by planting tubers individually in small pots of soil-based compost with added organic matter, transplanting as required. Place in 20–23cm (8–9in) pots for the rest of the growing season. Feed and water regularly.

Growing

In spring, plant the tubers vertically 4–7.5cm (1½–3in) deep; on light soils up to 15cm (6in) deep. Plant large tubers only, 30cm (12in) apart each way or 20cm (8in) apart in rows 40cm (16in) apart. When 30–60cm (1–2ft) high, earth up round the stems to about 7.5cm (3in). Keep weed-free at first; as the plants mature, the leaf canopy naturally suppresses weed growth. Feed with a liquid general fertilizer every 2 weeks and remove flowering spikes to concentrate energy into fattening the tubers. Trim back the foliage. Rampant growth make Chinese artichokes an ideal low-maintenance crop for a spare corner of the garden.

Maintenance

Spring Plant tubers when the soil has warmed.
Summer Keep crops weed-free, water and feed.
Autumn Harvest after the first frosts, or about 5 months.
Winter Protect crops with hessian, straw or sacking to enable harvesting to continue.

Harvesting & Storing

Harvest as required from mid-autumn to early spring, after the foliage has died back or when plants have

A mass of tubers

been in the ground for 5–7 months. Lift them just before use as they quickly shrivel. When forking through the ground during the final harvest, you should remove even the smallest tubers or they will rapidly become weeds.

PESTS & DISEASES

Chinese artichokes are usually pest-free, but you should take precautions against **lettuce root aphid**, which can cause wilting.

CULINARY

The tubers have a delicate, nutty flavour. Only about 5cm (2in) long, they are rather fiddly to cook. Boiling is simplest, but they can also be fried, stir-fried, roasted, added to soup or eaten raw in salads.

Creamed Chinese Artichokes
Serves 4

Jane Grigson, in her *Vegetable Book*, quotes this recipe from *La Cuisine de Madame Saint-Ange.*

500g (1lb) Chinese artichokes
1 tablespoon butter
½teaspoon lemon juice
300ml (½pt) double cream
Salt & freshly ground white pepper
Pinch nutmeg
Double cream, to serve

Boil the artichokes for about 5 minutes, drain, add the butter and lemon juice and cook gently for 5–7 minutes. Bring the cream to the boil, then add it to the artichokes, stirring in well. Season. Cover and leave for 15 minutes over a moderate heat, until the cream has reduced by a quarter. Just before serving, stir in 3 spoonfuls of double cream and quickly remove from the heat.

Tetragonolobus purpureus (syn. Lotus tetragonolobus). Leguminosae

ASPARAGUS PEA

(Winged Pea) Sprawling annual winged bean, ornamental but grown for edible pods. Half hardy. Value: small amounts of protein, carbohydrate, fibre and iron.

A wildflower of open fields and wasteland in Mediterranean countries, this plant may have arrived in Britain with imported grain. It has since become naturalized. Gerard records its cultivation before 1569 for its dark crimson, pea-like flowers; only later were its edible merits discovered, but it has never gained widespread popularity. The 1807 edition of Miller's *Gardener's Dictionary* notes: 'formerly cultivated as an esculent plant, for the green pods . . . it is now chiefly cultivated in flower gardens for ornament.'

The prominent winged pods illustrate the plant's other name

CULTIVATION

Propagation
Sow seed outdoors from mid- to late spring, once the soil warms and frosts are over. Drills should be 2cm (¾in) deep and 38cm (15in) apart; thin to 20–30cm (8–12in) apart once they are large enough to handle. In cooler areas, sow under cloches or in the glasshouse in trays or modules of moist seed compost. Harden off and transplant outdoors when plants are 5cm (2in) tall, spacing them about 20–30cm (8–12in) apart.

Growing
Asparagus peas flourish in an open, sheltered, sunny site on light, rich, free-draining soil. Keep weed-free and water as required.

As they are lax in habit, growing up pea sticks or a similar support saves space and makes harvesting easier. Rotate them with other legumes.

Maintenance
Spring Sow seed in mid- to late spring.
Summer Harvest regularly.
Autumn Harvest until early autumn.
Winter Prepare ground for the following year's crop.

Protected Cropping
In cooler areas sow under glass for transplanting later.

Harvesting & Storing
Harvest from mid-summer to early autumn, when pods are 2.5cm (1in) long. Pick regularly to prolong the harvest. Longer, older pods are 'stringy' and inedible. Pods which do not bend easily are unsuitable for eating. Harvesting is easier in the evening, when the leaves close and the small green pods are more visible.

Pests & Diseases
Protect crops from **birds** using 'humming line' or similar bird scarers. They can also suffer from **downy** and **powdery mildew**.

CULINARY

The subtle flavour is similar to asparagus. Wash the pods, 'top and tail' if necessary, then steam for up to 5 minutes (check them after about 3 minutes, as they need only light cooking). Drain well before eating. Mix with butter and cream or serve on toast. Alternatively, cook in butter until tender, drain and serve.

Asparagus pea flowers are blood-red and tiny

Tetragonia tetragonoides (syn. *T. expansa*). *Aizoaceae*

NEW ZEALAND SPINACH

Creeping perennial, usually grown as annual for edible leaves. Half hardy. Value: high in iron, beta carotene and folic acid.

This plant was unknown in Europe until 1771, when it was introduced to the Royal Botanic Gardens at Kew by the great botanist Joseph Banks after his voyage on board the *Endeavour* with Captain Cook. By 1820 it was widely grown in the kitchen gardens of Britain and France, but it did not appear in New Zealand literature until the 1940s, and there is no evidence of its use by the Maoris. It is unrelated to the true spinach, but its leaves are used in a similar manner – hence the borrowed name – though their flavour is milder than that of true spinach. A low-growing perennial with soft, fleshy, roughly triangular, blunt-tipped leaves, about 5cm (2in) long, it makes an attractive plant for edging and ground cover. It flourishes in hot dry conditions, without running to seed.

New Zealand spinach is seldom grown by gardeners, yet it is robust and a fine substitute for spinach

CULTIVATION

Propagation

The seed coat is extremely hard and germination is slow unless the seeds are soaked in water for 24 hours before sowing. Sow seeds individually, 2.5cm (1in) deep in 7.5cm (3in) pots indoors from mid- to late spring; repot as necessary. Plants are very cold-sensitive and so should be hardened off carefully before planting out once the danger of frost has passed.

Alternatively, sow seed *in situ* when there is no danger of frost, 1–2cm (½–¾in) deep in drills about 60cm (24in) apart, thinning to a similar distance between plants. Seeds can also be sown, 2 or 3 per 'station', 60cm (24in) apart, thinning to leave the strongest. Pinch out tips of young plants to encourage bushy growth.

Plants usually self-seed and appear in the same area the following year.

Growing

New Zealand spinach flourishes in an open site on light, fertile soil with low levels of nitrogen and grows well in dry, poor conditions. It tolerates high temperatures, but is very susceptible to frost.

Keep seedlings weed-free with regular hoeing. Once plants are established, their dense foliage will act as a ground cover and suppress weeds.

Water regularly during dry spells to encourage vigorous growth. It does not bolt in hot weather, but should be watered well to encourage growth. On poor soils, occasional feeding with a half-strength solution of general liquid fertilizer is beneficial, but take care not to over-feed.

The triangular leaves are striking

Maintenance

Spring Sow seed under cover for transplanting once frosts are over.
Summer Keep crops weed-free, water and harvest as required.
Autumn Protect plants to extend the growing season.
Winter Prepare the ground for planting in spring.

Protected Cropping

Protecting with cloches extends the harvesting season in cooler areas before frosts turn the plants into a soggy mess.

Container Growing

Crops can be grown in large containers of soil-based compost. Add grit to improve drainage. Water plants well throughout the growing season.

Harvesting & Storing

The first young leaves and shoots are ready to harvest from about 6 weeks after sowing. Pick regularly to maintain a constant supply of young growth and to extend the harvesting

The leaves can be eaten raw

CULINARY

The young leaves and shoots are steamed, lightly boiled and eaten with a knob of butter, or eaten raw in salads. They are better eaten fresh as the flavour deteriorates rapidly with age.

Cannelloni Stuffed with Chicken & New Zealand Spinach
Serves 4

500g (1lb) fresh New Zealand spinach
2 tablespoons butter
1 red onion, diced
2 tablespoons plain flour
450ml (¾pt) vegetable stock
1 bouquet garni
3 tablespoons thick cream
Salt & freshly ground black pepper
8 cannelloni shells
250g (8oz) cooked chicken, diced
100g (3oz) Parmesan, grated

Wash the spinach in several changes of water, place in a saucepan and cook for 3 minutes over high heat. Drain thoroughly and chop.

Melt the butter in a heavy pan, cook the onion until golden and stir in the flour to make a roux. Cook for 1–2 minutes. Stir in the stock, allow to boil, and add the bouquet garni. Season and stir in the cream.

Simmer without boiling for 10 minutes.

Meanwhile, boil the cannelloni until *al dente* and drain, setting aside to cool for a few minutes. Combine the chicken and spinach and half the sauce and season well. Use a large piping bag to stuff each cannelloni shell with the chicken mixture and arrange in a shallow, greased ovenproof dish.

Preheat the oven to 200°C, 400°F, gas 6. Reserve 1 tablespoon Parmesan and stir the balance into the remaining sauce. Pour this over the cannelloni and sprinkle with the reserved cheese. Cook for 20 minutes, until the top is browned and the dish hot through. Serve.

Cannelloni Stuffed with Chicken and New Zealand Spinach

season, which should last up to 4 months. Young leaves should be used immediately after cutting, can be stored for up to 2 days in a polythene bag in the fridge, or may be frozen. Wash, blanch for 2 minutes, allow to cool and drain before packing into polythene bags and placing in the freezer.

PESTS & DISEASES

New Zealand spinach is very robust but **downy mildew** may be a problem.

COMPANION PLANTING

It is sometimes grown as a 'green manure' to improve the soil structure.

Tragopogon porrifolius. Compositae

SALSIFY

(Oyster Plant, Vegetable Oyster, Goat's Beard)
Grown as biennial for shoots, flower buds and flowers;
annual for cylindrical tapering edible roots. Hardy.
Value: contains inulin, turning to fructose in storage;
small amounts of vitamins and minerals.

It is difficult to know whether to grow this plant for its delicious roots, or to grow it as a fragile ornamental by letting it flower (the flowers are also edible). Its Latin and common names are apt; *tragos* means goat and *pogon*, beard, describes the tuft of silky hairs on the developing seedheads; *porrifolius* means 'with leaves like a leek'. 'Salsify' comes from the old Latin name *solsequium*, from the way the flowers follow the course of the sun.

Salsify is a relatively recent crop. In the thirteenth century it was harvested from the wild in Germany and France. It was not cultivated until the early sixteenth century – in Italian gardens. The English plant collector John Tradescant the Younger recorded it in 1656. It was brought to North America in the late nineteenth century.

VARIETIES

The species *Tragopogon porrifolius* has a thin, creamy-white, tapering taproot up to 38cm (15in) long. It has narrow leaves and long, wand-like stems topped by beautiful dull purple flowers. These are followed by thistle-like seedheads.
'Geante Noire de Russie' is an extremely long, black-skinned variety with white roots and a superb flavour. **'Giant'** is consistently long-rooted with a delicate taste of oysters. **'Sandwich Island'** is a selected type with strongly flavoured roots and smooth skin.

CULTIVATION

Propagation
Always use fresh seed; its viability declines rapidly. Sow as early as possible, from early to mid-spring. Germination can be somewhat erratic, so it is better to sow 2–3 seeds in 'stations' 1–2cm (½–¾in) deep and 10cm (4in) apart with 30cm (12in) between the rows. After germination,

Salsify flowers vary from purple to near white

when the seedlings are large enough to handle, thin to leave the strongest seedling. Alternatively, sow the seeds in drills and thin to the above spacing.

Growing
Salsify thrives in an open situation on light, well-drained, stone-free soil which was manured for the previous crop (roots tend to fork when they are grown on freshly manured soil). On stony or heavy soils, dig a trench about 30cm (12in) deep and 20cm (8in) wide, filling it with finely sieved sandy soil or compost and sharp sand to give the roots room to grow. Lighten heavier soils by thoroughly digging over the area the autumn before planting, adding well-rotted organic matter and sharp sand. A pH of 6.0–7.5 is ideal; lime acid soils. Before sowing, rake the seedbed to a fine tilth and incorporate a slow-release general fertilizer at 60–90g/sq m (2–3oz/sq yd).

Regular watering ensures good-quality roots and, importantly, stops 'bolting' in dry conditions. It also prevents roots from splitting, which occurs after sudden rainfall or watering after a period of drought. Salsify should be kept weed-free, particularly during the early stages of growth. Hand weed, as the roots are easily damaged and inclined to 'bleed'. Alternatively, use an onion hoe or mulch moist soil with a layer of organic matter to stifle weed growth and conserve moisture.

Roots can be left in the ground to produce edible shoots or 'chards' the following spring. In autumn, cut back the old leaves to within 1–2.5cm (½–1in) of the soil and earth up to about 12.5–15cm (5–6in). In mid-spring the following year, the shoots are ready to harvest when they appear. On heavier soils, 'chards' can be blanched with a covering of bracken, straw or dry leaves at least 12.5cm (5in) deep when new growth appears in spring. An upturned bucket or flower pots with the drainage holes covered work just as well.

Maintenance
Spring Rake over the seedbed, incorporating general fertilizer. Sow seeds in 'stations'.
Summer Keep the crop weed-free, mulch and water during dry periods.
Autumn Lift crops as required. Cut back the tops and cover those being grown for 'chards'.
Winter Dig over soil manured for the previous crop. Lift and store crops grown in colder areas.

Container Growing
Salsify can be grown in containers, but it is impractical to produce them in large quantities. However, if you are desperate, fill a large wooden box, tea chest

'Sandwich Island' is the most commonly grown form

Tragopogon dubius, **a relative of the cultivated plant**

COMPANION PLANTING

Salsify grows well with mustard and planted near carrots discourages carrot fly.

MEDICINAL

Salsify is said to have an anti-bilious effect and to calm fevers. In folk medicine it is used to treat gall bladder problems and jaundice.

Salsify seeds, like a giant dandelion clock

or plastic drum with sandy, free-draining soil or a loam-based compost with added sharp sand. Ensure there are sufficient drainage holes. Keep crops weed-free and water regularly.

Harvesting & Storing

Harvest from mid-autumn. Lift as required; protect roots with a layer of straw, bracken or a similar material before severe frosts or snow. They can be lifted in autumn and stored in boxes of peat substitute, sand or sawdust, in a cool, frost-free garage, shed or cellar. Lift carefully with a garden fork; the roots 'bleed' and snap easily.

If you begin lifting and find the crop misshapen, leave the roots in the ground and harvest the shoots and buds the following year. Next time, grow them in sieved soil.

Harvest 'chards' in early to mid-spring: scrape away the soil and cut the blanched shoots when they are 12.5–15cm (5–6in) long. Or lift when 15cm (6in) tall, without earthing up, though they are not as tender.

Pests & Diseases

Salsify is usually trouble-free but may suffer from **white blister**, which looks like glistening paint splashes and can distort plants. Spray with Bordeaux mixture and destroy any plants which are badly affected.

Aster yellows cause deformed new growth and the leaf veins or whole leaf become yellow. Control the aster leaf hopper which spreads the disease.

CULINARY

Salsify has a delicate oyster-like flavour and can be cooked in a variety of ways (there is bound to be a recipe which suits you). Peel after boiling until tender, 'skimming' under cold running water as you would a hard-boiled egg.

Cut roots discolour, so drop them into water with a dash of lemon juice, then boil for 25 minutes in salted water with lemon juice and a tablespoon of flour. Drain and skin, toss with melted butter and chopped parsley and indulge.

Try them with a light mornay sauce, deep-fried or served *au gratin* with cheese and breadcrumbs. Perhaps sautéing them in butter and eating with brown sugar is more to your liking?

Roots can also be baked, puréed, creamed for soup or grated raw in salads. They stay fresh in a refrigerator for about a week.

'Chards' can be served raw in salads or lightly cooked. Young flowering shoots can be eaten pickled, raw or cooked and eaten cold like asparagus with oil and lemon juice. The subtle flavour makes them an excellent hors d'oeuvre.

Pick flower buds just before they open with about 7.5cm (3in) of stem attached, lightly simmer and eat when they are cool.

Salsify in Batter
Serves 4

750g (1½lb) salsify, topped & tailed, cleaned
Vegetable oil, for frying
Lemon wedges, to serve

For the batter:
110g (4oz) plain flour
1 teaspoon baking powder
1 egg
1 tablespoon olive oil
150ml (¼pt) water
¼ teaspoon harissa
½ teaspoon cumin
¼ teaspoon dried thyme
Salt & freshly ground black pepper

Cut salsify roots in half and boil in salted water for 30 minutes. Rinse under cold water. Peel and cut into 7.5cm (3in) pieces.

Make the batter: whizz all the ingredients in a food processor for 30 seconds.

Heat the oil in a large frying pan. Dip the salsify in the batter and fry in oil until crisp and golden, turning. Keep warm while cooking the remainder. Serve hot with lemon wedges.

Salsify in Batter

Salsify in Ham with Cheese Sauce
Serves 4

8 salsify, peeled & trimmed
8 slices cooked ham
2 tablespoons butter
2 tablespoons flour
1 teaspoon Dijon mustard
300ml (½pt) milk
4 tablespoons grated Gruyère
Pinch nutmeg
Salt & freshly ground black pepper

Boil the salsify for 5 minutes and drain. Cut into roughly 10cm (4in) lengths. When cool enough to handle, wrap each in a slice of ham and arrange in a greased baking dish.

Melt the butter in a heavy pan and stir in the flour to make a roux. Cook for a minute or two and stir in the mustard. Slowly add the milk, and then the Gruyère, and cook until the cheese is melted.

Season with nutmeg, salt and pepper and pour over the salsify. Bake in a preheated oven, 200°C, 400°F, gas 6, for 20 minutes, until browned.

Valerianella locusta (syn. Valerianella olitoria). Valerianaceae

LAMB'S LETTUCE

(Corn Salad, Mache, Lamb's Tongues)
***Low-growing, extremely hardy annual grown for edible leaves. Value: good source
of beta carotene, vitamin C and folic acid. Very few calories.***

'Jade' growing

In spite of its delicate appearance, lamb's lettuce is an extremely hardy plant, particularly valued as a nutritious winter salad crop. Its attractive bright green, rounded leaves have a slightly nutty taste. Depending on the authority, it was named lamb's lettuce because sheep are partial to it, or because it appears during the lambing season. Another name, corn salad, comes from its regular appearance as a cornfield weed.

Gerard wrote: 'We know the Lamb's Lettuce as loblollie; and it serves in winter as a salad herb among others none of the worst.' He also noted that 'foreigners using it in England led to its cultivation in our gardens'. It has been popular for centuries in France, where it is known as *salade de prêtre* (as it is often eaten in Lent), *doucette* ('little soft one', referring to the velvety leaves), and *bourcette*, describing their shape. In England it declined in popularity in the 1700s and a nineteenth-century commentator noted: '.... it is indeed a weed, and can be of no real use where lettuces are to be had.' Before the appearance of winter lettuce varieties, lamb's lettuce was the main winter salad; it was at one time classified in the same genus.

VARIETIES

There are two forms, the 'large' or 'broad-leaved' and the darker, more compact 'green' type, which is popular in western Europe, but less productive.

'Cavallo' has deep green leaves and crops heavily. 'Elan' is tender and mildew-resistant, as is the extremely robust 'Jade'. 'Large Leaved' is tender and prolific. 'Grote Noordhollandse' is very hardy. 'Verte de Cambrai', a traditional French type, has small leaves and good flavour. 'Verte d'Etampes' has unusual, attractive savoyed leaves. 'Vit' is very vigorous with a mild flavour. 'Volhart' is an old variety with bright green leaves.

CULTIVATION

Propagation

Lamb's lettuce can be grown as single plants or 'cut and come again' seedlings.

Sow seeds successively from mid- to late spring for summer crops in drills 10–15cm (4–6in) apart and 1cm (½in) deep, thinning

when seedlings have 3–4 seed leaves to about 10cm (4in) apart. Sow winter crops successively from mid- to late summer.

Seeds can also be sown in broad drills, broadcast, or in seed trays or modules for transplanting. Leave a few plants to bolt, and transplant seedlings into rows.

Growing

Lamb's lettuce flourishes in a sheltered position in full sun or light shade and needs a deep, fertile soil for rapid and continuous growth. It tolerates most soils provided they are not waterlogged. Create a firm seedbed and rake in a slow-release general fertilizer at 30–60g/sq m (1–2oz/sq yd) before sowing in spring and summer. Overwintered crops growing on the same site should not need it.

Keep crops weed-free, particularly during the early stages, and water thoroughly to encourage soft growth.

Maintenance

Spring Sow successively.
Summer Continue sowing and harvesting, keep crops weed-free and water well.
Autumn Sow crops under cover. Continue harvesting.
Winter When growth is slower, do not overpick.

Protected Cropping

Although it is extremely hardy, growing lamb's lettuce under cloches, polythene tunnels or horticultural fleece, or in an unheated glasshouse,

Lamb's lettuce can fill any space in damp corners of the garden

The silver-blue flowers of lamb's lettuce are delicate and attractive

encourages better quality and higher productivity. Make the first sowings in early autumn.

Container Growing

Can be grown in 25cm (10in) pots of loam-based compost with a low fertilizer content. Sow seeds thinly 1cm (½in) deep every 3 weeks from early spring to early summer and again from early to mid-autumn, thinning to leave the strongest seedlings at a final spacing of 10cm (4in) apart.

Keep the compost moist when plants are growing vigorously; reduce watering in cooler conditions.

Harvesting & Storing

Harvest seedlings, pick leaves as required, or lift whole plants when they are mature – about 3 months after planting.

Do not weaken by removing too many leaves at one picking. This is particularly important with outdoor winter crops.

Leaves can be blanched for a few days before picking by covering with a box or pot to remove any bitterness.

Young flowers can be eaten in salads.

Pests & Diseases

Some varieties are susceptible to **mildew**. Protect seedlings from **birds** and **slugs**.

Companion Planting

As plants take up very little space, lamb's lettuce is ideal sown between taller crops.

Medicinal

With its high beta carotene, vitamin C and folic acid content, it is regarded by many as a winter and early spring tonic, and is useful when other nutritional vegetables are scarce.

Culinary

Thinnings can be used in salads. Wash the leaves thoroughly to remove grit and soil. In seventeenth-century Europe, lamb's lettuce was often served with cold boiled beetroot or celery. The leaves are used as a substitute for lettuce and combine well with it, also complementing fried bacon or ham and beetroot. Leaves can also be cooked like spinach.

Lamb's Lettuce & Prawn Salad
Serves 4

A mixture of winter salad leaves, such as lamb's lettuce, endive & radicchio
Large fresh prawns, peeled
Toasted sesame seeds

For the vinaigrette:
Lemon juice
Balsamic vinegar
Virgin olive oil
Mustard
Salt & freshly ground black pepper
Fresh herbs – sage, parsley & chives, chopped

Wash the salad leaves and arrange on individual plates.

Season the prawns with salt and pepper and coat generously with sesame seeds. (Allow 4 or 5 per person if they are Dublin Bay or tiger prawns.) In a heavy-bottomed frying pan, gently cook them, turning after 3 minutes, when golden, to cook the other side. Then arrange on the salad. Make the vinaigrette, sprinkle over and serve.

Vicia faba. Leguminosae

BROAD BEAN

(Fava Bean, Horse Bean, Windsor)
Annual grown for seeds, young leaf shoots and whole young pods.
Value: low protein, good source of fibre, potassium, vitamin E and C.

Thought to have originated around the Mediterranean, the oldest remains of domesticated broad beans have been dated to 6800–6500BC. By the Iron Age they had spread throughout Europe. The Greeks dedicated them to Apollo and thought that overindulgence dulled the senses; Dioscorides wrote that they are 'flatulent, hard of digestion, causing troublesome dreams'.

They may be the origin of the term 'bean feast', being a major part of the annual meal given by employers for their staff to make merry. In the vernacular this has been changed to 'beano'. Britain has many folk sayings concerning the sowing date. Huntingdonshire country wisdom states: 'On St Valentine's Day, beans should be in clay', and it was generally accepted that four seeds were sown – 'One for rook, one for crow, one to rot, one to grow.' Flowers were considered to be an aphrodisiac – 'there ent no lustier scent than a beanfield in bloom' – while the poet John Clare wrote: 'My love is as sweet as a bean field in blossom, beanfields misted wi' dew.'

Hardy and prolific, they are the national dish of Egypt. An Arab saying goes, 'Beans have satisfied even the Pharoahs.' How about you?

VARIETIES

Broad beans are classified as 'Dwarf', with small, early-maturing pods which are excellent under cloches or in containers, 'Longpods', which are also hardy, and 'Windsors', with broad pods which usually mature later and have a better flavour. There are green- and white-seeded forms among the Longpods and Windsors.

'**Aquadulce**' is a reliable hardy Longpod for autumn and spring sowing. '**Aquadulce Claudia**'* is similar, with medium to long pods and white seeds. Ideal for freezing, it is less susceptible to blackfly. '**Bonny Lad**'* is dwarf, 45cm (18in) high, and good for small gardens, cropping well. '**Express**'* is a fast-maturing early Longpod. Pods are plump and beans tasty. '**Imperial Green Longpod**'* produces pods around 38cm (15in) long with up to 9 large green beans. '**Masterpiece Green Longpod**' is a good-quality, green-seeded bean. Freezes well. '**Red Epicure**' has beautiful deep chestnut-crimson seeds. Some of the colour is lost in cooking, but the flavour is superb. '**Sweet

The neatly spaced seeds of 'Red Epicure', a tasty variety

Lorane**' is a delicious small-seeded, prolific bean. Cold-hardy. '**The Sutton**'*, a Dwarf variety around 30cm (12in) high, is ideal for small gardens and under cloches. Excellent flavour, very prolific. '**Witkiem Vroma**'* is excellent for spring sowing, grows rapidly and has medium-sized pods.

CULTIVATION

Propagation
As they germinate well in cool conditions, broad beans can be sown from mid- to late autumn and over-wintered outdoors for a mid-spring crop. Seedlings should be 2.5cm (1in) high when colder weather arrives 'Aquadulce' cultivars are particularly suitable.

When the soil is workable sow every 3 weeks from late winter to late spring for successional cropping.

Plant seeds 5cm (2in) deep in rows or make individual holes with 30cm (12in) in and between the rows. Or grow in staggered double rows, with 23cm (9in) in and between the rows or in blocks 90cm (36in) square with 20–30cm (8–12in) between plants. Tall plants should be 30–45cm (12–18in) apart. Sow extra seeds at the end of rows, for use as transplants.

Growing
Broad beans flourish in an open, sunny site but overwintering crops need more shelter. Soils should be deeply dug, moisture-retentive and well-drained, having been manured for the previous year's crop. Alternatively, add well-rotted organic matter in late autumn before sowing. They need a pH of 6–7, so lime where necessary. Rotate with other legumes.

Rake a granular general fertilizer into the seedbed

1 week before sowing. Mulch, hoe or hand weed regularly, especially at first.

Watering should be unnecessary except in drought, but for good-quality crops, plants need 22litres/sq m (4 gal/sq yd) per week from flower formation to harvest end.

Support taller plants with stakes. Planting several staggered rows allows plants to support one another. Dwarf types can be supported with brushwood.

Maintenance

Spring Sow early crops under glass followed by later sowings until late spring. *Summer* Harvest from late spring to late summer. Keep crops weed-free and water after flower formation. *Autumn* Sow outdoor crops for overwintering. *Winter* Protect outdoor crops in severe weather.

Protected Cropping

Where plants cannot be overwintered outdoors, sow under cover in pots or boxes from mid-winter. Harden off and plant out in mid-spring. Remove cloches from protected early crops when the beans reach the glass.

Container Growing

Grow dwarf cultivars in containers of low-fertilizer loam-based compost at least 20–45cm (8–18in) wide by 25cm (10in) deep. Sow seeds 5cm (2in) deep and 10–13cm (4–5in) apart. Water regularly in warm weather, less at other times.

Harvesting & Storing

Pick when the beans begin to show, before the pods are too large (and tough). Pull with a sharp downward twist or cut with scissors.

Pods harvested at 5–7.5cm (2–3in) long can be treated as snap peas and eaten whole, but picking at this stage reduces yields.

Broad beans freeze well, especially green-seeded varieties. Wash, blanch for 3 minutes, freeze in

'Masterpiece Green Longpod' produces a high yield of smaller, thinner beans

polythene bags or rigid containers. Use within 12 months. Keep them in a polythene bag in the refrigerator for 1 week.

PESTS & DISEASES

Black bean aphid is the most common problem. Control by pinching off the top 7.5cm (3in) of stem when the first beans start to form. This also encourages an earlier harvest. **Mice** and **jays** steal the seeds.

COMPANION PLANTING

Plant with summer savory to discourage black bean aphid and among gooseberries to discourage gooseberry sawfly. The flowers are very attractive to bees. Broad beans are a good 'nurse' crop for developing maize and sweetcorn.

Interplant with brassicas, which benefit from the nitrogen-fixing roots. Dig in plant debris as a 'green manure' to increase soil fertility. Seedling beans protect early potato shoots from wind and frost.

CULINARY

Steam or lightly boil beans to eat with ham, pork and chicken. Eat with sautéed onions, mushrooms and bacon; dress with tomato sauce, warm sour cream or lemon butter and dill.

Bissara
Serves 4

An Algerian dish with subtle flavours, this recipe is based on one from the late, great foodie, Arto der Haroutian.

675g (1½lb) young broad
  beans, shelled weight
1 small green chilli, chopped
1 teaspoon paprika
1 teaspoon cumin seeds,
  pounded in a mortar
2 cloves garlic, peeled
8 tablespoons virgin olive oil
Juice of half a lemon
Salt & freshly ground black
  pepper

Garnish:
A little olive oil, lemon juice
  & paprika

Bissara

Boil the beans in lightly salted water until just tender. Drain and place in a food processor, together with the chilli, paprika, cumin and garlic. Purée by slowly drizzling in the oil and lemon juice. Season and pour into a bowl.

Garnish with a little olive oil, lemon juice and paprika. Serve bissara with warm bread.

Broad Beans with Summer Savory
Serves 4

A dish which reflects the pure tastes of summer.

500g (1lb) young broad beans,
  shelled weight
2 sprigs & 2 tablespoons
  summer savory
2 tablespoons butter
Salt & freshly ground black
  pepper

Put the beans into a pan of boiling, salted water with the sprigs of summer savory and cook until just done, about 3–5 minutes. Drain and put the pan back on a gentle heat. Add the butter and toss well as it melts. Season with more summer savory and salt and pepper.

Zea mays. Gramineae

SWEETCORN

(Maize, Corn on the Cob, Indian Corn, Baby Maize) Annual grown for kernels of edible seeds. Half hardy. Value: high in carbohydrates and fibre, moderate protein and B vitamin content.

'Sundance', an excellent early variety

Wild plants of maize have never been found, but it is believed that the crop was first cultivated in Mexico around 7000BC. Primitive types, smaller than an ear of wheat, were found in caves at Tehuacan in southern Mexico dating from around 3500BC, yet they were bred by Mayan and Incan farmers almost to the size of modern varieties. Early American civilizations were based on maize, and life for the Aztecs revolved round the milpa or cornfield. Multicoloured types with blue, scarlet, brown and almost black seeds predominated in South America. It became a staple crop in North America after AD800. The first types introduced to Europe in the sixteenth century from Central America were valued for both the 'cobs' and the yellow meal. Corn flourished in Spain, France, Italy, the Balkans and Portugal.

Sweetcorn is a sweet form of maize, a starchy crop used for grain and fodder. The yellow-golden varieties are commonly cultivated for the kitchen, but those with multicoloured seeds are extremely ornamental. Sweetcorn and maize are the third most important cereal in the world, after wheat and rice, and there are more than 500 different by-products. The seeds of corn also provide us with popcorn with its exploding grains; starch extracted after milling has been used as laundry starch; the inner husks are used for making cigarette papers and the pith has been used for making explosives and packaging material. Best of all is delicious fresh sweetcorn eaten from the cob dripping with butter; take the advice of Edward Bunyard: ' The principle of the lathe is adopted in eating them.'

VARIETIES

Sweetcorn has been developed over centuries and there are many varieties available, as you will see from your seed catalogue.

Traditional varieties
'**Earliking**' is very early, with good-quality cobs. Good for cooler climates. '**Golden Bantam**' is 180cm (6ft) tall with tasty golden cobs which are good for freezing whole. An early, very hardy variety. '**Summer Flavour**' is very early and ideal for cooler areas and later sowings. Very sweet, tender and tasty. '**Sundance**'* matures early and is good for cooler climates. It crops well in poor summers. Seeds are very sweet.

Supersweet varieties
These are sweeter and keep their sweetness longer than older varieties. They should not be sown with older types as there is a danger they will cross-pollinate and lose their sweetness.

'**Conquest**' is early and more tolerant of cold soil than most of this type. '**Honey and Cream**' is delicious and has white and gold seeds. For best results, isolate from other sweetcorns. **'Silver Queen'** is a late-season type with white kernels. **'Stowell's Evergreen'** is also white and needs a long growing season. Keeps well over a long harvesting period.

Popcorn & ornamental varieties
'Carousel' reaches 200cm (7ft) tall, producing 4–6 ears per plant, and has tiny red, white, yellow, purple and blue seeds. Dries well. **'Rainbow'** is large with richly coloured kernels; seeds are glossy red, yellow, orange and blue.

CULTIVATION

Propagation
Seeds do not germinate when soil temperatures are below 10°C (50°F). Better germination and earlier crops are achieved by sowing from mid-spring under cover in pots or modules. Plant 2–3 seeds 2.5cm (1in) deep in pots of moist seed compost from mid- to late spring, at 55°F (13°C). After germination, thin to leave the strongest seedling. Sweetcorn is sensitive to root damage and disturbance, so thin with care, holding the strongest seedling while removing weaker ones.

Male sweetcorn flowers

Harden off and plant out once there is no longer any danger of frost.

Plants should be 35cm (14in) apart in and between the rows or spaced 25–30cm (10–12in) apart in rows 60cm (24in) apart.

To avoid erratic germination, seeds can be pregerminated. Put a few sheets of tissue paper or similar material in the bottom of a seedtray, moisten with water, place seeds evenly over the surface, cover with another layer of moist tissue. Put the tray in a loosely knotted polythene bag in an airing cupboard or warm room. When the seeds swell and tiny rootlets have formed, sow a single seed 2.5cm (1in) deep in a 9cm (3½in) pot of seed compost or sow singly outdoors. Sow a few in pots to replace those which do not germinate outdoors.

Alternatively, sow *in situ* from late spring to early summer. When the soil is workable, make a block about 1.2–1.5m (48–60in) comprising 4 ridges of soil about 30cm (12in) high with 35cm (14in) between the top of each ridge. 'Station sow' 2–3 seeds in the furrow 35cm (14in) apart each way and thin to leave the strongest seedling.

Cut a square of thin polythene or similar slightly larger than the block. Spread it over the furrows, dig a shallow trench round the edge and weigh the margins down with soil to hold the cover in place. As the seedlings emerge, cut crosses in the cover so they can grow through, or remove it and earth up round the stem bases when plants are 45cm (18in) high.

Alternatively, sow on a level seedbed and protect crops with fleece or cloches, which should be removed as soon as the plants become too large.

'Supersweet' varieties need slightly warmer conditions for germination;

Flower corn, grown for its ornamental and practical value

soils should be at a minimum of 12°C (55°F).

Because sweetcorn is wind-pollinated, plants are sown in blocks for effective germination. The male tassels (flowers) at the top of the plant shed clouds of pollen on to the female tassels or 'silks' below. These are clusters of pale green strands on the ends of the cobs which become sticky before pollination and each strand is attached to a single grain. For high yields, each must be pollinated, and sowing in a block ensures effective pollination. On a calm day tap the stems to help pollination.

Growing
Sweetcorn needs a moisture-retentive, free-draining soil. Dig in plenty of organic matter several weeks before planting, or use ground manured for the previous year's crop. Ideally, the soil should be slightly acid with a pH of 5.5–7.0. Plants need a long, warm growing season to succeed, so grow fast-maturing, early cultivars in cooler areas. The site should be open, sunny, warm and sheltered from cold winds and frosts.

Rake in a slow-release general fertilizer after transplanting or when preparing the seedbed.

Keep compost moist throughout the growing season. Watering is particularly beneficial when they begin to flower, and when the grains begin to swell. Apply 22 litres/sq m (4 gal/sq yd) per week.

Stake plants when growing on exposed sites.

Sweetcorn is shallow-rooted, so take care when hoeing to avoid damaging the roots. It is much better to mulch with a layer of organic matter to suppress weeds and retain moisture. Mulch with black polythene on level ground. Do not remove sideshoots (tillers). Earth up to make plants more stable.

Maintenance

Spring Sow seed under cover or outdoors.
Summer Sow seeds; keep crops weed-free and water. Harvest.
Autumn Harvest.
Winter Prepare the ground for next year's crop.

Protected Cropping

When soil temperatures are below 10°C (50°F), sow from mid-spring under cover in pots or modules at 55°F (13°C). Harden off and plant out once there is no danger of frost.

Harvesting & Storing

Each plant usually produces one or two cobs. Those sown *in situ* mature later than seed sown indoors.

When cobs are ready to harvest, the 'silks' wither and turn dark brown. Peel back the leaves and test for ripeness by pushing your thumbnail into a grain: if the liquid runs clear, it is unripe; if it is milky, it is ready to harvest; if it is thick, then it is overmature and unsuitable for eating. To pick, hold the main stem in one hand and twist off the cob with the other.

After pollination the silks begin to turn brown, an indication that the cob is maturing.

Eat or freeze within 24 hours of picking, before the sugars in the seeds convert to starch. 'Supersweet' varieties hold their sugar levels longer.

To freeze, blanch cobs for 4–6 minutes, cool and drain, before wrapping singly in foil or cling film and placing in the freezer.

Cobs remain fresh for up to 3 days if they are stored in the refrigerator.

PESTS & DISEASES

Birds can pull up the seedlings and attack the developing cobs. **Slugs** attack seedlings. **Smut** appears as large galls on the cobs and stalks in hot dry weather. Cut off and burn immediately, or they will burst open and release a mass of black spores. Burn plants and debris after harvesting and do not grow sweetcorn on the site for at least 3 years. **Frit fly larvae** bore into the growing points of corn seedlings, which then develop twisted and ragged leaves. Growth is stunted and cobs are undersized. Use 'dressed' seed and rake a granular insecticide into the soil. **Mice** enjoy newly planted seeds, especially 'supersweet' types. Trap, or buy a cat.

A well-grown cob, packed full of mature seeds

COMPANION PLANTING

Grow sweetcorn with or after legumes. Runner beans can be allowed to grow over sweetcorn plants. Intercrop corn with sunflowers, allowing cucurbits to trail through them.

The shade they provide is useful to cucumbers, melons, squashes, courgettes, marrows and potatoes. Brussels sprouts, kale, Savoy cabbages, swedes and broccoli can be interplanted. Grow lettuce and other salads, French beans and courgettes between the crops.

MEDICINAL

Corn is said to reduce the risk of certain cancers, heart disease and dental cavities. Corn oil is reported to lower cholesterol levels more successfully than other polyunsaturated oils.

In parts of Mexico corn is used to treat dysentery. It is also known in American folk medicine as a diuretic and mild stimulant.

Planting in blocks gives higher yields, as plants are wind pollinated

CULINARY

To serve whole, strip off outer leaves, leaving 5–7cm (2–3in) of stalk on the ear. Pull off 'silks'. Boil in unsalted water, drain and eat hot with melted butter.

Roasted corn is a favourite with most children – it tastes wonderfully succulent compared with the sogginess of tinned corn.

Deep-fry spoonfuls of a mixture of mashed corn, salt, flour, milk and egg for 1–2 minutes or until golden brown to make corn fritters.

Seeds are ground, meal boiled or baked, cob can be roasted or boiled or fermented, maize meal is cooked with water to create a thick mash, or dough.

Tortillas are made by baking in flat cakes until they are crisp.

Dry-milling produces grits, from which most of the bran and germ are separated. Cornflakes are rolled, flavoured seeds. Multicoloured corn adds colour and flavour to sweet dishes and drinks.

Baby corns are particularly decorative and the perfect size for Oriental stir-fries, where they combine well with mangetout.

Polenta is made from ground maize.

Barbecued Corn on the Cob

This is the way to really taste the flavour of corn. Take 1 corn ear for each person. Boil them in salted water for 7–10 minutes and then drain.

Place each in the centre of a piece of foil. Use 1 tablespoon butter per corn ear and mix in

1 teaspoon fresh chopped herbs, sea salt and freshly ground black pepper; spread over the corn ears. Season well and then seal the foils.

Lay the corns on a medium-hot barbecue or in a charcoal grill (in which case keep it covered) and roast for 20 minutes, turning the cobs once halfway through the cooking.

Corn Maque Choux
Serves 4

Cajun cooking has become popular in recent years and this dish reveals the true taste of corn.

1 tablespoon butter
1 large onion, roughly chopped
1 green pepper, deseeded & diced
500g (1lb) corn, cooked & stripped from the cob

2 tomatoes, peeled, deseeded & diced
½ teaspoon tabasco sauce
Salt & freshly ground black pepper

Heat the butter in a heavy pan and sauté the onion until softened. Add the pepper and continue cooking for 3–4 minutes. Toss in the corn and the remaining ingredients and, over a low heat, simmer for 10 minutes. Adjust the seasoning and serve.

Succotash
Serves 4

The American Indians cooked succotash, and many recipes still exist for it. 'Silver Queen' is a particularly good variety to use for this dish.

3–4 tablespoons unsalted butter
300g (10oz) broad beans, cooked

3 or 4 ears roasted corn, husked
250g (8oz) French beans, topped & tailed
1 medium red onion, finely chopped
300ml (½pt) vegetable stock
½ red pepper, finely diced
1 beef tomato, peeled, deseeded & chopped
Salt & freshly ground black pepper

Melt the butter in a heavy frying pan and sweat the broad beans, corn, French beans and onion over a medium heat for about 3 minutes.

Then add the stock and continue cooking for 5 minutes before stirring in the remaining ingredients.

Taste for seasoning, mix thoroughly and continue cooking for 5 minutes more. Serve hot.

Succotash

Zingiber officinale. Zingiberaceae

GINGER

(Stem Ginger, Canton Ginger)
Herbaceous perennial grown for aromatic rhizomes.
Tender. Value: contains small amounts of vitamins
and minerals; ground ginger high in iron; fresh ginger
high in vitamin C.

Ginger has been grown in tropical Asia for at least 3,000 years and was one of the first spices brought to Europe along the Silk Road from China. Arab merchants controlled the trade in ginger and other spices for centuries until explorers like Marco Polo reached the Indian Ocean. The Portuguese took ginger to their colonies and the Spaniards introduced it to the New World; in 1547 they exported over 1,000 tons of rhizomes to Jamaica and Mexico, and by the end of the century had a thriving trade with Europe. Fresh ginger is cultivated throughout the tropics and is freely available.

The creeping, branched rhizomes growing near the surface, with pale yellow flesh beneath a thin, buff-coloured to dark brown skin, look like knobbly fingers and are often referred to as 'hands'. The stems can grow up to 120cm (4ft) tall, with narrow, lance-shaped leaves; the short-lived flowers are yellow-green and purple, marked with spots and stripes.

Freshly dug hand of ginger, Gaylephug, Bhutan

VARIETIES

Each centre of cultivation has its own forms. Several clones are found in India and three in Malaya. Two found in Jamaica are the high-quality white or yellow form and 'flint ginger', with tougher, fibrous rhizomes.

CULTIVATION

Propagation

Propagate in late spring just before growth begins, using sections of rhizomes. Lift parent plants carefully to avoid rhizome damage, shake off the soil and break off sections about 5cm (2in) long with at least one good bud. Dispose of older sections, keeping the young growth and trim the ends with a sharp knife. Dust the cuts with fungicide before planting, buds uppermost, 5–10cm (2–4in) deep with 15cm (9in) between rows. Water thoroughly with tepid water after planting.

Growing

Ginger needs an annual rainfall of at least 150cm (45in), high temperatures and a short dry season for part of the year.

The soil should be rich, moisture-retentive and free-draining; add well-rotted organic matter where necessary. It is essential that the ground is not compacted and all debris is removed, otherwise the rhizomes become deformed.

Water plants thoroughly during dry periods and keep them weed-free throughout the growing season. In the humid tropics, ginger can be planted at any time.

Maintenance

Spring Plant rhizomes under cover.
Summer Water, feed and keep weed-free. Maintain high temperatures and humidity.
Autumn Lift rhizomes carefully.

f rhizomes remain unused, they will sprout and rapidly develop

Protected Cropping

Ginger can be grown under cover, but as it needs high temperatures and humidity, this is not normally practical, and for optimum productivity it is better planted outdoors.

As a 'novelty crop' under glass, plant the rhizome just below the surface in peat-substitute-based compost in a 20cm (8in) pot. Keep it constantly moist, and feed with a liquid general fertilizer every 3 weeks during the growing season.

Harvesting & Storing

Younger tender rhizomes are harvested for immediate use and for preserving; they become more fibrous and pungent with age.

Harvesting can begin from 7 months after planting. Rhizomes for drying should be lifted about 9–10 months after planting.

Fresh 'root' can be stored in the refrigerator for several weeks wrapped in paper towels, foil or any container which allows it to 'breathe'. It can also be wrapped and frozen.

PESTS & DISEASES

Soft rot can appear as dark patches at the base of the shoots. To prevent, handle rhizomes with care, avoid waterlogging and treat with fungicide.

Cultivated ginger flourishing near Transvaal, South Africa

CULINARY

Ginger is used throughout the world as a flavouring for sweet and savoury dishes; it plays a starring role in foods like gingerbread, but is also an integral part of many spice mixes, appearing in biscuits, cakes, soups, pickles, marinades, curry powder, stewed fruit, puddings, tea, beer, ale and wine.

It is the most important spice in Chinese cookery. In Japanese cookery it is used as a side dish called 'gari' to accompany sushi. Besides being used fresh, dried and in powdered form, ginger is pickled, preserved in syrup, candied and crystallized.

Rhizomes should be lightly scraped or peeled to remove the tough skin before use.

MEDICINAL

Ginger has been used for centuries in Chinese medicine. In the Orient fresh ginger is a remedy for vomiting, coughing, abdominal distension and fever. Many Africans drink ginger root as an aphrodisiac, while in New Guinea it is eaten dried as a contraceptive and in the Philippines it is chewed to expel evil spirits.

In the Middle Ages it was believed to possess miraculous properties against cholera. Culpeper in his *Herbal* of 1653 says: 'It is profitable for old men; it heats the joints and is useful against gout; it expels wind.' It can be rubbed on the face as a 'rouge', stimulating circulation. Ginger is said to cleanse the body and lower cholesterol; it can be chewed to alleviate sore throats, is a digestive, relieves dyspepsia, colic and diarrhoea and prevents travel sickness.

Ginger tea

Agaricus bisporus and others

MUSHROOMS, EDIBLE FUNGI

Simple organisms growing on decaying substrate or symbiotically with living plants, some with edible fruiting bodies. Half hardy/tender. Value: low in calories, moderate potassium, linoleic and folic acid, carbohydrates, iron, niacin and B vitamins.

Fungi are extraordinary organisms: lacking both chlorophyll and root systems, they are more akin to moulds and yeasts than to traditional vegetable plants. The fleshy mushroom, or bracket, you eat is a fruiting body, dispersing spores in order to reproduce in the same way that plant fruits disperse seeds. Instead of drawing nutrients through roots, however, a fungus is sustained by a network of fine – often microscopic – threads (known collectively as the mycelium). This can extend over vast distances into rotting wood, soil or some other preferred medium. To help identify a fungus it is important to know the particular substrate on which it depends, or the higher plant species with which it lives in symbiosis (certain fungi, for example, grow only in the vicinity of specific trees such as birch or oak); when attempting to cultivate any kind of mushroom, you must provide similarly congenial conditions.

However, few of the many thousand fungus genera are amenable to cultivation. Even in nature, fruiting is wildly unpredictable: the organism depends on precise moisture and temperature variables to produce fruiting bodies, and more generally is sensitive to environmental changes such as recent air pollution and high nitrate levels.

Their erratic behaviour and mysterious origins – allied with the deadly toxins some contain – have given rise to a 'love-hate' attitude towards fungi. Some have been collected as 'wild food' since ancient times. The Romans esteemed them as a delicacy and the rich employed collectors to find the most desirable species. However, Gerard, writing in his *Herball*, remained unimpressed: 'few . . . are good to be eaten and most of them do suffocate and strangle the eater'. John Evelyn advised that all types of mushrooms should be kept well out of the kitchen.

By the late seventeenth century, varieties of *Agaricus* began to be grown in underground caves in the Paris region, in which giant heaps of manure were impregnated with soil taken from areas where field and horse mushrooms grew naturally. For many centuries cultivated mushrooms were a delicacy enjoyed only by the wealthy, and from the eighteenth century most stableyards had a shady corner where there was a mushroom bed. Some garden owners had outhouses converted to provide ideal growing conditions: George IV had a large mushroom house at Kensington Palace in London. In seasons when wild or cultivated crops were plentiful, surplus mushrooms were conserved in the form of sauces and ketchups, and only recently has the role of mushroom sauce in the kitchen been usurped by tomato sauce.

Cultivated *Agaricus* species have remained popular in northern Europe and the English-speaking world, yet elsewhere they are eclipsed by other mushrooms. In Japan, velvet shank, nameko, oyster and shi-itake mushrooms are established as the cultivated varieties, and some of them are slowly becoming popular in other countries. A number of species are commercially available, some of them to amateur growers, and usually work by inoculating the growing medium with mycelium or 'spawn'. Home growing of many fungus species is in its infancy, but gaining ground each year. As adventurous gardeners and mushroom eaters increasingly experiment, advances in mushroom cultivation will also help to conserve wild species.

Button mushroom growing in compost

Mushroom gathering has always had a strong following, from the Roman days to nineteenth-century Russia and France

SPECIES

The following lists include several of the more common and better known edible fungi.

Commonly available for home cultivation
These fungi are grown commercially and can occasionally be bought from specialist suppliers as kits, 'spawn' or impregnated dowels for inoculating logs. A notable advantage of buying mushrooms in this form is that you are assured of their identity. You should follow suppliers' detailed cultivation instructions carefully to increase the chances of success. Some producers have their own selected strains of these fungi.

Agaricus bisporus
(cultivated mushroom, champignon de Paris) has a smooth white to brownish cap and white stem and flesh. Excellent flavour raw and cooked. This accounts for 60% of the world's mushroom production. Available as kits or spawn (see 'Cultivation' below). Commercial growers are developing new races with colour variation in the cap: watch out for them in future as kits for amateur growers.

Flammulina velutipes
(enokitake, velvet shank, velvet foot, winter mushroom) occurs naturally on dead wood and is grown commercially on sawdust, particularly in Japan. Small tan-yellow caps on dark brown stems. Do not eat stems and wipe or peel off any stickiness from the caps before cooking.

Hericium erinaceus
(lion's mane, monkey head) produces large, rounded clusters of icicle-like growths that taste like lobster – delicious fried with butter and onions. Grows in the wild from wounds on living hardwoods such as beech, and can be cultivated on stumps or logs.

Lentinula edodes
(shi-itake) is a small to medium size mushroom with light brown stem and pale to dark reddish-brown cap. Documents record this strongly flavoured gourmet mushroom being eaten in AD199 and it is the second most important cultivated fungus. In Japan it is grown commercially on logs of chestnut, oak or hornbeam. Different forms tolerate warmer or colder conditions, and include Snowcap, a thick-fleshed form with a long fruiting season, grown on large logs, and West Wind, which is ideal for inexperienced growers, yielding well over a long period.

Oyster mushrooms developing in a grow-bag, India

Pholiota nameko (nameko, viscid mushroom) is among the four most important fungi cultivated in Japan. Grows in clusters on tree trunks or wood chips. Orange-brown caps atop paler stems are 5–6cm (2–3 in) in diameter. It is pleasantly aromatic.

Pleurotus (or oyster mushroom) is a genus with a number of distinct species and strains. Popular in Japan and Central Europe, they are increasingly available in kit form, or can be grown from plugs of spawn. Eat when small, discarding the tough stem. Sauté in butter until tender, season, then add cream or yoghurt. The first two are fairly common in the wild and are also offered in seed catalogues.

Pleurotus ostreatus (oyster mushroom) has large fan-shaped caps ranging in colour from slate-blue to white and with white or pale straw-coloured gills; used coffee grounds (sterilized as the coffee is brewed) are becoming a popular medium for inoculating with the spawn.

P. cornucopiae (golden oyster) has a white stem with a cream cap turning to ochre-brown. Grows on the cut stumps of deciduous trees, usually elm or oak. Other species may be harder to find, and some need warmth to fruit.

P. ergyngii (king pleurotus) has a concave cap, whitish becoming grey-brown. It tastes sweet and meaty and grows in clusters on the decaying roots of plants in the carrot family. It can be grown on chopped straw. **P. flabellatus** is an oyster mushroom with pink caps. **P. pulmonarius** has brown or grey caps. **P. samoneus-tramineus** from Asia is pink-capped. **P. sajor-caju** has brown caps.

Stropharia rugosoannulata (king stropharia) is a brown-capped, violet-gilled fungus commonly cultivated in eastern Europe; it is claimed to be capable of growing in vegetable gardens. It requires a substrate of humus containing rotting hardwood or sawdust. Grow spawn from reputable sources: look-alikes include deadly *Cortinarius* species.

Volvariella volvaceae (Chinese or straw mushroom, paddy straw, padi-straw) has a grey-brown cap, often marked with black, and a dull brown stem. Grown on composted rice straw, it is regarded as an expensive delicacy in China and other Asian countries. Needs high temperatures and humidity to grow well. Harvest when it is immature.

Naturally occurring edible fungi Many edible species of fungi may be found growing in your garden if it happens to provide the host trees or other conditions that form their natural habitat. In Continental Europe, fungi collected in the wild are often sold in markets; but local pharmacists or health inspectors are on hand to verify that those on sale are edible species.

NEVER EAT A FUNGUS UNLESS YOU HAVE FIRST HAD ITS IDENTITY CONFIRMED BY AN EXPERT

Agaricus arvensis (horse mushroom) and **A. campestris** (field mushroom) are cousins of the cultivated mushroom, found in clusters or rings in grazed or mown grassland. Dome-shaped white 'buttons' open to wide caps. Horse mushrooms can grow to soup-plate size with thick, firm flesh smelling of aniseed; the gills are pale greyish-pink darkening to chocolate-brown. Field mushrooms are smaller and rather more delicate in stature, with a 'mushroomy' smell; their deep pink gills become dark brown to black at maturity.

Boletus edulis (cep, penny bun) grows on the ground near trees, favouring pine, beech, oak and birch woodlands. The rounded, bun-like brown cap (often covered with a white bloom when young) sits on a bulbous whitish stem – also edible. Tube-like pores (rather than gills) beneath the cap are white, turning dull yellow at maturity. This delicious, fleshy fungus is highly prized in Continental markets and can be eaten fresh, pickled or dried. Related species of *Boletus* are also edible.

Cantharellus cibarius (chanterelle) is funnel-shaped; egg-yolk-yellow caps, fading with age, are thick and fleshy with gill-like wrinkles running down from the cap underside into the stem. Has a mild peppery aftertaste when eaten raw; excellent flavour cooked. True chanterelles grow on soil in broad-leaved woodland: similar-looking species are highly toxic.

Oyster mushrooms growing on a tree trunk

Hirneola auricula-judae, syn. **Auricularia auricula-judae** (Jew's ear, wood-ear) looks like a human ear and is date-brown, drying to become small and hard. Found on living and dead elder, beech and sycamore. Can be dried and reconstituted with water. Popular in Taiwan and China.

Hypholoma capnoides, syn. **Nematoloma capnoides**, is a gilled fungus found growing in clusters on conifer stumps. Caps 2–6cm (¾–2¼in) diameter are pale ochre with a buff-coloured margin. Check identity carefully: other *Hypholoma* species are suspect.

Laetiporus sulphureus, syn. **Polyporus sulphureus** (chicken of the woods) is a bracket fungus found on many hardwoods and softwoods, often on sweet chestnut, oak and beech. Has the flavour of chicken breast and is an orange to sulphur-yellow colour. Eat young, but only try a little the first time: it can cause nausea and dizziness in some people. The largest ever found weighed 45.4kg (100lb).

Langermannia gigantea (giant puffball) can be enormous: large and round with white skin, it sits on the ground like a giant soccer ball. The biggest ever recorded, according to the *Guinness Book of Records*, was 2.64m (8ft 8in) in circumference and weighed 22kg (over 48lb)! It is found on soil in fields, hedgerows, woodlands and gardens, often near nettles. Eat when young, while the flesh is pure white; it tastes good sliced, dipped in breadcrumbs and fried. Other related (and smaller) species of puffball are also edible while they remain white all through.

Lepista nuda (blewit, wood blewit, blue-stalk) is medium to large with a light

A basket of morel mushrooms

cinnamon-brown to tan cap; the gills and stems are violet to lavender. It is found in woodlands, parks and hedges. It can be grown in leaf debris around compost heaps. Better eaten young, it is well flavoured and particularly good in stews or fried. Never eat raw: cook thoroughly to remove traces of cyanic acid.

Marasmius oreades (fairy ring champignon) is found on lawns in a 'ring' of dark green grass with dying grass in the centre. Small with a bell-shaped light tan-coloured cap, matching gills and similar stem. Good in omelettes. Beware: similar looking species are toxic.

Morchella esculenta (common morel) is a delicious fungus that emerges annually in spring, earlier than most autumn-fruiters. The hollow cap has a surface covered in honeycomb-like pits and varies from round to conical in shape. (The many crevices of the cap often harbour dirt and insects – a rare instance when preparing by rinsing in water is advised.) Found on well-drained soils under deciduous trees, particularly in ash and elm woods, in gardens and near old hedges. Other edible species include **M. rotunda**, found on heavier soil, and **M. vulgaris**, on richer soil. Some similar-looking mushroom species are highly toxic.

Sparassis crispa (cauliflower mushroom, brain fungus) has a folded, rounded fruiting body, creamy-white when young, which looks more like a cauliflower than a conventional mushroom. It tastes nutty, with a spicy fragrance. Found at the base of pines and other conifers. As with morels, rinse to remove any debris.

Tuber melanosporum (the Perigord or black truffle), often found in oak woods, is highly desirable and the most valuable truffle. Pigs and trained dogs are used to sniff them out. Commercial growers are now developing truffle-inoculated trees; several closely related species are also edible – I have yet to try them!

CULTIVATION
(of *Agaricus* species)

Propagation

With the traditional commercial methods, indoor crops of *Agaricus* species are more reliable than those grown outdoors. Make a large heap of stable manure, preferably at least 150cm (60in) square, and moisten thoroughly. Cover until temperatures reach 45–60°C (140–160°F), turning once a week until it is crumbly and sweet-smelling. When it reaches that stage, fill boxes, buckets, containers or trays with a 23–30cm (9–12in) layer and firm. When the temperature falls to 25°C (75°F) and the surface is ready for spawning, push golfball-sized pieces about 2.5cm (1in) under the surface 30cm (12in) apart. After 2–3 weeks, white 'threads' appear on the surface. Spread a 5cm (2in) layer of 'casing' made from 2 parts peat substitute to 1 part chalk or ground limestone over the surface and keep it moist. When mushrooms start to appear reduce the temperature to 10–18°C (50–65°).

Two types of spawn are available – fungus-impregnated manure (block spawn) or impregnated rye (grain spawn). Block spawn is easier to use.

Alternatively, buy a bucket or bag of ready-spawned compost or a fungi-growing pack. Do not buy kits which have been in store for a long time and start the pack into growth within 3 weeks of buying it.

Growing

'Cultivated mushrooms' can be grown in or outdoors in the lawn or manure heap, though crops will be variable. Choose a shady position and enrich the ground with plenty of well-rotted organic matter. On a damp day in spring or autumn, 'plant' blocks of spawn, about the size of a golfball, 5cm (2in) below the soil and 30cm (12in) apart. A good crop of mushrooms often appears when spent mushroom compost is used as a mulch around other crops.

Maintenance

Indoor crops can be planted any time of the year. Plant spawn outdoors in spring or autumn.

Protected Cropping

Indoor crops grow well in an airy shed, cellar, greenhouse or cold frame. They do not need to be grown in the dark.

Container Growing

See 'Propagation'.

Harvesting & Storing

The first 'button' mushrooms are ready for harvesting 4–6 weeks after 'casing'; there may be another 2 weeks before the next 'flush'. Harvesting lasts for about 6 weeks. To harvest, twist and pull mushrooms upwards, disturbing the compost as little as possible, removing any broken stalks and filling the holes with 'casing'.

Mushrooms last in a ventilated polythene bag in the salad drawer of a refrigerator for up to 3 days.

Most species can be dried. Thread them on to a string and hang them over a radiator or in an airing cupboard, then store in a cool dry place. Reconstitute with water or wine.

After the final harvest, you can use the spent mixture as a mulch; you should never try to re-spawn for a second crop.

Shiitake mushrooms

PESTS & DISEASES

Mushroom fly can be a problem; pick mushrooms when young.

MEDICINAL

Edible fungi lower blood cholesterol, stimulate the immune system and de-activate viruses. Shiitake mushrooms are particularly effective. Jew's ear has been used in herbal medicine for treating sore throats.

WARNING

If you gather wild mushrooms, be certain of their identity before eating. Best of all, collect with an expert. Those which are highly toxic are often similar to edible species. **Mistakes can be fatal.**

CULINARY

Fungi should always be eaten fresh as the flavour is soon lost and the quality deteriorates. Avoid washing most kinds: the fruit bodies absorb water, spoiling the texture and flavour. Simply clean the surface by wiping with a damp cloth or brushing off any dirt. Peel only when necessary.

Both caps and stems of *Agaricus* species can be eaten. With some other fungi, stems may be discarded as inedibly tough. Check for any special instructions on preparation: some fungi, for instance, are toxic unless cooked.

Harvested cultivated mushrooms at the 'button' stage can be eaten raw, added to salads; more mature caps can be baked, grilled or fried whole, or sliced and stir-fried, made into soups, pies or stuffings, added to stews or the stockpot, or used as a garnish. Other fungi can be prepared in many similar ways. Large fruit bodies can be stuffed.

Try frying in butter and a little lemon juice for 3–5 minutes. Brush with oil and seasoning and grill each side for 2–3 minutes. Add yoghurt or cream before serving, or dip in breadcrumbs and fry. Garlic mushrooms are especially delicious.

Mushroom Soup
Serves 4

This is particularly satisfying on a cold winter's day. Open-capped cultivated mushrooms make a good alternative to the wild variety.

75g (3oz) butter
4 shallots, finely chopped
1 clove garlic, crushed
500g (1lb) field mushrooms, cleaned & sliced
1 litre (1¾pt) chicken stock
1 tablespoon plain flour
Dash soya sauce
A little thick cream
Salt & freshly ground black pepper

Heat 50g (2oz) of the butter in a heavy bottomed pan and sauté the shallots until softened; add the garlic and cook for 1 minute more. Add the mushrooms and stir to coat well. Pour in the stock and bring to the boil. Season and cover, simmering for 10–15 minutes, until the mushrooms are cooked. Remove from the heat.

In a separate pan, heat the remaining butter and stir in the flour to make a roux. Cook for 2 minutes and remove from the stove. In a liquidizer, blend the roux with the soup (this may need to be done in 2 batches or more). Add the soya sauce and check the seasoning. Garnish with a little thick cream and serve.

Mushroom Mélange

Grilled Shi-itake Mushrooms
Serves 4

Allow 2 mushrooms per person for a first course to be served with Italian bread.

8–12 shi-itake mushrooms
6 tablespoons olive oil
1 sprig rosemary
1 tablespoon fresh thyme leaves
2 tablespoons balsamic vinegar
2 tablespoons Barollo wine
1 small onion, finely chopped
4 slices toasted Italian bread
1 tablespoon butter
1 clove garlic, crushed
Salt & freshly ground black pepper

Wash the shiitakes, ensuring the gills are free from dirt. Discard the stems and add to a stockpot. Dry the caps.

Leave the mushrooms in a marinade of oil, rosemary, thyme, vinegar, wine, onion and seasoning for 30–45 minutes, turning them occasionally.

Grill under a preheated grill for 5 minutes each side, brushing with the marinade juices. Serve on slices of toasted Italian bread, buttered and rubbed with garlic. Pour over a little of the juices on each helping.

Mushroom Mélange
Serves 4

500g (1lb) oyster mushrooms
500g (1lb) shi-itake mushrooms
4 tablespoons butter
2 cloves garlic, crushed
2 shallots, finely chopped
4 tablespoons white wine
150ml (¼pt) double cream
4 tablespoons grated Parmesan
Salt & freshly ground black pepper

Wash the mushrooms well and chop them, including the stalks. Melt the butter in a heavy saucepan, add the garlic and shallots and allow to soften over a gentle heat. Add the mushrooms and stir well. Pour in the wine and the double cream and bring to simmering point. Then cover and leave to stew for 15 minutes.

Pour into a greased sauté pan, season with salt and pepper and sprinkle over the Parmesan. Put under a preheated grill on the highest setting for 3–5 minutes until the cheese is melted. Serve immediately.

PRACTICAL GARDENING

PLANNING YOUR VEGETABLE GARDEN

Is there a more glorious site for a garden than the foot of the Alps?

Several factors determine the planning and layout of a vegetable garden and the species which can be grown.

- the locality and climatic conditions
- the size and shape of the plot
- the number of people to be supplied with vegetables
- the duration of cropping
- the skill of the gardener, and the time available for maintaining the plot
- whether the vegetables are intended for use when fresh, stored, or both

It is a good idea to list the vegetables you like, then decide how and where they can be grown to achieve the best results. In large gardens a vast range and volume of tasty vegetables can be produced using crop rotation and protected cropping to extend the growing season. Smaller sites allow fewer opportunities for self-sufficiency, but it is still possible to grow a good selection or experiment with unusual varieties. Even the tiniest gardens, balconies or patios are suitable, particularly with the use of containers, while areas surrounded by buildings often create favourable microclimates for tender vegetables such as okra. Protected cropping provides further opportunities to defy the cold weather.

Before preparing a planting plan it is important to be aware of the advantages and disadvantages of the site, considering everything from aspect and shelter to soil quality and drainage. Choose a design which suits your site and taste: traditionally, plots were planned in beds and rows, but you may prefer the potager (or 'edible landscape')

developed by the French, or the raised bed system, which is ideal for intensive small or large-scale cropping. It is essential to provide the best possible growing conditions for optimum production and the old saying, 'the answer lies in the soil', is particularly relevant to vegetable growing.

Accurate timing is also a prerequisite. A cropping timetable should make full use of the ground all year round. It is advisable to plan backwards from the intended harvesting date to work out when crops should be sown. There is little advantage in having a garden full of vegetables which are cheap and plentiful in the shops; it is far better to plan your cropping dates for times when they are scarce and expensive.

Site and Soil

Most vegetables are short-term crops, which are harvested before they reach maturity. To achieve the necessary rapid growth, the ideal site is warm and light with good air circulation. This is particularly important for the fertilization of wind-pollinated crops such as sweetcorn, and to discourage pests and diseases which flourish in still conditions. However, it is worth noting that strong winds can reduce plant growth by up to 30%.

On a *gently sloping site* facing the sun, the soil warms faster in spring than in other aspects, making such an area perfect for early crops.

It is more difficult to work the soil on *steeper slopes*, especially if machinery is being used: crops should be planted across, rather than down the slope to reduce the risk of soil erosion during heavy rain.

On *very steep slopes*, the ground should be terraced.

A sloping site is ideal for early crops   **Kitchen garden (opposite)**

SOIL, SITES AND PREPARATION

Soils and Preparation

Vegetables can be grown successfully on a range of soils by selecting varieties which flourish in the existing conditions or by improving the soil with the addition of organic matter or other materials. A slightly acid soil, with moderate fertility and organic matter content is ideal, requiring only routine cultivation to produce a broad range of crops. Be aware of the compatibility between the selected vegetables and site, and choose the right plant for the right place for successful cropping: for example, don't grow asparagus on heavy clay. (See 'Growing' under vegetable entries.)

If necessary, gradually improve the soil by planting a ground-breaking crop like potatoes or Jerusalem artichokes and enrich the soil quality by adding organic matter. Potatoes are often used for this as they require a number of cultivations to 'earth up' and cover the tubers, so preventing weeds from becoming established. Potatoes also produce large leafy tops, blocking the light which is so essential for the germination of many weed species. Ensure that neglected, weed-infested sites are cleared thoroughly before planting, using translocated herbicides, cultivation and organic methods. It is better to start your garden clear from weeds than to tackle the problem halfway down the line.

Potatoes are good ground-breaking crops

Double digging and filling a trench with green manure

Soil Structure

Light, free-draining, sandy soils are ideal for early crops, as they warm up quickly in the spring. However, as they are open and free-draining, moisture and nutrients are quickly lost. This can be redressed by irrigation and by the addition of fertilizer and copious amounts of well-rotted organic matter.

Heavier clay soils become waterlogged and sticky during torrential heavy rain, are slow to drain, take longer to warm up in spring and become cracked and unworkable during prolonged drought. This makes the growing season shorter and cultivation extremely difficult. However, they retain water for longer periods and are usually very fertile; as a result they are suitable for hungry, leafy crops which require high nutrient levels. Incorporating well-rotted organic matter, sharp sand, horticultural grit and gypsum over several years gradually improves the soil structure.

A good soil structure can be easily damaged by cultivating when it is excessively wet or dry and by using heavy machinery – even walking on wet soil causes compaction and smearing. To reduce the impact, lay a plank on the soil to disperse the weight. Growing vegetables in 'deep beds' avoids this problem.

Soil Cultivation

The soil structure essential for successful growth is created by incorporating different materials into the soil: well-rotted compost improves moisture and nutrient retention, creates an open structure and aerates the soil; sharp sand helps drainage; and 'green manures' improve the structure.

Digging is the most important method of cultivation whereby debris from the previous crops is buried and the ground prepared for the following crop. Digging is an annual event and the timing can be critical.

On heavier soils in cooler climates, autumn digging is beneficial, as the winter frosts that follow help to break down these wet, sticky soils into a workable tilth. Sandy soils can be lightly forked over and it is advisable to cover them with compost or green manure to reduce the loss of nutrients during the winter rains. The depth of soil and fertility required depend on the types of vegetables to be grown. 'Root crops' such as parsnips and carrots penetrate deeply and the soil should be prepared and fertilized to a depth of at least 30cm (12in). Shallow-rooted salad crops do not need such deep cultivation and can be planted after deeper-rooted crops.

Single digging consists of cultivating the soil to about 30cm (12in): a good spade's depth and the average rooting 'zone' of many plants. The soil is systematically dug over in a series of trenches, with surface vegetation and debris often being buried in the bottom of the trench.

Double digging is used on poorly drained and previously uncultivated land, or where root crops are to be grown. It encourages deep rooting and promotes rapid drainage. 'Double' refers to the depth of cultivation, some 45–60cm (18–24in) deep or approximately two spades' depth. When double digging it is important to ensure that the topsoil and subsoil are not mixed; they should be cultivated, yet remain at the same level within the soil profile.

Lime and Liming

Soil acidity and alkalinity is measured on a pH scale ranging from 0 to 14; 0 is the most acid and 14 the most alkaline. The pH level affects solubility of minerals and their availability to plants. Acidic conditions encourage phosphorus deficiency and sometimes contain excess manganese and aluminium, while alkaline conditions can lead to a deficiency in manganese, boron and phosphorus.

Soil pH also influences the number and type of beneficial soil-borne organisms and the incidence of pests and diseases; worms dislike a low pH, but leatherjackets and wireworms are usually more common in acid conditions, as is the fungal disease clubroot. The pH range for healthy plant growth varies according to the preference of individual plants. Some plants and plant families have quite specific pH requirements; others are more tolerant. (See 'Growing' under individual vegetable entries.) The pH level can vary in different areas of the garden and even within the soil profile. In most soils, water percolating down through the soil leaches away soluble nutrients, making the area with the greatest acidity on, or just below, the soil surface.

The pH of a soil may need to be reduced, particularly when growing brassicas as a pH above 6.5 lessens the chance of clubroot. While it is difficult to generalize, to raise the pH of a loamy soil from 6.5 to 7.0 in the top 15cm (6in) of soil, apply 800 g/sq m (1.75lb/sq yd) of ground limestone.

To incorporate lime quickly, you need to add it while cultivating the soil; alternatively, spread it over the soil surface and wait for rainfall to wash it into the soil. Then leave the soil for about one month before planting. Do not apply lime at the same time as manure as this causes a chemical reaction, releasing nitrogen in the form of ammonia which is then lost to the soil.

Before applying lime, check the soil pH using a soil-testing kit or send soil samples to a laboratory for analysis.

Raking in lime

FERTILITY AND NUTRITION

Plants have varying nutrient requirements according to the species. Celery, leeks and members of the cabbage family are among the 'hungry' crops, requiring high levels of nitrogen to produce their leafy bulk. Others, such as peas and beans in the group known as legumes, are able to fix nitrogen from the atmosphere using nitrogen-fixing bacteria in swollen nodules on their roots. They can therefore flourish in a nitrogen-impoverished soil. If you leave the roots of legumes in the ground, they will release their nitrogen into the soil, which can then be used by the next crop. In so doing, you can plan a rotation so that a 'hungry' crop follows a crop of legumes.

There is no precise definition to describe a fertile soil, but ideally it has the following characteristics:

• a good crumb structure
• plenty of humus and nutrients
• good drainage, moisture retentive
• a pH which is slightly acid to neutral

Soil fertility is a key factor when growing vegetables as it is the source of essential nutrients needed for healthy growth. Nutrients are absorbed in solution by the roots and transported throughout the plant's system. The major elements include nitrogen, phosphorus, potassium, calcium, magnesium and sulphur. Minor, or trace, elements include iron, manganese, boron, zinc, copper and molybdenum. These are needed in minute quantities, yet are still essential.

Nutrients are present in the soil as a result of the weathering processes on the mineral particles and the chemical breakdown or decay of organic matter and humus by bacteria and other micro-organisms. These bacteria and micro-organisms release nutrients in a form available to plants. To function effectively they must have an open, well-drained soil with adequate supplies of air and water. Extra nutrients in the form of compost and fertilizer may be needed to provide sufficient nutrients to sustain healthy growth. For instance, young tomato plants require plentiful supplies of nitrogen until they flower and fruit, after which they need higher levels of phosphate and potash.

Freshly dug clay soil lumps will break up as weathering occurs

WATER AND WATERING

Vegetables consist of about 90% water and only crop to their full potential when water is plentiful. Yields are reduced when plants suffer from drought stress. The uptake of water is a constant process, with water being absorbed through the roots, flowing through the plant and evaporating via the stomata (pores) on the leaf underside. This is known as transpiration. Under favourable growing conditions, a mature lettuce transpires more than half its own weight in water every summer's day.

The soil is a plant's reservoir, and the volume of water available for plants to extract is referred to as 'available water'. Soils vary considerably in their ability to retain moisture, depending on the proportion of different types of materials which create their texture and structure.

Clay soils have the greatest moisture-holding capacity, due to the vast area of pore spaces between the fine soil particles. Sometimes they retain water so successfully that plants are unable to extract it.

Loam soils contain a balanced composition of variable soil particles, creating a variety of pore sizes and providing a good balance between drainage and moisture retention.

Sandy soils are open textured with a large number of sizeable pore spaces. Water is easily extracted but their free-draining nature makes them dry out rapidly.

Most soil water is lost either by evaporation from the upper regions of the soil profile, or transpiration from the leaves of crops or weeds. Moisture loss occurs most rapidly on hot sunny days with drying winds.

Water Conservation
Reduce the loss of water from a soil by:
• regularly incorporating well-rotted organic matter into the soil, to increase its moisture-holding capacity.
• deep cultivation to open up the soil and encourage deeper rooting. This allows plants to draw water from a greater soil depth where water reserves are held.
• covering the soil surface with organic or inorganic mulches such as well-rotted manure or black plastic.

Freshly dug clay/loam soil

Watering cucumbers using a drip-feed system

These prevent evaporation from the surface and upper layers of the soil.
• improving drainage on waterlogged soils. High water tables restrict root development, making plants prone to stress during drought. By improving the drainage system and lowering the water table the roots are encouraged to penetrate to a greater depth, thereby leaving them more drought tolerant.
• removing weeds, which compete with vegetables for water. They should be removed at seedling stage.
• reducing planting density, particularly on dry, exposed sites. This allows each plant to draw water from a greater volume of soil.
• providing shelter, especially on exposed sites. Reducing wind speed reduces moisture loss from the soil and from plants.

• being careful with accurate timing and frequency of application. Most plants have critical periods when adequate water supplies are very important for successful development and cropping. Vegetables are no exception.

Critical Watering Periods
Seeds and Seedlings
Water is essential for seed germination and rapid seedling development. Seedbeds should be moist, not waterlogged. Water seedlings using the fine 'rose' on a watering-can to provide a shower of tiny droplets and prevent plant damage.

Transplants
Plants often suffer from transplanting shock due to root damage after being moved, and the effects are more pronounced if the soil is dry. Water plants gently after moving them to settle moist soil around the roots.

Fruiting Crops
Peas, beans, tomatoes and other vegetables with edible fruit have two critical periods for water availability once they have established: when flowering (to aid pollination and fruit set) and when the fruit begins to swell.

Leaf and Root Crops
These need a constant water supply throughout their cropping life.

Frequency of Watering
This is difficult to assess as every soil is different and weather conditions are usually unpredictable. Always water thoroughly, soaking the soil to a reasonable depth. This encourages the roots to follow the water downwards, penetrating to a depth where the water supply is better. Deep-rooted plants are better at coping with drought. For long-term crops consider using irrigation systems. Seep hose and porous rubber matrix hose are very efficient as they apply water and fertilizer closer to the roots. Overhead sprinklers are extremely inefficient as only about 20% of the water ever reaches the plant.

Young vegetable plants being sprinkled with an irrigation hose, from a farm borehole

CROP ROTATION

Rotation is a system whereby groups of vegetables are grown on a different section of the plot each year, so maintaining the balance of soil nutrients for successive crops. Growing crops in this way avoids the build-up of pests and diseases, assists in weed control and prevents the soil deteriorating.

For crop rotation to be effective, a large area of ground is required, particularly when controlling soil-borne pests and diseases. White rot (which attacks the onion family), clubroot (which damages members of the cabbage family)

and potato cyst eelworm remain dormant in the soil for many years and can survive on any weeds which are relatives. This makes good husbandry just as vital as crop rotation.

Planning

Before planting, first list the vegetables you want to grow and group them together according to their botanical relationship. Allocate each group to a plot, then compile a monthly cropping timetable for each space.

Rotational groups	*Legumes* Broad bean French bean Pea Runner bean	*Onion family* Bulb onion Garlic Leek Salad onion Shallot	*Carrot & tomato families* Carrot Celery Pepper Parsnip Potato Tomato	*Brassicas* Cabbage Cauliflower Radish Swede Turnip

Next allocate each rotation group to a plot of land ('plot A' etc.), and draw up a month-by-month timetable for each space.

	Year 1	**Year 2**	**Year 3**	**Year 4**
Plot A	*Legumes* Broad bean French bean Pea Runner bean	*Onion family* Bulb onion Garlic Leek Salad onion Shallot	*Carrot & tomato families* Carrot Celery Pepper Parsnip Potato Tomato	*Brassicas* Cabbage Cauliflower Radish Swede Turnip
Plot B	*Onion family* Bulb onion Garlic Leek Salad onion Shallot	*Carrot & tomato families* Carrot Celery Pepper Parsnip Potato Tomato	*Brassicas* Cabbage Cauliflower Radish Swede Turnip	*Legumes* Broad bean French bean Pea Runner bean
Plot C	*Carrot & tomato families* Carrot Celery Pepper Parsnip Potato Tomato	*Brassicas* Cabbage Cauliflower Radish Swede Turnip	*Legumes* Broad bean French bean Pea Runner bean	*Onion family* Bulb onion Garlic Leek Salad onion Shallot
Plot D	*Brassicas* Cabbage Cauliflower Radish Swede Turnip	*Legumes* Broad bean French bean Pea Runner bean	*Onion family* Bulb onion Garlic Leek Salad onion Shallot	*Carrot and tomato families* Carrot Celery Pepper Parsnip Potato

This timetable fully utilizes the land and provides continuity of cropping. As space becomes available, plant the crops due to follow immediately: for example, Brussels sprouts and leeks cleared in early spring should be followed by peas, salad onions and lettuce. Crops may come from different groups, which means that rotation from one plot to another is a gradual process, rather than a wholesale change-over on a pre-set date.

GROWING SYSTEMS

Major paths between beds should be wide enough for a wheelbarrow; access paths can be narrower.

Rows
Traditionally, vegetables are grown in long straight rows, with plants close together within the rows, and pathways to allow access. This has some drawbacks. Competition between plants for space within a row means that much of the plants' extension growth tends to be into the pathways, causing leafy vegetables like cabbages, cauliflowers and lettuces to produce oval 'hearts' rather than round ones.

Row of good-looking ball-headed cabbages

Beds
These are effectively multi-row systems, with equidistant spacing of plants in and between the rows. Plants may be set in staggered rows, creating a diagonal pattern. Pathways between the beds are slightly wider than those on the row system, but closer plant spacing means that more plants are grown per square metre and their growth and shape more uniform. Close spacing ensures that weed growth is suppressed in its later stages and the soil structure remains intact, because there is less soil compaction when pathways are further apart.

Raised beds should be about 90cm (36in) wide so that it is easy to reach into the centre without overbalancing. After initial double digging and the addition of organic matter, they will not be trodden on, allowing a good soil structure to form. Layers of well-rotted compost added annually will be further incorporated by worm activity. Worms are recommended for intensive vegetable production and are particularly advantageous in wetter climates.

Bed system, with paths separating each

Random Planting
Vegetables can be grown as 'edible bedding plants' randomly scattered alongside flowering plants and borders in the ornamental garden. Swiss chard, cabbage 'Ruby Ball', beetroot 'Bull's Blood', fennel and the Brussels sprout 'Rubine' are particularly pleasing. (See pages 237–239, 'The Ornamental Vegetable Garden'.)

The Potager
This is the French tradition of planting vegetables in formal beds; a practical and visually-satisfying display.

Potagers can be extremely pleasing

Long-term Crops

Perennial vegetables such as asparagus are difficult to incorporate into a crop rotation programme. For this reason, they are often grown on a separate, more permanent site for a number of years before being replaced.

Growing for Continuity

The greatest challenge is to have vegetables ready for harvest throughout the year. Some, such as asparagus, have only a short harvesting period while vegetables like cabbage, cauliflower and lettuce are available at almost any time, provided that there is successional sowing. Careful selection of cultivars also helps to achieve continuity; growing a combination of rapidly-maturing and slow-growing types extends the cropping period. The season for many root vegetables such as parsnips can be lengthened by growing a portion of the crop for eating fresh, and the remainder for storage. These can slowly be used over the winter period.

Runner beans interplanted with a row of lettuces

Successional Sowings

It is usually quick-maturing crops that are prone to gluts and gaps, often 'bolting' and becoming inedible. To avoid this, sow sufficient seed for your needs a little and often, so that if something goes wrong, the problem is only a small one. A good guide is to sow a batch of seed when the first 'true' leaves of the previous sowing begin to emerge.

Intercropping

Spaces between slow-growing crops can be used as a seedbed for vegetables such as brassicas which will later need to be transplanted into permanent positions at wider spacings. This is only successful where the competition for moisture, nutrients, light and space is not too great. This can be partially solved by growing them between rows of deep-rooted crops, so that the roots are in different levels of the soil. To achieve this, it may also be necessary to space crops a little further apart than the usual spacings. Radishes sown on the same day as parsnips will have germinated, grown and been harvested before the parsnips have fully developed, achieving the maximum possible yield and covering the soil with vegetation and suppressing weed growth. This intercropping system requires some flexibility in the cropping plan, but still works within the overall framework.

Catch Crops

These are rapidly-maturing vegetables and include radishes, lettuce or salad onions which can be grown before the main crop is planted. Catch cropping is useful when growing tender crops such as tomatoes, sweetcorn and courgettes, which cannot be planted until the risk of late frost is well and truly over.

Extending the Season

The season for vegetables can be extended by growing them under cover at the beginning or end of their natural season; sowing early under cover hastens maturity while protection later in the season extends the cropping period. (For more detail, see pages 234–5, 'Container Culture' and page 236, 'Protected Cropping'.)

Pot-raised Plants

Raising plants in pots or modules is useful for those which are frost tender and allows plants to mature while the ground is cleared of earlier crops. This saves time and space and gives more control over the growth and development of young plants. Brassicas, lettuces, leeks and onions can be grown in this way.

'The Hungry Gap'

Few vegetables mature between late winter and late spring – a period often referred to as 'the hungry gap'. Although the choice of varieties may be limited, careful planning allows this gap to be bridged; spring cauliflower, winter cabbage, celeriac, kale and leeks can all be grown for harvesting during this period.

Vegetables in a random system, with aster, gladioli and plum

PROPAGATION

Most vegetables are traditionally grown from seed, and there is a wide choice available in the seed catalogues providing you have the time, space and facilities to do so. Gardeners with smaller gardens requiring fewer plants, or lacking the facilities to nurture tender vegetables through their vulnerable early stages, may find it economical and convenient to buy young plants from a grower or garden centre for immediate planting. Not all plants are grown from seed: onions and shallots can be produced from either seed or sets; Jerusalem artichokes and potatoes from tubers; and horseradish from root cuttings. Whatever you grow, it is important to obtain propagation material from a reputable, reliable source.

Seeds

The method of sowing depends on the crop, how it is to be grown, and the prevailing conditions for each season. Sowing systems include:

• *Direct Sowing*
Seeds are sown on the site where they will be grown to maturity. This is the simplest system, and is used where transplanting is either unnecessary (as with crops like broad beans and peas) or where the plants resent root disturbance (such as turnips, carrots and radishes).

• *Outdoor Seedbed*
Seeds are sown in relatively close rows and young plants are lifted and transplanted into their permanent positions a few weeks after germination. Cloches or crop covers can be used to promote early germination and growth. This system is ideal for vegetables with a long growing season, and can save space by not having small plants at their final spacing until they mature. Brassicas, particularly Brussels sprouts, cabbages and cauliflowers are usually raised in seedbeds. The plot which they will eventually occupy can be used for another crop until they are ready for transplanting.

• *Indoor sowing*
Seeds are sown in containers, usually pots, modules or trays, in a protected environment such as a greenhouse, cold frame, propagator or on a window sill. This system is expensive and often labour intensive, yet it is the most flexible as it allows seeds to be sown whatever the weather. It is most commonly used in cooler climates for tender crops such as cucumbers, peppers and tomatoes which cannot be planted out until there is no longer any danger of frost.

Crops with a long growing season, or those which are more valuable when produced earlier (such as celery, celeriac, leeks and onions) as well as those which resent root disturbance are grown in this way.

Seed Types
Seeds are usually bought as packets of individual 'naked' seeds but are available in other forms:

Pelleted Seeds
These were originally developed to create a uniform size and shape, so that a wide range of vegetable seeds could be machine-sown by commercial growers. Each seed is coated in a ball of clay which moistens and disintegrates in the soil. Pellets are easy to handle and sow at precise spacings, reducing the need for thinning. They should be sown at a depth of about twice their diameter. The soil should remain moist but not waterlogged until the seed germinates; should the soil dry out, the outer coating of the pellet sets hard, germination ceases, and the seedling may die. Pellets which are exposed to the air deteriorate rapidly and should be sown soon after the packet is opened.

Seed Tapes and 'Sheets'
Individual seeds are encased in tapes or sheets of tissue paper or gel and spaced several centimetres (inches) apart. When placed in the soil, these substances are soluble and so begins seed germination. Seed tapes and sheets allow seeds to be sown quickly and precisely. When sowing, they are laid on a seedbed or tray at the correct spacing, covered with soil or compost and watered as if sowing normal seeds. No thinning is required.

Primed Seeds
These seeds are in the first stages of germination. They are used mainly for plants which are difficult to germinate, or which need high germination temperatures, such as cucumbers. Seeds are posted to customers in tiny plastic packets to prevent moisture loss, and are pricked out into pots or trays on arrival.

Fluid Sowing
This is useful for sowing when weather and soil conditions make germination erratic. Seeds germinated under ideal conditions are sown, protected by a carrier gel and are germinated in the bottom of a plastic container lined with paper tissues or kitchen towel.

Thoroughly moisten the paper, scatter the seeds evenly over the surface, replace the lid or cover with cling film and place in a warm position at 21°C (70°F). When the seeds germinate and the rootlets are about 5mm (¼in) long, they are ready for sowing. Wash them from the paper into a fine mesh strainer, mix carrier gel made from half strength fungicide-free wallpaper paste, scatter the seeds into the paste and stir thoroughly. Pour into a clear polythene bag, cut off one corner and force the mixture through the hole by squeezing it as for an icing bag. Cover the seeds with soil or vermiculite.

Direct sowing, broad beans

Fluid sowing

Young courgettes ready to plant out

Protection
Germinating seeds indoors under controlled conditions makes it easier to achieve uniformity of germination and growth at times when external weather conditions are unfavourable. In cool temperate zones, warm sunny days, late frosts, gales, freezing torrential rain combined with cold, wet soil mean that germination can be, at best, erratic. Sowing seeds under cover for transplanting later also makes it much easier to achieve continuity with successional sowing and to determine the size of plant which will be harvested.

Multi-sowing
This speeds the growth of root and bulb vegetables. Sow up to 6 seeds (2 for beetroot) into a 7.5–10cm (3–4in) pot, leave the seedlings to develop and then transplant the potful of plants, allowing extra space within the rows. Thinning is unnecessary. A similar method can be used with modules. This technique works well for beetroot, cauliflower, kohlrabi, leeks, onions and turnips.

Vegetables which can be started in pots (months relate to cool temperate zones):

Vegetable	germination temperature °C	°F	when to sow in pots	when to plant out
Broad bean	5	42	Feb–Mar	Mar–Apr
French bean	10	50	Apr–Jun	May–Jun
Runner bean	10	50	Apr–Jun	Jun
Beetroot	7	45	Feb–Jun	May–Jun
Brussels sprout	5	42	Feb–Apr	May–Jun
Cabbage	5	42	Mar–May	Apr–Jun
Calabrese	5	42	Feb–May	Apr–Jun
Cauliflower	5	42	Feb–Apr	Apr–Jun
Celery	10	50	Mar–Apr	Jun
Courgette	15	58	Apr–May	Jun
Cucumber	15	58	Apr–May	Jun
Leek	7	45	Feb–Apr	Apr
Lettuce	5	42	Feb–Jun	Apr–Jul
Marrow	15	58	Apr–May	Jun
Onion	7	45	Feb–Mar	Apr–May
Pea	5	42	Feb–May	Mar–Jun
Pepper	15	58	Mar–Apr	Jun
Swede	5	42	Mar–Jun	Apr–Jul
Sweetcorn	10	50	Apr–May	Jun
Tomato	15	58	Mar–Apr	Jun
Turnip	5	42	Mar–Jun	Apr–Jul

Seed Storage and Viability
Immediately seed is harvested from the plant, it begins to deteriorate; even ideal storage conditions can only slow down the rate of deterioration. Viability (the ability to germinate) and plant vigour usually decline with age. Always use fresh seed, or store in cool, dark, dry conditions (definitely not the corner of the greenhouse) in airtight tins, plastic containers or jars, preferably with brown glass. These precautions can prolong seed viability for up to five years.

Plants
It is possible to buy pre-grown plants of many types from garden centres or seed companies. These are usually available in pots or modules.

Seedlings
These are sold in trays at the stage just before the seedlings have reached the true-leaf stage and when they require 'pricking out'. This is an ideal way to purchase vegetables which are difficult to germinate.

Plugs
These are usually small plants, just beyond the seedling stage, often with 3 or 4 leaves. They have already been 'pricked out' into small 'cell' trays where each plant has its own root-ball. They are easy to handle but may need to be grown on before transplanting.

Plants or Mini plants
These are available in strips or multi-packs similar to those used for bedding plants. The plants are quite large and are generally suitable for transplanting on arrival.

Tomatoes started in containers

MAINTAINING THE GARDEN

To ensure that plants are productive and the crops are of high quality, vegetables require careful nurturing and diligent husbandry. A neglected vegetable garden is neither productive nor ornamental and encourages pests, diseases and weeds which serve only to embarrass the gardener. It is certainly worth remembering that whatever the effort required, labouring in the vegetable garden has its own delicious rewards.

Garden Hygiene

Crop hygiene is essential for healthy growth, particularly among young or weak plants which are more susceptible to pests and diseases. It is vital to keep the vegetable garden free from sources of infection. Always use clean, sterile containers and compost, particularly when propagating plants. The best time to sterilize pots and containers is just *before* they are to be used; if they are sterilized immediately *after* use and put into storage, fungal spores or insect eggs may contaminate the container, especially if they are stored outdoors. Wash pots with a scrubbing brush in a mild solution of disinfectant and rinse thoroughly; warm water is preferable, if only for the comfort of the pot washer!

Check plants daily, if possible, as pests and diseases are easier to control before they become established. Instant eradication is the most effective remedy: either remove the affected part or wipe off the pest or disease, as with aphids or scale. Where possible, plants showing signs of problems should be isolated immediately. If you have space, it is a good idea to put new plants into quarantine for a few weeks before introducing them to the glasshouse, so preventing new problems from being introduced.

After harvesting, dispose of infected crop debris either by burning or putting it in the dustbin. Persistent problems such as nematodes and clubroot should be treated in this way: please note that they cannot be destroyed by composting as it only spreads the problem. Dig in or compost healthy remains before they become infected.

Glasshouses should be cleaned annually in winter: wash thoroughly with disinfectant to kill overwintering eggs and fungal spores. Winter is also the perfect time to disinfect plant supports, particularly bamboo canes which are hollow and often split with age, creating cracks and crevices which form suitable sites for fungi and insect eggs to overwinter. These can be sprayed or dipped in disinfectant. Plastic supports do not give rise to this problem.

Observation

Examine plants thoroughly and regularly, taking precautionary measures or trapping pests when they emerge. Sowing broad beans in autumn or pinching out the growth tips helps to control black bean aphid and a dusk patrol to trap slugs as they feed can be very effective.

Organic v Synthetic

Organic gardeners avoid the use of artificial chemicals, relying on good management and natural predators to control pests and diseases while working to create an environment in which they are unlikely to occur. Synthetic chemicals are often general rather than specific in their action and can kill pollinating insects or predators further down the food chain. Gardeners are at liberty to choose which system they use, but I find organic gardening to be very successful.

Organic substance	Pests/disease controlled
Bordeaux mixture (copper-based)	potato blight leaf spot (on beet, celery, spinach)
Derris (root extract)	aphids, flea beetle, red spider mite, weevils
Encarsia formosa (predator)	whitefly
Insecticidal soap (soft soap)	aphids, leafhopper, red spider mite, weevils, whitefly
Nematode	slugs
Pyrethrum (plant extract)	aphids, flea beetle, leafhopper, red spider mite, thrips, weevils, whitefly
Sulphur	powdery mildew

Transplanting

Vegetables are usually transplanted after they have been germinated in a greenhouse and have reached a stage at which they can survive outdoors. The timing depends on the prevailing weather and soil conditions. All plants suffer a check in their growth rate after transplantation. This is caused by inevitable root disturbance and by the change in environment as they are usually moved on to somewhere cooler. Younger plants tend to recover rapidly, while older plants take longer. It is essential to reduce stress; ensure there is plenty of water available, transplant on an overcast day into moist soil and provide shelter from strong sunshine until plants become established.

Watering with Liquid

It is vital to maintain rapid growth by watering regularly, otherwise plant tissues can harden and growth can be affected. Growth check in cauliflowers can cause young plants prematurely to form a small, poorly developed curd, while other plants will 'bolt'. Seaweed is also beneficial.

Plant Supports

These should be positioned before they are required by the plants, preferably before sowing or transplanting. Plants growing tall without a support can be damaged or suffer a check in growth. Supports should be selected according to the plants being grown. Peas climb using tendrils, preferring to twine around thin supports such as chicken wire or thin spindly twigs, while runner beans hug poles or canes. Plants without climbing mechanisms should be tied to stakes using garden twine in a loose figure-of-eight loop, positioning the stake on the windward side of the plant.

takes for vegetables such as broad beans are essential props in a well-maintained garden

WEED CONTROL

Any plant – even if it is ornamental – which grows in a place where it is not wanted is described as a weed, but the term is also used to refer to native plants which grow rapidly and successfully colonize gardens. These compete with crops for moisture, nutrients and light, acting as hosts to pests and diseases which can then spread to crops. Groundsel harbours rust, mildew and greenfly; chickweed hosts red spider mite and whitefly, while several species of nightshade in the potato family can carry viruses and eelworms, which cause severe damage to potatoes and peppers.

Types of Weed

Knowledge of a weed's life cycle enables the gardener to control weeds effectively.

Ephemeral weeds germinate, flower and seed rapidly, producing several generations each season and copious quantities of seed.

Annual weeds germinate, flower and seed in one growing season; the parent dies after seed has been produced for the following generation.

Biennial weeds have a life-cycle spanning two growing seasons; the parent dies after the seed has been produced in the second year.

Perennial weeds survive for several years, developing a perennating organ. They often spread through the soil as they grow, producing scores of new shoots and setting seed. New plants sprout from tiny fragments of root, rhizome or bulbils left in the soil, rapidly recolonizing the site.

Methods of Control

There are 4 main methods of weed control: manual, mechanical, mulching and chemical. Wherever possible, keep the garden weed-free and if germination occurs, remove weeds immediately before they flower and produce seed. The old saying, 'One year's seed is seven years' weed' is – unfortunately – scientifically proven. In some conditions, ephemeral weeds are capable of producing 60,000 viable seeds per square metre (10 ft square) per year. The vast majority of weed seeds are found in the top 5cm (2in) of soil, germinating only when exposed to sufficient light.

Thorough weed control is vital when preparing the soil for planting, particularly on new or neglected sites. Either fork through the area, removing weeds by hand, or spray with a systemic herbicide formulated for tough weeds. Both may need to be undertaken several times before complete control is achieved.

Manual Weed Control

Digging, forking, hoeing and hand weeding are often the only practical ways to eradicate weeds in confined spaces where herbicides can harm nearby crops.

Digging cultivates the soil to a depth of at least 30cm (12in). Soil is turned over in a series of trenches, burying surface vegetation and annual weeds. Perennial weeds should be removed separately; do not allow them to be buried among the surface vegetation. Trials have proved that the number of fat hen, cleavers and chickweed plants is considerably reduced when cultivation takes place at night,

Couch weeds flourishing among cabbages

Careful forking or raking when preparing the soil deters weeds

as many seeds are prompted to germinate after they receive a flash of light.

Forking cultivates the soil around perennial weeds before they are lifted by hand. If this is undertaken carefully, roots can be removed without breaking into sections and forming new plants.

Hoeing prevents weed seeds from germinating, reduces moisture loss and minimises soil disturbance. An old gardener once told me: 'If you hoe when there aren't any weeds, you won't get any.' He was right. Hoeing is effective against all weeds except established perennials, severing the stem from the root just below the soil surface. Be warned: hoeing too deeply can damage the surface roots of crop plants; if in doubt, hand weed. The blade should penetrate no deeper than 1cm (½in). Hoeing is better undertaken in dry weather.

Hand weed in dry weather when the soil is moist, so that weeds are easily loosened from the soil; always try to remove the whole plant. Remove weeds from the site to prevent them from re-rooting.

Mechanical Weed Control

Machines with revolving rotary tines, blades or cultivator attachments are useful for preparing seedbeds and can also be used to control annual weeds between rows of vegetables. They should be employed carefully to avoid root damage. When clearing the ground of perennial weeds, the blades simply slice through their roots and rhizomes. While this increases their number initially, several sessions over a period of time should gradually exhaust and eventually kill the plants. This is only viable when there is plenty of time.

Biological Weed Control

Mulching is the practice of covering the soil around plants with a layer of organic or inorganic material to suppress weeds, reduce water loss and warm the soil. Traditional mulching materials were organic, such as straw or compost, and gardeners still use anything from newspaper and cardboard to old hessian-backed carpets. Choose your material carefully; straw harbours pests such as vine weevil and flea beetle and contains weed seeds, but is effective as an insulating layer over winter. It also draws nitrogen from the soil in the early stages of decay. Using partially-rotted material like well-rotted farmyard manure or spent hops avoids this problem.

Organic mulches are also limited where crops need to be earthed up – a process which disturbs the soil. Inorganic materials like plastic sheeting, though effective, are unattractive but can at least be hidden beneath a thin layer of organic mulch.

Inorganic mulches:
• suppress weeds and prevent seeds from germinating.
• conserve soil moisture by slowing evaporation. If the soil remains moist, roots can continue to extract nutrients, which they are unable to do from dry soil. Plastic films are the most effective for this purpose, as many are non-porous.
• keep trailing crops such as bush tomato, marrow or cucumber clean by preventing soil from splashing up on to leaves and ripening fruit. This helps to prevent disease, but may encourage slugs.
• *white plastic mulches* hasten growth and ripening by reflecting light onto leaves and fruit. This also keeps the soil cooler.
• *black plastic mulches* warm the soil in the spring, as they absorb the sun's heat. (See photograph on page 228.)
• *sheet mulches* are most effective when applied before the crop is planted. Young vegetables are then planted through small holes made in the sheet.

Organic mulches:
• improve soil fertility and conserve its structure by protecting the surface from the splattering effects of heavy rain, cushioning the effects of treading on the soil, encouraging earthworm activity and by adding organic matter and nutrients to the soil.
• insulate the soil, keeping it cooler in summer and warmer in winter. Mulches can be packed around overwintering plants to reduce frost penetration into the soil, making root crops easier to harvest. Straw is ideal for this purpose.

Weeds which manage to push their way through are easily removed or spot-treated with a weedkiller. For effective weed control, organic mulches should be approximately 10cm (4in) deep, to block out the light. Organic mulches are applied after planting.

In general, organic mulches have the advantage of improving soil fertility as they decay, while inorganic mulches are more effective against weeds because they form an impenetrable barrier.

Organic mulch of straw around potatoes

Inorganic black plastic mulch protecting seedling bell peppers

Chemical Weed Control (Herbicides)

Choose and use herbicides with extreme care and ensure they are suitable for the weeds to be controlled. FOLLOW THE MANUFACTURER'S INSTRUCTIONS CAREFULLY.

Residual herbicides form a layer over the soil, killing germinating weeds and seedlings.

Contact herbicides only kill those parts of the plant that they touch. They are effective against annual weeds and weed seedlings but not against established perennials.

Systemic or *translocated herbicides* are absorbed by the foliage, travelling through the sap system to kill the whole plant, including the roots. Glyphosate is often the active ingredient. Individual weeds can be 'spot treated' using such herbicides in gel or liquid form.

Several chemical weed-control methods have been developed for use with vegetables. As many of the vegetables we grow have different tolerances to chemicals, no single chemical is suitable for all crops. This gives the grower three options: stock a range of chemicals and change the type regularly; use chemicals only as a last resort; or grow organically. I favour the latter!

Using and Storing Weedkillers Safely

Mixing
• Always wear adequate protective clothing, such as face mask, goggles, rubber gloves and old waterproof clothes when mixing weedkillers.
• Always dilute weedkillers according to the manufacturer's instructions.
• Never mix different chemicals together.
• Never dilute chemicals in a confined space, as they may give off toxic fumes.

Application
• Always wear the specified protective clothing, such as a face mask, rubber gloves and old waterproof clothes when applying weedkillers.
• Follow the manufacturer's instructions carefully and use only as recommended on the product label.
• Always apply weedkillers at the rate recommended on the manufacturer's label.
• Do not apply weedkillers in windy conditions; nearby plants may suffer serious damage.
• Do not apply weedkillers in very hot, still conditions when there is a high risk of spray travelling on warm air currents.
• If you are using a watering-can to apply chemicals, ensure that it is obviously labelled and at no times use it for any other purpose.

Storage
• Always keep chemicals in the original containers, making sure that the labels are well secured so that the contents can be positively identified.
• Mark the container with the date of purchase, so that you know how long it has been stored.
• Never store dilute weedkillers for future use.
• Always store out of the reach of children and animals, in a locked cupboard in a workshop or shed.
• Store in cool, frost-free, dark conditions.

After Use
• Always thoroughly wash protective clothing, sprayers, mixing vessels and utensils.
• Never use the same sprayer, mixing vessels and utensils for other types of chemical such as fungicides. The results could be disastrous!

PEST AND DISEASE CONTROL

Following good horticultural practices and upholding plant hygiene reduce the problem of pests and diseases, although these can never be entirely eradicated as so many are wind-borne or caused by prevailing weather conditions.

General Hygiene

Plant debris is a logical host for pests and diseases, particularly over winter, allowing them to survive in preparation for re-emergence and re-infection the following year. Do everything possible to keep plants healthy by cleaning your glasshouse and equipment regularly. Dispose of organic matter immediately; compost healthy material and get rid of infected plants at once by burning or placing in the dustbin. Aim to grow only the best-quality plants, as a healthy plant is better able to withstand pests and diseases. When buying plants, ensure they come from a reputable source and, if possible, keep them in quarantine for a short while before introducing them to the glasshouse.

Cultural Practices

Always use sterilized compost for seed sowing and potting. Seedlings are particularly vulnerable, especially when sown under cover. Sow seeds thinly, do not irrigate with stagnant or cold water, ventilate the glasshouse but avoid chilling plants or seedlings and do not allow compost to become waterlogged. Promote rapid germination and continuous growth to reduce the risk of infection at the time when seedlings and young plants are at their most vulnerable. Avoid overfeeding with nitrogen-based fertilizers as this produces soft, sappy growth which is particularly prone to attack. Inspect plants regularly, particularly if a variety is prone to certain problems. Grow pest- and disease-resistant cultivars where possible. Rotate crops and always keep the vegetable garden weed-free. Handle plants with care, particularly when harvesting, as this is a common cause of infection. Regularly check stored crops (notably onions and potatoes) as rot spreads rapidly in a confined space.

Soil-borne Pests

Cutworms

These grey-green caterpillars, approximately 5cm (2in) long, appear from late spring until early autumn.
Symptoms: they burrow into root crops including beetroot, carrot, parsnip and potato, and any plant with a soft taproot, eating through plant stems at soil level.
Prevention: plants grown under cover seem less prone to damage, and heavy watering in early summer often kills young caterpillars.
Control: incorporate a soil insecticide such as diazinon and chlorpyrifos or water pirimiphos-methyl into the top 5cm (2in) of soil.

Cabbage Root Fly

These white larvae, approximately 8mm (⅓in) long, are found from late spring to mid-autumn.
Symptoms: larvae feed on the roots of brassicas just below soil level, stunting growth and causing plants to wilt, seedlings to die and tunnels to appear in root crops.
Prevention: grow under horticultural fleece.
Control: place a 12cm (5in) collar of cardboard, plastic, carpet underlay or similar around the plant bases. Also incorporate an insecticide such as chlorpyrifos and diazinon or pirimiphos methyl into the top 5cm (2in) of soil.

Carrot Root Fly

These creamy-white maggots, approximately 8mm (⅓in) long, appear from early summer until mid-autumn.
Symptoms: these are a common problem with carrots, but can also affect celeriac, parsnip, celery and parsley. Larvae burrow into the roots, causing stunted growth and reddish-purple coloration of the foliage.
Prevention: sow thinly and lift carrots in late summer or in early autumn.
Control: place a barrier 60cm (12in) high around crops or incorporate a soil insecticide such as pirimiphos-methyl into the top 5cm (2in) of the soil.

Leatherjackets

These grey-brown, wrinkled grubs, can be up to 3.5cm (1½in) long.
Symptoms: they eat through roots and through the stems of young plants just below soil level. Most crops are vulnerable, including Brussels sprouts, cabbage, cauliflower and lettuce.
Prevention: ensure the soil is well drained, dig over the ground in the early autumn, especially if it has been fallow through the summer. The problem is often worse on new sites and usually diminishes with time.
Control: water vulnerable plants with piriphos-methyl and treat soil with diazinon and chlorpyrifos.

Nematodes (Eelworms)

(1) Potato Cyst Eelworm

These white to golden-brown, pinhead-sized cysts are found on roots in mid-summer. Each can contain up to 600 eggs which can remain dormant in the soil for up to six years.

Symptoms: growth is weak and stunted, fruits and tubers are small, foliage becomes yellow, with the lower leaves dying first followed by premature death of the plants. Potatoes and tomatoes are affected.

Prevention: rotate crops and grow resistant varieties like 'Pentland Javelin', 'Pentland Lustre', 'Maris Piper' or 'Kingston'. Do not grow potatoes or tomatoes on infected soil for at least 6 years.

Control: no chemical treatment available to the amateur.

Dead potatoes after potato cyst eelworm attack

(2) Stem and Bulb Eelworm

These are microscopic pests which live inside the plant and move around on a film of moisture; most active from spring to late summer.

Symptoms: weak, stunted growth, swollen bases on young plants, stems later thicken and rot. They affect a wide range of young plants from spring until late summer, particularly leek, onion, shallot and chives.

Prevention: rotate crops, practise good hygiene and management, and destroy infected crops. Do not grow potatoes or tomatoes on infected soil for at least 6 years, and any other vulnerable crops on the site for at least 4 years.

Control: no chemical treatments are available to the amateur.

Slugs

Slimy, with tubular-shaped bodies, up to 10cm (4in), from creamy-white through grey to jet-black and orange.

Symptoms: slugs are voracious feeders, making circular holes in plant tissue; damaged seedlings are usually killed. Tend to feed at night. Most soft plant tissue is vulnerable, particularly celery and lettuce.

Prevention: slugs are more of a problem on wet sites and clay soils; keep the soil well drained and weed-free. Remove all crop debris. Grow less susceptible cultivars. Create a barrier of grit, sand, eggshell or soot around plants or cut a 10cm (4in) section from a plastic bottle and place it as a 'collar' around plants. Make traps from plastic cartons, half buried in the ground and filled with milk or beer, or lay old roof tiles, newspaper or old lettuce leaves or other tempting vegetation on the ground and hand pick regularly from underneath. Attract natural predators like toads to the garden or use biological controls.

Control: apply aluminium sulphate in the spring as the slug eggs hatch. Use slug pellets. Apply Metaldehyde, if you must!

Wireworm

Wireworms

These are thin, yellow larvae, pointed at each end, about 2.5cm (1in) long.

Symptoms: holes in the roots and tubers, can cause foliage to collapse; seedlings are usually killed. A wide range of plants are attacked, particularly root crops and potatoes. Symptoms appear from spring until mid-summer.

Prevention: more of a problem on newly cultivated soil, wireworms usually disappear after 5 years; avoid planting root crops until the sixth year.

Control: lift root crops as soon as they mature, incorporate chlorpyrifos and diazinon into the top 5cm (2in) of soil. Cultivate the ground thoroughly.

Soil-borne diseases

Clubroot

This is a soil-borne fungus which can remain in the soil for up to 20 years.

Symptoms: leaves yellow and discolour, wilting rapidly in hot weather; the roots display swollen wart-like swellings, and become distorted. All members of the Cruciferae family are vulnerable, including brassicas and weedy relatives.

Prevention: clubroot is worse on acid soils, so lime to raise the pH, improve the drainage.

Practise strict crop rotation, good management and hygiene and grow your own plants instead of buying in or at least purchase from a reputable source. Raise plants in pots. Swede 'Marian' has good resistance to clubroot.

Control: dip the roots of transplants in a fungicidal solution such as thiophanate-methyl. Lift and dispose of affected plants immediately, and do not compost.

Scab on potato 'Red Desiree'

Common Scab

This fungus causes superficial damage to the underground parts of affected plants.

Symptoms: rough brown lesions on the surface of roots and tubers. More severe on alkaline soils and in dry summers. Common scab affects mainly potatoes but can be found on radishes, beetroot, swede and turnips.

Prevention: avoid liming, do not grow potatoes on soil recently used for brassicas, apply organic matter to the soil, and irrigate thoroughly in dry weather.

Control: grow resistant potato cultivars like 'Arran Pilot' and 'King Edward'. Avoid 'Majestic' and 'Maris Piper' which are very susceptible. Rotate crops.

Root Rot

This fungus is difficult to eradicate.

Symptoms: shrivelled, yellowing leaves, stems and pods; roots rot and stems rot at the base. Plants collapse. Attacks beans and peas.

Prevention: a minimum 3-year crop rotation; remove and burn infected plants.

Control: sow seed dressed with an appropriate fungicide, or water seedlings with a copper-based fungicide such as cheshunt compound or Bordeaux mixture.

Stem Rot

This fungus is difficult to eradicate.

Symptoms: yellow-brown cankerous lesions with black dots in and around the lesions, occurring at soil level. Attacks aubergine and tomato.

Prevention: remove and burn infected plants and crop debris, disinfect anything that comes into contact with diseased material, including hands and equipment.

Control: immediately after planting apply a fungicide such as captan to the bottom 10cm (4in) of the stem, repeating 3 weeks later.

White rot on maturing onion crop

White Rot

This fungus is almost impossible to eradicate.

Symptoms: discoloured, yellowing leaves which die slowly; roots rot and plants fall over, becoming covered with a white felt-like mould. Common on onions and leeks, but also attacks chives and garlic.

Prevention: do not grow susceptible crops for 8 years. Remove and burn infected plants immediately; do not compost any plant debris.

Control: apply a fungicide such as thiophanate-methyl to the seed drills when sowing.

Air-borne Pests

Aphids

Dense colonies of winged and wingless insects, from pale-green through pink to greeny-black.

Symptoms: shoot tips and young leaves distorted; sticky coating on lower leaves, often accompanied by a black sooty mould. Attack soft tissue on a wide range of plants, including brassicas, beans and peas, lettuces, potatoes and root crops.

Prevention: pinch the growth tips from broad beans, destroy alternative hosts, and take care not to overfeed with high nitrogen fertilizers.

Control: treat small infestations by squashing or washing off with a jet of water; spray with soft soap, derris, pyrethrum-based insecticide; encourage natural predators like lacewings, ladybirds and their larvae and small birds like blue tits.

Cabbage Caterpillars

These are small, hairy, yellow and black caterpillars up to 5cm (2in) long.
Symptoms: voracious feeders, the caterpillars eat holes in the leaves and in severe cases leave plants totally defoliated. A problem from late spring to autumn. Attack all brassicas.
Prevention: inspect plants regularly, squash eggs or caterpillars as they are found, pick off caterpillars and grow crops under horticultural fleece or fine netting.
Control: spray regularly with derris, pyrethrum, permethrin when eggs are first seen.

Cabbage Whitefly

Small, white-winged insects, usually found on the leaf underside. Clouds of insects fly up whenever the leaves are brushed.
Symptoms: puckering of the young leaves; sticky coating on leaves, often accompanied by a black mould. Whitefly attack all leafy brassicas. They can survive severe winter weather and are seen all year round.
Prevention: remove and burn badly infected plants immediately after cropping.
Control: spray with insecticidal soap or pyrethrum-based sprays, dimethoate or malathion; concentrate on the leaf undersides where they congregate.

Pea Thrips

Small, white to black-brown or yellow-bodied insects, usually on the leaf underside. Commonly known as 'Thunder Flies'.
Symptoms: distorted pods have a silvery sheen; peas fail to swell in the pod. The insects are often found on peas and also on broad beans.
Prevention: remove and burn badly infected plants.
Control: spray with a malathion or similar insecticide just as the plants start to flower.

Air-borne Diseases
Blight

This fungus infects leaves, stems and tubers and is worse in wet seasons. Severe epidemics led to the Irish potato famine.
Symptoms: in mid-summer brown patches appear on the upper and lower leaf surfaces, ringed with white mould in humid conditions; leaves become yellow and fall prematurely. In humid climates the fungus spreads rapidly over the foliage and stems which quickly collapse. Tubers show dark,

sunken patches. The fungus attacks potatoes, tomatoes and closely related weeds.
Prevention: remove and burn badly infected plant tops in late summer, avoid overhead watering and use resistant cultivars like 'Cara', 'Romano' and 'Wilja' potatoes. Do not store infected tubers. In wet seasons spray with fungicide before the disease appears.
Control: spray in summer with copper-based fungicide or mancozeb, and repeat at regular intervals as soon as symptoms appear.

Botrytis

This fungus infects flowers, leaves and stems and usually enters through wounds.
Symptoms: discoloured patches on stems which may rot at ground level; flowers and leaves become covered with woolly grey fungal growth. Causes shadows on unripe tomato fruit called 'ghost spot'. Soft-leaved plants are particularly

vulnerable including broad beans, brassicas, lettuces, potatoes and tomatoes.
Prevention: maintain good air circulation, handle plants with care to avoid injury and remove infected material.
Control: spray with thiophanate-methyl or carbendazim as soon as the disease symptoms are seen; remove and burn badly infected plants.

Downy Mildew

This is a fungus that infects leaves and stems, overwintering in the soil or plant debris.
Symptoms: discoloured, yellowing leaves, which have grey/white mouldy patches on the lower surface; plants often die slowly in the autumn. Attacks brassicas including weed species, lettuce, spinach, peas and onions.
Prevention: avoid overcrowding, remove and burn badly infected plants and maintain good air circulation.
Control: spray with zineb, mancozeb or copper-based fungicide when the first symptoms appear.

Methods of Control

Chemicals offer a quick and simple solution to many pest
and disease problems but, before using them, it is worth
considering the following:

Safety: Many chemicals are toxic and can be harmful to
humans, pets and wildlife. They should be applied with
extreme care.

Residue: chemicals may remain in soil and plant tissue for
long periods, affecting predators.

Tolerance: many pests and diseases, particularly whitefly and
red spider mite, are able to develop a resistance to chemicals
which are used persistently for long periods, so rendering
controls less effective. Applying a range of different
chemicals can overcome this.

Applying Chemicals

• Always follow the manufacturer's instructions and never
exceed the recommended dosage.
• Apply chemicals in still, overcast conditions, usually in the
early morning or evening.
• Protect surrounding plants from the chemical solution.
• Thoroughly clean all spraying equipment after use.
• Dispose of unwanted chemicals according to the
manufacturer's recommendations. DO NOT POUR THEM DOWN
THE DRAIN.

Biological Control

Several pests can be controlled using natural predators or
parasites. Apart from *Bacillus thuringiensis*, the bacterial
control for caterpillars, few are effective outside the closed
environment of a greenhouse. When this method is used,
populations of predators fluctuate with the available food

Carrots covered with fleece to protect from carrot fly

source. Most pesticides kill predators with the exception of
insecticidal soaps and pirimicarb (against aphids) and so
should be avoided.

Vegetable growers should be aware of *Phytoseiulus
persimilis*, the predatory mite which controls two-spotted or
red spider mite and *Encarsia formosa*, a parasitic wasp,
controlling glasshouse whitefly. This is ineffective against
brassica whitefly and other outdoor species.

Silver foil and other bird scaring devices over cabbages

CONTAINER CULTURE

The idea of growing vegetables in containers is not a new one: tomatoes and cucumbers have long been grown under glass in containers to prevent any contact with disease-infected soil. The main advantage is that the gardener gains almost total control over the contents and environment within the container. Portable containers give the flexibility to respond to weather conditions, moving plants outdoors once spring frosts end and putting them under shelter again at the onset of colder weather.

When room is limited, containers offer an alternative to ground space. They can be either functional or decorative. You can make good use of the patio, windowbox or even hanging basket: cherry tomatoes can be as ornamental as a conventional flower display, and even recycled plastic containers can be disguised within more attractive containers. It is worth remembering, though, that many vegetables are heavier feeders than the bedding plants which are usually grown in such ways. They also require regular and consistent watering to thrive and keep growing.

Selecting a Suitable Container

The chance of successful cropping is improved when large containers are used; they allow for a greater rooting depth, dry out slowly and provide adequate anchorage for crops which need staking. Composts should be moisture-retentive yet free-draining, reducing the likelihood of compaction due to heavy watering. Plastic containers (with drainage holes), while not always attractive, are more moisture-retentive than those made of wood or terracotta. To ensure good drainage, raise containers above the ground on bricks.

On the functional side, it is possible to grow early potatoes in bin-liners, dustbins or grow-bags in which tomatoes, peppers or cucumbers were grown in the first year. For the potatoes, remove most of the plastic from the upper surface of the bag to expose a larger surface area of compost. Salad onions, lettuces and radishes can also be grown in this way.

Rhubarb growing in black polythene bag

Selecting Crops

Vegetables most suited to container culture are either rapidly-maturing crops such as mini beetroot, carrots, lettuces, radishes and salad onions, or dwarf varieties of bush or climbing vegetables including aubergines, beans, cucumbers, peas, peppers and tomatoes, as these need little support. Deep-rooted vegetables like Brussels sprouts, maincrop carrots and parsnips can be grown in containers, providing they are at least 45cm (18in) deep.

Selecting a Compost

Use a 'potting compost' when growing vegetables in containers. Such compost has a good enough structure to encourage vigorous growth and contains the essential nutrients for healthy growth. Avoid using garden soil, unless it is a good loam, as most soils contain weed seeds, stones, pests and diseases and chemical residues. Their nutrient levels are also variable.

Composts for containers are either loam-based or loamless:

Loam-based Composts

A formula for loam-based composts was developed at the John Innes Research Institute, UK. Those used for containers are numbered 1, 2 and 3, each with a different level of nutrients. John Innes no. 3 is the strongest. Loam-based composts are much heavier, providing stability and support for the plants and better conditions for long-term crops. They release nutrients slowly, are free-draining and have a good structure. When using loam-based composts, place the container in its final position before filling with compost; once they are filled, the considerable weight makes them difficult to move.

John Innes compost formulation
The basic John Innes soil-based mixture (by volume):
7 parts sterilized loam
3 parts sphagnum moss peat
2 parts sharp washed sand

The John Innes Base Fertilizer (by weight)
2 parts hoof and horn
2 parts calcium phosphate (superphosphate of lime)
1 part potassium sulphate (sulphate of potash)

John Innes no. 1
36 litres (63pt) basic soil mixture
112g (4oz) John Innes Base
21g (¾oz) powdered chalk

John Innes no. 2
36 litres (63pt) basic soil mixture
224g (8oz) John Innes Base
42g (1½oz) powdered chalk

John Innes no. 3
36 litres (63pt) basic soil mixture
336g (10¾oz) John Innes Base
63g (2½oz) powdered chalk

Loamless Composts

These are traditionally based on peat with additional materials such as vermiculite, grit and shredded bark to improve drainage. With the ethical debate on peat, many compost manufacturers are using alternative materials such as coir or recycled organic waste. Loamless composts are generally lighter and cleaner to use than loam-based composts, combine moisture retention with good aeration, are long-lasting and cheaper. However, they are not as stable or moisture-retentive as loam-based composts and tend to decompose, reducing the volume in the container. They are also difficult to re-wet in drought conditions.

Overall, loam-based composts are recommended, and organic matter can be added if required.

Watering

A regular and adequate supply of water is essential for plant growth. Water stress due to drought, even for short periods, can greatly reduce the potential productivity of plants. When plants are actively growing, keep the compost constantly moist but not waterlogged by watering thoroughly and regularly. It is best to water containers in the early morning or in the evening, particularly in the summer, as this reduces the amount lost through evaporation. Gardeners with a large number of containers should consider investing in irrigation systems to save time when watering and feeding.

Sweetcorn growing in a container with garlic chives

PROTECTED CROPPING

Protected cropping extends the growing season in spring and autumn, accelerates growth and increases productivity. In cooler climates, crops sown earlier when external conditions are unfavourable will have grown considerably by the time the weather has improved, by which time they can be planted outdoors. This is particularly valuable when growing half-hardy vegetables like aubergines, sweet peppers and tomatoes. It also provides the option of growing crops of borderline hardiness under cover throughout the season; this makes cropping more reliable.

It is not only summer crops which benefit. Lettuce, spinach and other hardy winter salads produce more tender, better-quality crops when protected in an unheated greenhouse than those which remain outside.

Permanent Structures
These include *glasshouses*, either free-standing or lean-to, and allow almost total environmental control all year round if heat is provided.

Frames are ideal for raising seedlings or hardening off plants before transplanting outdoors. The lack of height limits the crops which can be grown in them. When covered with black polythene or layers of hessian, they provide a cheap and efficient method of forcing chicory and endive.

Cloches protecting spinach 'Jovita'

Semi-permanent Structures
Polythene tunnels are much cheaper to buy and easier to erect than glasshouses, but the plastic cover only lasts for about three years.

Cloches made of glass or plastic are easily moved to provide shelter to those individual plants or small groups which need it most.

Temporary Structures
Low *polythene tunnels* are like small cloches, are cheap, portable and versatile, but are of limited use because of their flimsiness and lack of height.

Fleece protecting newly planted sweetcorn

Crop covers or *floating film* were developed for commercial horticulture. These flexible covers can be laid immediately over the crop, or suspended on hoops as 'floating mulches'. As the plants grow, they are forced upwards.

Fleece is lightweight, soft-textured spun polypropylene, which lasts for a year provided it is kept clean, sometimes longer if cared for. It is ideal for frost protection and for forcing early crops. Many vegetables can be grown under this, from sowing through to harvesting and it is an effective barrier against pests and diseases. More light and air can penetrate through this than plastic film.

Plastic film is usually perforated with minute slits or holes for ventilation, but even the crop may overheat on sunny spring days. It is laid directly over the plants; as they grow, the flexible material is pushed upwards, splitting open the minute slits and increasing ventilation. It is often used in the early stages of growth.

Plastic netting has a very fine mesh, filtering the wind and providing protection, but has little effect on raising temperature. It lasts for several seasons.

As many of these materials are manufactured in long, narrow rolls, the most effective way to use them is to grow crops in narrow strips. Greatest benefit can be derived from such materials when they are used in conjunction with free-draining, thoroughly prepared, weed-free soil. Insect-pollinated crops like courgettes, cucumbers, marrows and tomatoes should have the protective covering removed or opened as the crop develops. This allows insects access to the flowers.

Protected Potatoes
Potatoes can be grown under black polythene sheeting. Cultivate the soil deeply, cover it with black plastic, burying the margins and sides to stop it blowing away. Make cross-shaped cuts in the plastic, push a potato through the hole and about 15cm (5in) into the soil. New tubers will form beneath the plastic, and are blanched without the need for 'earthing up'. When the 'haulm' turns yellow, the plastic can be removed and the tubers harvested.

THE ORNAMENTAL VEGETABLE GARDEN

Small fruiting gourd – attractive as well as edible

The sight of a neat, well tended vegetable garden burgeoning with healthy crops is immensely satisfying. Conditioned to believe that vegetables are functional, and flowers beautiful, many fail to appreciate the splendour and bounty of a vegetable plot with its contrasting colours, forms and textures, neatly framed by well kept paths.

The traditional design for a vegetable garden is based on a system of rows. This gives ease of access and maintenance, enables crops to be rotated regularly and for maximum production while preventing the build-up of pests and diseases. Large kitchen gardens were formerly attached to a 'great house', with the gardeners' task to cultivate a wide range of crops and supply the household with vegetables throughout the year.

By way of contrast, most gardeners now have smaller gardens, and the basis for what they grow and how they grow it is more a matter of choice than necessity. This provides them with the opportunity to grow vegetables for their ornamental values as well as utilitarian ones. For the same reasons, it may also be preferable to grow small quantities of a wider range of cultivars.

Colour

Vegetables are not only eaten for their flavour and nutritional value but add welcome colour to a meal. Consider the range of colour and tonal variation in a salad; it is generally greater than the range of flavours.

There are tones of green in lettuce, endive and cucumber, yellow in peppers, purple in beetroot and leaf lettuce and red in tomatoes and peppers. For centuries, only the French potager capitalized on this display of colours, but vegetables are at last more commonly used as design elements within ornamental planting schemes. The sight of vegetables dotted individually or grouped in the flower border has in recent years become a familiar sight. To the open mind and eye, all vegetables are ornamental, even if their attraction is more obvious in some than in others.

The contrasting red and green foliage of ruby chard is sumptuous, as is beetroot 'Bull's Blood', while purple- or yellow-podded French beans and the mauve leaves of Cabbage 'Red Drumhead' create their own exotic magic. Red-skinned onions like 'Red Barron' and the red-leaved lettuce 'Lollo Rosso' are equally stunning. Squashes impress with their bold shapes and colour (just look at 'Turk's Turban') while tomatoes like the golden 'Yellow Perfection' and striped 'Tigrella' delight the eye. Flowers and fruits add other colour accents.

Form

While you may not consider the shape of certain vegetables to be interesting (swedes or potatoes, for instance), a good many have appealing foliage or a distinctive habit. The bold architectural leaves and sculptured form of globe artichokes are prized by garden designers, a 'wigwam' of scarlet runner beans or trailing cucurbits makes a dramatic focal point, while the compact growth of parsley and chives is a neat edging for borders. Members of the onion family, leeks, and chives have spiky, linear leaves, which contrast well with the rounded shapes of lettuce and the feathery, arching growth of carrot tops. Celery and Brussels sprouts naturally have a distinguished upright habit. Perhaps the most unusual of all, 'Rubine', the purple Brussels sprout which is planted as a single specimen in a container, looks like an angular, alien sculpture.

Texture

Texture is rarely considered a design feature, yet the different colours and forms of vegetable foliage are underlined by their texture. Consider the solidity of a compact cabbage head, wreathed in glaucous, puckered leaves, or the soft billowing effect created by the dissected leaves of fennel or asparagus foliage. Exploiting such contrasts provides a foliage display as interesting as a bedding scheme or herbaceous border. Even after harvest the impact remains; the tall dried stems of sweetcorn look wonderful when frosted on a winter's day and the rustling sound as the wind blows through their dead leaves brings life to a desolate garden.

Vegetables as 'Bedding Plants'

Many vegetables are grown as annuals and, as each crop matures and is harvested, the appearance of the vegetable garden changes. Often, the only constant elements are the framework of paths and hedges and a few long-lived perennial crops.

   Such intensively grown crops are easier to maintain when grown in a formal pattern as this provides the ideal opportunity to arrange crops in brightly coloured, bold patterns or emphasize their subtle qualities. Brightly coloured chard, lettuce or kale or the shimmering foliage of carrots can be used to provide a foliage display rivalling any bedding plant.

   Vegetables which have run to seed look particularly spectacular; lettuces are upright and leafy, beetroot display their red veined leaves and bold flower spikes while onions and leeks produce symmetrical globes of flowers which are invaluable for attracting pollinating insects. Some gardeners allow a few plants to go to seed to enjoy such effects, but would you be daring enough to create a planting scheme with the specific purpose of featuring vegetables in their later stages?

   One approach to creating a 'bedding' scheme is to group together plants with a similar life span, for a long-term display. Alternatively, with skilful planning, it is possible to plant crops taking *different* times to reach maturity, filling any gaps with suitable vegetables after harvest, to retain the impact of the design. The time scale can vary considerably, with radishes taking a mere five weeks, and sprouting broccoli and winter cabbages remaining in the ground for

Globe artichoke flowers are prime examples of attractive vegetables

several months. Of course, the rapid changeover of these annual crops means that plant colours as well as flavours are constantly changing within the scheme.

   Perennial vegetables such as asparagus, globe artichoke and rhubarb can be grown in separate beds or used as permanent feature plants within the design. In smaller or irregularly shaped gardens, crop rotation allows a wide range of annual design patterns and planting arrangements. Growing vegetables purely for their ornamental value is an option which gardeners of such gardens should consider.

The Potager

Their love of food and appreciation of aesthetics motivated French gardeners to create the potager, or ornamental vegetable garden, with a more obvious visual appeal than the English kitchen garden. Simple, formal, geometric shapes such as four square-shaped raised beds dissected by straight paths form a permanent structure, enlivened with a succession of vibrantly coloured leafy crops chosen for their culinary and visual qualities. The main paths are wide enough for a wheelbarrow, but narrower ones, and stepping stones, allow access for maintenance and picking.

   Vegetables are placed according to their height and habit, larger vegetables forming centre pieces and smaller ones making up the rows. Climbing vegetables growing over ornamental tripods, arches or even canes provide height, and the whole area can be screened by trellis and can include vegetables in containers as additional features.

   To maintain the symmetry, harvest plants with an eye to pattern: work evenly from both ends and from the centre, or cut every other plant to keep the coverage balanced as far as possible. Make full use of successional cropping to ensure that the soil is always utilized and the pattern maintained.

Random Systems

Scattering vegetables individually or in groups among ornamental borders is becoming more popular. They should be planted according to their ultimate height with lower plants near the front of the border, using brightly coloured vegetables strong enought to stand up to their brightly coloured neighbours. Grow purple-podded climbing French beans through shrubs instead of clematis, runner bean 'Painted Lady' instead of sweet peas and purple-leaved cabbage alongside nasturtiums. Mini vegetables can be grown in window boxes or hanging baskets; try tomato 'Tumbler' or grow climbers as trailing plants.

The only requirement for successful growth of vegetables among ornamental plants is adequate soil or compost fertility, which can easily be maintained with well-prepared soil and careful feeding.

Vegetables planted alongside flowers

HARVESTING AND STORING

Some vegetables, like lettuce, cannot be stored for long periods and must be harvested and eaten fresh. Traditional methods such as storing in clamps, pickling and salting have been joined by freezing, which has revolutionized the lives of gardeners and cooks – even sweetcorn, traditionally eaten immediately after harvest – can be enjoyed out of season.

While the majority of vegetables are not harvested until they reach maturity, others, like lettuce 'Salad Bowl', are harvested while semi-mature and others, such as rocket, are harvested while juvenile.

The methods of harvesting and storing vegetables depend on several factors, particularly on the individual plant's storage organ and the winter climate. Many leafy vegetables such as Brussels sprouts and sprouting broccoli are hardy, surviving outdoors in the ground in freezing conditions. The flavour of Brussels sprouts even improves immeasurably after they have been frosted.

Some root vegetables with a high moisture content are easily damaged in winter, even when protected by the soil. This is usually caused by rapid thawing after a period of cold weather. Carrots, parsnip and swede are exceptions to this rule; they are extremely hardy and can be left in free-draining soils until required. In wet soils these crops would suffer winter loss by slug damage and rotting.

Outdoor Storage
In colder areas, vegetables overwintering in the ground need additional protection. This can be provided by spreading a layer of loose straw or bracken over them to a depth of 20cm (8in) and covering with soil. While this is labour saving, root crops stored in this way are susceptible to attack by pests and diseases throughout the winter.

The traditional method for storing root vegetables is in a clamp or 'pie'. Low mounds of vegetables are laid on a bed of loose straw up to 20cm (8in) thick. The top and sides of the mound are covered with a similar layer of straw, and then with a 15cm (6in) layer of soil or sand. Clamps can be made outdoors on a well-drained site or under cover in a shed or outhouse; for extra protection outdoors, they can be formed against a wall or hedge. If crops are to be stored for a long period, find a site which receives as little sunlight as possible during the winter. Although the storage conditions are very similar to those in the ground, harvesting from a clamp is much easier. However, losses from rodent damage and rotting can be high.

Longevity in Storage
The length of time that vegetables may be stored depends on the type and cultivar as well as the storage conditions. When traditional methods are used, the main cause of deterioration is moisture loss from plant tissue; for instance, beetroot and carrot desiccate very rapidly. Fungal infection of damaged tissue is a common problem; onions and potatoes bruise very easily. Vegetables for storage should be handled carefully; only store those which are disease-free, check them regularly and remove any showing signs of decay immediately. (See details under individual vegetables.)

Drying Vegetables
Peas and beans can be harvested when almost mature and dried slowly in a cool place. Either lift the whole plant and hang it up or pick off the pods and dry them on a tray or newspaper. Beans can be collected and stored in airtight jars until required. They will need soaking for 24 hours before use. Storage areas should be frost-free. Chillies, green peppers, garlic and onions can be hung indoors where there is good air circulation. Peppers, tomatoes and mushrooms can be cut into sections and sun dried outdoors where conditions allow, otherwise in the gentle heat of an airing cupboard or above a radiator. Vegetables which can be dried include beans, chillies, garlic, onions and peas. (See details under individual vegetables.)

Freezing
Only the best-quality vegetables should be frozen, and should always be thoroughly cleaned and carefully packed. Vegetables should be fast frozen. Most freezers have a fast-freeze switch and the freezer door should remain closed during freezing. Do not open the freezer door regularly or leave it open longer than necessary. (See details under individual vegetables.)

Vegetables Suitable for Freezing

Blanch	Shred, purée dice or slice	Freeze when young
Asparagus		
Aubergine	Aubergine	
Beetroot		Beetroot
Broad bean		
Brussels sprout		
Cabbage	Cabbage	
Calabrese		
Carrot		Carrot
Cauliflower	Cauliflower	
	Celery	
Courgette		
French bean		
Kale		
Kohlrabi	Kohlrabi	
Marrow	Marrow	
Parsnip		Parsnip
Pea		
Potato		
Runner bean		
Spinach		
Spring onion		
Sprouting broccoli		
Swede	Swede	
Sweetcorn		
Tomato		
Turnip	Turnip	Turnip

GROWING MINI VEGETABLES

Miniature, or baby, vegetables are either varieties which are suitable for harvesting when young or those which have been specifically bred to be naturally small at maturity. Initially mini vegetables were regarded as novelty crops, but they have now found a niche among small households where growing space is limited and are often grown for the pure virtue of being attractive. Many are ready to harvest in as little as 12 weeks and make a useful short-term crop.

Cultivation
Mini vegetables grow successfully in beds, pots, window boxes and hanging baskets but need at least 20cm (8in) depth of compost or soil. The growing medium must be fertile and crops should be watered regularly and thoroughly to maintain rapid growth. Weekly feeding throughout the growing season is recommended.

Planning
Most miniature vegetables are grown from seed, with successional sowing every two or three weeks extending the harvesting period. Always have a supply of young plants or seedlings growing in pots or modules for transplanting when space becomes available.

Plant Density
By increasing the number of plants per square metre, competition between plants can be used to restrict the growth of larger cultivars. This is not true of all vegetables: lettuce do not form a good heart at close spacings unless naturally small cultivars are chosen.

Selecting Varieties
The planting distances for varieties sold as mini vegetables are indicated on the packet. The spacing of larger varieties for harvesting when young can be gauged by experimenting.

Crops to Harvest Within 12 Weeks of Sowing
Beetroot
This is one of the oldest crops grown as small vegetables, mainly for processing. Sow thickly, thinning to 2.5cm (1in) apart with 15cm (6in) between rows. Mini varieties include 'Pronto', 'Monaco' and 'Action'.

Carrot
Amsterdam types can be grown for harvesting when small by sowing thickly and thinning to 1cm (½in) apart in rows 15cm (6in) apart. Mini varieties include 'Amini' and 'Ideal'.

Courgette
Most cultivars are suitable, especially F₁ hybrids. Allow 60cm (24in) between plants. Harvest several times a week to extend the cropping period. 'Peter Pan' is a mini squash. 'Sunburst' and its relatives can be harvested when small.

Kohlrabi
Harvest when the size of a golf ball for a milder flavour. Sow thickly, thinning to 2.5cm (1in) apart with 15cm (6in) between rows. The ultimate size is controlled by high-density sowing. 'Rolano' and 'Logo' are mini varieties.

Onion
Bunching cultivars like 'Ishikura' and 'Hikari' are ideal as they do not form bulbs, and their erect foliage means they can be sown at higher density. For pickling onions try growing 'Shakespeare'.

Turnip
Sow thickly, thinning to 2.5cm (1in) with 15cm (6in) between rows for table-tennis ball sized roots. Grow 'Tokyo Cross' or 'Arcoat' for mini vegetables.

Crops to Harvest Within 20 Weeks of Sowing
Brussels Sprout
Growing tall, old cultivars such as 'Bedfordshire' spaced 30cm (12in) in and between the rows provides a continuous supply of sprouts throughout the autumn and winter. Due to their height, make sure that the rooting depth is at least 30cm (12in).

Cabbage
Try the small savoy 'Protovoy' and 'Primero' as mini vegetables. 'Protovoy' should be planted 15cm (6in) apart in the rows with 5cm (2in) between rows, 'Primero' at 15cm (6in) square.

Cauliflower
Grown at 15cm (5in) spacings, it is possible to produce small-headed cauliflowers about the size of a tennis ball. These take an average of 17 weeks from sowing until harvest. The mini variety 'Idol' is suitable for freezing.

Kale
Allow 15cm (6in) square between each plant and harvest regularly to prevent the leaves from becoming stringy. Sow at 10-day intervals for successional cropping. 'Showbor' is a mini variety.

Leek
Spaced 1.5cm (¾in) apart in rows 15cm (6in) apart, mini leeks have a mild flavour and can be steamed or eaten raw in salads. 'King Richard' is a good variety.

Parsnip
The narrow-rooted 'bayonet' types are the best. Thin to 5cm (2in) apart in rows 15cm (6in) apart. Allow about 15 weeks from sowing. 'Lancer', a mini variety, is very resistant to canker.

Spinach
Sow every 2 weeks for continuous production. Protection may be needed for the early and late sowings. Choose cultivars with mildew resistance.

Sweetcorn
These do not need to be grown in a block as they are harvested before pollination when the tassels begin to show. They should be spaced 30 x 30cm (12 x 12in) apart. A good crop will depend on how sunny the summer is. Try the mini variety 'Minipop'.

VEGETABLES DYES AND OTHER USES

With vegetables being our primary food source, we often look no further than their use as food crops. However, many vegetables do have one (or more) other uses – as the basis for dyes, medicines, natural chemicals and even wines.

Dyes

Few vegetables contain plant juices with residual colours; all must be used with a mordant and the colour varies according to the type used. Most vegetable dyes fade with time, and can only be used on natural fibres. The following are worth trying:

Beetroot: although beetroot is notorious for staining skin, extracted juices produce only drab brown or fawn when used for dying.

Onion bulbs are covered with several layers of dry, brown, papery skins. Large quantities are needed for dying and although the natural colours, ranging from pale yellow to a copper-brown, are bold, they tend to fade rapidly when exposed to light.

Leeks: the 'flags' or foliage produce yellow and dull brown pigments.

Medicines

Food is considered by many as a potent medicine, providing the vitamins and minerals required for good health. It also contains pharmacological agents which act as medicines when ingested. The saying 'you are what you eat' is very true: a balanced diet promotes good health. With the popularity of 'fast food', vegetable intake has on average been reduced, thus creating an imbalanced diet. A good diet is one incorporating vegetables which ward off and relieve illness. Many vegetables, particularly 'greens' and carrots, contain beta carotene, a precursor of vitamin A which is believed to prevent cancer; others, like garlic, reduce cholesterol. A diet rich in fibre can help prevent bowel cancer, and researchers have suggested that soya can help against breast cancer. Studies are currently under way to examine whether diet can explain differences in cancer rates between northern and southern Europe. The nutritional value and medicinal uses of each vegetable are indicated under individual vegetable entries. Vegetables are the ideal way to eat your way to health.

Wine

Many vegetable gardeners are also keen winemakers. A good-quality vegetable wine certainly makes an interesting topic of conversation over a meal. Beetroot, carrot, celery, parsnip and rhubarb are all excellent – but guests should be reminded to leave their cars at home as the percentage of alcohol is usually high. Root vegetables with a high sugar content, such as parsnips, generally produce a wine which is very sweet.

Other Uses

Some vegetables make natural cosmetics, including face creams and packs. Cucumber and avocado are particularly good examples.

Soya-rich diets are regarded as preventative medicine

THE VEGETABLE GROWER'S CALENDAR

This calendar assumes that the vegetable garden lies in northern Europe, the average date of the last major frost in spring being April 1st and an average date for the first frost being October 20th. Gardeners with different frost dates can adjust this calendar accordingly. But, as any gardener knows, it is difficult to be precise – each year is different, likewise each garden. So use this calendar as a general guide.

JANUARY

(Mid-winter)

Prepare cropping plans and order seed. Lime autumn-dug plots if necessary. Place early seed potatoes in shallow boxes, with 'eyes' uppermost, and store in a light, frost-free place. Towards the end of the month, plant out shallots if soil is moist enough.

Protected cropping: sow radishes and carrots in grow-bags or in the borders of a cold glasshouse; sow lettuce for growing under cloches, and leek.

FEBRUARY

(Late winter/early spring)

Sow broad beans, early peas and spinach. Sow early-maturing cabbage and cauliflowers in pots from the middle of the month onwards. 'Chit' maincrop potatoes.

Protected cropping: sow cabbages, carrots, lettuces and radishes under cloches or in a polythene tunnel.

MARCH

(Early spring)

Plant onion sets in prepared ground. Sow beetroot, cabbage, carrots, parsnip, lettuce and maincrop peas.

Protected cropping: plant lettuce under cloches or in plastic tunnels, sow salad onions in grow-bags in an unheated glasshouse for early crops. Sow early cabbages and cauliflowers under glass for transplanting in mid-April and tomatoes from late March to early April.

Preparing seedbed with a measuring rod for spacing rows

APRIL

(Mid-spring)

Dig plots occupied by winter greens and prepare for leeks; plant maincrop potatoes, cabbages and cauliflowers (sown under cover in March). Make further sowings of beetroot, radishes, spinach, carrots, cauliflower, maincrop peas, broad beans and parsnips. Sow Iceberg lettuce, salad onions and seakale. From late April, sow winter cauliflower, Savoy cabbage, kale and broccoli into seedbeds. Transplant cabbages and cauliflowers sown in nursery beds in February. Pinch out the growing tips of flowering broad beans.

Protected cropping: tomatoes sown and pricked out in late March or early April should be transferred to a cold frame and hardened off. Sow marrows, squashes and sweetcorn at the end of the month. Prepare greenhouse borders or grow-bags for tomatoes, and plant towards the end of the month.

MAY

(Late spring)

Sow French and runner beans, carrots, courgettes, outdoor cucumbers, lettuce, turnips, spinach and parsley. Plant out celeriac, celery, sweetcorn and summer cabbage. Harvest asparagus, broad beans, cauliflowers, peas, radish and spinach. Earth up potatoes.

Protected cropping: transplant aubergines, outdoor cucumbers, tomatoes, peppers and sweetcorn.

JUNE

(Early summer)

Sow French and runner beans, Chinese cabbage, carrots, courgettes, outdoor cucumbers, lettuce, turnips, spinach and parsley. Transplant celery, summer cabbage and tomatoes. Harvest asparagus, broad beans, cauliflowers, calabrese, peas, radish, spinach and turnips.

Protected cropping: transplant aubergines and sweetcorn; pollinate tomato plants.

JULY

(Mid-summer)

Sow final crops of beetroot, carrots, lettuce, turnips, spinach and parsley. Sow salad onions, spring cabbage and seakale for overwintering. Sow keeping onions in a seedbed for transplanting the following March. In colder districts, plant leeks sown in cold frames in January at the beginning of the month. Remove basal suckers from early trench celery, thoroughly water and earth up.

Protected cropping: harvest cucumbers and tomatoes regularly to encourage further fruiting, and pinch out the growing point when each stem contains about 5 or 6 trusses of fruit.

Runner bean 'Painted Lady' climbing decorated frame

AUGUST

(Late summer)

Sow turnips for spring 'greens' and Japanese onions for overwintering. Sow spring cabbage in nursery rows. To prevent wind-rock in autumn and winter, draw soil around the stems of winter greens, particularly Brussels sprouts, kale and broccoli. Earth up trench celery. Harvest maincrop onions, ensuring that the bulbs' outer skins are well ripened before storing.

Protected cropping: harvest cucumbers and tomatoes regularly, self pollinate tomatoes.

SEPTEMBER

(Early autumn)

Order seed catalogues for the following year. Plant out spring cabbages into permanent positions. Sow spinach for harvesting in April. Lift maincrop carrots, beetroot and potatoes, and store in a cool, dark place: later sowings may be left in the ground. Earth up celery before severe frosts. Lift tomato plants with fruits still attached and store; ripen on straw under cloches or in the greenhouse. Wrap green fruits in paper and store in the dark.

Protected cropping: plant thinnings from late-sown salads in frames or under cloches to provide crops during winter. Lettuces reaching maturity should be covered with cloches or frames; sow further crops in a cold frame. The autumn is a good time to lay drains through waterlogged sites.

OCTOBER

(Mid-autumn)

Lift potatoes, beet and carrots for storing. Tie onions on to ropes when the skins have thoroughly ripened. Transplant lettuces sown in July to a well-drained, protected site to overwinter. Plant root cuttings of seakale in pots of sand and leave them in a sheltered place until the spring. Cut down asparagus foliage as it turns yellow. Tidy the vegetable plot, removing all plant debris. Double-dig, adding organic matter, and lime if necessary.

Protected cropping: protect July-sown parsley with cloches for overwintering. Sow lettuce in greenhouse borders or grow-bags for cutting in the spring. Continue harvesting green tomatoes, storing in a dark frost-free place to ripen. Clear grow-bags used for cucumbers, peppers and tomatoes in the summer and replant with winter lettuce.

NOVEMBER

(Late autumn)

Sow broad beans, and round-seeded peas in the open; protect with cloches if necessary. Remove dying leaves from winter greens, allowing air to circulate between plants. Check stored vegetables regularly and remove any showing signs of decay. Use those which are slightly damaged immediately. Sow green manure.

Protected cropping: lift and store crowns of chicory as well as seakale.

DECEMBER

(Early winter)

Plan next year's rotation of vegetables, ordering seeds as soon as possible. Prepare a seed-sowing schedule. Lift and store swede and late-sown carrots. If heavy falls of snow or prolonged frosts are forecast, lift small quantities of vegetables such as celery, leeks and parsnips and store under cover in a cool, easily accessible place. Finish digging before the soil becomes waterlogged. On clay soils, spread sand, old potting compost or well-rotted leafmould on the surface and dig in as soon as conditions are favourable, allowing the frost to break down the soil. Sow green manure on sandy soils or cover with compost to reduce leaching.

A covering of frost on a vegetable garden

GLOSSARY

Annual A plant completing its life cycle from germination to seed in one growing season.

Base dressing An application of organic matter or fertilizer, applied to the soil prior to planting or sowing.
Bed system A method of planting vegetables in close blocks or multiple rows.
Beta carotene The orange-yellow plant pigment and precursor of vitamin A which protects against certain cancers and heart disease.
Biennial A plant completing its life cycle in a two-year period.
Blanch To exclude light from leaves and stems and prevent development of green coloration. In the culinary sense, to immerse in boiling water for the removal of skin or colour, often as a preparation for freezing
Bolt To flower and produce seed prematurely.
Brassica A member of the cabbage family (Cruciferae).
Broadcast To scatter granular substances such as seeds, fertilizer or pesticide evenly over an area of ground.
Bulb A modified plant stem, with swollen leaves acting as a storage organ.

Capping A crust forming on the surface of soil damaged by compaction, heavy rain or watering.
Catch-crop A rapidly-maturing crop sown among slow-growing vegetables to make maximum use of the ground.
Chitting Pre-germination of seeds before sowing. The same term is used for sprouting potatoes.
Clamp A structure made of earth for storing root vegetables outdoors.
Climber A plant which naturally grows upwards covering supports or other plants.
Cloche A small portable structure, often made of plastic or glass, used to protect early crops grown outdoors.
Cold frame A low-lying square or rectangular unheated structure, with a glass or plastic lid.
Compost Decomposed organic material used as soil conditioner, mulch, potting or seed-sowing medium.
Crop rotation A system where crops are grown in different plots on a 3- or 4-year cycle, limiting the build-up of pests and diseases and making the best use of soil nutrients.
Cultivar A contraction of 'cultivated variety', a group of cultivated plants which retain desirable characteristics when propagated.
Cultivate The practice of growing plants in soil or compost. Can also be used to describe methods of soil preparation.
Cut and come again Seedlings, mature or semi-mature varieties, where several harvests can be taken from one crop.

Damp Down To wet the floors and benches in a glasshouse in order to increase humidity and lower high temperatures.
Deciduous Plants which lose leaves at the end of the growing season and redevelop them the following year.
Dormancy Temporary cessation of growth during the dormant season.
Double digging A cultivation technique which penetrates to 2 spades depth, also known as trench digging or bastard trenching.

Earth up To draw the soil around the base for support or to cover a plant for the purpose of blanching.
Evergreen Plants retaining their leaves throughout the year.

F1 Hybrid First-generation plants obtained by crossing two selected pure-breeding parents to produce uniform vigorous offspring.
Fanging A term used to describe the forking of a root vegetable.
Fertilizer A chemical or group of chemicals applied to the soil or plants to provide nutrition.
Fleece Lightweight, woven polypropylene cover used for crop protection.
Floating mulch (floating cloche) Sheets of flexible lightweight material placed over plants to provide protection.
Fluid sow A method for sowing germinated seeds into the soil using a carrier gel.
Folic acid Part of the vitamin B complex, found in leafy vegetables. Deficiency of folic acid causes anaemia.
Friable Used to describe soil with a crumbly, workable texture, capable of forming a tilth.
Fungicide Chemical used for the control and eradication of fungi.

Genus A taxonomic classification used to describe plants with several similar characteristics.
Germination The chemical and physical changes which take place as a seed starts to grow.
Green manure A rapidly-maturing, leafy crop grown for incorporation into the soil to improve its structure and nutrient levels.
Grow-bag A bag of compost used as a growing medium.

Half hardy Plants which tolerate low temperatures but not frost.
Harden off To acclimatize plants gradually, enabling them to withstand cooler conditions.
Hardy Plants which can withstand frost without protection.
Haulm The foliage of plants such as potatoes.
Heart up The stage at which leafy vegetables, like cabbage and lettuce, swell to form a dense cluster of central leaves.
Heavy soil A soil with a high proportion of clay particles, prone to waterlogging in winter and drying in summer.
Herbicide A chemical used to control and eradicate weeds.
Humus The organic decayed remains of plant material in soils.
Hybrid A variety of plant resulting from the crossing of two distinct species or genera.

Inorganic Term used to describe fertilizers made from refined naturally-occurring chemicals, or artificial fertilizers.
Insecticide Chemical used to eradicate insects.
Intercropping The practice of planting fast-growing vegetable crops between slower-growing varieties (see *Catch-crop*).
Inulin An easily digestible form of carbohydrate.

John Innes compost Loam-based growing medium made to standardized formulas.

Leaching The downward washing and loss of soluble nutrients from topsoil.

Leaf A plant organ containing chlorophyll essential for photosynthesis.

Leafmould Decaying leaves.

Legume A single-celled fruit containing several seeds which splits on maturity, e.g. beans and peas.

Lime Calcium compounds used to raise the pH of the soil.

Loam The term used for a soil of medium texture.

Maincrop The largest crop produced throughout the main growing season. Also used to describe the cultivars used.

Module A generic term describing the containers used for propagating and growing young plants.

Mulch a layer of organic or inorganic material laid over the ground which controls weeds, protects the soil surface and conserves moisture.

Nematacide Chemical used for the control and eradication of nematodes (eelworms).

Neutral Soil or compost with a pH value of 7 which is neither acid nor alkaline (see *pH*).

Nutrients Minerals which are essential for plant growth.

Organic Term used to describe substances which are derived from natural materials. Also used to denote gardening without the use of synthetic chemicals and composts, mulches and associated material.

Pan A layer of compacted soil that is impermeable to water and oxygen, and impedes root development and drainage.

Perennial Non-woody plants which die back and become dormant during winter, regrowing the following spring.

pH A measure of acidity or alkalinity. The scale ranges from 0 to 14, and is an indicator of the soluble calcium within a soil or growing medium. A pH below seven is acid and above, alkaline.

Pinch out To remove the growing tip of a plant to induce branching.

Potager An ornamental vegetable garden.

Pot on To move a plant in to a larger pot.

Prick out To transfer seedlings, from a seedbed or tray, to a further pot, tray or seedbed.

Propagation The increase of plant numbers by seed or vegetative means.

Radicle A seedling root.

Rhizome A fleshy underground stem which acts as a storage organ.

Root The part of the plant which is responsible for absorbing water and nutrients and for anchoring the plant into the growing medium.

Root crops Vegetables grown for their edible roots, e.g. carrot and parsnip.

Seed A ripened plant ovule containing a dormant embryo, which is capable of forming a new plant.

Seed leaves or *cotyledons* The first leaf or leaves formed by a seed after germination.

Seedling A young plant grown from seed.

Sets Small onions, shallots or potatoes used for planting.

Shoot A branch, stem or twig of a plant.

Shrub A plant with woody stems, branching at or near the base.

Sideshoot A branch, stem or twig growing from a main stem of a plant.

Single digging A cultivation technique which penetrates to one spade's depth.

Species A taxonomic classification of similar closely related plants.

Spore The reproductive body of a non-flowering plant.

Stale seedbed method A cultivation technique whereby the seedbed is created and subsequent weed growth is removed before crops are sown or planted.

Stem The main axis of a plant, from which lateral branches appear.

Subsoil Layers of less fertile soil immediately below the topsoil.

Sucker A stem originating below soil level, usually from the plant's roots or underground stem.

Systemic or *translocated* A term used to describe a chemical which is absorbed by a plant at one point and then circulated through its sap system.

Tap root The primary anchoring root of a plant, usually growing straight down into the soil. In vegetables this is often used for food storage.

Tender Plant material which is intolerant of cool conditions.

Thinning The removal of seedlings or shoots to improve the quality of those which remain.

Tilth The surface layer of soil produced by cultivation and soil improvement.

Top-dressing The application of fertilizers or bulky organic matter to the soil surface, while the plants are *in situ*.

Topsoil The upper, usually most fertile layer of soil.

Transpiration The loss by evaporation of moisture from plant leaves and stems.

Transplant To move a plant from one growing position to another.

Tuber A swollen underground stem used to store moisture and nutrients.

Variety Used in the vernacular to describe different kinds of plant. Also used in botanical classification to describe a naturally-occurring variant (*varietas*) of a plant.

Vegetative Used to describe parts of a plant which are capable of growth.

Weathering Using the effect of climatic conditions to break down large lumps of soil into small particles.

Wind-rock Destabilizing of plant roots by wind action.

ROYAL HORTICULTURAL SOCIETY AWARDS

After cultural trials, the R.H.S. grants an Award of Garden Merit (AGM) to plants of outstanding excellence. Some plants are judged Highly Commended (HC). An asterisk (*) beside a variety name in the A–Z indicates a vegetable which has received an award. The following list includes all awards made up until the end of November 1994.

Allium cepa (**Onion**) *Bulb type:* 'Buffalo', 'Centurion', 'Giant Fen Globe', 'Gion Festival', 'Hygro', 'Imai Early Yellow', 'Jagro', 'Jetset', 'Juno', 'Norstar', 'Sturon', 'Super Ailsa Craig', 'Turbo'
Salad type: 'White Lisbon', 'Winter Over', 'Winter White Bunching'
Allium cepa **Aggregatum Group** (**Shallot**) 'Atlantic', 'Giant Yellow Improved', 'Pikant', 'Sante'
Allium porrum (**Leek**) *Maincrop type:* 'Abila', 'Autumn Giant – Cobra', 'Berdina', 'Giant Winter – Catalina', 'Ginka', 'Glorina', 'Herfstreuzen', 'Longbow', 'Profina', 'Toledo', 'Verina', 'Winterreuzen – Ganada'
Apium graveolens var. *dulce* (**Celery**) 'Celebrity', 'Crystal', 'Galaxy', 'Giant Pink – Mammoth Pink', 'Green Cathedral', 'Ivory Tower', 'Lathom Self Blanching', 'Loret', 'Octavius', 'Starlight', 'Victoria'
Apium graveolens var. *rapaceum* (**Celeriac**) 'Monarch'
Asparagus officinalis (**Asparagus**) 'Connover's Colossal', 'Limbras', 'Lucullus'
Beta vulgaris (**Beetroot**) *Long red varieties:* 'Cheltenham Green Top', 'Forono'
Round red varieties: 'Action', 'Bikores', 'Bolthardy', 'Bonel', 'Mobile', 'Monogram', 'Pablo', 'Regala', 'Wodan'
Brassica oleracea **Acephala Group** (**Kale**) 'Bornick', 'Fribor', 'Winterbor'
Brassica oleracea **Botrytis Group** (**Cauliflower**) *Early Summer Heading type:* 'Alpha 5 – Polaris', 'Aubade', 'Perfection'
Summer Heading type: 'Dok Elgon', 'White Rock'
Autumn Heading type: 'Alverda', 'Belot', 'Castlegrant', 'Esmeraldo', 'Kestrel', 'Limelight', 'Lindon', 'Marmalade', 'Minaret', 'Plana', 'Red Lion', 'Talbot', 'Vernon', 'Vidoke', 'Violet Queen', 'Violetta Italia'
Brassica oleracea **Gemmifera Group** (**Brussels Sprout**) 'Cavalier', 'Edmund', 'Extent', 'Icarus', 'Igor', 'Patent', 'Roger', 'Stan'
Brassica oleracea (**Cabbage**) *January King type:* 'Marabel'
Late Summer/Autumn type: 'Quickstep', 'Stonehead'
Red type: 'Langedijker Red Early', 'Ruby Ball'
Red Winter Store type: 'Sapporo', 'Vesta'
Savoy type: 'Bolero', 'Ice Queen', 'Julius', 'Pageant', 'Taler', 'Tarvoy'
Spring type: 'Advance', 'Aladdin', 'Avoncrest', 'First Early Market 218', 'Jason', 'King Greens', 'Offenham 1 Myatts' Offenham Compacta', 'Pixie', 'Prince Greens', 'Pyramid'
Summer type: 'Derby Day', 'Duncan', 'First of June', 'Grenadier', 'Hispi', 'Hornet'
Winter Store type: 'Marathon', 'Multiton'
Brassica oleracea **Botrytis Group** (**Calabrese**) 'Shogun'
Brassica oleracea **Gongylodes Group** (**Kohlrabi**) 'Domino', 'Dynamo', 'Korist', 'Rowel'
Brassica rapa **Pekinensis Group** (**Chinese Cabbage**) 'Kingdom', 'Mariko', 'Nerva', 'Spring Sun 60'
Brassica rapa (**Turnip**) 'Milan Red', 'Milan White Forcing', 'Tokyo Cross'
Capsicum annuum (**Sweet Pepper**) 'Bellboy', 'Canape', 'Gypsy', 'Mavras', 'New Ace'
Cichorium endivia (**Endive**) 'Sanda', 'Wallone Frisee Weschelkopf'
Cichorium intybus (**Chicory**) 'Jupiter', 'Medusa', 'Pluto'
Cucumis sativus (**Cucumber**) 'Athene', 'Danimas', 'Femdan', 'Monique'
Cucurbita pepo (**Courgette**) 'Acceste', 'Astoria', 'Defender', 'Early Gem', 'President', 'Supremo'
Daucus carota (**Carrot**) 'Amini', 'Bangor', 'Bolero', 'Brilliant', 'Camberley', 'Campestra', 'Cleopatra', 'Evora', 'Ingot', 'Mokum', 'Nasha', 'Natan', 'Nanco', 'Nantes Express', 'Nantucket', 'Nantura', 'Napoli', 'Newmarket', 'Panther', 'Parano', 'Parmex', 'Rusty', 'Sytan'
Lactuca sativa (**Lettuce**) 'Beatrice', 'Becky', 'Bubble', 'Corsair', 'Debby', 'Delta', 'El Toro', 'Ice Cube', 'Jewel', 'Kelvin', 'Lakeland', 'Leopard', 'Lilian', 'Liset', 'Little Gem', 'Lobjoits Green Cos', 'Malika', 'Minigreen', 'Rolex', 'Roxette', 'Strada', 'Summit', 'Windermere'
Lycopersicon esculentum (**Tomato**) 'Blizzard', 'Counter', 'Gardener's Delight', 'Golden Sunburst', 'Gold Nugget', 'Outdoor Girl', 'Phyra', 'Shirley', 'Tigerella', 'Tornado', 'Yellow Perfection'
Pastinaca sativa (**Parsnip**) 'Cobham Improved Marrow', 'Javelin', 'Tender and True'
Phaseolus coccineus (**Runner Bean**) 'Achievement', 'Enorma', 'Kelvedon Marvel', 'Liberty'
Phaseolus vulgaris (**French Bean**)
Climbing – *Flat Pod type:* 'Algarve', 'Hunter', 'Kwintus', 'Musica'
Round Pod type: 'Benefic', 'Cunera', 'Diamant', 'Eva'
Dwarf – 'Annabel', 'Cropper Teepee', 'Delinel', 'Halco', 'Masai', 'Sprite', 'Talgo', 'Vilbel'
Pisum sativum (**Pea**) 'Cavalier', 'Coral', 'Early Onward', 'Edula', 'Honeypod', 'Hurst Greenshaft', 'Mammoth Melting Sugarpod', 'Oregon Sugar Pod', 'Reuzensuiker', 'Sugar Snap'
Raphanus sativus (**Radish**) 'Fluo', 'French Breakfast', 'Gala', 'Ribella', 'Robino', 'Rondar', 'Serrida', 'Short Top Forcing'
Solanum melongena (**Aubergine**) 'Galine', 'Rima'
Solanum tuberosum (**Potato**) *Early cropping:* 'Concorde'
Maincrop type: 'Avalanche', 'Croft', 'Famosa', 'Maxine', 'Navan', 'Picasso', 'Stroma'
Spinicia oleracea (**Spinach**) 'Dominant', 'Lavewa', 'Secundo', 'Sigmaleaf', 'Triade', 'Triathlon'
Vicia faba (**Broad Bean**) 'Aquadulce Claudia', 'Express', 'Imperial Green Longpod', 'Meteor', 'Relon', 'The Sutton', 'Witkiem Major', 'Witkiem Vroma'
Zea mays (**Sweetcorn**) 'Candle', 'Champagne Gold', 'Oracle', 'Pilot', 'Pinnacle', 'Sugar Boy', 'Sundance', 'Superstar'

Current information is available from the R.H.S., 80 Vincent Square, London SW1P 2PE, or from the Royal Horticultural Society Garden, Wisley, Surrey GU23 6QB, UK.

USEFUL NAMES & ADDRESSES

City & Guilds of London
  Institute
(Horticulture Courses)
46 Britannia Street
London
WC1X 9RG

Elm Farm Research Centre
Hamstead Marshall
Newbury
Berkshire
RG15 0HR

Friends of the Earth
(Information for organic
  growers)
26-28 Underwood Street
London
N1 7JQ

Henry Doubleday Research
  Association
(National Centre for
  Organic Gardening)
Ryton-on-Dunsmore
Coventry
Warwickshire
CV8 3LG

Horticultural Research
  International
(Kirton)
Willington Road
Kirton Boston
Lincolnshire
PE20 1EJ

Horticultural Research
  International
(Stockbridge House)
Cawood
Selby
North Yorkshire
YO8 0TZ

John Innes Centre
Norwich Research Park
Colney
Norwich
East Anglia
NR4 7UH

National Vegetable Society
56 Waun-y-Groes Avenue
Rhiwbina
Cardiff
South Glamorgan
CF4 4SZ

Rothamsted Experimental
  Station
Institute of Arable Crop
  Research
Rothamsted
Harpenden
Hertfordshire
AL5 2LQ

The National Council for
  the Conservation of Plants
  & Gardens (NCCPG)
The Pines
Wisley Garden
Woking
Surrey GU23 6QP

The National Society
  of Allotment & Leisure
  Gardeners Limited
Hunters Road
Corby
Northamptonshire
NN17 1JE

The Royal Horticultural
  Society (RHS)
80 Vincent Square
London
SW1P 2PE

The Royal Horticultural
  Society of Ireland
Thomas Prior House
Merrion Road
Dublin
Eire

The Soil Association
86 Colston Street
Bristol
BS1 5BB

USA
Rodale Research Center
Box 323 RD1
Kutztown
PA 19530
USA

Many agricultural colleges
and education centres have
demonstration gardens and
display areas which are open
to the public.

Seed Suppliers

Chiltern Seeds
Bortree Stile
Ulverston
Cumbria
LA12 7PB

Dobies Seeds
Broomhill Way
Torquay
Devon
TW2 7QW

Fothergill Seeds
Gazeley Road
Kentford
Newmarket
Suffolk
CB8 7QB

King & Co
Monks Farm
Coggeshall Road
Kelvedon
Essex
CO5 9PG

S E Marshall
Wisbech
Cambridgeshire
PE13 2RF

Suffolk Herbs
Sawyers Farm
Little Cornard
Sudbury
Suffolk
C010 0NY

Suttons Seeds
Hele Road
Torquay
Devon
TQ2 7QJ

Thompson & Morgan
London Road
Ipswich
IP2 0BA

Unwins Seeds
Histon
Cambridge
Cambridgeshire
CB4 4LE

USA
Atlee Burpee
Warminster
PA 18974
USA

Johnny's Selected Seeds
Foss Hill Road
Albion
Maine 04910
USA

The Cook's Garden
PO Box 65
Londonderry
VT05148
USA

SELECTED BIBLIOGRAPHY AND OTHER USEFUL BOOKS

Bio-dynamic Gardening
J. Soper
(Souvenir Press 1983)

*Collins Guide to the Pests
& Diseases & Disorders
of Garden Plants*
S. Buczacki & K. Harris
(Collins 1981)

*The Complete Know & Grow
Vegetables*
J. K. A. Bleasdale, P. J. Salter
et. al.
(OUP 1991)

The Contained Garden
K. Beckett, D. Carr
& D. Stephens
(Frances Lincoln 1982)

*Domestication of Plants in the
Old World*
D. Zohary & Maria Hopf
(Oxford Science
Publications 1994)

Dye Plants & Dyeing
J. & M. Cannon
(Herbert Press/Royal
Botanic Gardens Kew)

Early Garden Crops
(RHS Wisley Handbook)
F.W. Shepherd
(RHS 1977)

Encyclopedia of Gardening
C. Brickell (Ed)
(RHS/Dorling Kindersley)

*Encyclopedia of Garden Plants
& Flowers*
R. Hay (Ed)
(Reader's Digest 1978)

The English Gardener
W. Cobbett
(1833)

Four-Season Harvest
E. Coleman
(Chelsea Green 1992)

Jane Grigson's Vegetable Book
J. Grigson
(Penguin 1988)

Gardener's Dictionary
Phillip Miller
(1724)

Gardening without Chemicals
J. Temple
(Thorsons 1986)

Gardening on a Bed System
P. Pears
(Search Press/Henry
Doubleday Research
Association 1992)

Growing under Glass
K. A. Beckett
(RHS/Mitchell Beazley
1992)

Hints for the Vegetable Gardener
(Gardenway Publications
1990)

*The History & Social Influence
of the Potato*
R. N. Salaman
(CUP 1949)

*The Kitchen Garden:
a Historical Guide to
Traditional Crops*
D. C. Stuart
(Hale 1984)

*Maison Rustique, or the
Country Farm*
Estienne, C. Liebault
(1570)

Organic Gardening
R. Lacey
(David & Charles 1988)

*Organic Growing for Small
Gardens*
J. Hay
(Century 1985)

*Oriental Vegetables: the
Complete Guide for
Garden & Kitchen*
J. Larkcom
(John Murray Ltd 1991)

*The Ornamental Kitchen
Garden*
G. Hamilton
(BBC Books 1990)

*Queer Gear: How to Buy
& Cook Exotic Fruits
& Vegetables*
M. Allsop & C. Heal
(Century Hutchinson 1986)

The Salad Garden
J. Larkcom
(Frances Lincoln 1984)

Sow & Grow Vegetables
B. Salt
(MPC 1995)

Successful Organic Gardening
G. Hamilton
(Dorling Kindersley 1987)

*Tropical Planting
& Gardening*
H.F. Macmillan
(Malayan Nature Society
1991)

The UK Green Growers' Guide
S. G. Lisansky, A. Robinson,
J. Coombs
(CPL Press 1991)

The Vegetable Garden Displayed
J. Larkcom
(RHS 1992)

Vegetables
R. Phillips & M. Rix
(Pan Macmillan 1993)

Vegetables of South East Asia
G. A. L. Herklots
(Allen & Unwin)

*Vegetable Varieties for the
Garden (RHS Wisley
Handbook)*
J. R. Chowings & M. J. Day
(RHS/Cassell 1992)

INDEX